An Injury to All

V

An Injury to All

The Decline of American Unionism

KIM MOODY

V

VERSO

London · New York

This edition published by Verso 1988
© 1988 Kim Moody
All rights reserved

Verso
UK: 6 Meard Street, London W1V 3HR
USA: 29 West 35th Street, New York, NY 10001-2291

Verso is the imprint of New Left Books

British Library Cataloguing in Publication Data

Moody, Kim, 1940–
    An injury to all : the decline of American unionism. — (Haymarket).
    1. United States. Employment. Labour, history
    I. Title II. Series
    331'.0973

US Library of Congress Cataloging-in-Publication Data

Moody, Kim.
    An injury to all.

    (The Haymarket series)
    Bibliography: p.
    Includes index.
    1. Trade-unions--United States--History--20th century. I. Title.
    HD6508.M68 1988   331.88'0973   88-17283

ISBN 0-86091-216-7
ISBN 0-86091-929-3 (pbk.)

Typeset by Steven Hiatt Editorial Services,
San Francisco, California
Printed in the United States of America
by Bookcrafters, Chelsea, Michigan

Contents

The Haymarket Series

Editors: Mike Davis and Michael Sprinker

The Haymarket Series is a new publishing initiative by Verso offering original studies of politics, history and culture focused on North America. The series presents innovative but representative views from across the American left on a wide range of topics of current and continuing interest to socialists in North America and throughout the world. A century after the first May Day, the American left remains in the shadow of those martyrs whom this series honours and commemorates. The studies in the Haymarket Series testify to the living legacy of activism and political commitment for which they gave up their lives.

Already Published

POSTMODERNISM AND ITS DISCONTENTS: Theories, Practices
Edited by Ann Kaplan

AN INJURY TO ALL: The Decline of American Unionism *by Kim Moody*

THE SOCIAL ORIGINS OF PRIVATE LIFE: A History of American Families, 1600–1900 *by Stephanie Coontz*

Forthcoming

OUR OWN TIME: A History of American Labor and the Working Day *by David Roediger and Philip Foner*

YOUTH, IDENTITY, POWER: The Chicano Generation *by Carlos Muñoz, Jr.*

THE 'FIFTH' CALIFORNIA: The Political Economy of a State-Nation *by Mike Davis*

RANK-AND-FILE REBELLION: Teamsters for a Democratic Union *by Dan LaBotz*

THE MERCURY THEATER: Orson Welles and the Popular Front *by Michael Denning*

THE POLITICS OF SOLIDARITY: Central America and the US Left *by Van Gosse*

THE HISTORY OF BLACK POLITICAL THOUGHT *by Manning Marable*

To the sisters and brothers in Austin, Minnesota and Watsonville, California, who showed us what the labor movement can be

Acknowledgements

Like most books, this one is the result of the efforts of many people, one of whom was lucky enough to put it on paper and get most of the credit. Many of the people whose energy and work went into this book did so involuntarily, simply by doing research and publishing their results. They are credited in the notes or in the text itself. Others contributed to this book by virtue of the role they played in the various events and struggles described herein. I single out the fighters from Austin, Minnesota, and Watsonville, California, in the dedication to this volume, but their numbers are legion. I have been fortunate, largely in my role as a journalist at *Labor Notes*, but also as an activist in the labor and socialist movements over the years, to meet some of these contributors. What I have learned from them, no matter how brief the personal encounter, is completely interwoven with the assumptions and opinions I hold about organized workers in the United States and around the world.

Ultimately, however, there are those with whom I have had a closer collaborative relationship over time and/or those whose ideas have shaped the thinking that has gone into this book. In the first ranks of these would be the *Labor Notes* staff: Phill Kwik, Jane Slaughter, and Jim Woodward. A glance at the notes for the chapters dealing with recent events will give the reader a hint of how dependent I have been on the consistent reporting and analysis in *Labor Notes* of the trends of the past eight years. But the interaction with my fellow *Labor Notes* staff members has gone far beyond the acknowledgements in the newsletter or in my notes. Although not everyone on the staff would necessarily agree with everything in this book, it is, in my mind, a product of the *Labor Notes* experience.

Another special group of people who dedicated their efforts and, in many cases, lives to the advancement of organized labor and the working class were the many fighters, thinkers, and organizers who passed through the International Socialists (IS) from the late 1960s through the early 1980s. The IS experience was unique on the American political left, in my opinion, because of the depth and consistency of its commitment to the day-to-day struggles of the organized working class. It did not succeed any more than any other socialist group in building a genuine working-class–based socialist movement in the United States, but the richness of its interaction with the reality of class struggle and working-class life deserves at least a footnote in the history of the American working class. I could not possibly understand the workings of this economic system, of the trade unions, of the oppression of women and national minorities, or working-class life in America without having gone through that experience.

There are also people who deserve special mention for the influence they have had on my thinking about the subject of this book, even though some of them fall within one or another of these general categories. Among them are Steve Early, Suzanne Gordon, Mike Parker, Bill Parker, Wendy Thompson, David Finkel, Pete Kelly, Ilene Winkler, Don Bacheller, Tony Mazzocchi, Les Leopold, Anne Bastian, Sid Lens, Ken Paff, Steve Kindred, Pete Rachleff, Roger Horowitz, Mike Davis, Nelson Lichtenstein, Ray Rogers, Ed Allen, and Stan Weir.

Of course, having some ideas and writing a book are two different things. A very special acknowledgement, therefore, goes to the person who, chapter by chapter, edited, suggested, encouraged, and generally created order out of chaos in the most tactful and patient manner imaginable: Barbara Koeppel.

Introduction

In November 1986, as part of the celebration of the centenary of the founding of the American Federation of Labor, the Smithsonian Institution sponsored a two-day conference on work, technology and culture in industrial America. The discussion among a group of noted labor scholars centered primarily on the conflict between the values of collectivism and individualism in American culture and in the US labor movement. Historian Alice Kessler-Harris noted that 'two competing ideas have run through the labor movement, as they have run through the American past. The first is the notion of community – the sense that liberty is nurtured in an informal political environment where the voluntary and collective enterprise of people with common interests contributes to the solution of problems.'

Kessler-Harris cited town meetings and movements for social change as examples of collectivist activity in US history, arguing that 'the collective impulse lends itself to egalitarian values in that all citizens are deemed equal in their capacity to participate in democratic decision-making processes.'

On the other hand, American culture and history have also been characterized by a strong belief in individualism. In this discussion, *individualism* is used in a specific way. It does not mean the dignity of the individual per se, any more than *collectivism* means some Orwellian barracks society. Kessler-Harris described American individualism in its specific historical form:

> The second idea is that of individualism – a belief in the hard work and ingenuity characteristic of our Puritan forebears and of legendary frontiersmen and women; and faith in the capacity of people to rise by their own wills to the highest vistas of the American dream. Embodied in the notion of "free labor", the ideal assured the dignity of honest toil and posited that its results would be economic success.[1]

Perhaps the most obvious feature of the notion that honest toil assures economic success is its utter falsehood. American economic history, like that of all nations, demonstrates that wealth has not gone to the producers, but to the drones, the liars, and the ruthless. From the Robber Barons of the late nineteenth century to today's 'inside traders', the fruits of society have accrued to those who already hold wealth and power or to those unscrupulous enough to take it. Even the apparently honest businessman accumulates wealth through the exploitation of the labor of others. Acting as an individual, the honest worker typically gets what the employer is willing to give, which sustains a life-style considerably below the 'highest vistas of the American dream'.

For this reason, workers have always turned toward collective forms of action to increase the rewards of labor, and unions have been the major expression of working-class collectivism in American history. The history of such collective activity goes back to colonial days, but the birth of unionism as a mass phenomenon dates from the rise of a full-blown industrial capitalism in the aftermath of the Civil War. From that day to this, there has not been a decade in which workers did not strive to organize, expand, or defend trade unions. The forms of these unions changed as the shape of industry and the economy changed, but the impulse toward collective activity, mutual aid, and solidarity has been as much a part of the American landscape as the possessive individualism of the employers they confronted.

There is not much doubt, however, that throughout US history this conception of individualism has dominated official ideology and has thus long informed the thinking of workers and trade unionists as well as that of employers and entrepreneurs. Indeed, as Kessler-Harris also pointed out, the AFL was founded in 1886 largely with the view that the sole purpose of collective action was the advancement of the individual worker. This individualism reflected the consciousness of the skilled craft workers who composed the unions of the early AFL. The resort to mutual action was a necessary response to the collectivization of work itself that occurred with the rise of industrialism. But beyond the advancement of the individual members that composed the union, labor, in this view, had no broader responsibilities to the working class as a whole. They called themselves 'pure and simple unionists' and, in effect, invented business unionism – a unionism that sees members primarily as consumers and limits itself to negotiating the price of labor. This individualist approach to raising the price of labor expressed itself through attempts to limit the labor market to the skilled members of the various craft unions – resulting in exclusion rather than comprehensive organization in the new industries.

In contrast, the Knights of Labor, from whom the AFL's initial affiliates withdrew, attempted to organize all workers and saw unionism as a means of raising the well-being of the individual worker by elevating the condition of all 'toilers'. They did not counterpose individuality to the collective mass but saw that the fate of the individual was tied to that of all workers. Kessler-Harris described their view this way: 'In practice, protecting the dignity of the individual required what has come to be known as social unionism: collective activity in the community, the workplace, and above all in the political arena.'[2]

While the Knights failed to adapt their own collectivism in organizational modes adequate to combat the rising national corporate giants of the era, or to square their collectivist ideas with a modern understanding of social classes in capitalist society, their all-inclusive approach to organization and their embryonic social unionism foreshadowed the rise of the CIO half a century later.

The vast social movement that created the CIO and organized basic industry in the US has been the greatest achievement of the American working class to date. In a matter of a few years, what appeared to be a fragmented mass of individual workers paid at rates and worked at speeds imposed by the employers transformed themselves into an organized force that changed the economic and political fabric of society. Even before they formed unions, of course, the innate collectivism imposed on these workers by the conditions of modern industry expressed itself on the job through informal group actions. But these could not fundamentally alter the balance of forces that allowed employers to determine the living standards of the entire working class. That achievement required massive, all-inclusive organization: industrial unionism.

Like the Knights, the inclusive character of modern industrial unionism bred an egalitarianism that led it into the political arena and into alliances – albeit tentative in practice – with other oppressed groups in society. The CIO espoused a modern version of social unionism, in which organized labor was envisioned as a force that would lead to the raising of the living standards of an entire nation. This social unionism was half-formed and often contradictory, but it pointed to an egalitarian future for all that won the CIO respect far beyond its own membership.

The embryonic social unionism of the early CIO unions represented the only ideological expression of the democratic, collectivist thrust of the new industrial unions. In the US, unions remained the only form of working-class organization. Independent working-class parties did not take root in the culture of the American working class. Perhaps because of this, the inherent collectivist instincts of the working class rarely expressed themselves in socialist ideas. The egalitarianism of industrial unionism and the broader vision of social unionism were thus the only real potential springboards toward the development of an aggressive, class-based movement in post–World War Two America. But both the practical promise of egalitarianism and the ideological potential of social unionism were cut down in their youth.

This book is about the demise of the labor movement that was born in the 1930s and 1940s. Labor's decline as a force in US society is, by now, universally recognized, but it is seldom acknowledged that the roots of this contemporary decline lie in the struggles of that era and in the decisions and directions taken by the new industrial unions in their infancy – in the abandonment of the early social unionism of the CIO in favor of a modern version of business unionism.

Viewed from another perspective, the decline of unionism was rooted in a shift from a collectivist, egalitarian ethic to an individualist one. This change involved more than a style of unionism or of union leadership; it involved a historic change in the way working people in the US viewed themselves. A development as massive as the CIO upheaval of the 1930s is inconceivable without a certain measure of class consciousness, and it seems clear that for a brief moment in history the US working class, in its majority, thought of itself as just that – a working class.

The concept of social class, used in this manner, does not refer to income levels, educational attainments, or other static measures of social stratification. A social class in this sense is a social force acting in relationship to other social forces. In the case of the working class, it acts primarily in relationship to the capitalist class which employs the active workers in its ranks. Indeed, the working class is defined by its relationship to, dependence on, and opposition to the capitalist class. This relationship begins in the workplace at 'the point of production', but it extends throughout society, influencing politics, culture, and the quality of life in general.

Unions are a product of this social relationship. They appear everywhere the capitalist social order exists and are eliminated only by means of enormous repression or when they are unable to adjust to changes in the structure of capitalism itself. That was the fate of the Knights of Labor and other early union movements; that is the threat facing labor today. The changing structure of the economy and of work has disoriented labor in the past and is doing so today. But because the system itself tends to move workers toward self-organization, new labor movements typically spring up to replace failed ones.

This resilience on the part of the working class is sometimes cited as a reason for complacency about the current decline of labor. AFL-CIO President Lane Kirkland, for example, in an essay entitled 'It Has All Been Said Before…', reminds us that just as the Horse Collar Makers disappeared, so the United Auto Workers arose 'to meet new circumstances and needs.'[3] By implication, everything is under control and only hopeless nay-sayers bother droning on about the decline of organized labor.

The problem with this kind of smug retrospection is that a number of decades elapsed between the demise of the unions whose members catered to the horse-and-buggy trade and the organization of the mass-production automobile industry. A generation or two of industrial workers suffered indignity on the job and poverty at home because unionism could not adjust to the changes in work and business organization that capital wrought in a relatively short period of time. And it was difficult for labor to comprehend the changes that took place in the US economy, in part because of the very narrowness fostered by craft and business unionism in the late nineteenth century. The price in human terms was high.

There is a crude determinism in the view that unions simply come and go. This view sees unions solely as products of the organization of capital: capital acts, labor reacts. But social reality is far more subtle and complex. The very changes in business organization or the structure of work that threaten the existence of unions are themselves often a response to labor's organization. The captains of industry of the late nineteenth century responded not only to objective changes in the technology of transportation and production, but in addition shaped them in response to labor's own self-activity. The works of writers such as Harry Braverman and David Montgomery attest to this process in great detail.[4] The social relationship between capital and labor is a two-way street that involves constant interaction. Even allowing for lags in awareness on the part of labor, the inevitability that unions based solely on disappearing industries or occupations will themselves disappear like the Horse Collar Workers, the view that unions simply come and go, tells us very little about contemporary social reality or about the consequences of economic restructuring.

The direction of labor organization has never been a simple or inevitable one. Each change that has challenged labor has brought with it fierce debates within the labor movement about direction: craft unionism versus industrial unionism; business unionism versus social unionism; pressure politics versus independent class politics. The conditions imposed by capital at any moment, along with the broader economic and social context in which labor organizes, weigh heavily on the outcome of such debates, but there is no single, predictable outcome, nor is there anything inevitable about the decline of organized labor if it is understood in terms of social classes in conflict.

Some unions decline or disappear because of changes in the labor force, but the working class is not the same thing as the labor force. This is a common confusion in today's discussions of the crisis of the labor movement, and I will return to it at the conclusion of this book. For now, it is sufficient to note that while the part of the working class that is active in the labor market may change occupations, switch from declining industries to growing ones, or experience massive unemployment, the class continues to exist by virtue of its relationship to capital: it must sell its ability to perform labor in order to live. Since unions spring from this relationship and not from the particular nature of the work performed or the products produced, they can as well be organized in one industry as another. But this will not happen simply because time marches on. Different occupations and industries present different obstacles to organization. The workers and their leaders must analyze their situation and act on that understanding. Their organizations will have more or less durability and impact according to the accuracy of that analysis.

For some time now, capital has been responding to a variety of pressures, including unionism itself, in a more flexible manner than labor. Capital seeks to invest where it will get the greatest return and to organize the labor it employs in any investment to its greatest advantage. In pursuing this course, capital has proved highly mobile and organizationally experimental. Organized labor in the US has proved far less adaptable. Unions are not declining simply because of changes in the industrial landscape, they are declining as a proportion within all industries. There is no shortage of workers who toil under the regime of capital and who do so for increasingly smaller rewards, but the unions have lost sight of how to organize them.

Unfortunately, much of the literature available on the subject encourages the belief that the problem of declining unionism is simply one of changing occupations and shifts among industrial sectors. Ultimately, these definitions of the decline of the working-class organizations are based on the US Bureau of Labor Statistics' definitions of industry by product. Because many of the products of the growing sectors of the US economy are services rather than physical objects, some analysts have wondered whether those employed in them are really part of the working class at all.

In terms of the products produced by labor, the only social fact that is decisive is that labor produces commodities for the market. For some, the concept of the workers' collective product as a commodity sold on the market has been reduced only to objects that can be possessed and used over time – perhaps because that is the way Karl Marx and other economists of the nineteenth century usually discussed the labor process. Yet we know that most 'services' are organized on a capitalist/corporate basis, are produced by collective labor for the profit of the firm, and are sold on the market like so many shoes or pieces of cloth. Indeed, a growing number of commodities embody characteristics of both goods and services. Modern communications, for example, involves the purchase of traditional goods (computers, telephones, data transmitters and receivers), energy and transmission sources (electricity, microwaves, satellites), and services – often provided by the same firm. Without the collective labor of the workers in such an industry, the 'service' and the goods themselves are useless. In this case, we have bought a final commodity that is an inseparable melange of goods and services as defined by the Bureau of Labor Statistics. The commodity is no less a commodity for all the different types of labor that compose it; the workers are no less workers for the heterogeneous character of their collective product; and the capitalist who reaps the profits from the entire process is no less a capitalist because the total product cannot be held in one's hand or stored in a warehouse. All of this is to say that the changes that have occurred within the developed capitalist economies have not altered the fundamental condition of labor, which must still sell its capacity to work to an employer and must still work as part of a collective effort organized by capital, largely on the terms set by capital.

This book will also argue that the growth of the service sector is not a result of deindustrialization, but a function of the continued growth of goods-producing industries on a global scale. The locus of manufacturing will continue to change, more or less unpredictably, according to the economic and political situation in different parts of the world. US capital will flow to Brazil, South Africa, Mexico or Korea only as long as labor costs and political stability provide an above average rate of return on investment. Japanese capital, also faced with rising labor costs, has already turned toward industrial investment in Korea and even in the US. The rise of a new, militant trade union movement in South Korea could, in turn, make it less attractive as a focus of international investment. But within a given nation, the continued expansion or even the stability of much of the service sector depends heavily on manufacturing – domestic and foreign. Even in the US economy, manufacturing continues to provide a major source of national income. Thus, though goods-producing employment in the United States dropped from 36.1% of the labor force in 1965 to 25.6% in 1985, the proportion of the gross national product derived from the production of goods (measured in constant dollars) only dipped from 57.3% to 54.1% in the same years.[5]

The underlying assumptions of this book are therefore that we are seeing vast changes in the structure of the US and world economies and that these changes are reflected in the structure of both the labor force and the working class as a whole. We are not seeing the disappearance of the working class. If anything, the proportion of the population dependent on wage labor has increased, and as a result the most conscious workers will continue to seek ways to organize to better their lives. The success or failure of such efforts will depend in part on what those participating in them see as the problem and what they see as proper responses. Thus, the competing ideas that currently flow through the debates about the nature of the problems facing the unions and the directions to be taken to deal with them are of enormous importance to working-class people and all those who see the working class as a potential source of progressive social change.

The idea that the working class remains the central agency of progressive political and social change is also an assumption of this book. The concept of a social class as an 'agency' of change is, of course, rooted in the broader Marxist conception of how history is made – largely through the active intervention of people organized consciously along class lines. In this view, working-class self-activity and self-organization are both the means for changing society and the means of preparation through which working-class people learn to take on ever greater and more difficult historical tasks. A clear statement of the relationship between genuine class-oriented social unionism and the grander notion that working-class people can democratically control the process of production and even society as a whole appeared in the newspaper of FOSATU, the forerunner of the Congress of South African Trade Unions, the militant labor movement of Black South African workers that has taken center-stage in that people's struggle for freedom:

> The gains made by trade unions have been many. But more impressive than these gains has been the formation of an organization directed and controlled by the workers themselves. Workers are gaining experience in decision-making in their trade unions. They are able to have some control over their own lives. Such an organization opposes the strict authority of the capitalist bosses and trains workers for the role they will play in a future society. In South Africa trade unions have become schools for workers democracy.[6]

With rare exceptions, American unions cannot claim to have been schools of workers' democracy for decades. They are bureaucratic institutions that deny rank-and-file participation in decision-making and that have abandoned the fight against the authority of the capitalist boss both on and off the job. This, the heritage of nearly forty years of modern business unionism, explains much of their inability to respond to capital's initiatives.

The object of this book is to expose the roots of modern business unionism and explore the causes of its decline in the face of an epochal shift in productive forces and investment strategies. At the same time, I try to point to the active forces within the working class that have attempted to set new directions for labor and some of the potential lines along which working-class activists can fight to defend and advance the interests of their class as a whole.

This book is written for a variety of audiences. For some, the digressions into social history or theory, which are all based on a Marxist understanding of the many questions raised in the book, will seem unnecessary flights into intellectual abstraction. To others trained in such theories, these same sections may seem too simple, too pat. Aside from the obvious excuse that no book of this size can deal with everything adequately, there is a more important defense of this contradictory imbalance. I have attempted to apply my understanding of Marxism as a broad method of analysis to a subject that has, for the most part, received only empirical treatment. This empiricism is typical both of the thinking of the labor bureaucracy that presides over the decline of American trade unionism and of most of the academic literature that describes this decline. Since many of those for whom this book is primarily written, the conscious labor activists who daily face the problems described here, are not trained in the ideas that inform the analysis of this book, I felt compelled to make my assumptions as clear as possible without straying too far afield from the central analysis, and to provide a broader picture of the battlefield on which we are all engaged.

1

An Injury to All

On 17 January 1987 the five-and-a-half-month strike of 22,000 members of the United Steelworkers of America (USW) against USX ended when local union presidents approved a new contract by a vote of 38 to 4. The strike was the longest ever waged against a major steelmaker – but it was a lost strike. The new contract contained a $1.14-an-hour cut in earnings. In total hourly labor costs, USX saved $2.45 in the first year of the contract alone. The workers lost four paid holidays, a week of vacation in the first year of the contract, Sunday premium paid, and part of their shift differentials. The union also agreed to work-rule changes that eliminated 1,346 jobs. Larry Regan, president of USW Local 1014 at USX's Gary Works and one of the four local presidents to vote against the contract, expressed the bitterness of many steelworkers: 'Any time we're willing to give up jobs, the union is turning its back on the motto "An injury to one is an injury to all." We're going to give away this many jobs and [call the contract] an achievement? It's disgusting.'[1]

The USX agreement was the fifth concessionary contract negotiated by the USW during the bargaining round that began in 1986. The other major steel corporations, Bethlehem, National, LTV, and Inland, had also won wage cuts – without facing strikes. Steelworkers President Lynn Williams had said that USX would not get such treatment because of the corporation's financial health. The union offered a wage freeze. USX said it wanted what other steel firms had received and perhaps more. When it became clear that USX had no intention of backing down, the union offered to continue work under an extension of the old contract. The corporation said no. On 1 August 1986 the strike began with the union arguing that USX had, in effect, locked the workers out.

It was difficult not to note the contrast between the 1986–87 steel strike and the famous 116-day strike of 1959, the last great national steel walkout. In 1959 the major steel employers had demanded work-rule changes to increase productivity. The leadership of the Steelworkers judged the companies' demand to be an attack on the power of the union and turned it down. The strike that followed shut down 87% of steel production in the United States – virtually the entire unionized sector of the industry – and led to layoffs in many other industries. It took the intervention of the federal government in the form of a Taft-Hartley injunction to end the strike. And when the strikers returned to the steel mills, they did so with their work rules in place, with a wage increase, and with their pension and health insurance improvements and cost of living allowances (COLAs) and supplemental unemployment benefits intact.[2]

Before 1986, the USW had bargained simultaneously with the major producers. All of those employers were covered by the Basic Steel Agreement, a master contract that imposed standard wages, benefits, and conditions throughout the industry. This agreement, in turn, set a pattern for steel-fabricating, aluminum, copper, and can companies. By the mid-1980s this arrangement had come undone. Now wages, benefits and conditions differed not only between these USW-organized industries, but increasingly within them. In 1986, under pressure from the employers, the USW had dissolved the entire national pattern in the steel industry by agreeing to negotiate separately and on different terms with each company.

What happened in steel recapitulated union defeats in other sectors. The list of protracted but broken strikes ran from PATCO through Greyhound, Phelps Dodge and Hormel to Wheeling Pittsburgh and scores of lesser known labor struggles. Rollbacks in wages, benefits and conditions had characterized collective bargaining since the beginning of the 1980s. The average wage increase during the first year of contracts covering 1,000 or more workers fell steadily from 9.8% in 1981 to 1.2% in 1986. In manufacturing the trend was even more pronounced: first-year wage adjustments went from 7.2% in 1981 to -1.2% in 1986.[3] By the mid-1980s concessionary bargaining had spread to virtually every organized industry – from auto, steel, and rubber production workers to service employees in Las Vegas hotels, state hospitals, and city services.[4] There were occasional victories or partial successes by hotel workers in Boston, cannery workers in Watsonville, California and clerical workers at Yale University. But across the country the trend was unmistakably downward.

Seven years of concessions had eliminated master contracts and pattern bargaining in every major unionized industry. Pattern bargaining had been an institutional bulwark of collective bargaining; for decades, it was characterized by the regularity of its operation, the orderly re-

Impact Visuals/Mahmood Nadia

A locked-out steelworker pickets USX's Gary, Indiana plant, 1986.

negotiation of industry-wide contracts every three years or so, and the steady increases in worker earnings and benefits. The largest pattern agreements in auto, steel, rubber, coal, meatpacking, electrical equipment, telecommunications, trucking, and rail were emulated by smaller regional patterns, such as Western lumber and longshore on the East and Gulf coasts. By 1987, most of these had also broken up.

The fragmentation of collective bargaining and the wage deceleration of the 1980s were both symptoms and contributing causes to a more fundamental tendency in American society – the long-term decline of organized labor. The figures are unambiguous. The proportion of union members in the total nonfarm workforce fell from 32.5% in 1953 to 17.5% in 1986. In manufacturing, the density of unionization collapsed from 42.4% in 1953 to 24.8% in 1985. For transportation the comparable figures were 79.9% to 37.0%; for construction, 83.8% to 22.3%; for all kinds of mining, 64.7% to 14.6%.[5]

Declining union density, sometimes combined with shrinking employment in traditionally unionized industries, has in recent years been accompanied by an absolute decline in the number of union members, from a peak of 22.2 million in 1975 to an estimated 17 million in 1986.[6] As Table 1 shows, this loss of over 5 million members expressed a significant or even drastic loss of membership for most of the major industrial unions in the US.

Table 1
Paid Union Membership, 1967, 1979, 1985

Union	1967	1979	1985	Loss/Gain, 1979–85	
				Numbers	Change
UAW	1,325,000	1,499,000	1,010,000	-489,000	-32.6%
USW	952,000	964,000	572,000	-392,000	-40.6%
URW	166,500	158,000	106,000	-52,000	-32.9%
IAM	740,000	664,000	520,000	-144,000	-21.7%
IUE	304,000	243,000	198,000	-45,000	-18.5%
OCAW	142,000	146,000	108,000	-38,000	-26.0%
CWA	315,000	485,000	524,000	+39,000	+8.0%
UFCW[1]	892,000	1,076,000	989,000	-87,000	-8.1%
ACTWU[2]	416,000	301,000	228,000	-73,000	-24.3%

1. Combined membership of the Packinghouse Workers, Meatcutters, and Retail Clerks, which later merged to form the United Food and Commercial Workers.
2. Combined membership of the Clothing Workers and Textile Workers, which later merged to form the Amalgamated Clothing and Textile Workers Union.

Source: Bureau of National Affairs, *Directory of U.S. Labor Organizations*, 1984–85 edn., pp. 51–53 and 1986–87 edn., pp. 61–64.

Only a handful of unions such as the Communications Workers of America (CWA) and the Service Employees International Union (SEIU) could claim any growth – and then due to a strategy of organizing in numerous unrelated industries and jurisdictions. In most industries, the loss of union members reflected not only the loss of jobs due to deindustrialization but a trend toward deunionization as well.

This decline in unionization has had an inevitable correlate in a loss of union power in industry and society as a whole. The consequences of this loss of power are more far-reaching than the figures on wage deceleration suggest. Along with a number of important and usually well-noted changes in the US economy and workforce, the decay of union power has contributed to the first major, long-term decline in the standard of living of the American working class as a whole to occur in the twentieth century.

The Declining Union Advantage

When it comes to money, unions have always made a difference. In 1979, for example, unionized workers on the average made 30% more than their nonunion counterparts. This wage differential has varied over the years according to economic conditions. During World War Two, with virtually no unemployment and union wage increases controlled by the government, it was a low 6%. In the 1950s, the differential ranged from 12% to 16% and rose in the 1960s to 19% to 25%. Its climb to 30% by the end of the 1970s was a function of the unions' ability to chase inflation through both larger wage increases and cost-of-living allowances. In fact, until recently, the union wage advantage tended to be greater in hard times than in good. The largest gap between union and nonunion wages (46%) occurred in the early 1930s when relatively few workers were organized. Those who were organized, however, were better able to resist Depression-era wage cuts and short time.[7]

As might be expected, the union wage advantage is not the same for all social groups. In 1979, unionized women in the private sector of the economy made 15% more than women in nonunion jobs. The differential for men was 19%. The union wage advantage for Blacks was larger than that for whites, 25% compared to 17%.[8] The traditional gap between white and Black wages was much narrower in highly organized industries. In 1969 the average Black male made only 58% of the income of the average white male. In auto, Blacks made 84% of what whites made. In steel, the proportion was 83%; in primary nonferrous metals, it was 82%; and in rubber, 78%.[9] The average union advantage for all workers in benefits was even higher, varying from 30% to 68% depending on the wage level.[10] While these are only averages, it is clear that workers have greatly benefited from unionization.

This continued to be true into the 1980s, but the differential between union and nonunion earnings began to shrink under the pressure of concessionary bargaining. In the private sector, for which these figures are available, the 30% differential of 1979 fell to 28% in 1983, 25% in 1985, and rose slightly to 26% in 1986. In terms of overall compensation, the gap between union and nonunion workers may have closed even more. The employment cost index (which measures benefits as well as wages) for nonunion workers rose nearly twice as fast as the index for union workers from December 1984 to December 1986 – 8.4% compared to 4.8%.[11] Union members are certain to stay ahead of those without unions for a long time, but the general deceleration of union wage gains has reduced the union wage advantage. In previous periods of economic dislocation, the union advantage had tended to widen, but in the 1980s the unions were not able to muster the intensified resistance that would sustain their advantage.

The slowdown in union wage and benefit gains has had another impact. Higher union rates tend to bid up all wages up over time as union rates lead a general rise in earnings for all workers. This 'wage drift' is most obvious during booms, when the labor market is tightest, and its effect is always stronger on large employers than small ones. But as unions gain only small average wage and benefit increases or even take cuts, as they did for manufacturing wages in 1986, the growth of all wages and benefits will slow down. Indeed, even though nonunion wages and benefits (based on the employment cost index) outstripped union gains in 1985 and 1986, the rate at which they grew slowed from 23% during 1980–83 to 14% during 1983–86. The comparable rates in the growth of employment costs for all workers, union and nonunion, in the private sector were 24% for 1980–83 and 10% for 1983–86.[12]

When wage deceleration combined with even low rates of inflation, the result was a fall in real incomes. A study by the AFL-CIO's Industrial Union Department (IUD) shows that this has been the case since the early 1970s. From 1973 through 1979, real average weekly earnings declined 7.4% and from 1979 through 1985 another 7.6%, for a total drop of 14.4%. Real average hourly wages fell 4.3% in 1973–79 and 6.0% in 1979–85, a total decline of 10.1%.[13] There is a difference in the two periods, however. During 1973–79 inflation was rising fast, hitting double-digit levels, while in 1979–85 inflation was moderating, reaching a low of 1.9% in 1986. The decline in real income in the first period was primarily caused by inflation, that in the second period by wage deceleration. In 1987, wage deceleration continued, but inflation grew again: from January to April 1987, real weekly earnings fell 2.3%.[14]

Another factor in the decline of real wages has been the shift in the overall economy from previously unionized goods-producing industries to largely nonunion, low-wage service industries. Although this trend (with dramatic implications for the future of working-class life in the United States) has become more pronounced since the late 1970s, it has been unfolding for several decades. Moreover, because of the growing proportion of part-time jobs that is part of the shift to service industries, its impact is even greater on average weekly income than on hourly income. Thus, while real hourly earnings fell 6% during 1979–85, weekly earnings dropped 7.6%. The IUD study indicates that almost half of the decline in weekly income resulted from this sectoral shift. But only a third (two of the six percentage points) of the fall in hourly rates was attributable to the shift to services. Since inflation was relatively low during 1979–85, a good deal of the remaining two-thirds of the decline in real hourly income was a result of concessions and general wage deceleration – that is to say, a result of the behavior of unions during this period.

In the future, the proliferation of low-wage jobs will be even greater if current trends toward deindustrialization and deunionization continue. A study by the Children's Defense Fund revealed that the average real annual income of male workers between the ages of twenty and twenty-four years dropped from $11,572 in 1973 to $8,072 in 1984. The fund attributed this drop to the 'continuing shift in jobs in the US economy from goods-producing to service sectors and the reduced ability of young men to secure full-time, year-round employment.'[15]

Another facet of this downward trend is the fate of workers dislocated from better paying industrial jobs. The IUD study estimates that about 10% of the 6.1 million workers displaced from full-time jobs between 1979 and 1983 who were fortunate enough to find new employment by January 1984 ended up in jobs paying substantially less. For blue-collar workers, the average loss of income was 16%, but for 35% of them the loss was 25% or more. The figures for income loss by displaced female white-collar workers are identical, but these workers started at a lower pay rate. And Black blue-collar workers lost 50% more than their white counterparts.[16] Another study, prepared for the Joint Economic Committee of Congress, found that less than one-fifth of the new jobs created in 1973–79 were low-wage (jobs paying below $7,012 a year in 1984 dollars), but that nearly three-fifths of new jobs in 1979–84 were low-wage. Admittedly, in 1984 this increment was 8 million new workers out of a total of 113 million in the entire workforce, so the impact of this trend was still relatively small.[17] But the proportion of new jobs that were low-wage had increased so dramatically that a continuation of this trend would certainly depress average earnings.

Although the unemployment rate dropped during the 1980s from 9.7% in 1982 to 6.6% in March 1987, it remained high by postwar standards. For Blacks, the rates were invariably more than double those for whites, 18.9% in 1982 and 13.9% in March 1987. Latinos also experienced higher than average unemployment rates, 13.8% in 1982 and 9.0% in March 1987.[18] Moreover, the duration of unemployment was generally longer in the 1980s than in any previous decade since the 1930s. For example, the average length of unemployment during the 1980–83 recession was 25% longer than during the recession of the mid-1970s. By early 1987, after four years of recovery and growth, the average length of unemployment still lingered at around fifteen weeks. The proportion of workers experiencing fifteen weeks or more of unemployment grew from 26.2% in early 1986 to 27.8% in early 1987. The percentage of unemployed workers who received unemployment benefits fell from 72% during the 1975–76 recession to 45% during 1982–83. By May 1987, only 30.7% of those out of work were getting unemployment insurance benefits.[19]

Things were even worse for those workers who had permanently lost their old jobs and were regarded as 'displaced' by the Labor Department. A survey conducted in January 1986 estimated that 5.1 million of these displaced workers had held their lost jobs for three or more years. Of these, a third remained unemployed. The length of unemployment for all of these 5.1 million workers who were twenty years old or older averaged over eighteen weeks. For the third who were still unemployed in January 1986, it was over twenty weeks. For those who had given up looking for work, it was fifty-four weeks. In all categories, older workers faced longer periods of unemployment. Furthermore, of those displaced workers who had been covered by medical insurance, 32% remained without it in January 1986. Among those who had found new jobs, over 22% had no medical coverage, compared with 59% of those still out of work. Among Black displaced workers, about half had no medical insurance, while for Latinos the proportion was 44%.[20]

Not surprisingly, poverty grew in the 1980s. The number of people living on incomes below the official poverty level ($10,989 for a family of four in 1985 dollars) jumped by a third from 24.6 million in 1978 to 33.1 million in 1985. While two-thirds of these families were white, the incidence of poverty was predictably greater among minorities. Although 11.4% of white families lived in poverty in 1985 (according to the official definition), the rate for Latinos was 29% and that for Blacks over 30%. The growth of poverty was most dramatic among female heads of household, whose official poverty rate increased from 37% in 1970 to 48% in 1985. Because the government uses a somewhat arbitrary cut-off point to define poverty, families move in and out of 'official poverty' with relatively small changes in income. The reality of poverty is much more pervasive than these figures show. Furthermore, the poor were, indeed, getting poorer. The Center on Budget and Policy Priorities reported in 1986 that 'the proportion of the poor who fall below 50 percent of the poverty line has increased from 30 percent in 1975 to 33 percent in 1980 and to 38 percent in 1984. Likewise, the proportion of families with real (inflation adjusted) incomes below $5,000 a year increased by 39 percent since 1978.'[21]

Taken together, these trends have produced a substantial deterioration in the standard of living of the American working class. It can be measured by the decline in home ownership.[22] It can be seen in the closed plants and boarded-up stores in working-class communities throughout the country, whether inner-city slums and neighborhoods, working-class suburbs, or small industrial towns and cities. It can be heard in the widely voiced opinion that the next generation of working people will not make it to or hold their place in the 'middle class'. Ron Weisen, president of Local 1397 at USX's Homestead, Pennsylvania plant spoke of the fate of millions in the middle of the 1986–87 steel strike: 'When [USX President] Roderick put the padlocks on the gates of USX, he was telling the next generation of American workers that they too would be effectively locked out of American life.'[23]

The Rich Get Richer

Most Americans think of the conflict between working-class people and their employers as a struggle between labor and management, just as they conceive of the concentration of wealth as corporate aggrandizement. At one level these perceptions are real: the give-and-take of collective bargaining is conducted by management, and the boss on the job is management. The corporations command great wealth, whether they are manufacturers, banks, insurance companies, or fast-food chains. But these corporations and privately owned businesses are themselves owned and controlled by a smaller class of people. This class, which constitutes less than 10% of the US population, owns 72% of all the stock of these corporations, 70% of the bonds, and 78% of all business assets.[24] By virtue of this near monopolization of the means of production, finance, and commerce, they control the private capital assets of the nation. They are the capitalist class.

As workers saw their living standards erode and their futures grow bleak, this capitalist class saw its wealth multiply at spectacular rates. Measured as net personal assets (assets minus debts) of a household, the average wealth of 90% of American families grew by 52% from 1962 to 1983, according to studies prepared for the Joint Economic Committee of Congress. But for the richest .5% of US households the rate in the growth of net worth was 90%. For the next richest .5%, the growth rate was 72%, and for the remaining 9%, the merely rich, it was 57%. Thus, the richer they were, the faster their wealth expanded. As a result, the share of wealth controlled by the richest 10% of households increased from 65.1% in 1962 to 68.8% in 1983. This same study also noted that the acceleration of concentration was a recent phenomenon:'These data suggest that the dramatic increase in the share of national wealth held by the richest Americans, which is documented by the two Federal Reserve surveys, did not begin until late in the 20-year period between the two surveys (1962 and 1983).'[25]

The nature of the wealth of this top 10% is entirely different from the income sources of the rest of the population. Aside from 1.5 million farmers and those in the nonagricultural workforce who were self-employed (7.7% of the workforce in 1984), the vast majority of Americans derive their income and personal wealth from wages or salaries.[26] Some of those who earn salaries, including many lawyers, accountants, and management personnel, are well-off and, along with the better-off among the self-employed, compose what is usually called the 'middle class' (more accurately, 'the middle classes', since they perform a variety of different functions in relation to the capitalist class and the production of wealth in society). The vast majority of wage and salary earners, however, compose the working class, which produces the goods and services that are the real substance of the economy. The assets of working-class (and many middle-class) households consist of things like cars, homes, savings, checking accounts, and personal possessions, of which only savings provide any income. The members of the capitalist class, in contrast, own income-producing assets like stocks, bonds, various forms of speculative investment ('futures' in commodities or currencies or even 'futures' in 'futures'), or privately owned businesses. While they may draw large salaries as executives of corporations and may own expensive homes and cars, the bulk of their wealth derives from owning assets that produce profits or interest or that can be sold at a profit. Whatever they may do during the day, they do not work for or create the wealth that comes from these assets. Even the Internal Revenue Service calls this kind of income 'unearned'. One of the reasons why the personal wealth of the families of the capitalist class has grown is that the proportion of total income that is unearned has grown from 10.9% in 1973 to 16.3% in 1985.[27]

The 'work' of most active capitalists involves, above all, the manipulation of owned wealth. Not only do they not make any product or perform any service, but most are not involved in the day-to-day functions of management – except in matters of grand strategy. For most of the chores of management they employ a vast array of executives, supervisors, technicians and professionals to work out the details and smooth out the problems from marketing difficulties to labor relations. They employ or retain a legion of experts to handle legal, financial, accounting, technical, scientific, and even psychological matters. And, of course, they employ tens of millions of workers who actually mine, manufacture, transport, distribute, and sell the goods and perform the services that are the end products of labor. The entire process that results is geared to accumulate greater wealth: more money to invest, more business assets, more personal wealth. Because this is their true goal, they will at times abandon one particular line of production or economic activity for another. If greater profits can be made from building shopping malls or luxury condominiums, they will dump their factories. If returns on investment are higher in a foreign land and the political climate reasonably secure, they will direct their investments there. If management seems sluggish in the pursuit of these goals, the captains of capital will reorganize it, firing some managers and hiring new ones, or flirt with new theories of management – human resources management, participatory management, Japanese-style management. But the one aspect of their struggle to accumulate that remains constant is the attempt to reduce the cost of labor, at least in relation to other costs and, if possible, in absolute terms. The price of labor, it seems, is the one item which the capitalist, in his or her function as employer and ultimate controller of the process of production, has the power to influence in most situations. Their power to lower labor costs is, of course, affected by the extent and degree of organization among the workers.

Capital Takes the Offensive

The mass industrial unions formed in the 1930s and 1940s created a formidable institutional barrier to some of the older, more conventional forms of shaving labor costs, like cutting wages, lengthening the workday, reducing holidays or vacations, or not providing livable pensions. From the earliest days of capitalism through the 1920s, employers effectively promoted all these means of keeping labor cheap. Outside of industries where production was organized along craft lines and skilled workers were relatively scarce, few unions were able to hold their own until the organization of broad industrial unions with industry-wide contracts.

Another consequence of industrial unionism, along with brief periods of political reform in which labor played an important role along with other social movements such as the civil rights and women's movements, was the tendency away from the extreme concentrations of wealth and income that characterized the pre-1937 period. During the long postwar expansion, more Americans achieved middle-income status, and the incidence of poverty declined for a period.[28] So long as this trend did not greatly affect the ability of capital to accumulate, a majority of large industrial employers were content to avoid major confrontations with organized labor. When profits, figured as the return on invested capital, began to decline after the mid-1960s, however, capitalists began to seek ways to regain those profit margins – first as individual employers, then increasingly as a class.[29]

In general, the first response of capital took place at the company level and was left to management to carry out. In the late 1960s and early 1970s many companies began pushing for productivity increases rather than modifications in the basic terms of the labor contract. This produced several years of wildcat strikes, mostly at the local level, and a lot of academic literature about the 'blue-collar blues'. But ultimately long-term productivity gains could not be achieved simply by pushing the workers harder. Greater forces in the economy led to a decline in the rate at which productivity grew. Thus, in the 1970s, no longer content to leave matters to the sluggish management bureaucracies they had built during the postwar expansion, leading corporations began to organize more consciously and consistently to transform the entire atmosphere of labor relations and to redirect the pattern of investment.

Measured by the standards of previous growth periods, the performance of US corporations from the mid-1970s through the early 1980s was judged by most economists as mediocre to poor. Profit margins did not return to the mid-1960s level, productivity did not make any startling comeback, imported goods increased their share in several important markets, and corporate reorganizations, mergers and divestments only seemed to create burgeoning business debt. Other industrial nations passed the US in the application of advanced technology. Economists who analyzed these trends divided into those who saw the greater operation of the free market as the solution and those who advocated a modest turn toward national planning in the form of an 'industrial policy'. If there was a universal theme from the experts, however, it was that labor must abandon its adversarial posture, sacrifice some of the 'excessive' gains it had made, and learn to cooperate with management.[30]

Business performance as judged by most professional mainstream economists, however, is not necessarily an indicator of how well the owners of businesses are doing. In fact, while there were some losers, the capitalist class did very well during this period. Much of the wealth of capital in recent years has come from the rise of speculative investment and from the appreciation of stock prices resulting from merger and buy-out fever. It is an irony of the times that although the real assets of a corporation may shrink as it closes plants to make operations more efficient, the price of the company's stock is likely to rise. Thus, the capitalists were able to increase their wealth by closing plants and throwing hundreds or even thousands of workers into the streets. The increases in long-term unemployment and poverty of the 1980s that result from this deindustrialization have greatly benefited the owners of capital. What workers and communities see as destruction, the capitalist sees as creation.

The wage and benefit deceleration of the 1980s has certainly increased the profits of many firms, as has the higher productivity in manufacturing that has resulted from the destruction of union work rules. Cheaper labor is almost always a source of greater income to capital and its owners. While the magnitude of the transfer of income from the working class to capital can only be estimated, some figures allow a rough projection. The 1982 agreements covering 479,000 members of the United Auto Workers (UAW) at Ford and General Motors, which included a freeze in wage rates and other cuts in benefits, were said to be worth a total of $4 billion over three years. Similarly, the 1983 agreement between the USW and seven major steel companies, which included a $1.25-an-hour wage cut and additional benefit cuts for 260,000 workers, was estimated to be worth $3 billion to the employers.[31] Thus, nearly three-quarters of a million workers made concessions (modest by later standards) to nine corporations that netted capital about $7 billion over a three-year period. This was an average of about $9,500 per worker, or a little over $3,000 a year.

According to the US Bureau of Labor Statistics, major new contracts covering nearly 11 million workers were bargained in 1982–85. According to a Brookings Institution study, 37% of them – about 4 million workers – suffered a wage freeze or cut at least once during that period. Assuming that the freezes and cuts were of a similar magnitude to the steel and auto concessions ($9,500), these 4 million workers may have donated about $38 billion to capital. This figure is too low, however, because many other settlements included larger cuts and because it does not include the effects on profitability of work-rule changes that increase productivity. Also, the Bureau of Labor Statistics surveys only contracts covering 1,000 or more workers. The total number of workers covered by union contracts during that period was around 22 million.[32] The actual transfer of wealth from labor to capital during 1983–85 may well have been on the order to two to four times the $38 billion estimated above. Concessions may thus have netted capital anywhere from $76 billion to $152 billion in three and a half years. This later figure is greater than the average annual profits in manufacturing for that same period.[33]

Behind Shifting Wealth Is Shifting Class Power

A shift in wealth of this magnitude, along with the other aspects of the decline in the quality of working-class life in America, can only be explained by a dramatic shift in the power relations between organized labor and organized business and hence between the working class and capital. It is a major theme of this book that such a shift did, indeed, occur in a relatively short period of time. This shift was a complex one involving changes in the international economic order, in corporate structures, in the decline of American-based unions, and in the various policy options that both labor and capital deployed at different times. It was reflected in both the political and economic arenas. Reaganism was the visible tip of this political iceberg, but it included a general shift of both major political parties toward business priorities in legislation and economic policy. Together, these interacting forces provided the background for a historic change in the bargaining behavior of most US unions in the 1980s.

As crucial as the economic and political contexts are, however, they cannot fully explain either the rapidity or thoroughness of the collapse of many of the major institutions of collective bargaining that occurred in the 1980s. The disappearance of pattern bargaining and its replacement by competitive norms of wage and benefit bargaining took place within a few years. That is, an institutional system of income protection in use for four decades collapsed in half a decade. A rising standard of living achieved in over half a century of struggle, not only by unions, but by other mass movements, began an accelerated decline in a matter of less than a decade. Most of the conventional explanations, such as those invoking employment patterns, turn out to be partial at best or to explain only the new turf on which ancient struggles are being fought.

Historically, periods of dramatic shifts in class power and income distribution are characterized by social upheaval. The formation of mass industrial unions, which increased the relative power of the working class in American society, would have been unimaginable without the scale of social conflict that erupted in the 1930s. In past periods when capital has been on the offensive (such as the 1890s, the years just before and after World War One, and even the pre-CIO years of the early 1930s) there has been sharply increased industrial confrontation. This may yet be the case during the 1980s or 1990s, as the very existence of unions comes into question, but the stripping away of many of the major institutional defenses of union power has been accomplished to date without a significant increase in conflict on the part of organized labor as a whole. Indeed, the first half of the 1980s, during which much of the damage was accomplished, saw a decline in the traditional mode of resistance, the strike, without any real strategic reassessment or innovation in the mainstream of trade union thought or practice.

In the face of a major escalation of aggression by capital, unions and their leaderships have proved to be both rigid and feeble institutions – rigid in their inability to adapt to new conditions and feeble in their ability to defend the living standards of their members. Neither weakness nor rigidity resulted simply from a lack of new ideas or strategies, which have percolated at the grass roots and on the margins of the unions for years. Nor was the plight of organized labor from want of positive examples. Even in parts of the world where conditions were far more dire – such as South Africa, Brazil, the Philippines, and other developing nations – new, dynamic industrial union movements arose during the 1980s. Rather, the AFL-CIO's inability to respond effectively must be explained by the frozen ideological and institutional matrices of union leadership in the United States since the late 1940s and above all by the concept and practice of business unionism.

Business unionism as an outlook is fundamentally conservative in that it leaves unquestioned capital's dominance, both on the job and in society as a whole. Instead, it seeks only to negotiate the price of this domination. This it does through the businesslike negotiation of a con-tractual relationship with a limited sector of capital and for a limited por-tion of the working class. While the political coloration of American busi-ness unionism may range from conservative to liberal, it is the bread-and-butter tradeoff – wages and benefits defined in contractual language – that concerns the business unionist. Capital as a social class is irrelevant to this view. Only specific employers and their manage-ments are important, and they may be easy to deal with or resistant. They may abide by the laws and institutions that define American collective bargaining, or they may be lawbreakers and renegades. But they (whether corporations or 'bosses') are individuals linked only by mar-kets and lines of production. The parameters of bargaining are set by the conditions of those markets and lines of production, whether goods or services. The notion of a balance of class forces between labor and capi-tal as a whole is foreign to the business unionist – except possibly as the nostalgic trappings of a bygone era of labor relations. Thus, it is difficult if not impossible for the business unionist to comprehend a shift in power relations between social classes in any terms other than the profit margins or market shares of specific employers, votes taken by 'friends' and enemies in legislatures, or the dollars and cents of influence ped-dling.

As power has shifted over the past decade or so, the perspective of business unionism has become a disabling myopia. From this short-range and narrow view there appear to be only two lines of defense: circle the wagons or follow the dictates of the market and seek the labor-management cooperation that the 'experts' proclaim to be the future. In reality, American labor has attempted both courses of action. The choice of emphasis is usually at the initiative of the employer: capital acts, labor reacts. Neither course can possibly deal with the underlying power shift that continues to advantage capital. Business unionism has not simply failed to do its job as the institutions it once helped create (and became dependent on) collapsed in the 1980s. It has in fact become a barrier to the salvation of unionism and the defense of the working class in the United States.

It would be romantic and a gross oversimplification to see the current crisis of labor as one in which a tiny handful of business union leaders were restraining a combative membership possessed of a new social vision. The simple fact is that for many years the majority of union members have in most respects shared their leaderships' conception of unionism. It could hardly be otherwise. Business unionism did bring home the bacon for the majority of two to three generations of union members. And, as we have seen, unions still make a difference. The visible change in union practice is still new. The decline in working-class living standards is still relatively recent and is experienced somewhat differently by various sections of the working class. The nature and commonality of this experience is only now becoming apparent to a layer of trade union activists. The alternative to a failed business unionism is still less apparent.

To understand the decline of union power, we must look at the system of labor-capital relations in which modern business unionism was forged. While the roots of any important social development can be traced back almost indefinitely, the structure, ideology, and basic institutional arrangements that constitute modern business unionism emerged in the 1940s as the aggressive industrial unionism of the 1930s was tamed and institutionalized. This process was by no means automatic or simple, nor was its outcome predetermined. The resulting structure and perspective proved viable in an era of economic growth but ill-suited to meet the challenges of economic change or capitalist defiance.

2

The Postwar System of Labor-Capital Relations

Organized labor emerged from World War Two as a new force in American society, unprecedented in its size and organizational stability. Union membership had soared from 8.9 million in 1940, just prior to the war, to 14.9 million in 1946. By the end of the war, 35.5% of the civilian labor force belonged to unions and most basic industries were 80% to 100% organized. Public figures ranging from the president of the US Chamber of Commerce to liberal historian Arthur M. Schlesinger remarked on the rapid and apparently irreversible growth of unionism. Economist J. M. Clark put it sharply when he reported in 1946 that 'the balance of power has shifted radically in a generation.'[1]

Clark was referring to a shift in the balance of power primarily between the giant industrial corporations that dominated the immediate postwar economy and their workers. But labor's explosive growth from the mid-1930s to the mid-1940s signaled a more general change in the balance of forces between labor and capital in society as a whole. This new power was reflected not only on the shopfloor but in local and federal politics. It was a power earned through a series of strike waves and social mobilizations concentrated within little more than a decade.

The warning signs that labor would no longer remain the silent producer of the nation's wealth came first in 1934 when three American cities witnessed a level of bitter class conflict not seen since the end of World War One. In Minneapolis, Toledo, and San Francisco important strikes became rallying points for a broader mobilization of working-class forces, including the unemployed. There, in the depths of the Great Depression, previously unorganized and voiceless workers showed that the status quo of class relations could be challenged. Two years later, in

17

1936–37, the titanic wave of sit-down strikes that gave birth to the CIO swept American industry for more than a year. Beginning in the middle of World War Two, a different kind of strike wave took shape as industrial workers defied a wartime no-strike pledge to defend gains won on the shopfloor. The total number of strikes in this wave was impressive, reaching nearly five thousand in 1944, a record not beaten until 1946. But the number of days lost due to them was low because they were mostly on-the-job 'quickie' strikes.[2] The culmination of this process came in 1945–46 when virtually all the major industrial unions hit the bricks for wage increases. Over 4.5 million workers walked the picket lines in 1946 as the loss of workdays reached its historical highwater mark. Moreover, the shear momentum of the strike wave was all the more amazing because of the context in which it occurred. With the end of war, layoffs hit most of the industries in which the CIO was based. There were 2 million workers unemployed by October 1945, and 8 million veterans were on their way home. Under similar circumstances, a strike wave of comparable magnitude had been broken at the end of World War One, leaving organized labor powerless and disorganized in most of basic industry. In 1946, however, labor emerged intact and prepared to move on to new gains.[3]

A conventional explanation is that employers had come to accept unionism or perhaps even to value it as a way to make costs predictable and to discipline the labor force. Indeed, such ideas were in the air at the time. In 1945, Republican Senator Arthur H. Vandenberg proposed the formation of a President's National Labor Management Conference, noting that 'responsible management knows that free collective bargaining is here to stay.' The conference proposed by Vandenberg, however, seemed more a demonstration of capital's reluctance to accept unionism. For one thing, it took place just as the giant postwar strike wave began in the face of intransigent management bargaining positions. As historian David Brody has pointed out, moreover, this conference reflected management's nervousness about its 'right to manage' and the expansion of the scope of bargaining beyond wages, hours and basic conditions of employment.[4] Unionism had, in fact, been imposed on management, and its acceptance by most of capital had always been tentative and conditional.

The bargaining positions of the major industrial corporations in the 1945–46 round were hard and aggressive. General Motors led the way with a lengthy list of take-away demands. The resulting strikes were long and the results fairly meager, an 18.5-cent-an-hour raise in steel that was accepted by most other CIO unions. Still, the employers did not attempt to run production with scabs or to break the unions, as they had in meatpacking and steel at the end of World War One. The reason for this lies less in an ideological shift on the part of industrial capital than in the simple fact that the organizational position and stability of the major industrial unions by the end of the war was far greater than it had been at any previous time. The destruction of the new CIO unions and the greatly expanded AFL unions in basic industry would have required a virtual civil war. No one thought that a price worth paying.

The way in which the industrial unions had achieved this new strength is important because it explains much about the contradictory system of labor-capital relations that emerged after the war. The earlier attempt to establish order in labor-capital relations through the Wagner Act of 1935 had largely been a failure. The Wagner Act authorized the National Labor Relations Board (NLRB) to guarantee labor's rights to organize and bargain without interference from management. The law was immediately challenged by capital and not upheld by the Supreme Court until April 1937.[5] Even after this decision it was largely ignored by many big corporations. In fact, the CIO was not able to stabilize its membership base until the war broke out in Europe. The sit-down strike wave of 1936–37 more than doubled union membership in the US by 1938 – from 3.7 million members in 1935 to 8.3 million in 1938. But union membership remained virtually stagnant through 1940, while that of the CIO actually declined by 400,000. Only when the effects of war orders from Europe were felt throughout industry did union membership again rise significantly.[6]

The vast expansion of union membership that occurred during World War Two, from less than 9 million members to nearly 15 million by its end, proved to be stable even in recessionary conditions after the war. The foundations for this stability were the institutional arrangements that had evolved during the war as labor, capital, and the state attempted to work out procedures for guaranteeing the rapid expansion of war production. Basically, the leadership of the CIO offered the Roosevelt administration a no-strike pledge and a wage freeze in return for government pressure on the employers to allow the growth and stabilization of union membership. In the first year of the war, the CIO leaders, aggressively led by Sidney Hillman of the Clothing Workers, delivered their side of the bargain, and strike activity dropped dramatically as production and employment soared. The majority of employers balked, however, at granting the union shop to the CIO unions.

The federal government decided the issue in compromise form when the National War Labor Board (WLB) granted 'maintenance-of-membership' to one union after another. Maintenance-of-membership required workers to be union members and pay dues during the life of a contract. Unlike the union shop, however, it granted an escape period at contract expiration during which individuals could leave the union.

Maintenance-of-membership was presented by the War Labor Board as a way of creating labor-force stability for the employer as well as the union. WLB Chairman William H. Davis argued:

> Too often members of unions do not maintain their membership because they resent the discipline of a responsible leadership. A rival but less responsible leadership feels the pull of temptation to obtain and maintain leadership by relaxing discipline, by refusing to cooperate with the company, and sometimes with unfair and demagogic attacks on the company. It is in the interest of management, these companies have found, to cooperate with the unions for the maintenance of a more stable, responsible leadership.[7]

The social imagination of a lawyer and Democrat such as Davis, who collaborated regularly with such impeccably 'responsible' CIO leaders as Philip Murray and Sidney Hillman, was not always shared by the employers. In the end, the government often had to impose maintenance-of-membership on firms through the War Labor Board. By early 1944, the board had awarded maintenance-of-membership in 271 out of 291 cases. The dues checkoff also spread under state mandate as a means of enforcing maintenance-of-membership.[8]

The constant intervention of a variety of defense-inspired boards contributed another dimension to the postwar labor-capital relations system. Historian Nelson Lichtenstein spelled out the results of government intervention during the war:

> The NDMB (National Defense Mediation Board) and its successor, the National War Labor Board, were as important as the Wagner Act in shaping the American system of industrial relations. For the next four years, these boards were instrumental in setting for the first time industry-wide wage patterns, fixing a system of "industrial jurisprudence" on the shopfloor, and influencing the internal structure of the new industrial unions. They were a powerful force in nationalizing a conception of routine and bureaucratic industrial relations that had been pioneered in the garment trades but that the Wagner Act and the NLRB had thus far failed to implement fully.[9]

In sum, the major features of labor-capital relations as they were to be practiced for the next three and a half decades were well in place by the end of World War Two: national pattern bargaining, grievance procedures designed to remove conflict from the shopfloor, and bureaucratic unionism. The body of precedent and methods of functioning that established this system during the war were passed along through the National Labor Relations Board, the courts, the industrial wage and benefit pattern, the language of the labor contract, and the union bureaucracy to the postwar era.

Race and Sex: The New Social Dimensions of the CIO

The workforce and union membership that carried out the wartime strikes and the immediate postwar strike wave were significantly different from those of the 1936–37 sit-down movement. The war sent many white male industrial workers from Northern urban areas into the army. More important, war production nearly doubled manufacturing employment in durable goods over the course of the war. The number of production workers in durable goods manufacturing soared from 3.9 million in 1939 to 7.5 million in 1945.[10] Into these production jobs came Southern whites and, for the first time in many plants, Blacks and women. Blacks had been just 2.5% of defense production workers in March 1942 but accounted for 8% in November 1944. Total Black employment went from 2.9 million men and 1.5 million women in April 1940 to 3.8 million men and 2.1 million women in April 1944, a total gain of 1.5 million.[11]

The acceptance of Black workers by the major defense employers and much of the white workforce was by no means automatic. In 1941 the March on Washington Movement, led by A. Philip Randolph, president of the Brotherhood of Sleeping Car Porters, threatened to bring 10,000 demonstrators to Washington if employment opportunities in expanding war production were not opened to Blacks. Roosevelt established the Fair Employment Practices Committee (FEPC) in response. Resistance to Black employment was massive among both employers and white workers. In 1943, for example, nearly 100,000 white autoworkers in Detroit conducted 'hate strikes' in opposition to the hiring or promotion of Blacks.

The CIO, unlike the old AFL, favored organization of Blacks on an equal basis and supported federal efforts to ensure fair employment practices. The CIO leadership, however, had no active policy to promote the employment of Blacks within industry or, for that matter, Black membership within the CIO or its affiliated unions. Nevertheless, Blacks fought their way in and played an important role in several CIO unions such as the UAW, the Steelworkers, Shipbuilders, and United Packinghouse Workers, both during and immediately after the war. By 1946 there were 1.6 million Black union members, over 10% of total union membership. In the layoffs following the war Blacks fared two and a half times worse than whites, according to the FEPC, and lost most of the skilled jobs they had gained. Nevertheless, Black workers had secured a beachhead in the labor movement that would have been impossible before the rise of the CIO.[12]

Women also entered the wartime labor force in large numbers, the total number of women workers rising from 12.1 million in December

1941 to 18.7 million in March 1944. Of these nearly 7 million new female workers, about 600,000 were Black. Probably most women were drawn into traditionally female industries and occupations, such as the garment industry or clerical jobs in government, but the expansion of female employment in basic defense production was significant. The number of women production workers in the transportation equipment industry grew from 31,330 in 1939 to 777,400 in November 1943. By 1945, 28% (280,000) of the UAW's members were women.[13] But the new women industrial workers had no organizations to speak for or organize them comparable to the NAACP and the March on Washington Movement for Blacks. There was no feminist movement in the 1940s, and the left political parties of the time showed little sensitivity to women's problems or issues. That is not to say that the new women workers were passive. They played a role in numerous strikes, joined general union caucuses or factions, and some of them fought their way into local union office. In 1944 they forced the UAW to establish a Women's Bureau. Nevertheless, most of the CIO leadership accepted the view that women would return to the home after the war to make room for the men returning from military duty. According to the US Department of Labor, about 4 million women lost their jobs within eight months of V-J Day in August 1945.[14]

Although these postwar setbacks for Blacks and women were real and massive, they did not completely wipe out the advances that these two groups had achieved during the war in employment or union membership. For example, among Black workers some of the gains that had been made in employment and income during the war were sustained or recovered as the economy expanded again at the end of the 1940s. Black employment as craftsmen and operatives (factory workers) rose from 16.6% of the total in 1940 to 28.8% in 1950. In the same period, the proportion of the median income of 'non-whites' to that of white wage and salary earners rose from 41% to 60%.[15] The rate of participation of women in the labor force rose from about 28% in 1940 to 37% in 1945 and then fell to 30% in 1947. By 1950, it was around 32%, below the wartime peak but above the prewar level. The total female workforce rose from 13.8 million in 1940 to 18.5 million in 1944. By 1947, it had dropped to 16.3 million, a loss of over 2 million jobs. But it never returned to the prewar level. Furthermore, there were some permanent shifts in the nature of women's employment. The percentage of women working as domestic servants, for example, declined rapidly during the war and continued to do so in the postwar era. For Black women, this meant a drop in the proportion employed as domestic servants from 72% before the war to 48% by its end.[16]

Blacks and women were thus a part of the labor movement that emerged from the war, although their positions were precarious. Their presence as a significant and at times vocal section of the membership brought a change in the official position of much of organized labor toward race and sex discrimination. CIO practice on race and sex discrimination was much more advanced than that of the AFL craft unions, which had excluded Blacks from membership or segregated them into subordinate 'Jim Crow' locals and organized women only in trades considered 'female'. The CIO leadership held to a formal egalitarianism in relation to race and, to a lesser extent, sex when it came to membership rights. This included a genuine commitment to civil rights policies by the government such as establishment of the FEPC. Further, its stands on equal hiring regardless of race and sex and on equal pay for equal work were ahead of most of its Democratic Party allies of the day.

To be sure, the practice of the CIO leadership in fighting race and sex discrimination was limited. It did not include any conception of affirmative action, for example. Most important at the time, it did not include an activist policy of fighting discrimination within industry or even the union. The CIO leaders opposed the 'hate strikes' of 1943, but they did not put the weight of the union hierarchy behind the promotion of Blacks or women into the better jobs. When demobilization began in 1945 and government propaganda changed its tune from Rosie the Riveter to Rosie the Homemaker, the CIO leadership limited its efforts on behalf of women and Black workers to the pronouncement of legislative goals calling for equal employment rights, a position that could not save the jobs of low seniority minority or female workers. In general, the CIO leadership did not attempt to promote equality through special contractual language, although, because so much of the workforce was new, the formal equality built into many CIO seniority clauses sometimes benefited Black workers. Internally, formal equality did not bring much Black or female representation within the CIO. This created a festering problem within the new unions that would eventually explode as new social movements arose in the decades that followed the war.[17]

For all its limitations, the system of labor-capital relations that emerged in the 1940s had a social character different from anything that preceded it. Racism and sexism remained the dominant practice within the labor market and the unions, but the presence and pressure of Blacks and women in the ranks had moved much of organized labor toward a formal commitment to racial and sexual equality in hiring and pay. Blacks and women would still be relegated to the less skilled jobs, but under CIO contracts, unlike those of many earlier unions, all workers performing the same work would receive the same pay. The institutional arrangements that came to characterize the postwar system embodied this formal egalitarianism, dissolving the official segregation of the

workforce and trade union movement that had prevailed for generations. A variety of trends, including the conservatization of the CIO
unions, would open the road for further setbacks in the 1950s, but the
presence of minority and women workers in the major unions could no
longer be challenged.[18]

The CIO's formal egalitarianism brought it into a different relationship with the Black community than organized labor had ever known
before. Based particularly on efforts in Detroit, a political alliance was
forged between the CIO leadership, the NAACP, and other Black leadership elements.[19] For its part, the Black leadership saw an opening that
labor had seldom offered it in the past. There is no question that, at the
time, this alliance strengthened the position of organized labor as a
whole – a lesson that would later be forgotten.

Defining the Postwar Labor-Capital Relations System

With the institutional framework of the postwar labor-capital industrial
relations system largely in place, the attention of both labor and capital
turned to defining its content and limits. Foremost for labor in the immediate aftermath of the war was the wage question. Wage rates had
been restrained during the war, and when it ended the enormous overtime pay that had compensated for lower rates disappeared. Following
the precedents set during the war, the CIO leaders presumed that all industrial workers would receive basically the same increase. The model
for pattern bargaining had been established by the War Labor Board in
the 1942 Little Steel Formula, which had extended one industry's norm
to industry as a whole.

In 1945, Walter Reuther, then head of the UAW's General Motors
Department, tried to set the pattern with a demand for a 30% wage increase. In the face of GM opposition the resulting strike lasted 113 days.
Although Reuther was criticized for jumping the gun and not waiting
for the CIO unions to present their demands in unison, other CIO unions
joined the strike in 1946. In the end, it was the Steelworkers who set the
pattern, 18.5 cents an hour. The other CIO industrial unions soon followed suit. In the fall of 1946 another round was negotiated for all the
industrial unions for another 10 cents an hour, this time without a strike.
The increases were modest, but the CIO unions had established the
precedent that all industrial workers should receive the same wage increase. Pattern bargaining included all of basic industry.[20]

This continuation of wartime pattern bargaining was too much for
the leaders of American capital, and management vociferously resisted
the trend. Taking the lead in 1948, GM demanded that the UAW sign a

two-year agreement, ending the unified round of one-year contracts. Instead of a common bargaining round with a united wage demand, one or another union, usually the UAW or the USW, set a general pattern that the other unions attempted to match. By the early 1950s, pattern bargaining had become more a matter of emulation than of united action, a complex system of protection covering millions of workers that depended more and more on the power of a few large unions. In general, the biggest master contracts led the way, especially those in the auto industry's Big Three, Basic Steel, rubber, electrical equipment, meat-packing, and coal mining. Following closely were a variety of 'me-too' contracts, such as those in steel fabrication, auto parts, and mining other than coal. Using the argument of comparability, that workers performing similar work deserved similar rewards, workers in smaller firms were able to win wages and conditions akin to those of the leading master and me-too contracts. Eventually, the Teamsters established another master pattern agreement in freight, which in turn spawned new me-too agreements in other areas of trucking and warehousing, while the Communications Workers of America (CWA) set a pattern in telecommunications.

Alongside the growing network of master and pattern contracts in manufacturing were a number of different bargaining systems. Some, like those in construction and retail trade, both of which were tied to local labor-market conditions, were probably not much affected by the industrial patterns. Others were, such as the craft bargaining systems in railroads and air transportation. Although contracts in rail and air transportation were bargained along craft lines, these industries were federally regulated and the contracts were national in scope. Hence the doctrine of comparability, by which workers performing similar work in different industries were paid similar rates, created a certain linkage between these workers and those in basic industry.

Once the unions surrendered the idea of multi-industry (solidaristic) pattern bargaining, under which all the industrial unions received the same increase, the force of the patterns diminished and wage levels in different industries became more disparate. Pattern bargaining came to resemble less an army marching in unison than a train in which the most powerful pulled along the rest in a line that seemed to diminish in size according to the distance from the front. Nevertheless, it was a system of income regulation that provided a measure of protection for millions of workers, an insulation from the forces of the 'free' labor market that had depressed wages in earlier years.

If wages were the key question for labor in 1946, the issue that concerned capital was management prerogative. Far from seeing the union as an ally, capital saw its mere existence as an infringement on its inherent right to rule the production process through management direction. But the institutional protection of unionism, now firmly embodied in legal precedent, government practice, and the labor contract, made it too costly for capital to challenge unionism per se. Instead, the companies attempted to limit the scope of bargaining to wages, hours, and basic conditions of employment. The Wagner Act was vague on the content of bargaining, and no body of law or precedent as yet existed to define these limits.

Further, the contradictory nature of the institutions developed during the war seemed to point in different directions. On the one hand, the no-strike pledge seemed to provide capital a free hand to rule the shopfloor. Although labor was represented on the government boards that shaped labor policy during the war, that policy was to stay clear of questions of working conditions or workplace regime. Workers on the shopfloor took a different view. Since major economic issues were bargained through the War Labor Board, local union leaders had little to bargain over except the workplace regime and the loose ends of the wage deal, such as piece rates and turn-out. This kind of bargaining was mostly unofficial and was conducted increasingly on the shopfloor rather than across the conference table.

In addition, much of this sort of workplace struggle took place in the unusual and, for the workers, largely favorable conditions of cost-plus war production (under which the corporations were guaranteed a profit) and full employment. The wartime shopfloor union leaders had reason to stretch the limits of workplace bargaining. The local and shopfloor union officials and leaders tended to be higher seniority workers exempt from the draft. But a large portion of the workforce throughout industry was new. To win the loyalty of these workers and to maintain their own union offices, the local leaders had an incentive to fight for those things that the wartime system didn't recognize or hadn't defined. (This did not often extend to the idea of winning promotions above the level of production jobs for Blacks or women.) The result of these pressures was an escalating conflict which, according to Lichtenstein, 'contributed to the erosion of factory discipline and the rise of worker power, even control of the production process.'[21] The system of 'industrial jurisprudence' could not contain rank-and-file pressures under war production conditions.

Management saw all this as proof that unions would erode its authority. A study by Yale Professor Neil Chamberlain in 1946 found that executives in virtually all major corporations believed that more authority had been lost in the process of production than had been formally granted by contract. Capital was further incensed when, in 1945, Walter Reuther asked GM for large pay increases without increases in the prices of its cars. More alarming still, Reuther called on GM to open its books to the public. Far from fostering the blissful acceptance of unionism among employers, this incident and the declining authority of management sent many a boss off to Washington in 1947 to lobby for what became the Taft-Hartley Act.

The issue of union/worker power in the workplace proved intractable. It simply could not be settled through negotiations at the top, despite the willingness of most CIO leaders to negotiate away shopfloor power. As early as 1942, for example, the UAW had reduced the number of grievance committeemen at GM by half.[22] Since then, unions have consistently granted employers management rights and no-strike clauses in contracts and more and more 'flexibility' on the shopfloor. Nevertheless, through both official and informal organization and actions over the years, labor's rank and file maintained the workplace as contested terrain.

To address this problem from a new angle, GM President Charles Wilson made an innovative proposal in 1948 that later reappeared as a fundamental union position. Wilson proposed that wage increases be linked to the cost of living and to future increases in productivity. Emil Mazey, who led that year's bargaining while Reuther was in the hospital recovering from an assassination attempt, accepted this concept, and it became the pattern for UAW wage settlements for the next thirty years. Eventually, the UAW's annual improvement factor, as the productivity increase was known, became tied to increases in national productivity figures, but the precedent was set, and business felt confident that it had made a breakthrough. *Fortune* magazine praised the GM agreement for having recaptured management initiative: 'General Motors has regained control over one of the crucial management functions...long-range scheduling of production, model changes, and tool and plant investment. It has been so long since any big US manufacturer could plan with confidence in its labor relations that industry has almost forgotten what it felt like.' Annual improvement factor formulas similar to the UAW's covered 3.5 million workers by September 1952, but productivity bargaining was usually informal and often implemented as a wage increase in the expectation of productivity gains due to union cooperation in introducing new technology.[23]

As *Fortune* noted, the linking of wages to productivity, even if only informally in negotiations, was meant to create an economic incentive for the union and the workers to return workplace power to management and to accept the introduction of new technology. Productivity increases would bring regular wage increases. Resistance to technological change and conflict in the workplace would only thwart the smooth functioning of production which guaranteed higher productivity, or so the argument went. While this ploy never eliminated shopfloor resistance to management authority, it worked in terms of the cooperative behavior of the union leadership on matters of workplace regime. Perhaps most important for capital, it focused national bargaining on wages rather than on shopfloor issues. Eventually, the drive to increase productivity would push workers to test the limits of the postwar labor-capital relations system. But in the 1940s and 1950s the pay-productivity link contributed to industrial stability.

The Fight to Establish Bureaucracy in the CIO

In academic thought the development of bureaucratic rule within labor organizations is usually seen as a natural process associated with the growth of maturity in labor relations. Unions, the theory has it, proceed from their turbulent organizing phase, during which the labor leader is an agitator, to a mature relationship with management when the leader becomes an administrator. One of the earliest formulations of this theory appears in Robert Michels's 1911 study of German Social Democracy, *Political Parties*. Viewing the evolution of the trade union leader from the early days of the union, Michels wrote:

> During this period, propaganda is chiefly romantic and sentimental, and its objective is moral rather than material. Very different is it when the movement is more advanced. The great complexity of the duties which the trade union has now to fulfill and the increasing importance assumed in the life of the union by financial, technical, and administrative questions, render it necessary that the agitator should give place to the employee equipped with technical knowledge. The commercial traveler in the class struggle is replaced by the strict and prosaic bureaucrat, the fervent idealist by the cold materialist, the democrat whose convictions are (at least in theory) absolutely firm by the conscious autocrat.[24]

In this view, bureaucracy is simply an inevitable consequence of administrative complexity.

A similar theory developed in the US in the 1950s and 1960s. A classic formulation came from Richard Lester in his 1958 book with a telltale title, *As Unions Mature*. Lester described this maturation process in the same vein as Michels:

> As a union's growth curve begins to level off, subtle psychological changes tend to take place. The turbulence and enthusiasm of youth, the missionary zeal of a new movement, slow down to a more moderate pace. Increasingly, decisions are made centrally, as a political machine becomes entrenched, as

the channels of union communication are more tightly controlled from the top, and as reliance on staff specialists grows.... As the organization enlarges, the problems of management multiply and the emphasis shifts from organization to administration, negotiation, and contract enforcement.'[25]

Lester, like Michels, also notes that 'the good life on a sizable salary...may be part of a group of corrupting influences' and that 'democratic checks may have weakened with increasing size....' But – here the language is tentative – other things 'may' contribute to the problem. For Lester and most academic labor theorists writing before the late 1960s, bureaucracy is the gradual and inevitable result of an almost biological process of maturation. Viewed from the vantage point of the late 1950s, this scenario had a certain descriptive resonance. The labor movement had settled down, and bureaucracy was a more evident feature of unionism. Union members appeared to become complacent as their wages rose. Indeed, bureaucracy seemed the correlate of the very success of unionism and its acceptance by society, including acceptance by the employers.

But such a view confused cause and effect in the actual evolution of postwar industrial relations. Far from being the structural and temporal consequence of the stabilization of the bargaining process, bureaucracy was its necessary precondition. Bureaucracy was consolidated as wartime labor policy shifted collective bargaining to the level of the federal government, far from the shopfloor or local union. The primary consideration of the negotiators was war production, not the needs of workers. Rank-and-file interference, as we have seen, was viewed by the War Labor Board in a hostile manner.

Far from evolving gradually and peacefully, bureaucracy in the CIO had to be fought for and imposed against enormous resistance where it did not already exist, as in the UAW, and aggressively defended and expanded where it did, as in the Steelworkers. This fight began as war broke out in Europe and continued through the war years. It was not a product of the stabilization that emerged from World War Two, but an institutional foundation of it.

A decade before American economists and sociologists 'discovered' that union bureaucracy was a product of mature labor relations, an earlier generation discovered it was a desirable precondition. In a Brookings Institution study published in 1941, economist Sumner Slichter extolled the advantages of bureaucratic authority in labor relations:

Because the officers of the unions are both more willing and better able than the rank and file to take account of the consequences of union policies [on the competitive position of their employers], and because they attach less importance than the rank and file to immediate effects and more importance to long-

run results, unions are more successful in adjusting themselves to technological and market changes when the officers are permitted to make policies and
negotiate agreements without ratification by the rank and file.[26]

More likely than not this observation was based on the experience of
highly bureaucratic unions such as Hillman's Amalgamated Clothing
Workers and John L. Lewis' United Mine Workers of America (UMWA).
Indeed, Hillman, Lewis, and Philip Murray, who came to the CIO and
the Steelworkers from the UMWA, brought with them nearly two
decades of bureaucratic experience. All three shared Slichter's view that
authoritative leaders were better placed to deal with changing situations
than the membership. All were separated by decades from their roots in
industrial work. They lived and worked in a world more akin to that of
the employers and politicians they dealt with than that of the workers
they represented. In the 1920s both Hillman and Lewis ruthlessly suppressed opposition within their respective unions. Their disagreement
with the old-line leaders of the AFL was not over union democracy, but
over industrial organization. The new organizations they built, the national CIO and the Steel Workers Organizing Committee, predecessor
of the United Steelworkers, reflected their bureaucratic outlook. Most of
the new CIO unions, however, were built up from the grass roots in the
course of struggle. Until the war, most CIO locals and the newer national unions were highly democratic organizations – and, in the eyes of capital, unruly ones.

The CIO at the federation level, although bureaucratic, did not necessarily affect the internal regime of the affiliated unions so long as bargaining was an autonomous process conducted industry by industry.
The war changed that. Even before American entry into the war, Roosevelt had established the National Defense Mediation Board in March
1941. It attempted to centralize all further wage settlements through
federal mediation. After Pearl Harbor, the War Labor Board succeeded
the Mediation Board with greater powers of intervention. Wage settlements were determined centrally by a tripartite board of the federal
government, and the relationship of Hillman, Murray, and Lewis to the
overall bargaining process changed completely.

Hillman was the prototype of the bureaucratic labor statesman. According to labor historian Irving Bernstein, 'Hillman addressed himself
to the acquisition and manipulation of power.' C. Wright Mills singled
out Hillman as a leader among those seeking recognition in national
ruling circles: 'His lead during the early war years, his awareness of himself as a member of the national elite, and the real and imagined recognition he achieved as a member signaled the larger entrance...of labor
leaders into the power elite.' Even before the wartime boards were set

up he became an emissary of the Roosevelt administration, working hard to end strikes at defense-oriented plants.[27] When this role became embodied in official instruments of the government, notably the War Labor Board, Hillman, along with other top AFL and CIO leaders, achieved a new kind of power over the previously autonomous unions.

The War Labor Board lost little time in making national policy of Sumner Slichter's wish for more bureaucracy. In a 1942 case involving a strike at a small New England steel fabricating plant, the WLB ruled: 'If this union is to become a responsible organization acting through its leaders, it is necessary that it have some powers over its members.' A year later, when asked if the WLB recognized the right of union members to organize against the policy of their union leadership, WLB member William Davis replied that the board did not. In 1943 the Board also encouraged the leadership of the United Rubber Workers (URW) to control its locals and shopfloor organizations. Later the WLB upheld URW President Sherman Dalrymple when he expelled seventy-two members and fined several hundred others for their rebellious activity.[28]

The struggle to bureaucratize the CIO unions was inevitably long and politically complex. Far from being a natural tendency, bureaucratization met resistance again and again in virtually every CIO union, including the Steelworkers. In virtually all the new unions, administrations that upheld the no-strike pledge in practice or moved to discipline locals faced resistance, from the shopfloor to the national convention. Unauthorized strikes by millions of industrial workers, unofficial shopfloor bargaining by strong stewards' organizations, rebellion by locals, and factionalism at union conventions were the norm throughout the war and well into the postwar era. The economists' dream of a docile union membership led complacently through the contortions of a changing marketplace by an unchallenged leadership, always a myth, was not achievable in a period of rapid union growth and rising expectations. What bureaucratization eventually gave the leadership of most unions was the ability to defeat resistance or opposition under the conditions of the postwar labor relations system.

To obtain that ability, the bureaucracy had to take authority away from the workplace and the local union while at the same time fragmenting communications at the national level. Partly this was a structural problem. Over the years, the national leadership of the industrial unions centralized the issues that were negotiated in the national contract. This included issues once thought of as local, such as production standards and line speed. This process left the locals less to bargain over and increased the latitude of the top bureaucracy to control things. Such centralization, however, would have been difficult if more sophisticated, often political, means had not been found to concentrate decision-making power and to weaken the unions' shopfloor organization – always the center of resistance to bureaucracy.

Once again, the federal government, with the approval of the CIO leadership, took the first step, establishing what Lichtenstein called 'industrial jurisprudence'. This was the four-step wartime grievance procedure, which concluded with arbitration and during which strikes and direct action were barred. This system, accepted by the CIO in 1942, differed drastically from the old, largely informal, system of workplace negotiations, which rested in the final analysis on the threat of confrontation. The stewards had derived their power from this system and their ability to deliver under it. The War Labor Board's proposal was meant to undermine that power. According to Lichtenstein, the proposal had several implications:

> The system shifted disputes from the shopfloor, where the stewards and work groups held the greatest leverage, to the realm of contractual interpretation, where the authority of management and the value of orderly procedure weighed more heavily. In the meantime – possibly several weeks – the discipline and authority of management remained intact. As long as production continued on management's terms, workers with grievances were, in effect, guilty until proven innocent.[29]

In reality, this attempt to remove power from the shopfloor didn't succeed during the war. For one thing, management did not yet have the clear legal or contractual right to discipline rebellious workers in the face of intervention by the stewards or direct action by informal work groups. Indeed, disciplinary conflicts were a source of power for the stewards.

During the war the body of precedent defining what was grievable was not sufficient to establish universally accepted norms. Such a body of norms was built up after the war, when grievance procedures were incorporated into the increasingly complex labor contracts negotiated throughout industry. In the 1946 Ford and Chrysler contracts, for example, the UAW granted 'company security' – no-strike clauses that gave management the contractual right to discipline workers. An aspect of this process that would weaken workplace organization over the years was the inclusion of the steward representation system in the contract, a development that gave the company the right to bargain over the extent of shopfloor representation – and that also gave the union bureaucracy the right to cede its diminution. From a ratio that provided for a steward for every foreman in many CIO-organized industries, the proportion declined dramatically; by the 1950s each steward had come to represent hundreds of workers confronted by numerous supervisors.

In the extension of the bureaucracy's power, the weakening of workplace union organization was one side of the equation. The other involved extending the power that came from negotiating national contracts to control of the union's internal affairs. As extensive as the advance of union bureaucracy became during the war, it still largely depended on the centralizing role of the War Labor Board in wage determination. With the end of the war, further centralization of authority at the top would be needed if the wartime system was to survive the transition to a peacetime economy. The establishment of a viable national political machine that extended from the national headquarters to the local union was the key to that centralization in most unions. But bureaucratic authority in the turbulent atmosphere of the 1940s could not simply be imposed from above. Opposing political trends as well as recalcitrant shopfloor militants had to be defeated.

One course was for the leadership to take the initiative in forming the bargaining program. Walter Reuther, who was head of the UAW's GM Department in 1945 when he put forth his innovative idea of wage increases with no price increases, was a master at such maneuvering. Victor Reuther remembered years later that 'the GM strike was designed to take the ball out of the hands of the stewards and committeemen and put it back in the hands of the national leadership.' Indeed, the use of a militant program and the willingness to strike GM for a long time were important to Reuther's election as president of the UAW in 1946.[30]

The wartime CIO was alive with rank-and-file-based political trends, factions and caucuses. Communists, socialists of all kinds, Democrats, organized Catholics, and just plain militant trade unionists formed organizations within their unions that debated policy and contended for power. This ongoing political contest was a powerful source of union democracy. No matter how much bureaucratic authority they had accrued over the bargaining process, the top leaders of most CIO unions still had to contend with opponents whose roots among workers and support in the ranks were real and who had the ability to organize on a nationwide basis. This ability to organize nationally was often the result of alliances with national left-wing political groups or parties.

Each CIO union has its own complex history of the way in which opposition to entrenched leadership was divided, defeated, demoralized or co-opted. But central to the crushing of internal democratic life and political pluralism within most of these unions was the anti-Communist crusade of the 1940s. In March 1946 Winston Churchill, with President Harry Truman at his side, delivered his famous Iron Curtain speech, and a year later the Truman Doctrine was announced. A resolution at the 1946 CIO convention declared: 'Congress of Industrial Organizations resent and reject efforts of the Communist Party, or other political parties and their adherents, to interfere in the affairs of the CIO. This convention serves notice that we will not tolerate such interference.' Philip

Murray backed the resolution.[31]

Murray, Hillman, and other CIO leaders had for years been allied with the Communist Party forces in the CIO. They had shared a common, bureaucratic method of functioning in most respects. According to David Milton, who described the situation from a left-wing perspective, 'The Communist Party of the United States, in the final analysis, shared with its social-democratic rivals, Hillman and Murray, the same desire to secure positions of power by creating alliances at the top....'[32] For the duration of the war they also shared a commitment to worker discipline in the name of war production. The CP, in fact, had been among the most hard-line forces in the CIO in opposing strikes and urging use of piecework, speedup and whatever else was needed to maximize the war effort. But once the Cold War broke out, these alliances changed. The Hillman-Murray wing of the CIO leadership saw its alliance with the Democratic Party as too central to endanger – even though they were less than happy with Truman. The turn against the CP, therefore, was not at bottom a ploy to undermine union democracy. Nevertheless, it had just that effect.

The methods used against the Communists by the CIO leaders were demagogic, dishonest, and played into the latest initiatives from the right to limit labor's power. While the CIO opposed the Taft-Hartley Act, it did not shrink from using the act's requirement that union leaders sign an affidavit disclaiming membership in a Communist organization. By 1950, eleven CIO unions had been expelled because their leaders were alleged to be Communists. Rival unions were created in some cases, and bargaining in a number of industries was badly fragmented. For the purpose of this analysis, the most important outcome of the anti-Communist crusade and purges that raged from 1946 through the early 1950s was the chilling effect they had on internal debate within the unions. Red-baiting, relatively ineffective in the 1930s and during the war, became the universal tool for silencing dissent or isolating dissidents. Just as McCarthyism would silence radicals in the entertainment industry and tame liberals from academia to Congress in the early 1950s, the fight to ban Communists and other leftists from union office or even membership put all dissident forces in the CIO on the defensive.[33]

Perhaps the most debilitating aspect of the purges was the power of the bureaucracy to define who was a genuine trade unionist and who was an 'outsider'. The 1946 CIO convention resolution set this tone when it counterposed membership in the CP and 'other political parties' to membership in the CIO. In 1948 Reuther used this 'outsider' calumny to consolidate his machine in the UAW by asking, 'Are you going to be loyal to the CIO or to the Communist Party?'[34] Thus, disagreement with the CIO leaders translated into disloyalty to the organization. The argument was and is fundamentally antidemocratic. Political pluralism within a union is as much the basis of democracy as it is in society as a whole. But in this 'debate', the CIO leaders were able to define their side as the only legitimate one. All opponents were outsiders with conflicting loyalties – a demonic logic that prevails in most unions to this day.

In addition to the chilling effect of this new, monolithic view of policy-making, the defeat of the entire organized left by the CIO bureaucracy had another outcome. Rank-and-file workers in large national unions typically lacked the means to communicate with their counterparts in other areas. To a large extent, the left parties provided a viable national communications network for opposition formations in the unions. Even a very small party such as the Workers Party, a Trotskyist group with influence in some important UAW locals, could play a key role in working with broader forces to develop the Rank and File caucus in the UAW during 1943. This caucus led the fight against the no-strike pledge and was opposed by the UAW leadership and the CP, but the national structures of the Workers Party helped the caucus get off the ground.[35] Defining such groups as outsiders allowed the CIO bureaucracy to eliminate or delegitimize the major available alternative communications networks. In this way, the bureaucracies of the CIO unions came to monopolize communications above the local level by the early 1950s. Organized political pluralism within most unions was killed – all in the name of fighting totalitarianism.

The CIO's Political Bargain with Capital

To a large extent, the system of labor-capital relations that took shape during and immediately after World War Two was a political creation. Various arrangements with capital were negotiated in institutions created by the Roosevelt administration for the prosecution of the war. These were tripartite bodies in which representatives of the commanding heights of capital worked with the top leaders of the CIO and AFL under the auspices of the federal government. Since these top labor leaders had renounced the strike as a weapon 'for the duration', their authority in the give-and-take process that produced decisions during the war derived mainly from the personal influence that leaders like Murray and Hillman of the CIO, John L. Lewis of the United Mine Workers (whose contradictory role is beyond the scope of this narrative), William Green and George Meany of the AFL, and George Harrison of the railroad brotherhoods had with the Roosevelt administration. Their influence depended on a variety of political considerations: the administration's assessment of labor's importance in the electoral coalition that made the Democrats the majority national party; its need to appease capital both during the war and in the period of reconversion that followed; and its ability to deal with the growing fire from the Republican right.

The degree of labor's real influence can be measured by the fact that none of its proposals for a planned reconversion of the economy at the end of the war were taken seriously. The Truman administration did not heed its request in 1946 for the continuation of price controls after the removal of wage restraints. Even during the war, maintenance-of-membership was the sole tangible gain the labor leadership achieved. In fact, the CIO's political strategy for the period contained a deep contradiction.

Most of the top CIO leadership opposed the idea of a independent labor party. Instead, they opted for an organization that would attempt to mobilize the labor vote for the Democrats and to pressure for greater labor influence in party affairs. The vehicle for this strategy was the Political Action Committee (CIO-PAC), formed in 1943. As Lichtenstein describes it, 'In launching the new Political Action Committee, the CIO leadership specifically rejected any "ultraliberal party in the name of the workingman."'[36] For a few former socialists in that group, such as Hillman or David Dubinsky, president of the International Ladies Garment Workers Union (ILGWU), this had meant a change in political position, from advocating a labor or socialist party to accepting a subordinate role within the Democratic Party. This decision had already been made in 1936, when Hillman, Dubinsky and Lewis led the fledgling CIO unions into the Roosevelt campaign. For other CIO leaders, loyalty to the Democratic Party was simply a matter of long-time faith or ethnic heritage. Like most of the industrial workers who formed the base of the CIO, these leaders had grown up in the ethnically based urban Democratic machines of the big cities.

Labor party sentiment had been a real trend in the unions throughout the 1930s and 1940s. It surfaced occasionally, as at the 1936 UAW convention, where a resolution was passed calling for formation of a labor party. John L. Lewis, then head of the CIO, had to intervene directly to get the convention to endorse Roosevelt. In 1943, when PAC was formed, dissatisfaction with the Roosevelt administration was high in the CIO ranks. Labor party resolutions came up at state-level meetings in Pennsylvania and New Jersey. At the Wayne County (Detroit) meeting of the CIO-backed Labor's Non-Partisan League in June 1943, an angry resolution demanded that the Michigan state CIO convention that year form a state-wide labor party within ninety days of adjournment. The debate in Michigan continued throughout the summer of 1943. In fact, a resolution that supported both Roosevelt and the formation of a labor party passed the Michigan CIO convention in June over the opposition of CIO leaders.[37] But the labor party forces in the CIO of the 1940s lacked what Hillman and the leadership possessed: a national organization capable of conducting a fight throughout organized labor. For one thing, the CIO bureaucracy provided a national platform for Hillman's campaigns on behalf of Roosevelt and the Democrats. Almost as important was the active collaboration of the largest organization of the political left at that time, the Communist Party.

The Communists' Popular Front policy, suspended only momentarily while the Hitler-Stalin Pact was in force, brought them into alliance with the Roosevelt administration and its key backers in the CIO such as Hillman and Murray. Whenever labor party sentiment surfaced, the CP could be counted on to denounce it. The CP-Hillman alliance fought for control of the New York–based and Dubinsky-run American Labor Party (ALP) when it fielded an independent candidate for governor against the Democrats in 1942. The irony in this case was that the ALP had been set up in 1936 by Hillman and Dubinsky specifically to shift garment worker votes away from the Socialist Party and to Roosevelt. Later, disgust with the Democrats had pushed the ALP somewhat to the left. In the mid-1940s, the Hillman-CP forces worked to merge Minnesota's long-standing Farmer-Labor Party into the Democratic fold. Although a variety of left organizations with some members in the CIO unions, such as the Socialist Workers Party and the Workers Party, continued to push for a labor party, they were no match for the CP or the CIO bureaucracy.[38]

The victory of the Hillman forces and the establishment of PAC created new ironies. The labor relations system, as noted, was largely the result of a political process and therefore depended on a political balance of forces largely beyond labor's control. That political alignment was moving to the right even as the CIO leaders increased their dependence on the Democrats. Consequently, their decision to forswear direct action in pursuit of labor's goals in favor of this peculiar political alliance was made at the wrong time on the basis of a poor analysis of the balance of forces. In particular, they had failed to note, in spite of the massive business presence in Washington that came with the war, that the coalition on which Roosevelt based his wartime policies was far more business dominated than the electoral coalition of 1936.

More important, the PAC strategy disarmed labor for the future. American labor possessed no independent party with which to seek power or obtain direct representation in the political arena. Labor was thus entirely dependent on the good will of the leadership of the Democratic Party. Since labor lacked the ability to challenge the Democrats electorally, its only source of potential bargaining power was its ability to mobilize a Democratic voter turnout in national elections beyond the vote the urban machines could produce. That is, PAC had to deliver something new. This it failed to do in its first trial in the 1944 elections. Only 5% of the CIO membership contributed the dollar that PAC asked for. Seventy percent of the CIO's $1.4 million contribution to the Democratic campaign that year came from its middle-class spin-off, the National Citizen's PAC. Moreover, PAC's impact on working-class voter turnout was marginal. James C. Foster concluded that 'whatever bait the PAC had set out to lure labor voters into the Democratic fold had worked no more effectively than traditional political methods.'[39]

In spite of the poor labor turnout, PAC was pronounced a success. In their postelection assessment of PAC the CIO leaders wrote, 'We reaffirm that decision and reject any and all proposals for a third party.'[40] Yet the results of PAC efforts in the 1946 congressional elections were even more disappointing. Furious with Truman's policies, millions of workers had no other party to vote for and stayed home. Only 30% of the electorate voted and the Republicans captured Congress.[41] The PAC strategy did not gain the influence or legislation it was intended to achieve, but the contributions did pay the price of admission to a subordinate seat in America's higher circles for Hillman and his colleagues. That, perhaps, was what was most important to those who saw themselves more as powerbrokers than labor leaders.

The PAC strategy, and its AFL-CIO offspring, COPE, left labor dependent on political forces beyond its control. The absence of a labor party in US politics explains why the welfare state in the US has remained such a barebones operation compared with those developed by Labour and Social Democratic parties in Europe and Canada. Additionally, it meant that the balance of forces within the labor relations arena was different from and less favorable than that of other developed capitalist democracies. While wage determination in much of Europe was heavily influenced by active government policies in matters such as employment and training, as well as by favorable labor legislation, no US party had a consistent prolabor policy. Instead, US labor remained dependent on a body of legislation created in the 1930s and modified in favor of business through legislation in the 1940s.

Labor's political dependence on others laid the basis for its first great defeat, the Taft-Hartley Act. The purpose of Taft-Hartley, of course, was to limit labor's ability to act and therefore to organize effectively in the face of employer resistance. The elimination of the secondary boycott as a weapon made it more difficult to extend unionism generally. In the long run, however, the most important result of Taft-Hartley was that through the combination of the right-to-work provision and the banning of the secondary boycott, a large part of the US – above all the South –

became a nonunion haven for capital.

The passage of Taft-Hartley coincided with the failure of the CIO's first serious incursion into the South, Operation Dixie. This organizing drive collapsed largely because of the CIO's inability to confront racism in the South and, to a lesser extent, the obsession of the CIO leadership with its fight against its former Communist allies. The intersection of this geographic 'safehouse' for capital with racism in its most institutionalized forms continues to haunt organized labor. The migration of industry to the Sunbelt began in the wake of Taft-Hartley and the collapse of Operation Dixie.[42]

In contrast to the wealth of legislative developments throughout Western capitalism, labor in the US has been unable to win a single major piece of labor legislation since the Wagner Act of 1935. Subsequent labor legislation, such as Taft-Hartley or the Landrum-Griffin Act, was opposed by labor. Much the same can be said for the CIO's social unionist legislative goals of the 1940s. Proposals calling for full employment, national health care, comprehensive public housing, and economic planning were all defeated in the postwar period. Labor has been on the winning side only when broader coalitions have arisen, and then mostly when another social force such as the civil rights movement has been willing to operate outside the channels that the American labor bureaucracy accepts as normal. The CIO's essentially social democratic vision of the postwar world was not achieved in the US: it would seem that social democracy requires a social democratic party.

Without an independent political force, labor's line of defense fell back on the internally contradictory system of pattern bargaining. Without the solidaristic wage policy, this setup began a slow atrophy that would make resistance to increased employer aggression more and more difficult. Furthermore, the dependence of the whole structure on the good will of the Democratic Party made the American labor bureaucracy far more dependent on the government than its Social Democratic (or Communist) counterparts throughout the rest of Western capitalism. The labor bureaucracies in the rest of the developed capitalist world controlled or heavily influenced parties that, in or out of power, could defend their interests and thus create a different, more favorable, social balance of forces.

Despite these weaknesses, American labor emerged from World War Two as a powerful new force. Internally, it contained a tension between a bureaucracy which supported stability and a membership laboring under the growing demands of productivity bargaining and the unmet, socially explosive demands of Black and women workers. It based much of its new stability as a force in society on an institutional system of protection that was limited to the industrial arena, internally contradictory, geographically limited, and dependent on the good will of the federal government to a dangerous degree. These weaknesses were shored up, however, by an unprecedented period of economic expansion throughout the advanced capitalist world and by the unique position of US capital in that expansion.

3

The Making of Modern Business Unionism

At the end of the 1940s an enormous transformation took place in the CIO that created most of the bureaucratic, service-oriented content and practice of contemporary American industrial unionism. This metamorphosis involved the suppression of internal political life, the ritualization of the bargaining process, the expansion of the administrative apparatus to unprecedented levels, and the abandonment of the concept of social unionism that had been the public face of the CIO. The preconditions for this change lay in the labor-capital relations system that was shaped during World War Two and modified by the Taft-Hartley Act, the chilling effect of the anti-Communist crusade of the late 1940s and early 1950s on dissent within the CIO unions, and above all the postwar capitalist boom that allowed labor to make economic gains without constant confrontation.

The Postwar Boom

Like many business and government leaders, most labor leaders expected a new depression after the end of World War Two. It was partly this fear that prompted the search for some means of stabilizing union membership and the acceptance of maintenance-of-membership. Had a full-scale depression unfolded, with unemployment hitting the 20% to 25% range again, the bureaucratic system of labor-capital stability shaped during the war would probably have collapsed or, at the very least, evolved in a different direction. But a new depression did not arrive.

Neither the military demobilization of 1945–46 nor the recession of 1949 brought Great Depression–era levels of unemployment. The highest unemployment rate of the late 1940s was 5.9% in 1949, and unemployment did not reach this level again until the 1970s. Reflecting the relatively high employment level and some of the gains made during the war, the ratio of Black unemployment to white in 1949 was about 3 to 2, rather than the 2-to-1 ratio that became standard after the mid-1950s.[1]

Despite demobilization and recession, union membership remained more or less stable, actually growing from 1945 through 1947. The recession cost labor half a million union members, but even during the worst years, 1949 and 1950, total union membership was well above its wartime high at 14.3 million.[2] In fact, the 1949 recession was mild by the standards of US economic history. The immediate reason for the absence of the expected postwar collapse was the pent-up consumer demand that had been frustrated by wartime shortages and rationing. Also contributing to the boom in the US was demand based on the vast job of rebuilding the ruined economies of Europe and Japan.

This last point is important because it indicates a feature of capitalism as an economic system that explains much about the prolonged period of growth following World War Two and about the apparent intractability of the crisis that emerged at the end of the 1960s. This feature is destruction or, to put it another way, waste. War is one way to destroy capital and create economic waste. Depressions and recessions are more normal ways. Sometimes the downside of the business cycle is mild, as in 1949; sometimes it is deep and long lasting, creating a general crisis of the system such as the Great Depression. Historically, depressions play a cleansing role for the economic system. They destroy or devalue large amounts of accumulated capital and reduce wages. The waste involved in such a process may bring massive misery to the population, but for the capitalist it is only a temporary setback. With the value of capital low and labor costs down, it again becomes profitable to invest.

Of course, this cyclical recovery can be aborted. If the depression is very deep and a great deal of capital is destroyed, where is the new investment to come from? Private capitalists may well be wary of committing the large amounts of capital needed to create a recovery. And, since capitalists usually do not act in a coordinated fashion, who is to take the lead? British economist John Maynard Keynes thought he had found an answer in government spending: Let the government take the lead by pumping borrowed money into the economy. Although it was only barely aware of the theory behind Keynes's project, the Roosevelt administration attempted to do some of this though the various New Deal welfare measures. It didn't work. The US economy slumped again in

1937 after a brief and shallow recovery of a year.

What did produce a new wave of investment was World War Two. Investment resumed as war orders began to pour into the United States from Europe. US entry into the war created an unprecedented industrial expansion, and profitability was restored. The Great Depression had destroyed and devalued capital, providing the conditions for new investment. Government war spending provided the seed money to pay for it. While the US economy grew, the economies of Europe and Japan experienced the massive destruction of total war. Thus, the United States emerged from the war as the strongest economy in the world, and the economic wasteland of Europe provided a new investment opportunity for US capital. Once again, the government provided the seed money for investment in the form of the Marshall Plan beginning in 1948. The Marshall Plan was meant to help the governments of Western Europe resist Communism by stimulating economic growth, but it also had the long-range effect of inducing large-scale US investment in Western Europe for the next two decades. In the 1940s and 1950s, Europe was a low-wage market, and profits were high for American investors. The postwar boom was on.[3]

The rebuilding of Europe, however, was a temporary opportunity for US capital, which soon came into competition with the very European capital it had helped to sustain. To keep Western capitalism as a whole growing for three decades without a serious recession required another economic regulator, another source of destruction. A new world war was not part of a viable economic policy in the nuclear age. Small wars like Korea and Vietnam were not sufficient to regulate an increasingly integrated world economy. But massive arms spending was. According to a United Nations study, by the early 1960s, arms production accounted for about 10% of the total production of goods and services in the world.[4]

With or without war, arms spending is pure waste in an economic sense. It produces neither capital goods nor consumer goods. With the advent of the arms race, it produced highly expensive items that couldn't be used even in a conventional war. On the one hand, arms production stimulates the economy by providing jobs and profits that private industry might not create. On the other, it dampens the physical accumulation of capital in the economy as a whole by pouring vast amounts of wealth into products that do not reenter the cycle of production in any form. The use of this wasteful regulator of capitalism was not limited to the United States. After a brief interlude in the late 1940s, the permanent arms economy became a global phenomenon that helped prevent the return of economic depression by moderating the accumulation of capital on a world scale.[5]

The results for Western capitalism were spectacular. As British economist Michael Kidron pointed out in the late 1960s, 'The system as a whole has never grown so fast for so long as since the war – twice as fast between 1950 and 1964 as between 1913 and 1950, and nearly half again as during the generation before that.'[6]The US economy grew apace. From 1950 to 1964, the gross national product expanded by 83%, corporate profits more than doubled, and the amount spent each year on new plant and equipment rose by 138%, indicating business confidence in the future.[7] Productivity in the private economy as a whole and in the manufacturing sector both rose by about 50% in this period, but in some of the industries organized by the CIO productivity growth was even greater.[8]

Unionism grew in this economic atmosphere. From 1950 to 1956, union membership in the US grew by 3 million, hitting 17.5 million in the latter year. Through this period the proportion of union members to all nonagricultural workers remained about one-third. In manufacturing, the proportion of union members grew from 40% in 1947 to almost half in 1956.[9]Furthermore, the average hourly earnings of manufacturing production workers nearly doubled, from $1.07 in 1946 to $1.95 in 1956.[10]

US entry into the Korean War in mid-1950 did not bring the atmosphere of national sacrifice that had accompanied World War Two. Labor did not offer a no-strike pledge. Indeed, labor leaders walked out of Truman's War Stabilization Board in opposition to a wage freeze limiting new settlements to 10% above the January 1950 level.[11] Expanded war production brought more jobs and more union members in industry. Manufacturing jobs rose from 12.5 million in 1950 to 14 million in 1953. The end of hostilities destroyed over 1 million factory jobs, but industrial employment remained above the 1950 level in 1954 and surpassed it in 1955 with manufacturing employment hitting 13.4 million in 1956. Nor did union membership decline at the end of the Korean War.[12]

Not even the election of a Republican president brought setbacks. For the first time in its history, the CIO had no 'friend' in the White House. For all but the oldest AFL officials, Republican rule was but a distant memory. But the Eisenhower administration generally took a laissez faire attitude toward labor and collective bargaining. In 1953 its Council of Economic Advisers continued the tradition, initiated by Truman's Council and perpetuated by all subsequent administrations, of calling on labor and management to tie all contracts to national, as opposed to industry, productivity gains.[13] But it made no effort to implement an incomes policy or other forms of direct intervention. Indeed, organized labor experienced more difficulty with the federal government during

Truman's second term than during Eisenhower's first.

The economic conditions faced by labor after 1950 were thus unusually favorable. Moreover, except for a shallow recession in 1959, the expansionary bargaining atmosphere was unbroken. Lasting a decade and a half, this new industrial environment laid the basis for a fundamental transformation of the CIO unions into the bureaucratic, business unionist mold already predominant in the AFL craft unions. Backed by the largess of an ascendent capitalism, this transformation appeared justified to the leaders who shaped the system. Each contract promised an improvement in the standard of living and most delivered. There were strikes to persuade a reluctant management and to demonstrate to the membership that union leaders still knew how to fight when circumstances demanded it. Genuine confrontation, however, was viewed as archaic, a vestige of another era. Employers, for their part, lent authority to the practice of business unionism by measuring their opposition to union demands carefully. Union busting was rare. Routine functioning was good enough most of the time. Criticisms of the labor bureaucracy were ignored as the carping of a few disgruntled intellectuals. As the end of this idyll approached in the mid-1960s, one observer commented, 'The American labor movement is sleepwalking along the corridors of history.'[14]

The Elimination of Opposition and the Transformation of the Political Culture of the CIO

The CIO unions that grew during the 1950s were very different organizations from those that fought through the stormy 1940s. In virtually every major CIO union the bureaucratic ascendancy accomplished gradually in the 1940s was rapidly converted into one-party or one-man rule. The last vestiges of opposition were expelled, crushed or co-opted in a period of two or three years. The anti-Communist crusade legitimized the elimination of opposition, but not all those who were silenced or defeated were members or sympathizers of the Communist Party.

The United Auto Workers presents the most dramatic example of this process because its internal political life from its birth in 1935 to the end of the 1940s was rich and democratic. As in most CIO unions, bureaucratic control over union administration and contract bargaining grew during the war. But the UAW was alive with independent local leadership, political currents, and national caucuses. Every policy had to be justified and fought for at annual conventions. Debates were often long and heated. But all of this changed rapidly once Walter Reuther took the helm in 1947.

The 1947 UAW convention saw not only the election of Reuther but the defeat of the union's other major organized force, the Thomas-Addes caucus. This caucus had been supported by the Communist Party, and anti-Communism was a major theme of Reuther's campaign. But he was not satisfied with the defeat of the Communists or those they had supported. In the next two years, he moved to eliminate the remaining non-Communist opposition and to limit the ability of any future opposition to form. Jack Stieber, writing in the early 1960s, described Reuther's campaign: 'By the end of 1947 the Reuther forces were in complete control of communications, finances, and staff resources of the UAW. There followed a 'mopping-up' operation in which the administration brought to bear the full power of the international union – sometimes exceeding its constitutional authority – against opposition locals and their leaders.'[15] Among the incidents in this mopping-up operation was the expulsion of Tracy Doll and Sam Sage, leaders of the Progressive-Unity caucus, at the 1949 convention for distributing a report that alleged racketeering in the UAW. The convention justified this expulsion on the grounds that there was a difference between 'honest opposition' and 'treason'.[16]

Far more damaging to union democracy were the structural changes imposed by the Reuther forces in those years. In 1949 Reuther began the push to eliminate annual conventions, which had long been the focal point of intense political debates. In fact, although the constitution specified annual conventions, each convention since 1944 had voted to hold them twenty months apart. Nevertheless, the resistance to eliminating the institution of annual conventions was strong enough to defeat the Reuther amendment in 1949. In 1951, however, Reuther got his way in a motion to make the next two conventions two years apart. In 1953 the UAW's constitution was amended to make conventions biennial.

Most of the dissension at the 1949 convention came in fact from Reuther's supporters. Seeking to contain further dissension in his own ranks, he moved to reverse his 1947 decision to disband the Reuther caucus. In 1949 the caucus was revived. But the new caucus, eventually known as the Administration caucus, was a far cry from the contentious political grouping that brought Reuther to office. It was instead an administration machine. Run with iron discipline from the International Executive Board, it carried top-level decisions all the way down to the local level. Staff members were disciplined to carry out administration policies and denied the right to run against administration candidates at any level. Bert Cochran described the effect of this change on the UAW's internal affairs: 'A scattered membership thus found itself confronted by a solid phalanx of a disciplined and drilled officialdom of some 700 labor professionals commanding the services of a variety of experts, and in full control of the levers of power.'[17]

The next step was to gain control of the union's local press, which had often been a forum for dissenting views. This was done administratively and without convention discussion. Stieber relates how control was achieved: 'Further attention was directed at the union's publication policy when, in September, 1950, the International Executive Board informed local union editors whose papers were printed in conjunction with the *United Automobile Worker,* an official UAW publication, that an international publications committee would review their newspapers for possible libel and conformity with international policy.'[18] This was followed by the suspension of those papers that didn't take the message to heart.

By 1951 Reuther could boast that organized debate and opposition in the UAW was dead. Of course, he didn't call it 'debate'. He called it 'factionalism' and vowed it would never occur again. He told the 1951 UAW convention: '…we are never going back to those old factional days; we are going ahead, and we are all going ahead together…. the past is dead, as far as factional considerations are concerned.'[19]

There were, to be sure, a handful of critics such as Carl Stellato of Local 600. But organized opposition was no longer considered legitimate. In the eyes of the International Executive Board there was no 'honest opposition', only 'treason'. Individual dissent might be tolerated. Indeed, in 1957, when the McClellan Committee's investigation of labor corruption brought abuses of union democracy to light, the UAW set up its own Public Review Board. This board was composed of public figures supposedly beyond the influence of the UAW leadership and was charged with protecting the rights of individual members. But genuine opposition was not tolerated, and the UAW remained a one-party 'controlled democracy' until the social and economic conditions of the 1960s provoked a new wave of opposition.

Unlike the UAW, the United Steelworkers was born with a bureaucracy intact. The Steel Workers Organizing Committee was formed in 1936 by John L. Lewis, president of the United Mine Workers. A section of the Mine Workers' bureaucracy was passed on to the SWOC, giving it a bureaucracy even before it had much of a membership. The SWOC became the United Steelworkers of America in 1942, and Philip Murray its first president, while Murray was still a vice president of the UMW; in this manner, the USW inherited a central administration. But its political structure, also modeled on the UMWA, was decentralized. The biennial convention did not deal with bargaining policy at all, which was handled by a separate wage policy committee, nor did it elect officers, as in the UAW. The top officers were elected by national referendum, as in the Mine Workers, and the district directors, who composed the rest of the International Executive Board, were elected in district elections. Furthermore, except during the reign of the War Labor Board, bargaining was remarkably decentralized throughout the 1940s. President Murray bargained with US Steel, which set a pattern for the others, but all other bargaining was conducted by the local leaders. Thus, lacking any central focus, the USW did not develop a system of national caucuses like the UAW.

Opposition, political debate, and rank-and-file organization in the USW focused on the local and district level, where they were quite widespread. Because bargaining was conducted at the plant level, the locals had a great deal of power and autonomy.[20] Thus, the conflicts between the Murray administration and its opponents tended to take the form of fights to limit or preserve local autonomy. To achieve control, the Murray leadership fought to centralize every aspect of union functioning except its political structure. To provide the central administration with economic power, first SWOC and then the USW required that dues be paid to the International. To enforce this rule, the constitution was amended in 1948 to require the employers to send dues checkoff funds directly to the International. This made dues increases a focus of most convention-based opposition to Murray.

More important, the International was determined to take the substance of bargaining out of the hands of the local leadership. It achieved this in 1950 when the constitution was amended to make the International the sole contracting party in all contracts. Regular attempts to gain the right to ratify contracts throughout the 1940s and 1950s were defeated at tightly controlled conventions.[21]

The Communists had been supporters of the Murray machine. Lee Pressman, a party member, was the USW's legal adviser and CIO general counsel and a supporter of the bureaucratic center of the union. But as the general rift between the mainstream CIO leaders and the Communists grew in the early days of the Cold War, Murray moved to purge the CP.

The political culture of the CIO was still such that real political issues had to be found to use against the Communists. Murray, as well as many other CIO leaders, used the Marshall Plan and the 1948 presidential campaign of Henry Wallace on the Progressive Party ticket. Wallace, who was backed by the CP, threatened to pick up support among unionists beyond the CP membership who were disgusted with Truman. In response, the CIO Executive Board passed a motion declaring that support of Wallace was against CIO policy, and Murray waged a fierce campaign throughout both the CIO and the USW against Wallace supporters. Lee Pressman was forced to resign in 1948. Lacking any organized vehicle of opposition or any record of disagreement with Murray's administration, the Communists (and in their wake, other leftists) were disarmed.[22] Murray's further moves to centralize authority and limit local autonomy defused any potential opposition. Though carried out in a different way, the suppression of opposition in the Steelworkers was every bit as complete as that in the UAW by the early 1950s.

As in the USW, opposition in the United Rubber Workers came largely from leaders of important locals. During the war several large Akron locals had led wildcats, opposed the no-strike pledge, and mounted an opposition to the administration of Sherman Dalrymple. The Communists were a minor factor, and they supported the Dalrymple administration, including its suppression of wildcat strikers and insurgents. After the war, Dalrymple was succeeded by L. S. Buckmaster, a conservative unionist. Opposition to Buckmaster broke out in 1948. Its leader was George Bass, president of Local 5 in Akron. Buckmaster narrowly won reelection at the URW convention that year, but the Bass forces won an majority on the Executive Board and removed Buckmaster from office. Using the Cold War and red-baiting, even though the Bass forces were not leftists, Buckmaster recaptured control at the 1949 convention. Thereafter, the URW fit the new one-party mold.[23]

The elimination of opposition within the National Maritime Union (NMU) was more ruthless than most. NMU President Joseph Curran had been a Communist and had used the party's opposition to strikes and insurgency during the war to build a powerful machine. With the beginning of the Cold War, Curran changed sides and mounted a fight against his former comrades. In 1948 he beat the Communists and immediately moved to rid the union of other opposition elements. Curran expelled his opponents within the leadership one by one, fired union representatives for opposing 'union policy', and used loyal staffers to intimidate members. The fight was raucous, and at one point four hundred oppositionists sat-in at NMU headquarters. Curran had the police remove the demonstrators. Bert Cochran summarized the results in familiar terms: 'By the 1950s, with all major critics expelled from the union, and others properly intimidated, the NMU settled into the…pattern of pure-and-simple unionism.'[24]

Curran's success points to a problem with the Communists' role in the CIO. Wherever they participated in the leadership of the CIO unions, they helped to shape the bureaucratic system of labor-capital relations and to entrench bureaucratic practices within the unions. Thus, Curran could defeat both Communist and non-Communist opponents in a period of two years because of the bureaucratic apparatus he had helped build when he was a Communist Party member. Despite all the clashes between Communist and non-Communist CIO leaders and members in the late 1940s, they had no real differences over the practice of collective bargaining or union structure.

Within the top CIO leadership, non-Communists and Communists alike could justify one-party rule. With two-thirds of his union's districts in receivership, Lewis gave this answer to critics at the 1936 convention of the United Mine Workers: 'It is not a fundamental principle that the Convention is discussing. It is a question of business expediency and administrative policy as affecting certain geographical areas of the organization. It is a question of whether you desire your organization to be the most effective instrumentally...or whether you prefer to sacrifice the efficiency of your organization in some respects for a little more academic freedom.'

Lewis spoke the language of business unionism. When Harry Bridges, a party sympathizer, justified one-party rule in the ILWU he turned to a roseate model of the Soviet Union under Stalin. In 1947 he defended his autocratic regime by asking: 'What is totalitarianism? A country that has a totalitarian government operates like our union operates. There are no political parties. People are elected to govern the country based upon their records.... That is totalitarianism...if we start to divide up and run a Republican set of officers, a Democratic set, a Communist set and something else, we would have one hell of a time.'[25]

Thus, in the United Electrical Workers (UE), where the Communists held power beginning in 1941, the anti-Communist opposition took on a rank-and-file character with the formation of a national opposition caucus in 1946. The political direction of this movement was largely set by Father Charles Owen Rice and the Association of Catholic Trade Unionists, but its appeals against bureaucratic practices in the UE won support in the ranks.[26] This conflict was resolved by the expulsion of the UE from the CIO in 1950 and the establishment of a rival union, the International Union of Electrical Workers (IUE) – a split that created two bureaucratic unions with little internal opposition. Around 1950, the leaders of the CIO unions, including those that were expelled or those, like the Miners, that had left, could rest secure that no such 'hell of a time' was at hand within their own organizations: Opposition was dead.

The crushing of opposition and the expulsion or suppression of the Communists did more than simply solidify the bureaucratic character of industrial unionism in the United States. It killed the political culture that had made the CIO unions so different from those of the AFL. Because of their reliance on bureaucratic methods, the Communists played an ambiguous role in this culture. But as part of an ideological trend distinct from liberalism, they contributed to the pluralism of CIO political life despite their frequent efforts to blur any such distinction. Inadvertently, the presence of the Communist Party throughout the CIO legitimized the existence of other left trends, such as the two Trotskyist groups (the Socialist Workers Party and the Workers Party), the Socialist Party of Norman Thomas, a myriad of smaller groups, and well-known independent leftists. Because of this political pluralism and the left character of the debates of the day, virtually every tendency in the CIO attempted to portray itself as politically progressive and/or industrially militant. Anti-Communists such as Murray and Reuther consistently characterized themselves as social unionists and political progressives.

Throughout the CIO and its affiliates, the fight to suppress opposition was conducted in the name of CIO policy, often demagogically as CIO policy versus Communist Party policy. Not only were dissident political trends defeated organizationally, but the practice of debate around differing political strategies or ideologies was delegitimized. Murray re-enforced the suppression of political life in the CIO when support for Wallace was declared a violation of CIO policy. The message was that the CIO supported Democrats and that third parties were beyond the perimeters of legitimate political discussion. Political leftists or union dissidents of any stripe were now defined as 'outsiders'. Red-baiting worked long after the Communists were driven from influence. As Ed Mann, a non-Communist radical in the Steelworkers, noted, 'The McCarthy days of the 1950s killed everything that even looked like an independent organization; anybody who got two people together was immediately red-baited or run out.'[27] The vibrant and democratic political culture of the CIO became history.

The New Cultural Setting of American Labor

An important result of McCarthyism in the unions was the dissolution of the previous connection of insurgent workers with political intellectuals. Reform activist Herman Benson, who was a rubber worker and socialist activist in the 1940s, wrote: 'In those days, radical intellectuals and radical workers were bound in a fraternity nowhere dreamed of in contemporary talk about a new "alliance". They shared more than common ideals; they often shared membership in the same party or group.'

This 'fraternity' gave union activists access to the same information and analysis their bureaucratic rivals had. It also gave intellectuals a grounding in the realities of work and unionism. But, as Benson also noted, 'Around 1950, intellectuals and union dissidents went rocketing off in opposite directions.' With criticism from intellectuals as unacceptable as opposition from the ranks, 'laborite intellectuals made peace with the labor movement, reconciled themselves to its limitations, and stopped nagging for reforms.'[28] The labor intellectuals of the 1950s either became union staffers and kept their thoughts to themselves, or went to work at universities where labor studies were limited to technical analysis.

The cross-fertilization of ideas among leftist intellectuals and union activists had contributed much to the political culture of the CIO prior to 1950. Active or inquisitive workers were not solely dependent on the union's house organs or the capitalist mass media. Independent analysis and ideas, which are crucial to any social movement, were available to the ranks of most CIO unions through a variety of left publications, both those of groups and independents, and through the many local union publications to which these intellectuals contributed. The purposeful suppression or marginalization of such publications left the rank and file dependent on the media of a national culture that was moving to the right, adopting business ethics as universal values, transforming the organized working class into an 'interest group', and introducing a concept of individualism in the guise of a critique of 'conformity' that repudiated the notion of labor solidarity.

Bert Cochran summed up this process exactly when, in the late 1950s, he described the 'businessman's intellectual reconquest of America'.[29] The literature of the late 1930s reflected the fact of class conflict, and books on the new growth of unions abounded. The intellectual atmosphere of the early 1950s, on the other hand, reflected the rise of US business to world hegemony. The labor scholarship of the period proclaimed the evolution of bureaucracy and the abandonment of confrontation to be a natural and, therefore, unopposable process of maturation. The political science of the decade discovered that there were no classes, only contending interest groups. The concept of a plurality of 'countervailing forces' was popularized by John Kenneth Galbraith in his *American Capitalism: The Concept of Countervailing Power* in 1956. Organized labor was one such group, legitimate so long as it stuck to its narrowly defined role of negotiating wages and hours, illegitimate if it overstepped its relationship to the other 'countervailing forces' that composed modern capitalism. The concept of the capitalist class was replaced by the innocuous concept of management in the works of Adolf Berle, Gardner Means and Peter Drucker. Reinforcing this classless social pluralism – but indirectly justifying the suppression of genuine political pluralism in the unions – was Daniel Bell's 1959 pronouncement of the end of ideology. Serious political debate was no longer needed in the unions because there was presumably nothing worth debating anymore.

During the 1950s most labor experts apologized for and defended the contemporary practice of the union leadership. Among members of the Wisconsin school, the major school of labor economists and historians founded before World War One by John R. Commons, bureaucratic unionism was a given scarcely worth reflecting on. This school had been shaped in the defense of the AFL against both its socialist and management critics. Commons, Selig Perlman and Philip Taft had dismissed the notions of class and class consciousness decades before. Their economic analysis was concerned with the behavior of unions in labor markets rather than with labor and capital as contending forces, and their histories were self-conscious defenses of AFL practice. When Philip Taft wrote *The Structure and Government of Labor Unions* in the early 1950s, he described a world in which union leaders respected the opinions of members and members supported their leaders. There were no heated contests for leadership in Taft's labor movement because there was no real disagreement. He explained the bureaucratization of unions as a function of market changes: 'If the labor or product market in which a union operates undergoes a change, the leaders may try to adapt the union's structure and operations to the new needs.'[30] Union leaders, in Taft's view, were just doing what was necessary.

But the market-oriented analyses of the Wisconsin school could not explain the changes the CIO had undergone in the 1940s. Industries like auto, steel, rubber, and electrical equipment were quite large and centralized when the CIO was born. Other than simple growth, these industries recorded no structural changes from the late 1940s to the early 1950s. Thus, Richard Lester and the other theorists of union maturity saw the transformation of unionism so evident in the early 1950s as an inevitable function of conflict itself. Lester wrote that 'collective bargaining institutionalizes conflict by gradually building up orderly processes, joint machinery, and other administrative restraints against unruly or precipitate action.'[31] Lester's language reveals that he, as much as Taft, was concerned with justifying the behavior of the labor bureaucracy. The difference is that Lester's focus was not on markets but on institutions. In rediscovering Robert Michels's 'iron law of oligarchy', the union maturity theorists justified the elimination of opposition and political debate as fully as the Wisconsin school had.

Unlike the liberal labor economists of the 1950s, the popular sociologists of the period were social critics. Their work, however, replaced class conflict as a social problem with a focus on the individual. The subjection of the individual to the group became the theme of those sociologists most critical of modern mass organization. *The Organization Man* by William Whyte, Jr., and *The Lonely Crowd* by David Riesman both bemoaned the growth of conformism in the age of mass organizations. While primarily concerned with the new middle class caught in an impersonal corporate world, Riesman did take note of the 'indifferent mass of nominal union members' who characterized the working-class versions of his 'other-directed' conformist. Riesman's idea of the good 'inner-directed' worker was the pre–Civil War 'self-educated workman' whose Mechanics Association 'did not look at everything from a labor angle'.[32] These critiques of conformity were by no means off the mark, but their methodological approach artfully changed the discourse of social analysis from one of conflicting social classes, so evident in the 1930s and 1940s, to one of individuals and organizational structures.

This view of society was endorsed in the mass culture of the 1950s by the 1954 Marlon Brando movie *On the Waterfront*. The film was inspired by New York State hearings on union corruption on the waterfront in the 1940s. It portrayed a lone wolf longshoreman taking on a mob-run union. The longshoremen of *On the Waterfront* were an 'indifferent mass of nominal union members' if ever there was one. The real story of the New York waterfront of the 1940s and early 1950s was another matter. Members of the International Longshoremen's Association fought the leaders' corruption and the sweetheart contracts that underwrote it with a series of wildcats that paralyzed the port of New York in 1945, 1947, 1948, and 1951. These wildcat strikes and not corruption triggered the state investigations.[33] But reality did not fit the new social paradigm of individuals coping with the imperatives of modern organization.

In the second half of the 1950s, the public was further exposed to this worldview in the highly publicized hearings on labor racketeering conducted by the McClellan Committee. With the mass media hanging on every word, the committee painted a picture of organized labor as a den of thieves. Its targets were a small number of AFL unions or former AFL affiliates like the Teamsters and the ILA, most of which had been corrupt for half a century. While the focus was on criminal and financial misdoings, the hearings also addressed the abuse of union power by top officials. The object of the McClellan hearings, and later the Landrum-Griffin Act, which they helped produce, was to weaken the power of unions in relation to employers. In line with the thinking of the time, the politicians who led this effort believed that the good, conservative American workingman (in the imagined world of the 1950s, women were homemakers) would restrain the power of corrupt leaders like Hoffa if only they had the democratic right to do so. The Labor-Management Reporting and Disclosure (Landrum-Griffin) Act, with its Title I Bill of Rights, was written entirely in the language of individual rights.

Nothing, however, dominated the culture of the 1950s so much as the notion that affluence had arrived in the land and if every last man, woman and child wasn't well-off yet, the means were at hand. In the popular literature, this usually meant that blue-collar workers had joined the middle class in an orgy of consumption. As William Manchester wrote in the 1950s, 'Assembly line workers with working wives [are]… driving expensive new cars and buying stock.' In 1954, *For-*

tune magazine declared that the average middle-class consumer was no longer the businessman but 'the machinist in Detroit'.[34] Of course, *Fortune*'s Detroit machinists were skilled tradesmen who composed only about 15% of the auto workforce and, as a 1960 study showed, were almost entirely white.[35]

The most sophisticated advocates of the worker affluence theory, however, didn't claim that poverty had been eliminated or that every worker consumed like a businessman. John Kenneth Galbraith argued instead in his 1958 book *The Affluent Society* that United States now had the means to generalize affluence. Galbraith's view is important because it contained an idea that provided theoretical coherence to productivity bargaining and business unionism. It was not a new idea – it had been part of Keynesian economic theory as it was laid out in the 1930s – but Galbraith popularized it. In one sentence he abolished the economic roots of class struggle for a whole generation of liberals and labor leaders: 'Increased real income provides us with an admirable detour around the rancor anciently associated with efforts to redistribute wealth.'[36] In other words, as long as the postwar boom continued and the economy grew, everyone could experience rising living standards without recourse to class conflict or social struggle. As one of the more important countervailing powers in the economy, labor had a legitimate role to play in guaranteeing that the employers allowed the workers to maintain their share in the growing economy in line with productivity increases. This idea justified both the existence of unions and the adaptation of CIO leaders to business unionism.

The theories of affluence and the individualist ethics of the 1950s could not have taken root without the transformation that took place in the CIO in the late 1940s. The existence of an aggressive, democratic labor movement engaged in solidaristic bargaining, alive with political debate of a largely left character, and committed to the pursuit of broader egalitarian and welfare goals would have been incompatible with these views. But as opposition was eliminated, political discourse stifled and trivialized, and the goals of social unionism quietly abandoned in favor of defensive self-justification, the CIO leadership silently, often inadvertently, ratified the great celebration of American business values. The cultural environment in turn stamped the CIO's new business unionism with the Good Housekeeping Seal of Approval.

Modern Business Unionism Takes Root

Business unionism was of course not new in the 1950s. Most AFL unions had practiced it for decades. The growth of business unionism began when most of the top leaders of the AFL repudiated socialism before the turn of the century. In 1890, AFL President Samuel Gompers declared: 'The trade unions pure and simple are the natural organizations of the wageworkers to secure their present material and practical improvement and to achieve their final emancipation.'[37] Adolph Strasser, another early AFL leader and friend of Gompers, said, 'We have no ultimate ends. We are going on from day to day. We are fighting for immediate objects – objects that can be realized in a few years.'[38] The McClellan hearings revealed in the 1950s that some AFL officials had stretched this concept to include a variety of illegal but personally profitable ventures. But, as Sidney Lens pointed out in 1959, 'The overwhelming majority of business unionists have never received a pay-off, nor carried a gun or a pair of brass knuckles. They are simple, direct, practical.'[39]

The business unionist was content to negotiate, sign, and administer labor contracts. The politics of that process concerned nuts-and-bolts legislation that affected collective bargaining, not social reform per se. Business unionists were more likely to be political liberals than the employers they dealt with, but in normal times they did not see the union as a vehicle for social change. Indeed, until the mid-1930s, the AFL rejected most forms of national labor or social legislation. For the typical AFL official prior to the labor upsurge of the 1930s, 'politics' meant a relationship with a local political machine. At the national level, business unionism dealt with politicians in much the same way it did with employers: through a process of negotiation and implied threat. The AFL slogan 'Reward your friends and punish your enemies' certainly implied that those who opposed labor's legislative goals would suffer its wrath at election time. But political favor or disfavor was a practical matter of give-and-take, not one of ideology or social philosophy.

AFL business unionism was ideological on one point: it supported the capitalist system. Gompers was rhapsodic on the subject. In the view of business unionism, capitalism, unionism, and democracy were inextricably linked. Unions could not function without political freedom, and capitalism was thought to be the basis of that freedom. As George Meany put it in 1955, 'We are dedicated to freedom… through a system of private enterprise. We believe in the American profit system.'[40] For most business unionists, capitalism was simply a given. Unlike Gompers, who faced a strong socialist opposition in the early AFL, they felt no need to philosophize about the system. Their job was to strike a bargain within it.

The acceptance of the business enterprise as the immutable expression of the system led naturally enough to the notion that 'the trade unions pure and simple' were themselves businesses. No one put it more eloquently than John L. Lewis: 'Trade unionism is a phenomenon of capitalism quite similar to the corporation. One is essentially a pooling of labor for the purpose of common action in production and sales. The other is a pooling of capital for exactly the same purpose. The economic aims of both are identical – gain.'[41]

The idea of the union as a business led in turn to the conclusion that it should be run like one – from the top down. As Teamster President Dave Beck asked in the 1950s: 'Unions are big business. Why should truck drivers and bottle washers be allowed to make big decisions affecting union policy? Would any corporation allow it?'[42] Few union officials made the point that crudely, but the belief that the businesslike functioning of a union required bureaucratic norms of organization was a basic article of faith for the AFL business unionist.

John L. Lewis was an ardent, self-conscious business unionist, but, unlike most AFL unions of the mid-1930s, Lewis's United Mine Workers was an industrial union. Lewis understood that the new mass production industries could not be organized along craft lines and took the initiative in forming the CIO as a committee of eight union presidents within the AFL in November 1935. However, this step did not signal a fight between business unionism and social unionism, much less between business unionism and socialism. Of these eight, three were nominal socialists who abandoned the Socialist Party within a few months. Irving Bernstein's description of them is accurate: 'The only conviction they all shared was faith in industrial unionism, and an impatient belief that the Federation was permitting a historic opportunity to slip through its fingers.'[43]

The CIO that emerged from World War Two was the product of more than a decade of massive social upheaval. Millions of workers flowed into new organizations, stamping them with their own democratic aspirations and shaping a new generation of leaders from the shopfloor to the international union headquarters. Previously existing unions, such as the Mine Workers or the many AFL unions that grew during the upheaval, could absorb new members without basically altering their bureaucratic structures or the philosophies of their leaders. But the new CIO unions were mostly built from the ground up, or, like the Steelworkers, were a hybrid of rank-and-file democracy and bureaucracy. Furthermore, the leaders who were shaped in those turbulent years despised the routine business unionism of their AFL rivals, whom they often fought in the streets. Many of these leaders were leftists who influenced the way the active rank and file viewed unionism, even if they failed to recruit many workers to socialism or Communism. Classes and class conflict were accepted facts that were reflected deeply in the culture of the period. The wartime debates and internal union factional struggles were waged on this intellectual terrain – inhospitable soil for the philosophy of business unionism.

In this environment, where socialist ideas flourished among an active minority but could not serve as a consensus alternative to the business unionist outlook, the concept of social unionism arose. Former socialists like Walter Reuther were among its more articulate proponents, but Catholics like Philip Murray, formerly a business unionist in the Lewis mold, and the anti-Communist members of the Association of Catholic Trade Unionists shared the idea. Although vaguely Social Democratic in outlook, social unionism was not really a consistent political philosophy. Rather, it was a statement about the role of unions in society that differed strikingly from that of business unionism.

Unlike the AFL business unionists, the leaders of the CIO saw labor as a force for broad social and political change. The changes they envisioned were not revolutionary or even anticapitalist, but the idea that unions had a social responsibility beyond improving their members' living standards was itself a break with AFL business unionism. Philip Murray described this outlook in 1944: 'It is a new departure for American labor to lead... a national movement devoted to the general welfare just as much as to the particular interests of labor groups.'[44]

During the war, the CIO and its allies put forth a program calling on the nation to take responsibility for the health, education and housing needs of the people. This was written into the Economic Bill of Rights that Roosevelt used in his 1944 campaign. In that year the CIO went farther and demanded economic planning to secure full employment: 'When the war is over we will have a people anxious to have jobs for all. What we must not lack is a plan to keep our industries going full blast, and a president and Congress who will assume the responsibility for all the people's needs.'[45]

As this statement indicates, the top leaders of the CIO saw this social unionism in the context of the PAC/Democratic Party strategy. But this concept of unionism also spawned a revival of labor party and third party sentiment during and after the war. Indeed, a poll taken in 1947 indicated that 23% of the CIO officials interviewed favored setting up a labor party within the next two or three years.[46] The majority opposed breaking with the Democrats but often felt the need to argue in the language of independent political action. In 1946, for example, Walter Reuther declared:

A party serving the true interests of the common people cannot be declared into existence; it must grow. The time must be ripe, the people must be ready. Labor's political responsibility is neither to close its eyes to the necessity of new alignments nor to surrender to doctrinaire moves to launch a new party prematurely on a too-narrow base. It is rather to recognize the transitional, the stop-gap nature of its present political activity, to reach out into the community for natural allies with farm and progressive middle class groups, and to lay the organizational and programmatic groundwork for a people's party.[47]

A socialist pamphlet of 1948 advocating the formation of a labor party used similar language in describing how to start one. Writing for the Workers Party, Jack Ranger proposed that progressive unionists form labor party caucuses in their local unions. Then, 'As soon as the movement has a base among the unions, try to draw in representatives of other organizations in the locality that might naturally be disposed to a labor party – consumers' cooperatives, the Farmers' Union, parents groups, tenant leagues, Negro organizations, etc.'[48] The concept of a political alliance with other working-class and oppressed groups was central to social unionism.

The social unionism of the CIO also involved a different attitude toward the Black community than that of the AFL. The AFL's business unionists made no real changes in their discriminatory policies during the war. They even supported cuts in funding for the Fair Employment Practices Committee that Roosevelt had established in response to A. Philip Randolph's threatened March on Washington. In contrast, the CIO opposed efforts to cripple the FEPC. More important, it set up the Committee to Abolish Discrimination, which conducted large-scale educational campaigns among the CIO's membership. Ten CIO affiliates established similar committees. The formal stands of the CIO against discrimination were strong for the time, although their enforcement was weaker than their rhetoric. As a result, an alliance between the CIO and the NAACP emerged that lobbied aggressively for government action against racial discrimination. This alliance was active through the end of the 1940s. The alliance was flawed by both its top-down character and its limits as a lobbying coalition removed from either the CIO's rank and file or the grass roots of the Black community.[49] Nevertheless, the racial egalitarianism advocated by the CIO through the 1940s was an important element of social unionism.

However, the social unionism of the 1940s declined rapidly during the 1950s. It lived longer in the political rhetoric of Walter Reuther and in the UAW's official mythology than elsewhere, but in practice the concept that the unions should lead a broad movement for social change was dead by the second half of the 1950s. The conditions for the CIO leadership's transformation to modern business unionism are clear in retrospect: the extent of bureaucracy throughout the CIO by the end of the 1940s; the suppression of political debate, accomplished by 1950; the routinzation of pattern bargaining in the first half of the 1950s; and the expansive economic environment that made all this possible. Writing at the end of the 1950s, Sidney Lens provided a summary of the changing mood of the CIO leadership:

> The transformation of "social unionism" has been subtle but extensive. In both its moral overtones and its intrinsic philosophy it has tended to blend with the very forces of Big Business which it fights so steadily on the narrow economic front. Instead of remaining a maverick force within the social stream, as it has grown older, it has become "responsible", sluggish toward new ideas, practical rather than idealistic, legalistic rather than militant, more conformist than anti-conformist.[50]

Nothing symbolized the change more than the CIO leadership's retreat from its alliance with the Black leadership. According to Meier and Rudwick:

> During the late 1950s the close cooperative relationship between the black community and the industrial unions gradually broke down. The merger of the CIO with the AFL in the middle of the decade indicated to many blacks a declining commitment to the battle for job equality. And this came at the very time that the multiplying NAACP legal victories and the dramatic rise of Martin Luther King to public prominence signified a revolution of expectations that was spawning a new militance among blacks.[51]

The belief that the 1955 merger of the AFL and CIO reflected an adaptation by the CIO leadership to business unionist norms was widespread. The merger convention reflected the current state of the labor leadership as a whole. Whereas CIO conventions in the 1940s included a large number of local leaders, the first AFL-CIO convention was, according to one left journalist, composed of 'paid functionaries many years away from the trade or industry they presumably represent today.' The merger statement was a masterpiece of ambiguity which granted equal status to industrial and craft unionism. Its section on racial discrimination was a toothless statement that left the door open to Jim Crow unionism by offering minority members the right 'to share in the full benefits of trade union organization', but said nothing about equal rights within the Federation or its affiliates.[52]

While a variety of political differences remained among and between the leaders of the CIO and the AFL, the framework and practice of most CIO leaders had narrowed sufficiently to make functional unity possible. Reuther, for example, no longer argued that it was the wrong time for a labor or people's party. At the 1954 CIO convention that approved the merger, he argued that it was the wrong idea in the first place. His reasoning was instructive as well. He told the delegates:

In Europe, where you have society developed along very classical economic lines, where you have rigid class groupings, there labor parties are a natural political expression. But America is a society in which social groups are in flux, in which we do not have this rigid class structure.... A labor party would commit the American political system to the same narrow class structure upon which the political parties of Europe are built.... Basically what we are trying to do is work within the two-party system of America and bring about within that two-party system a fundamental realignment of basic political forces.[53]

The realignment Reuther referred to was evidently not a class realignment. Rather, in the 1950s and 1960s it generally meant driving the Dixiecrats out of the Democratic Party to make it more consistently liberal. This idea, ironically, made its debut in the US of the 1930s in the Popular Front strategy of the Communist Party. By the end of the 1940s it was common coin in CIO circles.[54] But even this vision was far from the practice that soon came to characterize the AFL-CIO's new Committee on Political Education (COPE).

With the elimination of political debate throughout the CIO, labor's role as a pressure group within the Democratic Party – rather than as the leader of a broad movement – was unchallenged policy. No special transformation was needed to dissolve CIO-PAC into COPE: the new Federation was now simply a bigger pressure group. The function of COPE, like that of PAC, was simply to raise money and turn out the labor vote. The actual brokering and pressuring were done by the highest officials of the Federation, such as Meany and Reuther, supplemented by a cadre of professional strategists and lobbyists. The AFL leaders did not fear that Reuther and his CIO allies would abuse the strategy by promoting radical social legislation because the former AFL unions held twice the votes of the former CIO unions. In reality, Meany ran the Federation and Reuther occasionally complained.

The real change that made the AFL-CIO merger possible was a simple one: the CIO leaders had abandoned their social welfare legislative agenda as impractical. They shared with the AFL leaders a commitment to legislative goals that directly affected unions, such as employment programs and minimum wage legislation, but they no longer put such goals as civil rights, national health care, federal public housing, and economic planning on the active agenda of the CIO or the new Federation. Such goals appeared merely as ritual in the ceremonial events that most union and Federation conventions had become, but no longer made their way to the halls of Congress. Even calls for the repeal of the Taft-Hartley Act receded to the corners of convention rhetoric. Instead, politics meant having a say about who the Democrats ran for president, though the leaders seldom got their way, and supporting those candidates with good COPE ratings, though these ratings measured only major congressional floor votes, not commitment to labor's overall agenda. This move to the politics of business unionism was not a complete return to the Gompers era only because the AFL had itself moved away from its old opposition to social legislation during the 1930s.

Ironically, the CIO's retreat from social unionist politics helped to modernize collective bargaining. Some of the goals of social unionism were modified and transferred to the collective bargaining field in the late 1950s. Reuther's 1955 demand for the guaranteed annual wage, which led to the introduction of supplemental unemployment benefits, is an example. Typical of the ambiguity of this change, it was put forward by Reuther as an alternative to the popular '30 for 40' demand for a shorter work week. Another example was the UAW's turn toward profit sharing in 1958. Reuther dropped the demand in the face of company resistance, but he helped to establish the trend toward benefits bargaining. Bargaining for benefits such as pensions and medical care was in one sense a part of the social unionist heritage, but it also reflected a narrower vision of politics, heralding withdrawal from genuine social alliances, and the return to a practice of contract unionism that was not much different than that employed by pre-CIO industrial unions such as the Miners and Clothing Workers.

Toward the end of the 1950s a group of former CIO leaders and ideologues, including IUE President James B. Carey, could record how complete the retreat was for some in a publication called *Trade Unions and Democracy*. Referring to Gompers in describing their own business unionist view of the role of labor in society, they explained that 'adhering to the precept of Samuel Gompers to emphasize economic actions, US unions have not consciously sought to change society; however, they have materially assisted in achieving fundamental transformations as a by-product of their economic action.'[55] This was certainly an inversion of Murray's statement about labor leading a movement for the general welfare.

In the realm of collective bargaining, the new business unionism meant the routinization and further bureaucratization of the bargaining process itself. From the start, the CIO unions had dealt with industries in which a small number of companies dominated. In auto, General Motors and later the Big Three set the pattern, whereas in rubber it was the Big Four, and in meatpacking, the Big Three. In steel, six companies dominated, and in electrical equipment, General Electric and Westinghouse led the way. But the actual bargaining process was quite decentralized, and local leaders played significant roles. Grass-roots participation, combined with annual renegotiation of contracts, kept the union an active focus of membership involvement and sharp debate, the antithesis of routine business unionism. To change this, the CIO leaders moved rapidly to centralize control over bargaining and to replace the one-year bargaining cycle with long-term contracts.

In 1947 the Rubber Workers required that all locals 'submit their contracts to the General President of the International Union for approval before such agreements were to be signed.'[56] In the UAW, any relative bargaining autonomy the various departments (GM, Ford, Chrysler, Ag-Imp, and others) might have had ended as the Administration caucus became the disciplined tool of the International Executive Board. The common – now universal – practice of making the international unions the sole contracting agent, adopted by the Steelworkers in 1950, was advocated at the time as a way to protect local unions from lawsuits for damages made possible under the Taft-Hartley Act.[57] This argument had legal merit, but it also gave the internationals final control over contract bargaining and administration.

The increased control of the internationals over contracts coincided with the end of the annual bargaining round and its replacement by the long-term agreement. John L. Lewis began this trend in 1950 when he ended a decade of intense conflict in the coal industry by signing a three-year agreement with the newly formed Bituminous Coal Operators Association (BCOA). The purpose behind both the lengthening of the contract and the centralization of bargaining was to allow the operators the stability they needed to introduce new technology into the mines in order to increase productivity. Productivity increases thus became an unofficial index for wage increases.[58]

The USW followed Lewis's lead later that same year with its first three-year contract. After USW President Philip Murray died in 1952, his successor David J. McDonald pressed to centralize basic steel bargaining. In 1955 he proposed that bargaining with the six top companies take place in Pittsburgh with his personal involvement. In 1956 the process went further. The twelve major steel firms chose a four-member committee, with US Steel taking two of the seats, to bargain with the union. Unlike the situation in coal mining, however, the centralization of bargaining in the steel industry was accompanied by growing employer hostility that produced a 36-day strike in 1956 and the bitter 116-day strike of 1959.[59]

The UAW had taken the first step toward ending the annual bargaining round in 1948 when it signed a two-year agreement with GM. In 1950, GM proposed to extend this note of stability by offering a five-year contract with the same annual improvement raise and cost-of-living formula as in 1948. Reuther agreed to it, but widespread dissatisfaction because of the inflation created by the Korean War obliged him to reopen the contract in 1953. Calling the contract a 'living document', he negotiated a 10-cent-an-hour wage increase plus improvements in the annual wage increase and cost-of-living formulas. In 1955 Reuther signed a contract containing a by then standard three-year clause.[60]

Both the three-year contract and the tendency toward centralized bargaining increased throughout the 1950s. According to Charles Craypo, 'the three year contract, which was nearly non-existent in 1948, by 1957 accounted for roughly one-third of all contracts.'[61] By the end of the 1970s, about three-fourths of all contracts surveyed by the Bureau of National Affairs (BNA) had three-year terms.[62] Centralization also increased in many industries; the most notable example was trucking, where the Teamsters brought two hundred contracts and 180,000 workers into an expanding master contract that would eventually cover 500,000 Teamsters across the country.[63]

The routinzation of bargaining through the establishment of the three-year contract and the administrative centralization of pattern bargaining brought with it a vast expansion of the administrative apparatus that supported the power of the top leadership and increased its independence of rank-and-file influence. By 1964, US national and international unions employed over 13,000 people on their national headquarters payrolls. One standard explanation for this huge army of 'labor professionals' was that the growing complexity of the contract required a legion of experts. In fact, when the US Department of Labor categorized these employees according to occupation in 1970, only 6% were 'professionals', whereas half were organizers or representatives ('reps').[64]

A large number of these full-time staffers were employed by the former CIO unions and other unions that administered the major pattern agreements. Their growing numbers were a function of the top leaders' efforts to stabilize bargaining and enforce labor peace between contract negotiations. Although the UAW's membership did not increase, its staff grew from 407 in 1949 to 780 in 1958 and 1,335 in 1970. The Steelworkers' staff reached about 850 in the early 1960s and 1,122 in 1970.[65] Observing this process in the 1950s, Sidney Lens commented, 'The "reps" speak as one voice with the top leadership.' Indeed, they became not representatives of the members, but enforcers for the international executive boards. The industrial union reps of the postwar era repeated the social evolution of the bureaucrats who employed and deployed them. Lens's description of the process is classic:

> The professional representative, necessary though he is under current conditions, develops a whole set of special attitudes. Since he is appointed by the regional directors or top officers rather than elected by the membership, he tends to lose a feeling of responsibility. His post is now a "job," and he is no

longer as vitally concerned about pleasing his own sense of mission as in pleasing his regional director, or at least keeping clear of his lash. His own salary and benefits become progressively larger by comparison with the members who still work at the lathe, and his economic stake tends to make him moderate just as the secure doctor or lawyer tends in the same direction. He is now an "organization man."[66]

In the 1940s and 1950s reps were recruited from the cream of local leaders, sometimes even from the opposition, and were usually articulate. In unions where debate was dead and information the monopoly of the bureaucracy, the rep became not only the enforcer but the sole source of information. In this capacity the rep served as the unopposed tribune of modern business unionism.

Modern Business Unionism at Work

In its own terms, modern business unionism worked well within the system of capital-labor relations shaped during and after World War Two. Its own terms were wages and benefits. Average hourly earnings for production workers in manufacturing rose by 81% from 1950 to 1965. Those in bituminous coal mining rose by 80%, in steel by 102%, in electrical equipment by 79%, in auto by 88%, in meatpacking by 114%, in oil refining by 79%, in rubber tires by 96%, and in Class I railroads by 91%.[67] In the same period, the real, spendable weekly earnings of a production worker with four dependents rose 31% in manufacturing and 32% in mining.[68] Although these gains fell somewhere short of affluence, the postwar boom nonetheless saw an unusually long period of unbroken wage gains.

The benefits bargaining that substituted for the expansion of the welfare state following World War Two became a trademark of modern business unionism. While the Labor Department did not record 'package' settlements until 1965, making it hard to quantify the change, benefits bargaining clearly gave a substantial boost to the living standards of union members and their families who were covered by high-benefit contracts. Before and during World War Two, the term *fringe benefits* referred almost exclusively to paid holidays and vacations. But benefit bargaining expanded enormously in the 1950s. Whereas in 1951 'fringes' accounted for 17% of the value of compensation of blue-collar workers, by 1981 the average was 30%. In large industrial firms of the sort covered by the former CIO unions, benefits were over 50% of labor costs.[69]

Today, virtually all labor contracts contain one or another kind of pension plan. Before 1946 very few did. Once again, Lewis and the Mine Workers set the direction when they established the UMWA Health and Pension Fund in 1946. Similar in some respects to the older craft union funds and controlled by the union, it was unique in that it was employer financed. The UMWA fund was the model for the Teamsters' Central States Pension Fund negotiated by Dave Beck in 1955. Most industrial union pension plans, however, were company based and set up to supplement social security payments. This kind of plan was first won by the Steelworkers in 1949 and generalized very rapidly to the other CIO unions.[70]

Before the establishment of the UMWA's fund, health care expenses had been entirely a private burden in the United States. A few large companies like Ford provided company clinics or doctors in the spirit of the 'welfare capitalism' of the 1920s, but these schemes were hardly comprehensive and did not cover hospitalization. In the early 1980s, however, the Bureau of National Affairs found that 75% of the contracts it surveyed had health care programs and 60% had major medical benefits. By 1980 over 130 million Americans were covered by a partly (72 million) or wholly (58 million) paid employer or union health care plan.[71] While nearly 100 million people remained without health benefits, this dramatic change brought improved health and longevity to a significant portion of the working class.

Still speaking the language of social unionism in 1955, Walter Reuther advocated a guaranteed annual wage. Opposed to any sort of forced level of employment, or 'featherbedding', and to the demand for a shorter workweek with no reduction in pay, Reuther proposed that auto workers receive a minimum annual income regardless of layoffs. He first proposed the idea to Ford management, which replied, 'never'. In the end, Reuther gained supplemental unemployment benefits – payments above those provided by state unemployment insurance. Some of the major ex-CIO unions adopted this demand, but it did not become general like pension or health benefits. By the mid-1960s, according to BNA, only 14% of the contracts surveyed had such provisions. Most 'income maintenance' provisions were simple severance pay schemes, and only 29% of contracts had those by 1966.[72]

Income maintenance was modern business unionism's substitute for job or employment security. Economist Sumner Slichter noted industrial unionism's preference 'for income security rather than employment security' as a source of 'a basic conservativism in the American labor movement'. By emphasizing money compensation over employment, the unions 'avoided the neccessity of bargaining over such essential management decisions as production schedules, capital improvement plans, and plant localtion', giving management 'its freedom to make these decisions.'[73]

Craft unions had always emphasized maximizing work through a variety of contractual clauses, including elaborate job classifications and descriptions. For the skilled trades, this practice carried over somewhat into CIO contracts. But to protect production workers, who were most vulnerable to periodic layoffs and to the impact of new technology on employment, the CIO had looked to government social and economic policy. When the CIO abandoned social unionism, it turned to income maintenance schemes as a substitute.

Rejecting the old craft union approach, Lewis again set the trend in the 1950 agreement with the BCOA. In return for a steady growth in wages and benefits, Lewis, in his own words, encouraged the operators to produce coal 'at the lowest possible cost permitted by modern techniques.'[74] Although it did not acknowledge the link to technology, Reuther's plan shared this spirit. In 1957, Harry Bridges, still regarded as a Communist sympathizer, reversed the policy of the ILWU on mechanization. Speaking as bluntly as any business unionist, he asked his members, 'Do you want to stick with our present policy of guerilla resistance to the machine or do we want to adopt a more flexible policy in order to buy specific benefits in return?' It took him three years to negotiate it, but Bridges knew which he wanted. The 1960 Mechanization and Modernization Agreement with the employers' Pacific Maritime Association granted the shippers a free hand on the job in return for a minimum of thirty-five hours pay for those on the job. Older workers were encouraged to retire with a lump sum bonus in addition to their pension.[75]

The spread of the economic gains and new benefits in manufacturing, mining, and transportation to other industries was partly a function of pattern bargaining. The influence of the major contracts in steel, auto, coal mining and later trucking had significant influence on thousands of other contracts covering related or comparable work. However, a variety of factors began to reduce the influence of the pattern agreements. Economist Charles Craypo summarized the process succinctly: 'Interindustry patterns faded after the 1940s. The trend favored decentralization. Long-term contracts resulted in staggering expiration dates, and formula bargaining put some industries on different projections.'[76] Similarly, within an industry the original solidaristic pattern tended to weaken during the 1950s. A 1960 study by Harold Levinson of the impact of the Big Three pattern on the rest of auto showed that the number of firms that adhered exactly to the pattern declined drastically from 1946–49 to 1955–57, while the proportion of contracts that were below pattern agreements increased.[77]

Nevertheless, so long as the economy grew, the weakening of pattern bargaining did not really become apparent. By 1965, for example, average hourly earnings in coal mining, steel, auto, and rubber were still within pennies of each other. Only in electrical equipment did wages for production workers fall way behind, and this was the result of intensified competitive bargaining in the wake of the expulsion of the UE from the CIO, the creation of the rival IUE in 1950 (which badly fragmented bargaining), and a high level of employer resistance.[78]

In a labor movement now devoid of national political tendencies and debates that crossed union lines, the degeneration of pattern bargaining from a method of multiunion solidarity in the 1940s to a looser 'demonstration effect' in the 1950s and after, reinforced parochialism and insularity throughout the unions. One no longer belonged to the labor movement, just to a union. Bargaining was the business of one's own union, and that business ended in the councils of that union. If the other guy did all right, well and good, but it wasn't your concern.

The growth of real income and the expansion of benefits were not won without some conflict. Strikes were common in steel throughout the 1950s, and the 116-day strike of 1959 was a bitter affair provoked by US Steel.[79] In fact, the number of strikes during the 1950s was not much lower than in the second half of the 1940s. But these strikes were shorter on average, and fewer workers were involved, so that as a percentage of the workforce or of workdays lost, strike figures were lower in the 1950s than in the 1940s and declined even more in the first half of the 1960s.[80]

Modern business unionism could not abolish the conflicting interests of labor and capital. Rather, it could only attempt to manage the conflict. So long as the leadership was in control, the legitimate contract strike was institutionalized when it couldn't be avoided. It occurred, in theory at least, only when the contract expired. It had to be authorized by the leadership, and it was run as a passive affair with token pickets at the gate and the majority of members at home watching TV. Bargaining was conducted in secrecy, of course, so the members just waited for reports. Rallies or even meetings became infrequent, usually only convened when a 'tentative' settlement was reached.

In the hands of the modern business union bureaucrat, the strike even became a means to win membership compliance. As journalist William Serrin noted in his book on the 'civilized relationship' between GM and the UAW, strikes became not only a way to put pressure on the company but also a way for the workers to let off steam. UAW Secretary-Treasurer Emil Mazey put it bluntly in 1970: 'I think that strikes make ratification easier. Even though the worker may not think so, when he votes on a contract he is reacting to economic pressure. I really think that if the wife is raising hell and the bills are piling up, he may be more apt to settle than otherwise.'[81]

In its heyday, from 1950 through the mid-1960s, modern business unionism brought a significant improvement in living standards to millions of workers. As increases in benefits freed wage income for expanded consumption, more workers participated in the era of affluence to a degree no working class had previously experienced. By 1960, for example, 60% of American families owned their own home.[82] But this working-class prosperity was built on an increasingly routinized set of institutions and practices in which the role of the union membership became increasingly less important. Further, business unionism had left a number of complex industrial and social problems unaddressed in the celebration of a new consumerism. These unattended problems festered beneath the facade of success. Even before the motor of the postwar boom faltered, they would challenge bureaucratic business unionism on its own turf.

4

Blue-Collar Blues
Blue-Collar Rebellion

The modern business unionists of the AFL-CIO chose to struggle only on the safe terrain of wages and benefits. In the minds of the leaders of the industrial unions of the AFL-CIO and of the major independents such as the ILWU and the UMWA, the question of workplace regime was settled. Capital had the right to manage, to introduce new technology, and to discipline its employees on a 'guilty till proven innocent' basis. The employers had to pay for these rights, at times dearly. But overall, the employers came out ahead as profits rose faster than labor costs and the rate of return on capital grew. This was accomplished in part by constant shopfloor pressure to raise productivity and increase the number of hours worked. Modern business unionism left this problem to the routine procedures of the 'shopfloor jurisprudence' supplied by the grievance procedure and administered by the diminished workplace organization of the local union. Life on the job grew worse.

As the former CIO leaders discarded their social agenda in all but ceremonial rhetoric, the earlier gains of Black workers were eroded. The old ratios of income and unemployment that symbolized the political economy of racism asserted themselves, and the Black working class experienced economic decline even as the nation celebrated its affluence. By the end of the 1950s, poverty in general had not abated despite the increase in real wages. The AFL-CIO's research department estimated that nearly a quarter of the population lived in poverty and that a third of the country was ill-housed.[1] The comparable figures for Blacks were significantly worse, of course. Yet organized labor turned its back on the problems of poverty and racism precisely at the moment that Black America began its fight for justice on a massive scale.

71

The growing insularity of business unionism's industry-by-industry, company-by-company focus on wages and benefits, along with the racism and sexism that dwelt in the house of labor, blinded it to new developments. Labor ignored the growing proportion of minority and women workers in the workforce, concentrated as they were outside the existing bastions of unionism. True, the AFL-CIO's legislative department usually supported civil rights legislation, but only if it didn't threaten an existing labor practice or institution (like limiting apprenticeships to white males) – and then only after demonstrations, civil disobedience and even violence had made some reform unavoidable. No John L. Lewis stood up to demand the organization of these new millions of workers. Unions might organize new workers within their jurisdictions (or even outside if dues-paying membership slumped enough), but there was no coordinated strategy or pooling of resources like the one that had launched the CIO. The barrier was not financial but ideological. In effect, modern business unionism disarmed itself rather than prepare for the struggles to come.

White Promises, Black Deeds

After 1950, the socio-economic position of the Black working class declined rapidly. The gap between white and Black earnings had narrowed from 1939 to 1950 (Black earnings grew from 41% of white earnings to 60%), but this trend reversed during the 1950s. By 1952, Black earnings had fallen from 60% to 57% of white earnings, and by 1962 this figure was down to 53%.[2] Similarly, the unemployment ratio, which had been 3 to 2 against Blacks, increased during the first half of the 1950s to 2 to 1 in spite of the addition of 3 million jobs to the nonfarm economy and 1.5 million to manufacturing by 1953.[3] The growth of manufacturing employment during the Korean War did not have the same impact as it had had in World War Two. An Urban League study issued in 1952 found persistent discrimination against the hiring of Blacks in defense jobs. Nor did the housing boom of the 1950s help Blacks. In 1955 it was estimated that less than 1% of the 9 million new homes built since 1935 were available to Blacks.[4] The continued migration of Blacks from the South, often cited as a cause of Black urban poverty, did not really explain this decline. For one thing, the migration of Blacks in the 1950s was slightly smaller than that of the 1940s, 1.5 million compared to 1.6 million, and, as the famous 1967 *Kerner Report* noted, was 'relatively small when compared to the earlier waves of European immigrants.'[5] The real explanation lay elsewhere: in systematic racial discrimination.

On 1 December 1955 the AFL and CIO convened separate conventions in order to approve the terms of their merger. On that same day, Rosa Parks defied racial segregation on a bus in Montgomery, Alabama. On 5 December the AFL and CIO met in joint convention for the first time. Also on that day, the Montgomery bus boycott commenced, and American history took a new course. The AFL-CIO's founding convention did not take note of the event. Indeed, the new AFL-CIO Executive Council remained silent throughout the year-long boycott in spite of the fact that one of the earliest leaders of the boycott, E. D. Nixon, was a local official of the AFL Brotherhood of Sleeping Car Porters.[6]

In fact, the AFL-CIO's founding convention slapped Black workers in the face. Its statement on racial discrimination left open the continuation of Jim Crow locals, separate seniority lists, and segregationist practices. It called only for minority workers to 'share in the full benefits of trade union organization', but made no provision for equal rights within the Federation or its affiliates. The consequence was clear. As a historian generally sympathetic to the AFL-CIO leadership put it, 'Through the 1950s and into the 1960s, the AFL-CIO failed to compel some of its affiliates to stop discriminatory and segregationist practices.' These practices involved not only the segregated locals of the South but all of the skilled building trades unions. Because these unions controlled entrance to employment in the majority of construction jobs, Blacks were excluded from the nearly 1 million new construction jobs created from 1950 to 1965.[7] The AFL-CIO thus played an active role in perpetuating the position of Black workers at the bottom of the workforce, and the former CIO leaders went along.

The record of the AFL-CIO Executive Council throughout the second half of the 1950s reinforced the suspicion in the Black community that the Federation would not be an ally in the expanding civil rights movement. To begin with, the ouncil refused to endorse the 1956 National Day of Prayer in support of the beleaguered civil rights movement in the South and the 1957 Prayer Pilgrimage for Freedom to Washington demanding a strong civil rights act. In 1957 the council approved the admission of the Brotherhood of Locomotive Firemen and Enginemen and the Brotherhood of Railway Trainmen to the Federation, even though both unions had constitutional bars to nonwhite membership. Only A. Philip Randolph, president of the AFL Brotherhood of Sleeping Car Porters and a vice president of the Federation, voted against it.[8]

The disaffection of the Black community and its leadership grew in the late 1950s. A sharp critique of AFL-CIO practices was issued in 1958 by the NAACP's labor secretary, Herbert Hill. In 1956 Hill had urged NAACP chapters to cooperate with the AFL-CIO's new Civil Rights Committee. Frustrated by the lack of progress, Hill wrote at the end of 1958 that 'all too often there is a significant disparity between the declared public policy of the national AFL-CIO and the day-to-day reality as experienced by the Negro wage-earner in the North as well as the South.' Hill's critique launched a public debate between Hill and various AFL-CIO leaders that would go on for years. It brought to public attention the reality of racial discrimination, not only in the building trades but in former CIO unions such as the ILGWU.[9]

Spurred by the civil rights movement in the South and frustrated by the intransigence of the AFL-CIO Executive Council, Black labor leaders and activists in the North began to organize. Rank-and-file steelworkers in Pittsburgh formed the Fair Share Group of Steelworkers in 1957 to fight for the advancement of Blacks into the better jobs in steel from which they were barred by discriminatory seniority lines. In the same year, a group of Black UAW officials and staffers in Detroit formed the Trade Union Leadership Council (TULC) to demand Black entrance into the skilled trades and into the leadership of the UAW.[10] The development was significant because both Walter Reuther of the UAW and David McDonald of the Steelworkers were among the more liberal and vocal leaders on civil rights questions. Thus, the revolt that began to take shape in their own backyards indicated the distance between rhetoric and practice.

The Black revolt within the unions went public on a national scale when A. Philip Randolph attacked AFL-CIO racial practices at its 1959 convention. The delegates from Randolph's union, the Sleeping Car Porters, put forth a resolution calling for the expulsion of the two railroad brotherhoods admitted in 1957 unless they dropped their racial bars within six months. Randolph included the International Longshoremen's Association (ILA) in his attack, charging it with discrimination against its six thousand Black and Puerto Rican members in the shape-up system. All of the Sleeping Car Porters' resolutions were defeated, and George Meany counterattacked by angrily asking Randolph, 'Who in the hell appointed you as the guardian of the Negro members in America?'[11]

In May 1960 the Negro American Labor Council (NALC) was founded with Randolph as president and Cleveland Robinson, then vice president of District 65, as vice president. The NALC took a militant stance against segregation in the labor movement and grew rapidly. In 1961 it endorsed the NAACP's attack on AFL-CIO practices, which had been drafted by Herbert Hill. Hill's report went beyond criticizing unions with formal racial bars to state that racist union policies were not isolated cases, but a 'continuation of the institutionalized pattern of anti-Negro employment practices that is traditional with large sections of organized labor and industrial management.' This time Meany had the entire Executive Council censure Randolph, with no dissent but

Randolph's. The NAACP, Martin Luther King, Jr., and many other Black leaders came to Randolph's defense.[12]

The militant pressure tactics of the TULC and NALC did have some impact in the early 1960s. In 1962 the UAW elected its first Black to the International Executive Board, Nelson Jack Edwards, and the following year supported the March on Washington, which the AFL-CIO Executive Council refused to support. By the mid-1960s, all AFL-CIO affiliates had dropped their formal racial bars and had declared their policy to be one of nondiscrimination. While the AFL-CIO refused to endorse, much less organize, demonstrations or direct actions, it gave its active lobbying support to the Civil Rights Act of 1964 and the Voting Rights Act of 1965. In one sense, the Black pressure groups of the early 1960s forced the AFL leaders to support civil rights legislation. Unlike the social unionists of the 1940s, however, they had no intention of taking the lead in such battles. Instead, they responded to the initiatives of the civil rights movement. Nor would the AFL-CIO or most of its affiliates go as far as the movement did. For example, even Reuther and the former CIO unions that supported the 1963 March on Washington opposed the demand raised by a number of Black leaders for a 'Jobs for Negroes' program. This precursor of affirmative action was too much for the ex-social unionists, who saw it as 'discrimination in reverse'.[13]

TULC and NALC had their limits, however. Both were led by labor professionals. Horace Sheffield, head of the TULC, was a UAW staffer. The TULC turned to electoral politics in Detroit, defeating the UAW's candidate for mayor in 1961. However, the TULC-backed candidate lost to John Conyers, Jr., in the 1964 congressional elections. After this defeat, Sheffield returned to the Reuther fold. Randolph was a vice president of the Federation. Like Sheffield, he saw himself as pressuring for reform from within the bureaucracy, not as part of a force dedicated to some fundamentally new conception of unionism. As the Black civil rights leadership began to break up and move in different directions, King toward direct action around economic issues in the North, others toward Black Power, Randolph made peace with the rest of the AFL-CIO Executive Council. He tried to convince Meany to recognize the NALC as a voice for Blacks within the higher circles of the Federation, a role like that of the Jewish Labor Committee. In 1965 he declared that the AFL-CIO had made enough progress toward elimination of discrimination to warrant a cessation of hostilities between the labor leadership and the Black community. He resigned from the NALC in 1966. By the second half of the 1960s both TULC and NALC had declined as significant forces.[14]

Randolph's split from the NALC and from the direction of the more militant sectors of the Black leadership, including King, represented a strong political accommodation to the norms of bureaucratic coalition politicking. In 1965 Bayard Rustin, once an aide to King and then assistant to Randolph, wrote an article for *Commentary* entitled 'From Protest to Politics'. It argued that the days of protest were over and that henceforth a mature coalition politics within the Democratic Party was appropriate. The argument was based on Rustin's experience as an organizer of the 1963 March on Washington, where he had worked closely with Reuther and Randolph to forge an alliance – and abandoned the jobs-for-Negroes idea in the process. Rustin's strategy was nothing other than the operating method of the AFL-CIO's COPE. It was a recipe for accommodation to the needs and concerns of the labor bureaucracy and the power brokers of the Democratic Party. In their move away from independent protest, both Rustin and Randolph not only abandoned the fight against discrimination, but became spokespersons for the AFL-CIO's support for the Vietnam War. They were rewarded by George Meany with the formation of the A. Philip Randolph Institute, a wholely owned subsidiary of the AFL-CIO Executive Council; Randolph became the institute's chair and Rustin its executive director.[15]

The NALC and TULC accomplished something in their militant heyday. They put Blacks on the agenda of the AFL-CIO when the majority of international union officials would rather have avoided addressing the concerns of Blacks. Their pressure was instrumental in ending some of the worst discriminatory practices, but in the end it did not terminate racial discrimination within the labor movement. The return to the fold of bureaucratic business unionism by the best-known leaders of these organizations in the mid-1960s stripped Black rank-and-file union members of a channel of protest or communication. The withdrawal of these leaders from critical opposition occurred just at the moment when the direction and experience of many Black leaders and that of the AFL-CIO hierarchy began to diverge sharply.

A Golden Era?

In the experience of most of the white labor bureaucracy, the Kennedy-Johnson years figure as a golden era. The major indicators of business union success held up well enough. From 1960 to 1968 union membership grew by almost 3 million, while the proportion of union members to the total nonfarm workforce slipped only a couple of percentage points. Overall unemployment rates declined over the decade. Average real spendable earnings for production workers rose for most of the 1960s, leveling off only after 1967.[16]

What was perhaps most rewarding for the top leaders of the AFL-CIO and most of its affiliates was their return to grace in Washington. Growing Democratic majorities in Congress appeared to justify COPE efforts and COPE dollars, which had reached an average of $2,000 per Democratic congressman and $10,000 per senator by 1964. The AFL-CIO's Legislative Department, headed by Andrew Biemiller, was in charge of the traditional business of fending off antilabor legislation such as attacks on the Davis-Bacon Act and was generally successful. But perhaps the biggest prize was the return of welfare legislation in the Kennedy-Johnson era. Leaving the narrow stuff to Biemiller, COPE became the specialist in welfare legislation and from its vantage point in Washington believed its normal lobbying methods to be very effective. It was as though the goals of the social unionism of the 1940s could be achieved with the business union methods of the 1950s.[17]

In the trail of Lyndon Johnson's 1964 victory over Barry Goldwater and the new wave of Democrats he carried into Congress, the labor bureaucracy and its political apparatus experienced what seemed to it a rebirth of the New Deal. Historian Robert Zieger describes this period as the AFL-CIO leadership saw it themselves:

> Through the first half of 1965, the Democratic majorities passed a dozen key administration bills. Legislation attacking air and water pollution, expanding federal aid for education, establishing a massive scholarship program for college students, and providing funds for programs aimed at elimination of poverty made seasoned observers recall the fabled "hundred days" of the first Roosevelt term. AFL-CIO operatives particularly welcomed legislation that provided important health care benefits for the elderly and indigent, for it represented the first significant congressional defeat of a powerful medical lobby that had thwarted labor-led national health initiatives for over thirty years. Although Johnson's congressional career in the 1940s and early 1950s was steeped in the anti-union world of the Texas Democratic Party, laborites collaborated eagerly with administration aides and hailed Johnson's "Great Society" as the culmination of the New Deal's uncompleted agenda.[18]

It was utterly remarkable that these labor leaders could see this response to a decade of Black upheaval and mass movement as the accomplishment of their timid bureaucratic methods.

Ironically, the very success these top labor official experienced in Washington created a rift among them. The social legislation of the period was, in fact, far beyond the demands or expectations of George Meany and most of the AFL wing of the bureaucracy, which was still the majority. For them the war in Vietnam was important as contributing to the achievement of full employment, their real goal. But things seemed different to the leaders of unions with a large and/or growing Black membership. Reuther, whose UAW now had a large Black membership, and the leaders of unions such as 1199, District 65, and AFSCME saw that, in fact, the war precluded the sort of massive expenditure they saw as necessary to reduce Black poverty. Long-standing differences with the Meany wing over foreign policy now coincided with a concern about further economic programs.

Reuther saw the question of Black deprivation as an economic one, not a fundamental question of racism. He was, on the one hand, totally hostile to the new Black nationalism taking shape in America and soon to appear in his union's ranks. But he still saw the value of supporting some of the initiatives taken by Martin Luther King, Jr., such as the 1966 Chicago Freedom Movement, that addressed the problem in economic terms. For a period Reuther lavished the language of social unionism on the public and even his membership. In 1966 he resigned from the AFL-CIO Executive Council, and in 1967 broke with the AFL-CIO to enter into an inexplicable alliance with the Teamsters. The new Alliance for Labor Action, as it was called, languished and died after a couple of years. The split over the war was real enough on its own terms, but no challenge to the methods of business unionism was involved in Reuther's decision.[19]

For Black America, the late 1950s and early 1960s had been a time of rising expectations and growing hopes. The civil rights movement in the South brought down much of the edifice of segregation and in 1964 and 1965 achieved the two most sweeping pieces of civil rights legislation in the country's history. The defeat of Barry Goldwater in 1964 and Lyndon Johnson's declaration of a war on poverty in the same year seemed to indicate that the American political system was ready to accommodate the aspirations of millions of Blacks. Yet despite the proliferation of antipoverty programs and the modest expansion of the welfare state through medicare and medicaid, the plight of the mass of Blacks scarcely changed at all. From 1964 on, one urban ghetto after another erupted in violent uprisings. Martin Luther King, Jr.'s attempt to carry the civil rights movement into the North in 1966 revealed a depth of racism that even the Black leadership had not understood. White 'backlash' captured the attention of politicians trying to secure reelection in majority white constituencies. The escalation of the war in Vietnam drained economic resources, causing cutbacks in the new poverty programs and, increasingly, costing Black lives.

For most Black leaders and activists, the second half of the 1960s was a time of frustration or a time of radicalization. A year before Bayard Rustin romanticized the 'Negro-Labor Alliance', the activists of the Student Nonviolent Coordinating Committee (SNCC) and of the Mississippi Freedom Democratic Party (MFDP) experienced the reality of Democratic coalition politics as labor joined the party machine to support the regular, racist delegation from Mississippi against the MFDP's attempt to unseat it at the 1964 Democratic Convention. In the face of such frustration, the demand for 'Freedom Now!' gave way to the search for Black Power; and the quest for civil rights to that for Black Liberation. To be sure, a thin layer of the Black middle class found a way upward through the programs designed to aid the poor. In 1968 the Kerner Commission cited poverty, deprivation, and frustration as the causes of urban civil disorder. No matter where one looked in society, Black people were still at the bottom. Economic expansion based on demand generated by the Vietnam War kept unemployment relatively low, but Black unemployment was still twice that of whites. The *Kerner Report* summed up the all too familiar situation of Black workers: 'Negro workers are concentrated in the lowest-skilled and lowest-paying occupations. These jobs often involve substandard wages, great instability and uncertainty of tenure, extremely low status in the eyes of both employer and employee, little or no chance for meaningful advancement, and unpleasant or exhausting duties.'[20]

The accomplishments of the civil rights movement had been real, but had not gone deep enough. A sense of betrayal by liberal allies pervaded the traditional Black leadership, and a mood of desperate anger grew among the radicalized activists and the Black masses. The complacence of most of the AFL-CIO leadership stood in sharp contrast to the emerging militance among Black workers.

Labor's Missed Opportunity

Political scientist Manning Marable was right when he wrote, 'It cannot be overemphasized that the Civil Rights and Black Power Movements were fundamentally working class and poor people's movements.'[21] So were the urban ghetto uprisings that swept the nation in the second half of the 1960s. Beginning in Harlem in 1964, but first capturing national attention in Watts in 1965, they were outpourings of frustration and anger at the lack of change in the day-to-day life of the most impoverished section of the American working class. They were not 'race riots' like those in Chicago in 1919 or Detroit in 1943, in which white civilians attacked Blacks. From Watts through Detroit in 1967, they were confrontations with the authorities through the one channel of communication always open to the urban poor – concerted violence.

To most white Americans and 'civic leaders' of all races, the uprisings appeared irrational and pointless. No specific demands were made, no negotiations for their resolution were proposed. But in fact, as the Kerner Commission would later acknowledge, specific grievances preceded virtually all the upheavals.[22] The demands of those who participated were perfectly clear to anyone who cared to listen. For the masses of Blacks in the ghettoes of the North, neither racial nor economic barriers had yielded to the Civil Rights Act's Title VII, which promised equal employment opportunity. The same was true for housing, transportation, medical care, and so on. As for the vote: they had it, and it had not made a difference. These 'rioters' were poor working-class people demanding attention to their needs. They got attention. But it came in form of committees, commissions, and reports. What they needed to solve their problems was organization.

Here was the biggest outburst of working-class anger since the demonstrations of the unemployed in the early 1930s and the mass pitched battles of the 1934 strikes in Minneapolis, Toledo, and San Francisco. Thirty years before, in the wake of those events, John L. Lewis had stood before the AFL and demanded, 'Prepare yourselves by making a contribution to your less fortunate brethren. Heed this cry from Macedonia that comes from the hearts of men. Organize the unorganized....'[23] In 1965 the modern business unionists of the AFL-CIO saw only chaos. The voice they heeded came not from the 'hearts of men', but from the established leaders of business and government.

With few exceptions, US labor leaders across the country adopted a strategy of 'civic improvement' when the times demanded new organization. The responses of Reuther and the UAW leadership, including Sheffield and the former TULC leaders, were typical: They denounced the 1967 Detroit uprising. Reuther offered the services of the UAW's 600,000 Detroit-area members as a 'cleanup' detail. The UAW, along with Detroit AFL-CIO leaders, joined with the leading businessmen of the area in the New Detroit Committee to lobby the state legislature for a fair housing bill and emergency school aid. The Big Three auto companies understood the situation a little better and began hiring thousands of people in the months after the uprising. The UAW cooperated in this effort, but its role was that of social worker, not advocate. In the hiring that followed more whites were hired than Blacks. A couple of years later, layoffs erased most of these gains.[24]

Some labor leaders did heed the cry. In 1967 Cleveland Robinson, the Black secretary-treasurer of District 65, told an NALC convention that there were still 50 million unorganized workers, most of them low-paid service workers, and that 'except in rare instances the mainstream of labor has not seen fit to put forward the efforts necessary to organize in these areas.' Robinson proposed that the NALC initiate conferences in large urban areas to plan the organization of these workers into 'unions that will be democratic institutions, unions whose program will respond to our needs, unions which will be a force to reckon with.'[25] But neither

District 65 nor the NALC had the resources for such a project. As far as the leadership of the AFL-CIO was concerned, Robinson might as well have been in Macedonia. In those circles, the cry went unheeded.

One person who heard and understood this cry 'from the hearts of men' was Martin Luther King, Jr. For a long time King had understood the problems of Black people to be, in part, those of working people. Addressing the AFL-CIO convention in 1961, he said: 'Negroes are almost entirely a working people. There are pitifully few Negro millionaires and few employers. Our needs are identical with labor's needs – decent wages, fair working conditions, livable housing, old age security, health and welfare measures, conditions in which families can grow, have education for their children and respect in the community.... The two most dynamic and cohesive forces in the country are the labor movement and the Negro freedom movement.[26]

Until the second half of the 1960s King's work focused on civil rights, but after the passage of the Voting Rights Act in 1965, his attention turned toward economic issues and a class conception of society. This is not to say that he joined Rustin in reducing the liberation of Black people to a matter of business unionist routines and liberal coalitions. Quite the contrary: King developed a moral and economic critique of American capitalist society, which toward the end of his life led him to advocate democratic socialism – in his words, a 'socially conscious democracy which reconciles the truths of individualism and collectivism.' Unlike Rustin and Randolph, King understood that this would mean taking on the Democratic administration and many of the former liberal allies of the civil rights movement. In planning the Poor People's Campaign, he told his supporters, 'We will be confronting the very government, and the federal machinery that has often come to our aid.' King's new direction included opposition to US intervention in Vietnam, which he openly opposed against the advice of many mainstream Black leaders. But at its heart was the idea of organizing poor people and working-class people of all races into a movement capable of prying economic justice from an unwilling society.[27] King's path led to two events that highlighted the opportunity labor was missing in terms that even the AFL-CIO Executive Council should have understood.

On 12 February 1968, 1,300 sanitation men in Memphis, Tennessee all but five of them Black, walked off the job in a dispute over lost-time pay. The strike was actually the culmination of a four-year organizing effort by the American Federation of State, County and Municipal Employees (AFSCME). King's presence in Memphis in March and April made this strike a national event. He seems to have seen Memphis as the opening event of a broader campaign to organize Southern workers into unions. On 4 April, the day he was murdered, he told AFSCME President Jerry

Wurf, 'What is going on here in Memphis is important to every poor working man, black or white, in the South.'[28] King did not live to carry out his plans to help build the hospital workers' organizing drive and strike in Charleston, South Carolina the following year. However, Corretta Scott King became the chair of Local 1199's National Organizing Committee, and the Southern Christian Leadership Council vigorously supported the strike.

Both Memphis and Charleston pointed to the very real possibility of an organizing breakthrough in the South with Black workers playing a leading role. If the urban uprisings in the North had been one cry for help, the struggles in the South pointed to an answer. Furthermore, they demonstrated that the Black community would turn out again and again in massive numbers to support such struggles. There was a power there in American society waiting for direction. King had seen this possibility, but had not lived to act on his vision. The US labor leadership, which had the resources to turn a vision into a massive campaign, didn't get the message. In 1968 it cared more about nominating and electing Hubert Humphrey than organizing the unorganized. Indeed, labor's ability to mobilize resources was demonstrated by its efforts on behalf of Humphrey. As one historian described it, 'Thousands of union volunteers manned telephone banks, distributed literature, and canvassed neighborhoods.'[29] Had those thousands been linked to tens of thousands of Black community activists in a national organizing drive, the balance of class forces in the US today would be completely different.

There was a significant growth in public sector unionism during the 1960s. From 1962 to 1970, public employee union membership doubled to over 4 million, accounting for virtually all union growth in that period.[30] Black public workers were a large proportion of those new union members. Women also began to account for a growing proportion of union membership due to organizing in the public sector.

However, the growth of public employee unionism was accomplished mainly with the methods of modern business unionism, in particular lobbying for state collective bargaining laws. In some cases, the large inflow of Black and women workers helped to transform conservative AFL unions into more modern liberal business unions that allied themselves with the civil rights movement in the 1960s. This wave of public sector organizing was, however, the product of the separate efforts of only a few unions, such as AFSCME and SEIU, rather than of any general campaign by labor as a whole. In fact, private sector union leaders were often hostile to their publicly employed brothers and sisters. The growth of public employee unions and the transformation of the National Education Association (NEA) from a professional association to a real union demonstrated more than realized the potential for public and service sector organizing. For the most part, labor remained true to the norms of business unionism, seeking security through legal means, protecting its prior gains by lobbying, and engaging in broader social alliances only at the respectable level of Democratic Party coalitionism.

A Decade of Rank-and-File Rebellion

There was an anomaly in the position of labor in the 1960s that few labor leaders were able to perceive. On the one hand, much of the labor bureaucracy experienced the decade as a return to grace in Washington and, hence, the enhancement of their own power. Yet most analysts described organized labor as a declining force in US industry. In 1963, for example, industrial relations expert George Strauss described a shift in the balance of power in the plant and in collective bargaining:

> How strong are the unions today? Certainly, economic factors – automation in particular – have tended to shift the balance of power toward management's side, and the balance has switched most radically where economic pressures have been greatest. In addition, unions have lost much of their vitality and forward motion; they are playing an essentially conservative role in the plant community, seeking to preserve what they have rather than to make gains.[31]

B. J. Widick, writing in the mid-1960s, discussed this decline at length. In one sense, he offered an answer to the paradox by arguing that the unions had, by emphasizing the Democratic Party as labor's savior, created a 'leaning on government' that was 'destructive of the self-confidence and independence of labor'.[32] This emphasis was, of course, the heritage of labor's experience in World War Two.

The problem of dependence on government became more apparent during the Kennedy administration. Kennedy appointed Arthur Goldberg, formerly top attorney for the Steelworkers, as secretary of labor, seemingly a victory for labor. But the Kennedy administration, with Goldberg as point man, proceeded to intervene in collective bargaining to limit wage gains to the level of national productivity increases. Goldberg's major intervention was in the steel industry in 1962. USW President David J. McDonald went along without resistance or complaint.[33] In fact, the former CIO leaders had no principled objection to government intervention or to productivity guidelines. Unlike McDonald, they might argue over the formula or seek exemption for their own union, but on principle, government involvement in bargaining was just the other side of the coin of 'leaning on government'. Resistance to this practice would come from the ranks, but every Democratic administration from Kennedy on attempted to impose some form of wage control.

For most of the 1960s the usual indicators of business unionism held up well enough for officials to feel at ease. Their elevated position in society as bureaucrats living on upper middle class incomes who moved in a world of businessmen and politicians did not prepare them to understand the decline of union power at the base. The frontline of labor was left to the grievance procedure and the weakened shopfloor organization that survived from the early 1950s. Further, a decade of management pressure and technological change had created a burden on this system of 'shopfloor jurisprudence' that it was not designed to deal with. For one thing, management could remove an issue from the shopfloor to a higher level simply by denying any grievance at the first step or two of the procedure. Grievances then piled up at higher stages and were either arbitrated if they were regarded as important by higher levels of the union or bargained away at contract time. As a consequence of the time delay inherent in this system, management initiatives, even when blatantly in violation of the contract, could not be stopped through the grievance procedure. This included, of course, the disciplining of militants, even shopfloor officials. The contract, with its management rights and no-strike clauses, prevented the rank and file from taking direct action within the legal framework of this system.[34]

One reflection of this problem was the growing complexity of local bargaining in industry. At GM, for example, the number of local demands grew with each contract period from 11,000 in 1958 to over 39,000 in 1970. The general business unionist response to the proliferation of grievances was to increase the specifity of the contract's language. As David Brody has pointed out, the growing specification on worker *rights* in the contract actually narrowed the *freedom* of the shopfloor union to work these matters out and hence restricted its power. What had previously been a matter for negotiation was now strictly one of interpretation. The steward ceased to be a leader and became increasingly a shopfloor lawyer – and shopfloor organization suffered from this 'Perry Mason syndrome'.[35]

Technology had much the same effect. Since the days of 'scientific management', capital has used the introduction of new technology to reduce the power and influence of the workforce in a variety of ways. A machine- or computer-driven work process is less open to worker contestation than one driven by supervisory personnel.[36] Since the industrial unions accepted capital's right to introduce new technology, negotiating only over 'income maintenance' or economic compensation for jobs lost, the shopfloor union organization had little to say in the matter.

In line with the precepts of modern business unionism, capital took its right to manage seriously and organized itself appropriately. Industrial relations departments proliferated and experts were brought in. George Strauss described this trend in the early 1960s: 'Less emphasis is being placed on "making friends and influencing people", much more on the ability to bargain and engage in power politics.' Shopfloor supervision was given more training and authority. All of this was meant to 'eliminate the necessity for constant bargaining with the union, and to permit management to make decisions unilaterally.'[37] So armed, management proceeded to take full advantage of the right to increase productivity that business unionism had granted it.

The results were good for capital, but never good enough. From 1955 to 1967, unit labor costs in nonfarm business rose 26%, while after-tax corporate profits rose 108%. In manufacturing, the same figures were 23% and 93%, respectively. Rates of return on capital, the capitalists' most important indicator of success, rose in manufacturing, with only a slight slip in the 1958 recession, to new heights in the mid-1960s. Productivity growth rates in the nonfarm economy and in manufacturing, however, were only comparable to the rise in real compensation; they did not move ahead of labor costs. Thus, management pressure to increase productivity was constant. In addition, employers pushed for extra profits by trying to lengthen the workday, while workers accepted the overtime so that they could finance their new levels of consumption. During this period employee hours worked increased by 18% in nonfarm business and 14% in manufacturing.[38]

A combination of conditions, in addition to this new management pressure, contributed to an outburst of rank-and-file action and organization from the mid-1960s through early 1970s that challenged both management and the existing leadership of many unions. In the mid-1960s a series of wildcat strikes broke out and a number of union reform movements took shape. Toward the end of the decade, the productivity push coincided with sharp rises in the cost of living that put enormous pressure on contract negotiations. In the same years, Black militancy and nationalism penetrated the workforce, producing a fusion of Black radicalism and economic militance that confronted the remaining social unionist pretensions of the UAW leadership and, in the minds of managers and union bureaucrats alike, introduced the ethos of the urban uprisings into the heart of industry.

The new rank-and-file rebellion of the 1960s was, above all, a wildcat strike movement. Wildcats were not new – they had been around since World War Two and had broken out from time to time in the 1950s. In fact, UAW members began wildcatting after the 1955 GM settlement, when Reuther refused to pursue contract provisions to limit speedup.

In 1961 a bigger wildcat broke out over the same issues, and in 1964 GM workers again walked out. This time Reuther made the strike official. The strikers distributed bumper stickers reading Humanize Working Conditions. Stan Weir, a former longshoreman and union dissident, was one of the first writers to chronicle these new developments. In an essay entitled 'A New Era of Labor Revolt', Weir pointed out that five major unions experienced wildcats in 1964. In 1966 airline mechanics belonging to the International Association of Machinists (IAM) struck a number of airlines, halting 60% of the nation's airline service. They defied their own top union leaders and President Lyndon Johnson as well. Using as their slogan 'We're working under chain-gang conditions for cotton-picking wages', they stayed out for five weeks. Over the course of the 1960s the frequency of wildcat strikes grew: the number of strikes that occurred during the life of a contract went from about 1,000 in 1960 to 2,000 in 1969. Contract rejections, which had been rare before the 1960s, soared to over 1,000 in 1967.[39]

Strike activity of all kinds rose dramatically in the second half of the 1960s, exceeding by most measures the level of strike activity of the 1930s and, with the exception of 1946, the 1940s. This strike wave climaxed in 1970 when over 66 million days were lost due to strikes, a record exceeded only by 1946 and 1959 in the postwar era.[40] The strike wave of 1970 bears examination because it illustrates both the explosive militance of the time and the difficulties faced by rank-and-file workers trying to shape to their own needs a system built on bureaucratic business unionism. Among the strikes of 1970 that best manifested these problems were the GM strike, the tristate wildcat of 40,000 coal miners, and the national wildcat strikes by Postal Workers and Teamsters.

The GM strike was a legal strike well under the control of the UAW's International leadership. Nevertheless, it bore the marks of the era. For its part, the UAW leadership (now bereft of Walter Reuther, who had died in a plane crash earlier that year) had learned a lesson from the postcontract wildcats of the 1960s. Instead of treating local issues as a by-product of national economic negotiations, the UAW determined to settle the 38,000 to 39,000 local grievances and demands first under the direction of the International. But with 155 locals involved, the process was not completely under the International's control. According to William Serrin, local bargaining committees heaped demands on top of demands, some quite frivolous, thus prolonging local negotiations and indirectly pressuring the International. These tactics did prolong the strike, which lasted sixty-seven days, but the tools for pressure were blunt. On its side, the International saw the strike as a means of gaining ratification from a tired membership.[41]

Employees of the US Postal Service are legally prohibited from striking. Furthermore, the terms of their contract were not really negotiated in the usual sense. Congress set the basic terms of pay and employment. In 1969 and early 1970, Congress was dragging its feet, and matters were further confused by Nixon's proposal to reorganize the Post Office as an 'independent' corporation, a move that threatened the civil service status of postal workers. Leaders of both the National Association of Letter Carriers (NALC) and the American Postal Workers Union (APWU) appeared indecisive. On the night of 18 March 1970, postal workers in New York City took matters into their own hands and walked off the job. Within days the strike spread across the country, closing down postal service in at least two hundred cities. There had never been anything like it. Attempts to use the National Guard to move mail failed as guardsmen openly fraternized with strikers. The strike lasted two weeks, with the postal workers winning an immediate 14% wage increase and an improved upgrading system.[42]

Even before the postal wildcat ended, members of the International Brotherhood of Teamsters began walking off their jobs as the National Master Freight Agreement expired on 1 April. The next day, Teamster President Frank Fitzsimmons ordered them back to work. Many returned, but workers in several areas stayed out, some for a long time; St. Louis Teamsters struck until May. In Ohio the Teamster walkout lasted for two weeks and led to confrontations with the National Guard. In Los Angeles, where local leaders helped organize the strike, the walkout lasted a month. Fitzsimmons was forced back to the bargaining table, and a long strike by the independent Chicago Truck Drivers Union helped force a larger settlement.

One of the issues that sparked the strike in Los Angeles was elimination of a clause that allowed locals to conduct 24-hour strikes without facing discipline. This clause had been a powerful tool for defending working conditions in the hands of a militant local like 208 in Los Angeles. But Local 208 could not force that issue; instead, it ended up in a long fight over attempts to put the local into trusteeship. The wildcat had a positive effect on wage bargaining, but not on the more fundamental issue of working conditions.[43]

The strike of 40,000 coal miners in West Virginia, Ohio and Pennsylvania in June 1970 was the culmination of a series of strike movements in the coalfields. Like the massive Black Lung Strike of 1969, the 1970 wildcat was semi-political in nature and did not occur around expiration of a contract. The strike was called by the Disabled Miners and Widows, one of a number of coalfield organizations that, like the Black Lung Association, arose to address problems that the UMWA under President Tony Boyle refused to deal with. The strike demanded hospital and pension benefits for miners forced out of work because of disabilities. It had the full support of the working miners, but was unable to win its demands.[44]

The strikes of 1970 and their outcomes reflected the problems faced by workers forced to function according to the rules of modern business unionism. Tactically, the wildcats stepped outside the legal framework of US labor relations, but they could not force their real concerns onto the union agendas. In each case, the union was able to ignore the strike movement through its bureaucratic control of the negotiating process or to defuse the strike by getting better economic terms. The postal strike, which was a strike of lower paid workers for better wages, was the most successful. The attempts by autoworkers, teamsters and coal miners to address working conditions were not successful.

Control of the bargaining process was, of course, a major factor in allowing the international unions to ignore the demands of their members. But of equal importance was the ability of the internationals to preclude effective opposition through their monopoly of national organization – thus keeping centers of local opposition isolated. Decentralized and relatively democratic unions like the NALC and the APWU were not able to do this, which is one reason why the postal strike held strong for two weeks although it lacked any real national organization or center other than the New York City locals. On the other hand, both the IBT and the UMWA were highly bureaucratic, corrupt organizations. More important, however, their structures and monopolization of internal union communications helped to minimize contact between locals under the same contract and thus to fragment local or regional bases of the strike movement.

The only possible way to counter the bureaucratic power of the internationals was to build a national organization at the rank-and-file level. This was indeed the lesson many of the wildcaters of the 1960s drew toward the end of the decade. In the UAW a number of single-issue pressure groups, notably the skilled-trades-based Dollar-An-Hour-Now movement and the 30-And-Out committee came together to form the United National Caucus (UNC) in 1968; it played a significant role in UAW affairs into the early 1970s. Out of the Teamster wildcat of 1970 came the first national opposition group in that union, Teamsters United Rank and File (TURF). The most impressive of these rank-and-file organizations was the Miners For Democracy (MFD), which formed in 1970 shortly after the 30 December 1969 assassination of Jock Yablonski, opposition candidate for UMWA president.

The MFD was the only national opposition organization to successfully challenge an international union administration and beat it. In this challenge, it had a number of advantages that its counterparts in other unions have often lacked. First was a tradition of solidarity. To coal miners the picket line has always been sacred. 'Stranger pickets', that is roving pickets from other mines, have been recognized without question. Thus, the powerful strike movements of the late 1960s, which broadened geographically as time went on, laid the basis for a trust often lacking among other groups of workers. Furthermore, the bureaucratic machine the MFD faced, while brutal, was not sophisticated or adept at co-opting issues or diverting workers into other channels: Tony Boyle was no John L. Lewis. In the end, after rigging an election against Yablonski, Boyle turned to murder. This brought the MFD enormous public sympathy, even among labor leaders. The MFD also received a good deal of support from the outside, and was able to recruit some talented people to its staff. Nevertheless, the MFD remained an isolated phenomenon even after it won control of the UMWA in 1972. The new leaders democratized the union, but they had no model beyond versions of business unionism from which to learn. Consequently, they proved unequal to the new challenges the employers confronted them with later in the decade.

In the UAW and in the Teamsters, the new rank-and-file organizations did not become strong enough to contest for power. TURF, in fact, died an early death due to the opportunism of one of its main leaders and the subsequent internal fight it provoked. Unable to establish a recognized leadership or a national center, TURF collapsed within a year of its foundation. TURF also suffered from the local isolation of the 1970 wildcat. Because different areas struck for different lengths of time and had little contact, workers in some places felt that those who went back early had sold out. With no previous national network on which to base itself, TURF was easily pulled apart by its first leadership squabble.

The United National Caucus was an attempt to pull together several quite distinct dissident groups within the UAW. Its initial base and numerical strength came from two single-issue movements, the 30-And-Out movement for early retirement, and the Dollar-An-Hour-Now movement among skilled tradesmen. These two movements had clear economic goals well within the framework of the UAW's modern business unionism. The leadership of the UNC, which included leaders from Ford Local 600, GM Local 160, and Chrysler Locals 3, 7, 212, and 961, had a broader vision of an opposition movement, incorporating some of the UAW's previous social unionism. The UNC also had some Black support and attempted to relate to the rising Black consciousness movement in the Detroit plants. But the UNC confronted the most politically sophisticated union leadership in the country. In spite of some of the advanced social ideas in its program, the appeal of the caucus had been its economic militancy. In the 1970 negotiations, the UAW leaders were able to take the wind out of the UNC's sails by co-opting some of the demands that gave it its initial strength, such as 30-And-Out, reintroduction of the COLA, and a big enough wage increase to muddy the waters on that issue. This prevented the UNC from becoming a mass movement, although the organization continued to exist until about 1974.[45]

Symptomatic of the limits of the rank-and-file upsurge of this period was the virtual absence of any contact or cross-fertilization between the massive strike movements of 1970 and the organizations of the era such as MFD, TURF, and the UNC. Almost as a given, the leaders and activists of these movements accepted the isolation that went along with business unionism. Such outside support as came, for example, to the MFD did not include mutual aid between various groups or strikes. This was, in part, a reflection of how successful the American labor bureaucracy had been in abolishing the practice and even legitimacy of labor solidarity and of any active conception of a labor movement.

In spite of its mass character, the rank-and-file rebellion of the late 1960s and early 1970s didn't receive much public attention until the Lordstown strike of 1972. Lordstown was GM's newest plant and part of its new General Motors Assemby Division (GMAD). GMAD was organized to increase productivity, and its managers took a tough stance toward the workers. At Lordstown, young white workers who often sported the long hair of the period resisted and fought back. Lordstown came to symbolize the alienation of younger workers confronted with the latest in automation. In fact, Lordstown was but one of a number of plants reorganized by GM into GMAD in order to increase productivity. GMAD plants in Norwood, Ohio and in St. Louis had similar experiences, as did dozens of Ford and Chrysler plants.

The typical young worker at Lordstown was white, but Blacks increasingly formed a significant part of the production workforce in the auto industry. In the late 1960s, as the civil rights movement gave way to the Black Power movement, Black nationalism and radicalism appeared among Black workers. The concentration of Blacks was particularly high in the older Chrysler plants of inner city Detroit. Although Black workers came to form a large part or even a majority of the workers in many plants, the locals were still dominated by whites. The first of a number of Black caucuses was formed in May 1968 as the Dodge Revolutionary Union Movement (DRUM). DRUM was a joint effort by Black workers at Chrysler's Dodge Main plant and a group of radical Black intellectuals. Not surprisingly, DRUM was born out of a wildcat strike in which several Black workers were victimized by management.

The movement toward Black self-organization grew with the perception by Black autoworkers that the UAW did not have their interests at heart. By the end of 1968 several other 'revolutionary union movements' (RUMs) had taken shape in other plants. The Detroit-based groups joined together to form the League of Revolutionary Black Workers, and similar organizations were formed in other parts of the country. The Black Panther Party, for example, founded a caucus at GM's Fremont, California plant, and the United Black Brothers functioned at Ford's Mahwah, New Jersey, plant. Unlike the UNC or MFD, these Black groups saw themselves as part of a broader revolutionary movement for Black liberation. They responded to the horrible working conditions in the plants and put forward practical demands as well as broader political ideas, leading and participating in wildcats. Although these groups proposed joint action with white workers, racial polarization prevented the sort of coalition that they envisioned. Eventually, the UAW Administration caucus artfully sponsored more moderate Black candidates in local union elections throughout the Detroit area. In addition, the Black liberation movement itself faced serious government efforts to suppress it, as well as internal factionalism, and was already on the decline by the end of the 1960s.

By the early 1970s the managers of American mass culture no longer wanted to hear about Black militancy, or anybody's radicalism. So the problem of rank-and-file rebellion was trivialized as the 'blue-collar blues', and the more passive phenomena of absenteeism, long hair and drug abuse replaced wildcat strikes and Black caucuses as marketable trademarks of working-class dissatisfaction in the media.

But there was nothing new about the 'blue-collar blues' in postwar America. Writing in 1957 about his experience as an autoworker a year earlier, Harvey Swados presented the problem more bluntly than the 1973 Special Task Force report *Work in America* ever dreamed of putting it: 'The plain fact is that factory work is degrading.' In language that did not allow for ambiguity, he told his readers that 'the men with whom I worked on the assembly line last year felt like trapped animals', and that 'they were sick of being pushed around.' The factory Swados worked in was 'aswarm with new faces every day; labor turnover was so fantastic and absenteeism so rampant...that the company was forced to overhire in order to have sufficient workers on hand....' As Swados also noted, no one was interested in these conditions in 1957.[46] But in 1973 this sort of passive disaffection made a better news story than real social rebellion.

Lordstown was presented as a case of generational and stylistic rebellion against the new technology. But what had really been new about the rank-and-file rebellion – its militancy, its organizations, its multiracial character – was largely ignored. The leading official document of this period, the *Report of a Special Task Force to the Secretary of Health, Education, and Welfare: Work in America*, published in January 1973, makes note only of Lordstown.[47]

A few months after the publication of *Work in America*, three strikes broke out in Detroit-area Chrysler plants that embodied the worst fears of media hucksters, corporation managers, and union bureaucrats alike. On 24 July 1973, two Black workers locked themselves into a power gage in Chrysler's Jefferson Assembly plant in Detroit. When management attempted to remove them, the two were surrounded and protected by their fellow workers. The action was the culmination of months of conflict with a racist supervisor over speedup . The conflict was like many others in Detroit's older inner-city plants – a combination of speedup and racial slurs that one of the RUM groups called 'niggermation'. Organized groups in the plant including the United Justice Caucus had agitated around the issue. They had fought through union channels for months, and finally two workers, Isaac Shorter and Larry Carter, took direct action. But instead of walking out, the workers took over a part of the plant and demanded the dismissal of the supervisors. After a day's occupation, they won.

In early August two industrial accidents, amputations resulting from a faulty crane, brought things to a head at Chrysler's Lynch Road Forge plant. The union met with management and was told that everything had been checked out. The workers knew better, and the midnight shift refused to report to work on 7 August. Doug Fraser, just recovering from the Jefferson sit-in, accused 'outside' radicals of starting the strike. Not even Chrysler management backed him on that one. There was a caucus in the plant, the Forge Revolutionary Union Movement (FORUM), one of the last surviving RUM groups, but the strike was now supported by the overwhelming majority of the workers. All shifts were out – 1,300 workers. Fraser, realizing that he couldn't talk the workers back to work, said he would personally investigate conditions in the plant and authorize a strike if one was warranted. Ironically, Fraser's attempt to gain control of the strike backfired. When a judge confirmed the legality of an injunction against the strike, the workers stayed out, encouraged by Fraser's promise to call a strike if conditions were as bad as they claimed. At a 12 August meeting of the local, Fraser again demanded a return to work, and for two hours local leaders argued with the members in favor of a return. A close vote was declared to be a majority in favor of going back, and by the next day the strike was broken.

The next day, two workers at Chrysler's Mack Avenue stamping plant found another way to halt production. This action had, like the others, followed months of attempts to resolve plant problems through union channels. The United Justice Caucus, a UNC affiliate which published the Mack Avenue Health & Safety 'Watchdog' had pressured for action for a long time. Even the UAW International had told Chrysler in official negotiations that Mack was on the verge of a walkout if health and safety violations were not corrected immediately. As usual, the company told the union it would take care of the problems but actually did nothing. So, on 14 August, Bill Gilbreth and Clinton Smith sat on a conveyor belt. When the authorities tried to remove Smith and Gilbreth, workers gathered around to protect them. On 15 August, police and security guards removed the small number of occupiers, but the problem of getting the workers back to work still remained. What the police could not do, the UAW could and did. At 4:30 am on 16 August, about one thousand UAW officials from all over the area, some carrying baseball bats and other weapons, gathered at Mack Avenue to escort the workers back to work. Those who tried to picket were attacked. The performance was repeated the following day. The International thus organized to break the strike at a plant that it had acknowledged was the most dangerous in the Chrysler system. The UAW's modern business unionism had come to resemble that of the Teamsters. It would not be the last time strong-arm tactics would be used in defense of the International's policy.[48]

The 1973 wildcats symbolized the whole unresolved problem of the shopfloor regime. The workers couldn't take the increasing pressure on the line, but the International didn't want any part of contesting management prerogative. Because nothing was resolved, the 1973 Chrysler wildcats looked like an escalation of the upheaval that had begun a few years before. In fact, they were the final act of that upsurge. There continued to be rank-and-file movements and occasional wildcats, but the massive phenomenon that took shape in the late 1960s and early 1970s disappeared after the summer of 1973, and along with it most of the rank-and-file organizations of that era. The history of each organization, each union, and each movement revealed weaknesses, mistakes, failed hopes. But behind the general collapse of militance was a bigger change already in the making.

The industrial context of most of the large strike or reform movements of this period was on the verge of a change that few suspected at the time. For all their political differences, the rank-and-file movements had accepted this context as a given. So, too, the practices of modern bureaucratic business unionism had been taken for granted. Their shortcomings were a target for criticism or even opposition, but no one suspected that the institutions upon which business unionist practices were based would collapse before the practices themselves could be defeated or changed. The internationals had done their best to defeat their own shopfloor insurgencies, but in doing so had simply weakened the unions further by handing the employers a new round of victories. The business unionist could not understand the one thing that all the rebels of the 1960s and 1970s had said: In the end, the union is its members.

Nixon's wage freeze in August 1971 had not broken industrial insurgency. A seven-and-a-half-month strike by 40,000 telephone workers at the New York Telephone Company began, over the opposition of the leaders of the Communications Workers of America, on the day the wage freeze was announced. Detroit's Summer of '73 lay ahead. Wildcats in the coalfields continued into 1974. What halted the rank-and-file insurgency was the recession of 1974–75, which was the deepest recession since the 1930s. Manufacturing capacity utilization collapsed from 83% in 1973 to 65% in March 1975 at the bottom of the recession. The index of industrial production fell from 129.8 in 1973 to 117.8 in 1975. The index of iron and steel production for those years fell from 122.3 to 95.8; motor vehicle production fell from 148.8 to 111.1. Reflecting these large slumps in production, unemployment rose from 4.9% in 1973 to 8.5% in 1975, by far the highest rate of the postwar era. The unemployment rate rose from 8.9% to 13.9.% for Blacks. For blue-collar workers, the rate rose from 5.3% to 11.6%, and for factory operatives, from 5.7% to 13.2% – compared with 2.9% to 4.7% for white-collar employees.[49] For the young workers from Lordstown to the coalfields, from the steel mills to the telephone company, the 1974–75 recession was a quick education in the downside of capitalism and a blow to the confidence of youth. And as it turned out, the 1974–75 recession was the great divide between the insurgent world of the early 1970s and the new economic order beyond. That new order would have little place for either modern business unionism or the young rank-and-file insurgents.

5

Economic Power Shift

Modern bureaucratic business unionism was shaped in the economic expansion of World War Two and sustained for a quarter of a century in an era of continuing economic growth. The institutional framework that underlay union stability had never been tested by a drastic change in the economic environment. The practices of business unionism, which leaned heavily on these institutions, had never been challenged by concerted employer aggression. But in the 1970s the contours of the US economy began to change at an accelerating rate. The difficulties that arose did not take the form of a depression or simply a more severe downturn in the business cycle. Rather, the US economy had become part of an internationally integrated economy that renewed crisis was forcing through a process of restructuring. In the US itself this led to deindustrialization and drastic changes in the structure of industry and the workforce. These changes would demand of organized labor and its leadership a flexibility and a political awareness that was altogether missing in the routine of business unionism.

The US Economy under Stress

Long before the 1974–75 recession, signs of economic stress had emerged in the US and throughout Western capitalism. Average annual growth rates began to decline. For the developed capitalist nations as a group, real annual growth rates shrank from 5.2% in 1961–65 to 4.8% in 1966–70 and to 3.7% in 1971–75. For member states of the European Economic Community the comparable figures were 4.7%, 4.4%, and 2.7%. For the US, they were 4.6%, 3.0%, and 2.2%.[1] Along with increasing stagnation came inflation, beginning in the late 1960s in most Western capitalist nations and increasing throughout the 1970s. The US rate of inflation had averaged only 1.3% a year in 1960–65, but rose to nearly 6% in 1970 and to 11% in 1974. This combination of lower growth and faster price increases was a novel one that forced economists to create a new economic category: 'stagflation'. Among its major causes was an enormous growth of debt on a world scale.[2]

The rising role of debt within the US economy was a sign of its loss of dynamism. In the 1950s and 1960s, American corporations were able to generate the vast majority of new investment from their own profits. In the early 1960s, 70% of investment funds were internally generated. But in the 1970s this proportion dropped steadily, hitting 60% in mid-decade and falling to less than 50% by the end of the decade.[3] The increasing difficulty in generating investment funds from production was a classic warning sign of economic crisis, the falling rate of profit.

The falling rate of profit in the American economy became apparent in the second half of the 1960s. One of the first mainstream economists to note this trend was William Nordhaus. In a 1974 study for the Brookings Institution, Nordhaus concluded that profits as a share of gross national product had fallen since the mid-1960s. In September 1979 the *Morgan Guaranty Survey* reported that rates of return on investment had averaged 10.2% in the 1950s and 1960s but had declined to 7.1% in the 1970s. A similar study by the Paris-based Organization for Economic Cooperation and Development (OECD) in the same year showed that rates of return on industrial assets had tended to decline in most of the major industrial economies of North America and Western Europe.[4]

This falling rate of profit did not mean that either individual capitalists or corporations were going broke. Indeed, the size of profits still grew in most years, and many financiers and industrialists made unprecedented fortunes. But it did mean the system had once again run up against the problem of accumulating capital. Since the rate of profit is the ratio of profits to assets or capital invested, it is more difficult to sustain higher rates of profit as assets accumulate. Whatever regulating effects arms expenditures had on accumulation diminished as the Western economies grew and arms spending declined as a proportion of gross national product, even though it grew in absolute terms.[5]

These signs of crisis were also a function of the very success of US policy in helping the European and Japanese economies recover after the war. In the 1950s and 1960s many of these economies grew at a faster rate than the US. Their rates of productivity were higher and their unemployment rates lower.[6] This growth soon enabled them to become effective competitors of the US in markets throughout the world, including the US market itself. The new competition undermined the position of the US as the dominant force in world capitalism. Eventually, it forced the deregulation of the entire international monetary system that had been worked out at Bretton Woods the end of World War Two.

The economic crisis that has unfolded since the late 1960s has been different from most previous capitalist crises in that there has been no general collapse, such occurred in as the 1930s. Recessions have been deeper than those of the 1950s and 1960s, but have never reached the proportions associated with the Great Depression. One of the major reasons for the attenuated character of the crisis has been the internationalization of capital and capitalist production, which began before the first signs of crisis appeared and has accelerated since.

The motor of capitalist crisis is a decline in the average rate of profit throughout the system. When the system was made up of national economies with limited connections to one another, a slump in one nation's rate of profit would be sufficient to bring on a national crisis as capitalists stopped investing in the face of declining returns. But if the 'economy' is an almost limitless area in which rates of profit vary because of different conditions, such as widely different labor costs, then capitalists can seek relief by investing in an area offering a higher than average rate of profit. By the time profit rates in the West began slumping in the late 1960s, US and European multinational corporations and banks were already well positioned to invest throughout the world.

Capitalist investment became truly international in the 1970s on a scale not previously known. The globalization of investment created markets for capital and commodities far beyond the usual collection of national economies. Not even the collectivized economies of Eastern Europe and China remained immune to the reach of capital. Economic internationalization inevitably brought on a restructuring of industrial production that shifted the concentrations of basic industry from its previous centers to new locations around the world. It also increased competition between capitals and the corporations through which they were organized and the national markets in which they were based.

Competition, in turn, brought about further rationalization (closing of old facilities, introduction of new technology, etc.) in domestic industry and the constant reorganization and concentration of capital through vast merger and buy-out (and, conversely, divestment) movements. These enormous changes in the structure of the US economy confronted labor with a new agenda full of problems.

The Shift in Employment and the Decline of Unions

A common explanation for the decline of organized labor in the US is the shift from a goods-producing economy to a service economy. Since the heyday of the CIO in the 1940s, industrial work has declined as a proportion of the total workforce, while service employment has risen dramatically. For example, in 1940 industrial, goods-producing employment accounted for 40% of the workforce: in 1980, only 28%. This trend has been a long-standing one, general to Western capitalism, and modified only momentarily in times of war. To begin with, the tendency for the service sector to grow is inherent in an economic system that seeks to bring every sort of activity under the reign of profit. More recently, automation, the export of capital, and the replacement of domestically produced goods by imports have contributed to the trend as capitalism becomes an international system.

Historically, the rise of the service sector as a source of employment has been a result of the 'commodification' and capitalization of social functions previously performed in the home, conducted outside the market economy through barter, or carried out by self-employed individuals. These include food production and preparation, clothing production and repair, health services, grooming services, home and farm equipment repairs, and many other services customarily bought in the market today. Well into this century the growth of service businesses was a result of the shift from a rural, farm-based economy to an urban, industrial society. As more of the population became wage earners with cash incomes, the larger the market for services became.

The development of mass production industry created a new group of service and retail businesses. Historically, the rise of service employment is not a negation of industry or industrial employment, but a function of it. By the mid-1980s, the federal government reported that, 'Twenty-five percent of US GNP originates in services used as inputs by goods-producing industries.'[7] Mass production industry also created a new market of working-class consumers able to pay for services previously done in the home. Further, as services increasingly become organized as large-scale capitalist enterprises, they become important consumers of industrial products. As the technology of industry progresses, a section of the workforce becomes 'freed' to work in the lower-paying service jobs that both consumerism and industry call forth. In the last two decades the growth of working-class consumer power and the increased availability of labor has been made possible by the increased entrance of married women into the workforce. The growth in service jobs that has accommodated that trend began with the expansion of public service jobs during the New Deal that continued through the 1960s and the rise of the headquarters functions of expanding US multinational corporations from the 1960s through today.

While the growth of service sector employment inevitably produces a proportional shift in the statistical status of industrial employment, it does not explain the slower growth and eventual absolute decline in the number of industrial jobs, much less the decline in the proportion of union members in the workforce. Large areas of the private service sector have been highly unionized in the US and elsewhere. Transportation, utilities, and wholesale distribution have been union strongholds, and the relative success in organizing government service employees since the 1960s suggests that there is no inherent barrier to the organization of service workers.

The strongest indicator that the shift to service employment does not, in itself, explain much about trends in unionization is the decline in the proportion of unionized blue-collar workers. Prior to the absolute decline in manufacturing jobs that began in the 1980s, the proportion of unionized workers in manufacturing dropped from a high point of 42.4% in 1953 to 32.3% in 1980, a decline of 24%. The percentage of union members in the entire nonfarm workforce dropped from 32.5% in 1953 to 23.2% in 1980, a drop of 29%. Thus, the decline of unionized workers as a proportion of manufacturing employees was comparable to that for the whole economy. In the 1980s the decline accelerated in traditional blue-collar areas. The proportion of organized workers in manufacturing fell from 32.3% in 1980 to 24.8% in 1985, a 30% drop. The decline in unionization from 1953 to 1985 was much greater in mining (64.7% to 14.6%), transportation (79.9% to 37%), and construction (83.8% to 22.3%). By the mid-1980s, the AFL-CIO Research Department reported that nonunion workers accounted for over 50% of metal, machine and equipment electrical workers; 69% of the chemical, rubber, oil, plastics, and glass workers; 69% of all garment and textile workers; 64% of wood, paper, and furniture workers; and 67% of food-processing workers.[8] These figures make it hard to explain the decline of unionization as a consequence of jobs lost to foreign imports, since the decline in the density of unionization is much greater than the loss of jobs due to any cause. However motivated by competition, the explanations for this degree of deunionization lie in the strategies and tactics of domestic employers and the inaction of domestic unions.

The decline of unionism in the US has resulted from the failure of business unionism to organize aggressively in the private service sectors and its complacency at the growth of nonunion sectors within the traditional industrial areas of union strength. Behind this failure, of course, were some very real changes in the structure of the economy, most of which provided a favorable shift in the balance of forces for capital. In fact, some of these changes were produced by conscious strategic responses on the part of capital to unionism and to shifts in the international economic climate.

The Migration of Industry

Even before the signs of economic crisis had become apparent, US corporations embarked on a migration away from the centers of unionism. The memory of confrontations with tens of thousands of workers in cities like Detroit, Flint, Toledo, Akron, Gary, South Chicago, and Pittsburgh haunted capitalists and managers alike in the years following the decade of class confrontation that climaxed in the 1946 strike wave. Beginning in the early 1950s, industry began to move away from those centers in search of areas without strong union traditions. The most obvious choice was to relocate in the 'right-to-work' haven of the South that the Taft-Hartley Act had helped to create. Some industries, like textiles, shoes, and furniture, simply picked up shop and moved. More frequent throughout the postwar period was a shift in investment, with major Northern corporations directing new investment to the South. One study of *Fortune* 500 corporations showed that during the 1970s, 34% of the older plants of these industrial firms were located in right-to-work states, but that half of the new plants built during those years were in them.[9]

In general, corporations sought to decentralize production by using smaller plants, geographically dispersed and located in semi-rural areas where they thought tradition would weigh against unionization. But even if unions tried to follow the corporate migration, companies believed that they could minimize the solidarity engendered by the earlier massive concentrations of workers and their families. Workers in the new plants would be hundreds or thousands of miles from the old centers of CIO strength and light years from the culture of its radical early years. One of the first industries to follow this strategy was the electrical equipment industry. Historian Ronald Schatz described this move:

> Starting in the mid-1940s, consequently, the corporations moved operations out of the older, large factories and into newer, smaller facilities in the border states; the South; the Pacific Coast; rural sections of New England; Puerto Rico; and other countries.... General Electric was one of the first major CIO-organized firms to carry out this strategy. In the 1920s all of GE's plants were located in the Northeast. In 1952, GE already had 117 plants spread out over 24 states. By 1961, it had 170 plants in 134 cities with much larger concentrations in the West and South than before.[10]

Other industries soon followed suit. Meatpacking, once heavily concentrated in Chicago and Kansas City, began closing its massive old urban-based operations and building new, smaller plants throughout the Midwest and Plains states. Tire plants left Akron for the West and

South. Auto production drifted away from Detroit. GM pioneered this strategy in the 1960s by building its new plants in relatively remote areas. The famous Lordstown, Ohio plant, built in the late 1960s in a rural area far from other auto centers, was an example. In the 1970s GM opened the majority of its US plants, nine out of fourteen, in right-to-work states. This was a reversal of the Fordist tradition of centrally integrated production associated with the introduction of assembly line production in the auto industry. But with the construction of the Interstate Highway System in the 1950s and 1960s, the new strategy became a practical alternative. The decentralization of production was one of a number of strategies for increasing management's power over labor. Closely related to the dispersal of industry were the allied strategies of multiple sourcing and parallel production. New technology installed in the new plants was also designed to enhance management authority as well as increase productivity.[11]

An overall measure of the change in industry that took place between the mid-1950s and the 1970s is the growth in the number of plants and the decrease in the size of their average workforce. In 1954 there were 31,800 plants belonging to multiplant manufacturing companies. By 1977 there were 81,200 such plants. But during the same years the average number of workers per plant declined from 233 to 124. And while industrial production grew by over 160%, the number of production workers in manufacturing grew by only about 10%.[12] Industrial workers were producing a great deal more, but they were dispersed geographically and isolated by the production process itself. Aside from the loss of union members, which was certainly substantial, this dispersal of industry presented business unionism with increased problems of communication, information gathering and, what was probably most important in the long run, the weakening of pattern bargaining. Countless plants paying a variety of wages and benefits could only increase the competitive pressure on union wage and benefit rates in one industry after another.

Corporate Concentration

The dispersion of domestic production facilities was by no means associated with a dispersion of ownership. The plants might be moving south or west or away from the cities, but ownership remained in the same hands in the traditional urban centers of corporate power. A study of new manufacturing jobs created in the South from 1969 through 1976 showed that 70% of the net job growth in the South occurred in branch plants of northern firms. A study using Federal Trade Commission data for 18,000 mergers and buy-outs between 1955 and 1968 showed that the vast majority reflected control by Northern-owned firms and that 'four out of every five states experienced an outward shift of corporate control.'[13]

There is a distinction to be made between the *concentration* of capital, defined as the growth in the size of units of capital (that is, corporations) and its *centralization*, the increased control of assets or markets by fewer firms. What has occurred in the US since World War Two has been the increased concentration of capital rather than its centralization, which did not change much by the usual measures. In terms of centralized control of manufacturing assets, for example, the top 100 manufacturing corporations controlled 49.1% of all manufacturing assets in 1968. By 1977, however, this figure had dropped slightly to 45.7%. To be sure, these top corporations controlled the commanding heights of industry, but even the merger movements of the late 1960s and 1970s did not change the degree of control much. What did change was the size of the corporations with which organized labor had to deal. In 1960 there were 28 manufacturing corporations with $1 billion or more in assets, representing 27.6% of the nation's total manufacturing assets. In 1970 there were 102 billion-dollar corporations controlling 48.8% of manufacturing assets. By 1979, 212 manufacturing firms could claim $1 billion or more in assets, representing 60% of the nation's manufacturing assets. Billion-dollar firms controlled more of industry's assets, but there were many more such firms.[14]

The concentration of capital was accomplished largely through corporate mergers and buy-outs. From 1953 through 1968, the top 200 US manufacturing firms, for example, bought 3,900 companies; most became part of conglomerates.[15] Labor in the late 1970s faced corporations with many times the plants, equipment, and financial assets they had when the CIO began organizing in the 1930s. The balance of power between labor and capital on the company level had changed in favor of capital in most cases. But the overall shift in this balance was much greater in society as a whole. The merger movements in combination with the rise in debt had intensified the interlocking nature of corporate and financial business in the US. For example, a 1978 Senate study concluded that the top thirteen financial corporations interlocked with 70% of the 130 corporations covered in the study. Even before the spectacular arbitrage deals of the 1980s, financial institutions had a major stake in the nation's nonfinancial corporations. By the mid-1970s, for example, bank trust departments accounted for 60% of all stock purchases. This stock ownership was further concentrated in a handful of Northern banks. Another Senate study of 122 corporations showed that New York's Morgan Guaranty Trust was among the top five stockholders of 56 corporations, while Citibank was among the top five of 25 corporations. Indeed, of the twenty-one institutions that were found to dominate stock ownership of the 122 corporations, eleven were banks, six were investment firms, and four were insurance companies.[16] While this sort of stock ownership does not necessarily imply direct control, it does mean that these powerful financial institutions have a stake in the functioning and profitability of these corporations. A major consequence of this development was a trend toward unification of industrial and financial capital.

In 1979 *Business Week* reported that corporate boards of directors were no longer 'rubber-stamp' operations directed by management. Increasingly, they were dominated by business leaders from outside the corporation, many of them from financial institutions. By the end of the 1970s, 97% of the firms surveyed by *Business Week* had outsider-controlled audit committees, while the executive committees of 80% of these firms were dominated by people from outside the management of the corporation. The corporate board of directors was becoming a class-conscious, activist center of business direction. The 'managerial revolution' projected in the 1950s was stillborn as corporations reacted to economic stress and the signs of a coming economic crisis. *Business Week* pointed to the Penn Central failure of the mid-1970s as the turning point in the reemergence of the board of directors. The new management outlook included a shift from the traditional productionist or even marketing view of industrial activity to a more financially oriented approach to decision making. Overall company profitability was no longer a sufficient guide to investment decisions; instead, profitability had to be considered right down to the plant or even department level.[17]

Who's the Boss Today?

Activist capital not only possessed greater concentrations of wealth, but more and more corporations had become diversified businesses with numerous sources of income and a much greater ability to endure a strike in one line of production. In 1959 US Steel took a 116-day strike, but in the end the company withdrew its demands for concessions. In 1986–87, USX, US Steel's sinister-sounding descendent, derived over half its income from such nonsteel holdings as Marathon Oil. This time, it beat the union after nearly six months of what the union termed a lockout. In spite of all the talk about foreign competition, USX preferred to humble the USW rather than protect its market share. There was even speculation that USX had changed its name in preparation for leaving the steel business if it did not get this third round of concessions. USX had other businesses to lean on. In fact, one of its divisions, POSCO, which produced tin and steel, was allowed by the USW to function during the strike on the grounds that it was a separate company. The USW also tried to fight USX in the same limited way it had fought US Steel in 1959. The union rejected the idea of a boycott or corporate campaign against the entire USX corporation or any of its products. The union did leaflet some Marathon gas stations in Indiana and Ohio, but a Steelworkers spokesperson let it be known that 'we are not – repeat not – calling for a boycott.'[18]

As a diversified corporation, USX was not unique in the steel industry. Armco Steel had diversified into nonsteel operations include energy and changed its name to Armco Inc. National Steel had turned itself into a subsidiary of a larger holding company known as National Intergroup. LTV, of course, was a conglomerate before it entered the steel business. Indeed, by 1981 nonsteel operations accounted for 38% of the assets of steel-producing corporations, 27% of sales, and 34% of operating profits.[19] Even before the companies broke with coordinated bargaining, the USW was facing a set of employers with resources far beyond their steel facilities. The leadership of the USW knew this as well as anyone, but the knowledge had little or no effect on the strategic or tactical thinking of the union.

The meatpacking industry provides another example of how changes in ownership affect labor relations and the underpinnings of industrial unionism. According to a study by the UFCW, the top six meatpackers, who were under pattern agreements, were bought out in the late 1960s and early 1970s or became diversified companies (see Table 2).

Table 2
Conglomerates in Meatpacking

Conglomerate	Meatpacker
Esmark	Swift & Co.
Greyhound	Armour & Co.
LTV	Wilson Foods
United Brands	John Morrell
General Host	Cudahy Foods
Hansen Trust	Hygrade Foods

Source: UFCW, *1986 Report on the US Meat Packing Industry and the Challenges Workers Face*, Washington 1986, Section I, p. 4.

As conglomerates interested in maximizing returns on their new investments, these corporations engaged in the standard practices of milking the division for profits, closing less efficient plants, selling plants, or closing down all or most operations, as in the case of Morrell, Cudahy, and Hygrade. By the early 1980s, many plants that had been under the union's pattern agreements no longer existed. Some, like Greyhound's Armour plants, were closed and sold to another firm, ConAgra, which reopened them as nonunion plants. By that time, Hormel, one of the few firms not bought up by a conglomerate, began transforming itself by entering into marketing agreements with FDL and by beginning operations in South Africa. The shape of the industry and of the system of bargaining that had been established in the 1940s and 1950s was completely changed. Many of the plants and even companies on which the industry's patterns were based had closed, and new firms like Iowa Beef Packers (IBP) had entered the industry. The major union in the industry, the Amalgamated Meat Cutters, which had absorbed the United Packinghouse Workers in 1968, was slow to respond to these and other changes. In fact, the merged union began losing members after 1973. Its solution was to merge again in 1979, this time with the Retail Clerks International Union, a union based mainly in the retail grocery industry and with no experience in meatpacking. This merger did not address the problems of industry restructuring, and within a few years the companies had succeeded in cutting wages and destroying the system of pattern bargaining in meatpacking.

Furthermore, in the second half of the 1980s an entirely new wave of restructuring swept through the meatpacking industry as the older packinghouse firms were completely replaced as industry leaders. The first firm to restructure was IBP, which became the number one beef packer and moved on to make gains in the pork segment of the industry. Two vertically integrated grain and feed companies, Cargill and ConAgra, made an aggressive entry into the industry by buying up existing plants in the mid–1980s. In 1987 Conagra leapt into second place in the industry by merging with Monfort of Colorado, Inc. Cargil became number three with the acquisition of Excel, Swift Independent and Val-Agri. Unlike most other meatpacking companies, ConAgra and Cargil had feedlot and feed capacity as well as slaughtering and processing plants. The change was significant because these three companies were aggressively antiunion and owned nonunion plants.[20]

Another example of how seriously changes in ownership can affect bargaining was the coal mining industry. John L. Lewis's productivity deal with the Bituminous Coal Operators Association (BCOA) in 1950 began the transformation of that industry. With the widespread introduction of mechanization productivity grew and employment fell. The United Mine Workers dropped from 350,000 members in 1950 to 150,000 in 1965. Thousands of small coal operators went out of business as the larger companies mechanized. In the second half of the 1960s national and multinational corporations began buying up coal operations. In particular, large oil companies acquired many of the large coal operators. Utility companies bought up coal operations to expand the number of 'captive mines', those directly operated by industrial corporations that use the coal themselves rather than sell it on the market. Table 3 shows what the acquisition drive of the late 1960s did to the ownership of the top fifteen coal producers. The industry and its bargaining arm, the BCOA, were now dominated by firms many times the size and financial worth of those John L. Lewis had bargained with. Further, many of these companies no longer derived the majority of their revenues from coal production.

Table 3
Ownership of the Top Fifteen Coal Mining Operators

	Coal Producer	*Owner (1966–78)*
Owned by Oil Companies	Consolidation Coal	Continental Oil
	Island Creek Coal	Occidental Petroleum
	Arch Mineral	Ashland Oil & Hunt Oil
	Old Ben Coal	Standard Oil (Ohio)
Captive	US Steel	
	Bethlehem Steel	
	Pacific Power and Light	
	American Electric Power	
	Western Energy	
Other Owners	Peabody Coal	Williams Companies, 27.5%; Newmont Mining, 27.5%; Bechtel, 15%; Boeing, 15%; Fluor, 10%; Equitable Life, 5%.
	Amax Coal	Amax
	Peter Kiewit Sons	
Independent	Pittston	
	North American Coal	
	Westmoreland Coal	

Total tonnage of top fifteen producers: 296 million tons
Total US production, 1976: 665 million tons
Production share of the top fifteen: 44.5%

Sources: *Business Week*, 28 November 1977; US Bureau of the Census, *Statistical Abstract of the United States, 1977*, Washington 1977, p. 751.

Unlike many other unions during this period, the UMWA grew rapidly. From 150,000 members in 1965 it grew to 277,000 in 1976. The number of working miners in the UMWA grew from 90,000 in 1965 to 171,000 in 1976. Even more impressive, the UMWA's percentage of the industry's workforce increased from 67% in 1965 to 82% in 1976. But the new owners of the coal industry put most of their new investment into stripmining operations in the West. By the mid-1970s UMWA contracts covered only about 50% of the coal mined in the US; even in the Eastern states the union share of production declined from 75.3% in 1973 to 68.8% in 1976. The leading companies in the BCOA decided that it was time to take on the UMWA. In 1977 the BCOA presented a long list of concessionary demands including the gutting of the elaborate community health system provided by the UMWA contract and a number of disciplinary measures meant to end wildcat strikes in the industry. The miners struck for 110 days, defied a Taft-Hartley injunction, rejected two offers, and finally approved a contract by only 57%. But in the end the employers forced the UMWA into its first retreat since 1950.[21]

The BCOA won as much as it did largely because UMWA President Arnold Miller, elected in 1972 as part of the Miners for Democracy slate, turned out to be, as former UMWA Research Director Tom Bethell put it, 'a tower of indecision'. Even though the leadership collapsed in the face of the BCOA's assault, it finally took a split in the ranks of the employers to end the strike. In February 1978, after the UMWA's bargaining council rejected the BCOA's first offer by 25 to 13 against Miller's recommendation, several of the large coal operators moved to replace J. Bruce Johnston of US Steel, long the leader of BCOA, as chief negotiator. His successor was Nicholas Camicia of Pittston. Camicia was no softy, but Pittston, like a number of the other noncaptive operators, was hurting from the strike. The new BCOA committee presented a slightly modified second offer, but the UMWA membership rejected it against Miller's recommendation by 74,957 to 32,641.[22] The new committee further modified its demands in March, and the membership accepted this offer in the belief that they could not do much better as long as Miller was in command. Although modified twice, the contract was still a major setback for the UMWA. As in other industries, the perception that the power of the union was declining and that concessions could be won eventually led some companies to pull out of the employers committee and demand substandard wages or conditions. For example, the strike against A. T. Massey began in 1984 when Massey refused to sign the master agreement. Massey, itself the owner of several coal operations it claimed were independent companies, was jointly owned by Fluor Corporation and Royal Dutch Shell.[23]

The protection of industrial unionism extended beyond those workers and companies directly covered by the major pattern agreements. They tended to provide a common reference point for industrial workers performing similar work in different industries or for employers outside the master agreement. Until the late 1960s many such companies were small independent producers, but with the merger wave thousands of these firms became subsidiaries of giant corporations. Almost invariably, their labor policies changed. When the major patterns began to fall apart in the early 1980s, tougher labor policies turned into demands for concessions and threats to close plants.

One such company was Morse Cutting Tool of New Bedford, Massachusetts. Morse was an independent manufacturing firm producing drill bits and cutting tools, mainly for the auto and other heavy industries. The workers had been represented by Local 277 of the United Electrical Workers since the late 1930s and gone on strike only once, in 1976. In 1968 Gulf & Western bought Morse along with other plants as part of an expansion program. For years, G & W milked the plant and then in 1981 began a drive for concessions aimed mainly at working conditions in its plants around the country. Unlike many of Morse's previous owners, who bargained by reference to standards set in their own line of production in basically regional markets, G & W took a more global view of what wage levels were competitive. In January 1982 it arrived at Local 277's door with a list of take-away demands and threats to move equipment and production to other plants unless they were met. Morse's wages and benefits were standard for the cutting tool industry in the area, and G & W didn't dispute this point. Morse President David Cameron argued the G & W view in May 1982: 'Morse management realizes that by agreeing to fair and reasonable settlements by comparison to other New England Tool Companies, Morse has become noncompetitive. The real competition today is in the low Labor Rate areas where wages are $3.00 to $4.00 per hour less.'[24]

Here the failure to organize the entire industry and establish a national standard returned to haunt the union. This problem was compounded by the conglomerate nature of the employer. As in so many such conglomerates, workers at the company's various plants were either non-union or represented by different unions. There was no coordination across union lines. The UE obviously did not have the kind of leverage over G & W that the UAW has had over GM, Ford or Chrysler. And it had no national standard from which to argue comparability.

Nevertheless, the UE, unlike many other unions, didn't collapse. Instead, it initiated a unique campaign in the community of New Bedford. Morse's market problems were laid at the company's feet as the union argued that G & W had milked the plant rather than investing in it and had run down its sales department. The UE appealed to the community by accusing G & W of disinvesting in New Bedford and hurting a city that had served Morse well since 1864. It shifted the focus of the fight from concessions to G & W's irresponsibility toward the entire community. A Citizens Committee to Support the Morse Workers was formed with wide support, including thirty-five local unions in the area. When Local 277 struck the plant in 1982, it had the backing of much of the town of New Bedford.[25]

The plan worked even though Gulf & Western continued to make the same threats. Eventually, the union persuaded New Bedford's mayor to threaten to use the city's power of eminent domain if G & W tried to close the plant or move equipment. This idea was borrowed from the Tri-State Conference on Steel, a labor/community alliance in the Pittsburgh area that was attempting to keep steel plants open there. In 1985, unable to beat the UE and the community, G & W sold the plant to a new owner. The plant was losing money and, after four years of creative resistance, the UE agreed to wage cuts in 1986. Although the union eventually had to grant concessions to the company, it is certain that if it had simply granted concessions to Gulf & Western in 1982 or conducted a conventional strike, it would have faced a second round of concession demands in 1986 and quite likely a whole or partial plant closing.[26]

The Morse story is unusual only because the union found new ways to fight a multinational conglomerate. Otherwise, the very dates that punctuate the Morse experience mark an era when countless numbers of workers at small firms began to have to deal with conglomerates. The year 1968 saw the climax of the first great round of corporate mergers and acquisitions. In 1981 scores of multinationals, inspired by Chrysler's second and third round of concessions, took the offensive against their unions. As the major patterns disintegrated, the attack on these isolated plants and operations grew.

Changing ownership, usually accompanied by an increased concentration of capital, was an aspect of the power shift that allowed Corporate America to accelerate the concessions trend and eventually destroy all of the major industrial pattern agreements. This spelled the end to the wage standardization that has always been a central characteristic of industrial unionism. For workers outside the major patterns, the shift in capital ownership combined with the decline of pattern bargaining or the lack of any national standard also ended the industrial union practice of stronger unions setting a standard that organized workplaces could try to achieve in their own bargaining.

The Industrial Union Department of the AFL-CIO recognized the problem of dealing with merged companies and conglomerates even before the collapse of pattern bargaining. An IUD pamphlet noted that

> the ability of unions to bargain effectively is being threatened by the changing character of American business and industry. When these employers expand or combine, whether into giants of the traditional type or into

conglomerates, the unions that were formed to deal effectively with the separate plants or the original firms find that their ability to deal with the employer has been diluted. Union pressure, even a strike by one part of the giant's workers, is only a minor annoyance if the rest of the company continues to produce profits.

The IUD further notes that in this new situation the employer can 'whip-saw the unions' and 'pressure the weakest union into accepting less than is justified.'[27]

The IUD's program for dealing with this situation is coordinated bargaining. In the IUD's definition, coordinated bargaining can range from joint, simultaneous bargaining by all the unions in the same corporation to, at a minimum, the sharing of information and the development of a more or less common bargaining program. Coordinated bargaining in its fullest form would obviously represent the extension of industrial union methods to the problems presented by changing ownership patterns. It is, by any standard, a sound idea. For the most part, however, it is just that – an idea.

The one long-standing example of coordinated bargaining is in the electrical equipment industry, where bargaining at GE and Westinghouse has been on a fully coordinated basis since the 1960s. There are a few examples of partially coordinated bargaining – for example, at Colt Industries. Coordinated bargaining beyond the sharing of information is rare. No conglomerate operating in the US has a fully operating system of coordinated bargaining. Indeed, locals of the same union in conglomerates seldom coordinate bargaining unless they were already functioning jointly in a firm that was bought out.

An example of the extent of the problem was a bitter eight-month strike by UAW Local 1663 at Essex Wire's Elwood, Indiana plant in 1977–78. In 1976 Essex became one of several divisions of United Technologies as a result of an acquisition. Essex had about 115 plants in North America, 70 of which were organized by seven different unions. Not only was there no coordinated bargaining at the level of United Technologies, but there was none at the Essex level either. The nine UAW locals within Essex did not coordinate or communicate. In fact, while Local 1663 was on strike, there were five different strikes by UAW locals in the Essex system, and no effort was made to coordinate them or their goals. In fact, UAW policy in 1978 was quite the opposite. International Rep Carolyn Forest stated at the time that 'we usually try to negotiate wages on the basis of that plant's ability to pay.' In other words, the UAW already practiced at Essex and other parts suppliers what it would later concede at GM, Ford and Chrysler – competitive bargaining.

One reason for the scarcity of coordinated bargaining is simply that the conglomerates resist it militantly. The avoidance of union power was one of the reasons many major industrial corporations shifted from dependence on a single line of production in the first place. For coordinated bargaining to work, the unions involved must have common contract expiration dates. Without common contract expiration dates, a joint strike is illegal if the contracts have no-strike clauses, since some unions would still be under contract. To avoid common expiration dates, the employer can stall negotiations or provoke a long strike with one union while amicably settling with others, and so on. Coordinated bargaining requires a level of coordinated militancy and tactical innovation still beyond the imagination of most business unionists.

But even beyond the problem of company resistance and union timidity are the self-imposed barriers that make coordinated bargaining inaccessible to local unions that need it most. The IUD's pamphlet *Coordinated Bargaining: Labor's New Approach to Effective Contract Negotiations* reflects bureaucratic business unionism's obsession with protocol and hierarchy. The pamphlet says nothing about common expiration dates, joint actions, or other real problems. It focuses on procedures. Procedure number one sends a clear message to any embattled local union that the day when coordinated bargaining will become a reality is far away. If only to understand the mind of the business unionist, it is worth tracing the byzantine course through which a request must go.

To begin with, no local union can make such a request of the IUD. The pamphlet states that 'requests for coordinated bargaining may be made only by international unions and only in writing.' This written request must include a list of locals and all the relevant information about them. Upon receipt, the IUD's staff will assess the feasibility of the request. Should the request be deemed feasible, the IUD will draw up a list of plants, expiration dates, etc., and forward the information to all the internationals involved. The internationals will check out the information and return it, corrected if necessary, along with a plan for talking to their own officials and locals. Once each international has cleared its own diplomatic hurdles, the procedure then moves to the first real piece of business in the whole process. Again, to grasp the cautious mentality involved, it is worth quoting the IUD's description of this step:

> Before calling a full committee meeting [of local leaders], the assigned coordinator shall meet with the international presidents only or their designees, who, together, will decide on behalf of their respective unions whether or not to call a full committee meeting. If the decision is in the affirmative, this group will develop into an International President's Committee and the coordinator will take the necessary steps to implement the first full committee meeting. The responsibility of the International President's Committee will be to guide the future activities of the full committee.[28]

The international presidents are also given control over communications between unions and committees. Initiatives from below are out of order in this view of coordinated bargaining.

A feature of bureaucratic unionism is that all important decision making is left to the international presidents and their executive boards. They have given themselves power over all the union's contracts, which number from a few hundred to many thousands in today's major unions. They control all decisions and negotiations concerning political affairs. They orchestrate conventions. They direct the union's considerable finances. To take responsibility for a new, complex area of endeavor like coordinated bargaining means more time, more intricate 'politics', more headaches as the targeted corporate giant resists and maneuvers in return. There is the apprehension that coordinated bargaining might involve a new mode of functioning with unforeseen repercussions on the internal life of the union. Most of all, it points to a new level of confrontation (on the part of the employer if no one else) that gives ulcers to modern business unionists. So coordinated bargaining remains rare throughout industry and partial where it is attempted. It is a great idea awaiting a leadership with the courage, imagination, and appreciation of rank-and-file initiative to carry it out.

The Internationalization of Corporate Power

Because profit rates differ between nations due to their different conditions and cost structures, capital has always tended to look abroad for better opportunities. As the domestic migration of industry ceased to yield above average rates of return on new investment toward the end of the 1960s, US capital turned increasingly abroad. US private assets abroad rose from $19 billion in 1950 to $49.2 billion in 1960 and to $118.8 billion in 1970. This was an average increase of 150% per decade. But by 1980, US private assets abroad had risen to $579 billion, a gain of 335% – over twice the rate of growth of the previous two decades.

The proportion of profits made by US firms overseas followed a similar course. In 1950 profits made abroad were 3.4% of total profits. By 1965 they had risen to only 5.9%. But by 1970 they were 9.4% and by 1980, 15.6%. Thus, in the fifteen years from 1950 to 1965 overseas profits as a proportion of total profits didn't even double, but in the decade and a half after 1965 they nearly tripled.[29]

The declining rate of profit throughout the industrialized world altered the direction of much US overseas investment after the mid-1960s. For most of the postwar era the bulk of US investment abroad went to Europe and Canada. By the end of the 1970s, however, US assets in Latin

America and the Caribbean ($150 billion) nearly equaled those in Europe ($167 billion) and surpassed those in Canada ($96 billion).[30] Much the same can be said of European capital, which tended to flow to Asia. The direction of US and European capital to the Third World was highly selective, however. A few key countries of Latin America and Asia were the recipients of the lion's share of this investment, notably Mexico, Brazil, Hong Kong, South Korea, Taiwan, and the Philippines.

For capital, the development of new areas of large-scale investment at above average rates of return provided new opportunities, thus preventing a collapse of investment and a full-scale depression. The growth of the proportion of profits made overseas noted above is an indication of the relative success of this strategy for US capital. In the long run, it also created a mammoth debt problem in both the Third World and the US. By the end of the 1970s, Third World debt was estimated at about $250 billion.[31] This burgeoning debt could itself lay the basis for a massive depression, but so far that possibility has been avoided by the regular rescheduling of debt payments and the extension of still more loans.

This investment strategy accelerated the internationalization of capital and the integration of both the advanced capitalist nations and the developing Third World countries. Capital markets were increasingly global markets, including the Eurodollar and petrodollar markets of the 1970s. Even industrial production became integrated as the industrial capacity of a small number of Third World nations grew. A consequence and cause of this internationalization of the economy was the growth of the multinational corporation. That is, most of the $516.6 billion in US assets abroad in 1980 was organized as divisions or subsidiaries of US-based industrial or financial corporations. Increasingly, US companies were building their production capacity outside the US or becoming the financial partners of foreign industrial firms. For example, the proportion of plant and equipment located outside the US by American companies in the metal and machinery industries rose from an annual average of 14% in the late 1950s to 28% in the late 1960s. Another indication of how important overseas production had become to these multinationals was revealed in a congressional report that by 1970, 'close to three-quarters of total US exports and upwards of one-half of all imports [were] transactions between the domestic and foreign subsidiaries of the same [US and foreign] multinational conglomerate corporations.'[32] The import problem was largely a creation of US capital.

The multinationalization of American business accelerated the concentration of capital already under way as part of the domestic migration of production. As US firms entered international product and capital markets more aggressively in the 1960s, they soon discovered they were not alone. European and Japanese firms were pursuing the same strategy. Ironically, many of them did so with US money behind them. Nevertheless, the competitive position of the US multinationals soon came under intense attack. In 1959 US-based firms accounted for 111 of the top 156 multinational corporations. By 1976 only 68 US-based firms qualified for the top 156. Of thirteen international industries surveyed in a 1978 study, American multinationals had lost ground in twelve.[33]

Among the many strategies for improving their position in global markets, these US multinationals turned toward greater concentration of capital at home in order to create a stronger base from which to compete. In terms of assets and income, the top 500 industrial corporations in the United States dwarfed even the resources of the federal government. In 1983 these top 500 corporations controlled $1.4 trillion in assets and had an annual sales of $1.8 trillion, compared to the federal government's mere $132 billion in real property and $600 billion in annual receipts.[34] The financial and industrial sectors of US capital had increased their power through concentration of these massive assets. With a new sense of class solidarity and urgency, they turned their attention to American labor.

US industrial employers now possessed the resources, both in terms of money and productive facilities beyond the reach of the traditional bargaining agent, to counter union pressure. To compound matters, these corporations often produced their income through systems of multinational production and sourcing. The example of Litton Industries is typical. Economist Charles Craypo conducted a detailed study of Litton, a superconglomerated multinational that soared from 249th place among the *Fortune* 500 in 1960 to 35th in 1972. Litton skillfully moved work among its international network of plants, closing some plants and putting the unions representing the surviving workers in a nearly hopeless situation. Craypo summed up the impact of this form of corporate organization on unions: 'The impact of conglomerate, multinational structure on collective bargaining is to give the employer, under certain conditions, the capacity to make the institutionalized bargaining system an ineffective method of resolving industrial disputes.'[35] Business unionism, unable with rare exceptions to cooperate across union lines in the US, was hardly able to develop effective international links capable of countering the concentrated power it faced.

The Domestic Impact of Internationalization

Increased investment abroad by American and European corporations affected the structure of employment in their domestic economies. As capital moved outward in the 1970s from the old industrial nations to

new corners of the world, one consequence was a decline in the proportion of gross national product generated by industrial production in
most nations of North America and Western Europe. The converse was
a significant rise in the proportion of GNP generated by industry in a
number of Asian and Latin American countries in the same period,
notably the major targets of overseas investment: Mexico, Brazil,
Venezuela, South Korea, Taiwan, and the Philippines.[36]

For the US economy, this meant an acceleration of the long-standing
decline of industrial, goods-producing jobs and a rise in service-sector
employment as corporations internationalized production and as administrative, financial, communications, technical and marketing tasks
in the US-based headquarters grew. In the 1980s some industries such
as auto and steel lost a portion of employment to imports. Imports,
however, were a relatively small piece of the puzzle of international
competition, which was having an impact in markets all over the world.
Even within the US economy, intensified competition was not simply a
contest between domestic and foreign firms. Intensified competition
from any quarter will increase market rivalry among all producers,
domestic as well as foreign. The fight for market dominance among US-
based capitalist firms knew no nationality, no regard for US workers or
their communities, and no rules other than those imposed by outside
forces. A far greater loss of industrial jobs can be explained by the
measures that domestic employers took in response to competitive pressures in markets around the globe than by imports per se. Indeed, a 1984
study showed that between 1973 and 1980 productivity and international outsourcing accounted for a loss of over 4 million manufacturing jobs,
compared to about a quarter of a million lost to direct imports.[37]

Behind the loss of jobs to productivity was new technology. The introduction of new technology is capitalism's historic response to anything that undermines profit margins. That can be foreign or domestic
competition in either foreign or domestic markets, or simply slumping
profit margins resulting from the internal dynamics of the production
process. In the auto industry, for example, GM's move in the 1960s to
spread new, technologically advanced plants spread around the country
began prior to any real threat by imports. It was, rather, part of a global
strategy for improving GM's position in all corners of the world by
reducing costs through drastic modernization and increased labor discipline. Eventually, Ford and Chrysler had to follow suit to some extent.
It was not Japan that set this dynamic in motion, but the search for increased profits. Even when today's automakers are willing to accept a
reduced share of the market (limited to mid-sized and larger cars) and
to invest in Japanese firms, they will introduce new technology to increase profits. In meatpacking, the introduction of technological change

occurred in the context of the dispersal of production in the 1960s and was entirely a response to domestic competition. On the other hand, the garment industry has been under siege from imports for a long time but has never experienced sweeping technological change.

While there have always been those who argue that new technology creates as many or more jobs than it replaces, there is little evidence to support this contention. In assessing the impact of robotization on the auto industry, for example, *Business Week* concluded in 1983 that while robotization would create perhaps 3,000 to 5,000 jobs to make the robots, it 'will replace up to 50,000 auto workers.' Overall, new jobs in manufacturing high-tech equipment 'will account for only a fraction of total US employment by the mid-1990s.' The same year, the Congressional Budget Office estimated that by 1990, 'a combination of automation and capacity cutbacks in basic industry will eliminate three million manufacturing jobs.'[38]

In the mid-1970s, Harry Braverman pointed out in his ground-breaking study *Labor and Monopoly Capital* that the long-term growth of technology naturally contributes to the proportional shift from production work to clerical and service jobs because technology tends to be applied first to the production process and because service occupations are less susceptible to automation. More recently, clerical work has itself seen the application of much electronics technology, but his observation was nonetheless correct for much of the accelerated shift in employment structures that has taken place since World War Two. As Braverman pointed out, the pay of this new mass of clerical workers is held down by the vast number of people (mostly women) available for this kind of work. So long as this labor is relatively cheap, capital has little incentive to automate.[39]

In an earlier chapter, I argued that technology was one cause of the deterioration of the union power in the workplace. Technology is also a key aspect of both the dispersal of industry and the internationalization of capital, and as such it plays an important role in the unfavorable shift in the overall balance of social forces in US society as a whole. David Noble, a social historian of automation, has eloquently described the overall impact of the new industrial technology, placing it in context with other changes of the past three decades:

> Computerized monitoring and surveillance systems, remotely controlled and satellite-linked plants, CAD/CAM [computer-aided design and manufacturing] systems, robotization – all are being designed precisely to serve management's efforts to neutralize the power of unions and workers and to guarantee decisive control over far-flung operations. The concentration of corporate power, the internationalization of enterprises, the ability to play one country's work force off against another's in a global division of labor,

the unprecedented mobility of capital, and the direct assault upon organized labor's right to exist in the United States, all give to management great advantages in this contest. Moreover, the official trade union challenge itself is handicapped from within, by a union leadership distrust and fear of its own more militant rank and file and equally important, by an abiding faith in technological promises.[40]

Another strategy common to most corporations in the last twenty-five years has been rationalization. In the wake of the merger movements of the late 1960s and again from the late 1970s through today, corporations weeded out the least efficient of the operations they had bought. A study covering the early 1970s compared the employment patterns of independently owned companies and firms that had been bought by other companies. The acquired companies showed a vastly greater propensity for reducing employment levels.[41] An example in the steel industry occurred with the merger of the conglomerate LTV and Republic Steel in 1984, which was accompanied by the integration of compatible operations and the elimination of duplicate and less efficient ones.[42] Using the acquired firms as 'cash cows' or simply closing all or part of an acquired plant and integrating what can be salvaged with some other operation is basic strategy in the era of corporate mergers.

In the 1980s rationalization intensified and took a somewhat new direction. Corporate mergers and acquisitions accelerated, but their purpose changed from conglomeration to an increased emphasis on buying firms in the same line of production. In its 1983 'Deals of the Year' survey, *Fortune* magazine noted: 'The movement away from conglomeration was evident in 1983's grand-scale deals. Corporate acquirers tended to go for the industries they knew best – their own. Among the mergers and acquisitions in *Fortune*'s directory, same-industry deals predominated.'[43] To be sure, there were exceptions to this trend, like US Steel's purchase of Marathon Oil. But in general, this turn in merger strategy reflected the need for industrial corporations to retrench in search of profitability.

Whether rationalization occurs in the context of slimming down to one major line of production or branching out into new businesses, as in the steel industry, it always involves plant closings. But in an era when the average rate of profit is falling, closing plants is not simply the traditional question of closing obsolete operations. In the 1960s and 1970s stock market prices for industrial companies were well below what it would cost to build new plants. Hence, many corporations went on buying sprees. But the newly purchased facilities were expected to meet certain profit goals. A profitable plant might well be closed if it did not meet the goal set for it. Since average rates of return were slumping, the goals of the new corporate owners were certain to include above average profitability. This meant that corporations closed efficient plants in efforts to sustain their rates of return. The pressure for such decisions often came from financial associates of the industrial firm. The *Wall Street Journal* cited such an example in the decision of Uniroyal to close its Indianapolis tire plant in 1978. The *Journal* reported:

> The factory has long been the country's leading producer of inner tubes. It operates profitably.... The company, in a formal statement, cited "high labor costs" and "steadily declining demand". Union and management officials who worked at the plant tell another story. They say that Uniroyal could have kept the plant operating profitably if it wanted to but that under pressure from the securities markets management decided to concentrate its energy on higher growth chemical lines.[44]

On the basis of extensive studies, Barry Bluestone pointed out:

> It is important to recognize that consistent with this corporate strategy, the vast number of plants being closed (other than very small family-owned businesses) are not shut down as a result of bankruptcy. Instead the phenomenon of disinvestment involves multi-unit firms choosing to close down particular plants or divisions in order to use their cash flow (profits plus depreciation reserves) for more profitable investment elsewhere, or in some cases to move the plant or division to what management believes is a low-cost area.[45]

Through the end of the 1970s, the opening of new plants still outstripped the closing of old ones, and the number of production jobs still rose somewhat, even though the new plants on average employed fewer people. From 1967 to 1977 the number of plants rose from 51,700 employing 9.8 million production workers to 81,200 plants with 10.1 million production workers. But in the early 1980s the creation of new plants leveled off, and the number of production jobs slumped. In 1982, the latest year for which figures are available, there were just 81,700 plants employing only 8.8 million production workers, a loss of 1.3 million production jobs.[46] Rationalization and plant closings have not only eliminated jobs; they have increasingly become a tool for disciplining labor and, in the 1980s, a corporate lever for blackmailing reluctant workers into making major concessions on wages, benefits, and work rules.

Containment and the New Employer Activism

By the 1960s, the migration of industry was more or less consciously conducted to minimize union influence. The increased cash resulting from the concentration of capital and multinationalization made this course affordable, and sagging profit margins in the second half of the 1960s made it seem imperative. The rule of law in labor relations, so long sought and so recently achieved, gradually eroded. Defeating new union organizing attempts became, for two decades, a strategy sufficient to produce declining union influence within all but a few industries.

Through the first half of the 1950s, unions maintained or even increased the degree of unionization within their traditional jurisdictions. Unionization efforts in the 1950s became largely routine campaigns to follow runaway shops or organize new ones within the same industry. The method of organizing in the private sector was largely defined by the procedures of the National Labor Relations Act and overseen by the National Labor Relations Board, which conducted union representation elections. Under this procedure, the need for a recognition strike was, theoretically, eliminated.

During the 1950s management opposition was minimal. Perhaps slightly overstating the case, Professor Richard Freeman told a congressional hearing in 1984, 'In the 1950s many managements did relatively little to discourage their workers from unionizing – after all, did not the law specify that the decision was the workers' to make?' In general, the filing of an unfair labor practice charge with the NLRB was enough to make the employer play by the rules. During the 1950s the number of unfair labor practice charges filed against employers was less than one per election. So long as employer resistance remained at this level, unions could do well through the legal procedures of the NLRB. During the 1950s unions won 65% to 75% of the elections they petitioned for with large numerical majorities.[47]

But as industrial migration took on momentum in the 1960s and the employers intensified their fight for control of the workplace, the desire to contain unionism grew. Professor Freeman went on to describe the employers' change of heart: 'In ensuing decades, however, management has come to contest hotly nearly every significant NLRB election.' As unions attempted to follow capital to new areas, the number of representation elections grew from 4,729 in 1957 to 7,576 in 1965 and to 8,061 in 1975, almost doubling. The number of unfair labor practice charges against employers, however, grew from 3,655 in 1957 to 20,311 in 1975, growing by five and a half times. It grew again to 31,281 in 1980 in spite of a small decline in the number of elections. Most unfair labor practice charges involved the firing of workers who openly supported the union. One of the pacesetters of this tactic was J. P. Stevens, a giant textile firm. A National Council of Churches study found that when the Textile Workers Union of America, responding to the movement of textile jobs to the South, launched an organizing drive against Stevens in 1963:

The company responded with a campaign of harassment and surveillance of pro-union workers, and dismissals of Union leaders. In every one of the twenty-one plants, workers were discharged for union activity. The leaders of the union movement were fired, and other workers were intimidated to prevent their joining. One procedure used was to post a list of the Union organizing members on a plant's bulletin board. Then, as members were fired, or frightened into quitting the Union, their names were publicly scratched off the list.[48]

The workers unfairly fired or disciplined would eventually be reinstated or get back pay, but the companies could easily afford to pay such settlements. The number of prounion workers fired rose until fully one out of twenty workers involved in an organizing election was being fired. The chilling effect was strong. Union victories slumped to 55% in 1970 and 45% by the end of the 1970s. The percentage of workers who were covered by a union victory declined even more – from 83% in 1950 to 52% in 1970 and 37% in 1980.[49]

Companies soon discovered they could delay elections almost indefinitely. Representation elections cannot be held while there are outstanding unfair labor practice charges, so that the union's means of defending itself becomes the company's way of delaying an election and demoralizing the prounion workers. J. P. Stevens, for example, was able to put off a vote at its Roanoke Rapids, North Carolina plants for over a decade. From 1963, when the Textile Workers Union initiated its organizing drive in Roanoke Rapids, to 1976, Stevens was cited for 1,200 violations of the National Labor Relations Act and found guilty 111 times. Back pay awards to the workers involved came to $1.3 million, peanuts for a multinational with annual sales of over $1 billion.[50]

As more companies pursued this strategy, the caseload of the NLRB became a problem in itself. Designed to preempt class struggle through its procedures, the NLRB's channels became clogged as the employers pursued the struggle from their side. The number of days between the filing of an unfair labor practice charge against an employer and the issuance of a decision grew steadily. In 1980 this procedure took 484 days; by 1983, 627 days. If the decision was challenged in the courts, the total time was likely to be three years.[51]

The task of unionization in some ways only begins after winning an NLRB election. The law requires an employer to bargain in 'good faith', but does not require it to sign a contract or grant any of the union's demands. Indeed, it is estimated that only about 50% to 60% of the unions that win representation elections are able to get a contract. Again, J. P. Stevens provides an example. After eleven years of organizing and litigation, the Textile Workers finally won elections at seven of the

Stevens plants in Roanoke Rapids in August 1974. Stevens refused to bargain in good faith in spite of many more NLRB charges. A contract was not signed at these plants until 1980. It took years of a massive national boycott and corporate campaign to force Stevens to sign these contracts. The boycott was the largest and best publicized since the lettuce boycott by the United Farm Workers. The corporate campaign, newly devised by ACTWU staffer Ray Rogers, used the financial power of the unions and churches to get some of Stevens' leading banking partners to add their pressure to normalize labor relations.[52]

Without the aid of such a massive national pressure campaign, many unions faced with intransigent employers don't achieve very much. With the union unable to produce any gains, company-organized employees are free to petition for decertification. If there had been a strike in hopes of forcing a contract, the scabs could petition for a decertification election after a year. But even preventing the union from accomplishing anything and harassing union militants was often enough to bring on decertification, particularly if the employer had hired a union-busting consultant to help manage the process. Decertification elections soared from about 100 a year in the early 1950s to over 800 by the late 1970s. The number of workers denied union representation through decertification is not massive – 22,680 in 1977, for example – but it is a way of draining union resources and discouraging other labor militants in the area as well as those in a particular workplace.[53]

The impact of the Taft-Hartley Act on these trends carries the problem even a step further in those states with right-to-work laws. Even assuming a union could win an election and a contract, it could not by law have a union shop in such states. An aggressive employer can continue to put pressure on workers not to join the union, and decertification moves thus remain a constant threat. Not surprisingly, the growth of employer resistance to union organizing meant that the South's role as a nonunion haven actually grew after the 1950s. During the 1950s and 1960s, employment in the South rose as a proportion of national employment from 19.9% in 1953 to 26.9% by 1978. But successful resistance to unionism meant that the percentage of unionized workers in the South actually dropped during those same years from 17.1% to 12.8%.[54] Clearly a piecemeal approach to organizing in the South, even one that involved such a large campaign as the J. P. Stevens organizing drive, was not enough to reverse this trend.

The reduction of unionism as a force within any given industry in the 1960s and 1970s was carried out on the company level by the combination of buying or building new nonunion plants, migration, and the prevention of unionization. While it was unfashionable to admit it until recently, nonunion status has been a prime factor in corporate decisions to buy a plant in the US. In an interview with the *Wall Street Journal* in the late 1970s, Donovan Dennis, a vice president of the plant location consulting firm Fantus Corporation, noted the single biggest factor in plant location decisions: 'Labor costs are the big thing, far and away. Nine times out of ten you can hang it on labor costs and unionization.'[55] With the increased ability to resist unionization, a corporation could weaken its unions simply by diluting their influence within the firm.

A detailed study of one corporation by Anil Verma and Thomas Kochan gives a interesting insight into how large industrial corporations have accomplished this goal. The corporation studied was not named, but its description as a corporation employing 94,000 workers in 300 locations with a sales of $6 billion in 1982 placed it in the same league as conglomerate giants like Litton, United Technologies, Gulf & Western, and General Dynamics. In 1957 this company had eight plants and was 80% unionized, although most of them were independent unions tolerated by the company. Following a merger with an aerospace firm in 1958, the new company bought thirty plants in the 1960s, half of which were union, and ten more in the 1970s, none of which were union. While denying that unionization per se was a major factor, a company vice president told the researchers, 'In reviewing a candidate for acquisition, we look much more at the employee relations component now than we did in the 1960s.'[56]

The company applied the same criteria to new plants when it shifted its growth emphasis to new construction. Verma and Kochan describe the strategy as a whole:

> In labor relations, the late sixties and seventies also signaled the development of the nonunion or union-free strategy within the company. Of the seventeen plants opened between 1970 and 1982, all except one have remained unorganized. As we have seen, this was not a completely new idea in the company; management's philosophical opposition to unions was long-standing. What was new in this period was a unique strategy for implementing this philosophy. In fact, this firm, along with several others, was shaping a kind of industrial relations so unique and innovative that its impact would fundamentally alter the practice and understanding of industrial relations in the United States.[57]

A consequence of this strategy was that the company's unionized plants were, on the average, much older than its nonunion facilities, 47.23 years compared with 18.40 years. Not surprisingly, employment in the union sector declined much more over the years than nonunion employment: Union jobs dropped from 80% in 1957 to 59% in 1979 and to 50% in 1982. Wage rates, benefits, and work rules in the unionized plants were superior to those in nonunion plants, but the company was not adverse to raising nonunion wages enough to prevent unionization. One aspect of its antiunion philosophy that placed this firm ahead of most others was its early adoption of 'worker involvement' schemes in its nonunion plants. [58]

The company had not engaged in union busting, but it had reduced union influence simply by containing unionism – almost exclusively through buying or building nonunion plants. While comparative data are not available, the *Labor Relations Handbook* by Corporate Data Exchange (CDE) records the percentage of unionized employees for eighty corporations using data from 1975–81. It also records the number of representation elections won and lost. A look at a few major corporations known to have been highly unionized in the 1940s and 1950s prior to conglomeration and expansion should give some indication of how widespread this strategy was (see Table 4).

Table 4
Representation Elections, 1975–81

Company	Percent Union (US)	Number of Unions	Elections Won	Lost
Caterpillar Tractor	55%	3	3	0
Firestone Tire	35%	4	42	21
General Dynamics	50%	10	7	5
General Electric	40%	14	30	49
Goodyear Tire	50%	9	22	22
Gulf & Western	40%	22	24	14
McDonnell Douglas	50%	6	2	3
Rockwell International	40%	13	4	8
Uniroyal	25%	3	3	3
United Technologies	40%	15	13	9
Westinghouse	50%	10	20	16

Source: Corporate Data Exchange, *CDE Handbook: Labor Relations*, New York 1982.

In 1958, 81% of production workers in tire and rubber were organized, 73% in electrical machinery, and 89% in petroleum refining. By the end of the 1970s the leading firms in these industries were 50% union or less. The energy (oil, gas, coal) companies listed by CDE show an even lower proportion of union members, 20% to 45%. While most extreme in the case of the conglomerates, the trend typifies most firms that now deal with a number of unions. In a few cases these unions coordinate bargaining. Usually, however, bargaining is fragmented and increasingly ineffective. Also, many of the unions listed by CDE as petitioning for elections were not necessarily those with an existing jurisdiction in the company, indicating that at least some of these are raids rather than new organizing efforts by current bargaining agents.[59]

The declining proportion of union members within so many industries and corporations shoots more than a few holes in the two most common explanations for the decline in unionism: the growth of imported industrial goods and the employment shift from goods-producing to service-producing industries. Imports and employment shifts do, of course, account for part of the overall decline in the proportion of union members in the total workforce. But neither of these phenomena explains the declining proportion of union members within existing US industries, including those that are not significantly affected by foreign competition such as transportation and meatpacking. A large part of the explanation is clearly the failure to organize the new, nonunion sectors of these domestic industries.

The explanation from the AFL-CIO Executive Council is that legal barriers have thwarted organizing. According to the AFL-CIO's report *The Changing Situation of Workers and Their Unions*, the Wagner Act worked well in the 1950s and 1960s, but in recent years employers have been allowed to avoid unions 'by a law that has proven to be impotent and a Labor Board that is inert.' But in fact, the law has always been impotent when employers chose to ignore it. The decline of union fortunes under the procedures of the law began in the 1950s and was well under way in the 1960s. Like most laws governing labor relations, the NLRA works for labor only when labor 'enforces' it through its own efforts.

Business unionism was in no way prepared to deal with increased employer confrontation. Consequently, throughout most of the 1960s and 1970s, union efforts to organize the unorganized receded, even in familiar jurisdictions. The number of petitions for all kinds of NLRB certification elections leveled off during the 1970s, and a growing proportion of them were company-inspired petitions for decertification elections. The number of actual representation elections also fell during the 1970s, and then plunged downward to half their previous level in the 1980s. In 1980 there were 7,296 representation elections, but in 1983 there were only 3,492.[60]

In the private sector, organizing was simply not a priority for bureaucratic business unionism. A study of the organizing expenditures of twenty international unions by Paula Voos revealed a relative decline in the efforts these unions made from the early 1950s through the mid-1970s. Measured in real dollars per unorganized worker, union spending on new organization dropped from $1.03 in 1953 to $.83 in 1965 and $.71 in 1974. Using Voos's figures, Richard Freeman suggests this decline in organizing programs was responsible for a 21% decrease in the number of newly organized workers over that period.[61]

In 1972, AFL-CIO President George Meany made his views on new organizing clear:

> Why should we worry about organizing groups of people who do not want to be organized? If they prefer to have others speak for them and make the decisions which affect their lives without effective participation on their part that is their right.... Frankly, I used to worry about the membership, about the size of the membership. But quite a few years ago, I just stopped worrying about it, because to me it doesn't make any difference. It's the organized voice that counts – and it's not just in legislation, it's any place. The organized fellow is the fellow that counts.[62]

Thus, even in the routine, union-by-union terms of business unionism, organizing became less and less of a priority precisely as business was gaining new power through its own growth and the expansion of a non-union workforce in industry after industry.

The problem, however, is even greater than these figures indicate. With rare exceptions, the approach of most unions to organizing since the 1950s has been a routine, shop-by-shop approach which could not organize large numbers of workers even if it were well financed. In a round table discussion on the difficulties of organizing, Charles McDonald of the AFL-CIO's Organizing Department pinpointed one of the problems: 'What many people fail to recognize, however, is that few unions have a national organizing strategy; instead most organizing efforts are initiated and carried out at the local level.'[63] Obviously, such a parochial approach is ill-suited to dealing with today's conglomerate, multinational corporations.

The Industrial Union Department of the AFL-CIO has initiated three multiunion coordinated organizing drives in Sun Belt centers in two decades. These efforts, in Greenville/Spartanburg, South Carolina, Los Angeles, and Houston, brought together organizers from different unions under one command in an attempt to organize on a geographic basis. None was very successful. They were generally underfunded – but one also suspects the heavy hand of business unionism. For example, these organizing drives were invisible. The techniques that social movements use to gain them visibility were absent. There were no major attempts to publicize the case for unionism in terms of the social, racial or national issues of importance to the unorganized. By official accounts, the efforts were thwarted by the employers' willingness to break the law. Employer resistance, however, is not an explanation; it is a given. Comparison of the IUD's efforts with recent successful organizing drives provides a more accurate explanation of why the IUD failed.[64]

Business unionism's habit of 'leaning on government' led labor in the 1970s to look to the political arena for help in organizing the unorganized. Labor prepared its agenda and focused on passage of full employment legislation, a bill allowing building trades unions to shut down an entire construction site for organizing purposes (known by the legal term *common situs picketing*), and above all else the reform of the nation's labor laws so that recalcitrant employers could be brought to heel. But labor did not seem to notice that business was directing its massive new resources toward the political arena and organizing aggressively on behalf of its own agenda.

6

Business Organizes as a Class

The influence of business money on politics is as old as the republic. But at certain points in US history business has put aside its usual laissez-faire approach to political influence, creating new vehicles appropriate to the social and economic changes it confronted. Elite policy-formulating organizations have a long history in twentieth-century America. The Conference Board dates back to the Progressive Era before World War One, while such prestigious bodies as the Business Council and the Committee for Economic Development (CED) originated in the 1940s to guide postwar policy.

Similarly, the liberalism of the Kennedy years found many of its policy guidelines in late 1950s in studies commissioned by the Rockefeller brothers; these studies argued for more aggressive Keynesian policies to stimulate domestic growth and free trade to promote international expansion. These ideas were carried into the Kennedy-Johnson administrations by such business notables as Secretary of State Dean Rusk, a Rockefeller associate; Secretary of the Treasury C. Douglas Dillon of the investment firm Dillon Reed; and Secretary of Defense Robert McNamara, previously president of Ford.[1]

Class Consciousness and the Business Agenda of the 1970s

In response to the onset of economic crisis during the 1970s, business launched new organizations, revived some of the old ones, and formulated a new economic agenda for the United States. Thomas Byrne Edsall described one key aspect of what business accomplished in this period:

During the 1970s, business refined its ability to act as a class, submerging competitive instincts in favor of joint, cooperative action in the legislative arena. Rather than individual companies seeking only special favor in the reward of a contract, in the dropping of an antitrust case, or in State Department assistance in gaining exclusive franchising rights in a foreign country, the dominant theme in the political strategy of business became a shared interest in the defeat of bills such as consumer protection and labor law reform, and in the enactment of favorable tax, regulatory, and antitrust legislation.[2]

The leader of this development was the Business Roundtable. Founded in 1972 through the merger of two antilabor business groups and reenforced in 1973 by the joining of another, the Business Roundtable became an activist organization with a clear economic and legislative agenda.

The origins of the Business Roundtable are worth examining because they parallel business's growing resistance to unionization in the face of declining profit rates. Long before the leaders of the AFL-CIO discovered that the nation's labor laws were 'impotent', business leaders had decided they were too strict. In 1965 a group of corporate executives came together to form the Labor Law Study Group. Their goal was to curb union power by 'reforming' those aspects of labor law that seemed to underwrite that power. Among the leaders of the Study Group were executives from AT&T, GM, Union Carbide, US Steel, General Dynamics, General Electric, Exxon, International Harvester, and B. F. Goodrich. In addition to 'study', these executives spent time in Washington, where they introduced no less than twenty-four proposed 'labor law reforms'.

Construction costs were a chief concern of these large corporations, and a number of the major actors in the Study Group went on to form the Construction Users Anti-Inflation Roundtable in 1969. This new organization included a broad list of big industrial corporations, but also several major national construction contractors such as Fluor, Bechtel, and Dravo. In 1972 the new organization merged with the Labor Law Study Group, broadening its agenda. The March Group jointed in 1973; it was 'devoted to strengthening the American business system' and was particularly concerned with world trade. The new Business Roundtable that resulted from these mergers was an all-encompassing organization led by representatives from 125 corporations in industry, finance, and commerce, but with over 1,000 other firms involved. It had its own task forces of lawyers, economists, and consultants. But its key source of influence in Washington was the 'deep personal involvement of chief executives'.[3]

Based on its concern with labor costs and the costs of those industries

Striking PATCO members join the 1981 Labor Day parade in Detroit.

which served business, such as construction, transportation, energy, and finance, the Roundtable and other probusiness thinktanks developed a political agenda for the decade. At its heart was the reform of labor law (including NLRA, the Davis-Bacon Act and other prevailing-wage laws); the deregulation of transportation, energy, and finance; restraint on government social spending; and the restructuring of the tax system in ways thought to encourage investment and increase profits. The business agenda of the 1970s was, of course, the core of the Reagan agenda of the 1980s. But business did not wait for the return of the Republicans to the presidency and in fact accomplished a good deal of this agenda while the Democrats controlled both houses of Congress and the White House.

Unlike many earlier business organizations, such as the Business Council, which limited its activity to policy formulation and education, or the National Association of Manufacturers, which was composed of second-string business leaders, the Roundtable was both activist and elite. It represented virtually every facet of big business, and among its leading members were both Republicans and Democrats. Unlike the Business Council or the CED, the Roundtable came out slugging. As Edmund Littlefield, the chairman of the Business Council put it in 1976, 'We leave the advocacy to the Business Roundtable.'[4]

The Roundtable engaged in more than advocacy, however. Unlike previous policy groups, it mobilized its business constituents to carry through its more important lobbying efforts. The high point of this strategy came in 1978 when the Roundtable flew small businessmen from around the country to Washington in corporate jets to lobby Congress in the successful fight against labor law reform. Although the Roundtable represented big business, its class consciousness was such that it attempted to lead all of capital into the fray. The actions of the Roundtable also helped transform somnolent groups such as the National Association of Manufacturers and the US Chamber of Commerce, showing them how to act beyond the narrow confines of their sectoral interests. Like the Roundtable, the Chamber learned to mobilize its constituents – for example, by holding 'town meetings' across the nation to build support for its positions. One Chamber official told the *Congressional Quarterly:* 'At one time I think the unions had it all over business in terms of grass-roots activity. That is now reversed.'[5]

The other major organizational change in the way business intervened in politics was the rise of the corporate political action committee (PAC). Ironically, it was a post-Watergate reform that breathed life into the PAC movement in 1974 and made it legal for corporations to contribute to candidates and parties. No less ironically, PACs were the invention of the labor movement. But once the legal road was clear, business created hundreds of PACs, far outstripping labor in their ability to mobilize money for candidates. In 1974 there only 89 corporate PACs. But in 1978 there were 784, and by 1982 1,467 corporate PACs were able to throw money at needy and deserving candidates. Trade association PACs were also formed. The amount of money contributed by these two kinds of business PACs rose from $8 million in 1972 (mostly from trade associations) to $39 million in the nonpresidential year of 1978 and $84.9 million in 1982.[6]

Capitalists, of course, have always tried to control politicians through generous contributions. But certain changes in US electoral politics that began prior to the 1970s gave their money a new significance and a new degree of control. In the 1960s American election campaigns ceased to be the exercise in block-vote mobilization they had been in the days of the political machine – whether urban or county-courthouse-based. Political contests became media events. If the evening news did not provide a candidate with enough exposure to give him the edge, then paid TV advertisements could. By the 1970s a politician who lacked a hefty media budget didn't stand much of a chance in national or state-wide contests. Labor, too, increased its PAC contributions. Indeed, labor made an unusual effort to increase Democratic strength in Congress in the 1982 elections. But its $35 million, although impressive by comparison with labor efforts of the past, could not hope to match the $84.9 million raised by business.[7]

Money and the dependency it encouraged were major factors in the political shift to the right that occurred among politicians in the second half of the 1970s. This money was not randomly spread around, of course. Business PAC contributions tended to flow in a common direction. In presidential elections the lion's share of PAC money flowed to Republican presidential candidates. When the Republicans captured the Senate, business PACs tended to favor Republicans. But in contests for the House of Representatives, almost as much corporate PAC money went to Democrats as to Republicans. The reason was control by Democratic incumbents of House and Senate committees of great importance to business. In 1984 business PACs handed Republican congressional candidates $23.6 million and Democratic candidates $20.7 million.[8]

Organized, aggressive business pressure in combination with bountiful corporate PAC money had great influence on both the voting patterns and political thinking of more and more Democratic politicians. This was particularly true of the new generation of congressional Democrats who replaced the liberal old guard in the second half of the 1970s and throughout the 1980s. The political impact of capital's new aggressiveness became apparent during the Carter administration. The *Wall Street Journal* noted the phenomenon in 1978:

> Business PACs aren't experiencing any difficulty in finding outstretched hands, and they seem to be getting their money's worth from a growing contingent of Democrats. Many observers, looking at the pro-business tone of the current Congress, have concluded that PAC dollars have something to do with it. Says one Democratic member of the House Ways and Means Committee: "These PACs are influencing a lot of House Democrats. You're seeing

people from mainstream Democratic districts, elected with labor support, who are now voting with business."[9]

Four years later the *Wall Street Journal* could report much the same thing in spite of a Republican White House and Senate. PAC money continued to flow to incumbents of both parties who sat on important committees of both houses. So far as the Democrats were concerned, according to the *Journal*, the contributions were so effectively tied to legislative results that even Republican Robert Dole complained. After the 1982 elections even Wall Street, a Republican bastion, was broadening its PAC contributions across party lines.[10]

The fact that the Republicans had developed a superior fund-raising capacity among small contributors before the rise of the PACs meant that the Democrats were actually more dependent on business money than were the Republicans. The loss of the White House and Senate in 1980 accelerated the Democratic quest for business money. James Shannon, a Democratic member of the important House Ways and Means Committee from Massachusetts, explained that

> We on the Democratic side came out of the 1980 election and saw we got clobbered, in large part because of money. So the whole subject has come out of the closet. There has been all too much discussion around here about how what we do in the House and on our committees is going to affect our ability to raise money. I mean, people aren't embarrassed about saying this anymore. I'm not a virgin on this: I take PAC money – that's part of the process. But what happened after 1980 was that a lot of special interests swooped down on the Democratic Party and said: "Look, fellas, we're good Democrats, and we should play the same game the Republicans played, and we're going to show you how to do it." I'm no Common Causer, but this stuff has really been bothering me. But Shannon added, "You go where the money is, and its not going to be with the traditional Democratic constituencies."[11]

The post-1980 effort to corner business money was led by the new Chairman of the Democratic National Committee, Charles Mannatt. Mannatt's reorganization of the party's relationship to big money was accurately described by Ferguson and Rogers: 'Under Mannatt, who before he became DNC chair was mentioned as a possible future head of the American Bankers Association, the party's financial structure soon bore more than a faint resemblance to that of a debt-encumbered LDC being run under IMF surveillance. Major banks, including Bank of America and Chase, helped float the loans, which prominent business leaders of the party guaranteed.'[12]

Mannatt's reorganization included the founding of the Democratic Business Council in 1981. This project was originally the idea of Byron

Radaker, chief executive officer of Congoleum, a large multinational conglomerate. By the summer of 1983, the council had recruited 111 businessmen, each of whom paid $10,000 for the honor. The council met with Democratic presidential hopefuls and advised Democrats on Capital Hill. By its own description, the council promised its members quarterly meetings in Washington 'where members can share their respective business, professional and political interests with the political leadership of America.'[13]

The ease with which so many Democrats bent to the will of business was also a consequence of important changes in the traditional base of the Democratic Party. The organized base of the New Deal coalition was the contradictory alliance of the Northern urban political machines and the 'Solid South' – that is, the white vote in the pre–civil rights South. The New Deal coalition is often romanticized as a combination of labor, minorities, and liberals. In fact, the Black vote was too small to count on a national scale before the 1960s, while labor only acquired the organizational strength to be a factor in the 1940s. It was Southern racism and Northern corruption that mobilized Democratic majorities in the era before the end of World War Two. Both these dubious institutions decayed rapidly after the war, which is one reason why the Democrats have had so much trouble gaining presidential majorities. Southern whites increasingly voted for Republicans in presidential elections, while Northern working-class voters simply dropped out of the electoral process altogether. Working-class abstentionism carried over into congressional elections as well. According to Walter Dean Burnham, 'By 1976 blue-collar and service workers constituted only 48.5 percent of the active electorate, but fully three-quarters of the "party of the non-voters."'[14]

Along with this well-known trend, the upward social climb of people from Democratic backgrounds and their move outward into the once Republican suburbs created a new kind of Democratic voter – a voter who saw himself or herself as a member of the educated middle class and who voted with greater frequency than most working-class people. In primary elections, the proportion of upper-middle and upper-income voters was even higher. The new Democratic constituency produced a generation of Democratic politicians with no loyalty to labor or other traditional Democratic groups that favored liberal economic policies. Indeed, much of this increasingly middle-class electorate had a material interest in the perpetuation of the near poverty of service workers, whose low wages subsidized the consumer preferences of the newly affluent. Redistributive income policies, like labor unions, were anathema to them. The resulting political discourse, as Burnham points out, is a debate between factions of the upper-middle and upper-income strata –

one in which the interests of the working class play no role. Such a discourse is obviously opened to increased business influence.[15]

PAC money, business pressure, and the key role of the affluent in primary elections produced an ideological shift among Democratic politicians at both federal and state levels even before the term *neoliberal* became common. The well-known collapse of Keynesian policy options in the 1970s and the subsequent theoretical disarray and disrepute of liberal economics that became highly visible during the Carter years left the liberal Democrats ideologically confused and programmatically paralyzed. It was in the late 1970s that the Republican supply-siders took the offensive and began winning a growing number of Democrats to many of the general ideas and policy conclusions, if not the precise theoretical propositions, of supply-side economics. PAC money, of course, did not require ideological conformity. Indeed, it is doubtful if most business leaders were aware of the rigors of supply-side theory. But business knew it wanted a break in taxes, deregulation, and an end to other alleged barriers to investment.

This the Democrats gave willingly in the final years of the Carter administration. In 1977 and 1978, labor's major legislative goals were defeated one after another. An increase in the minimum wage and the Common Situs Picketing bill went down in 1977, and labor's major agenda point of the decade, labor law reform, was defeated in 1978 – all with the Democrats firmly in control of the White House and both houses of Congress. In 1978 the Democratic Congress shaped a tax bill that virtually reversed Democratic policy by shifting the tax burden away from business and the rich and toward middle- and lower-income groups. Tax rates on personal income were reduced across the board in pure supply-side style, the investment tax credit was increased and the capital gains rate lowered. It was during this tax battle that Jack Kemp (Rep.-N.Y.) emerged as the champion of supply-side tax policy. The air transport industry was deregulated in that same year. Federal grants-in-aid to the cities were cut for the first time in 1979, and trucking deregulation followed in 1980.[16] The business agenda was already engraved on the Congressional tableau by the end of the decade, well before Reagan's first term began.

In 1979 congressional Democrats acknowledged the new balance of power in that year's *Report of the Joint Economic Committee of Congress*. For the first time in twenty years the Republicans and Democrats endorsed a single report rather than the usual practice of producing majority and minority reports. In the introduction to the report, Democratic Chairman of the Joint Committee Lloyd Bentsen wrote: 'This year's report illustrates an emerging consensus in the Committee and in the country that the federal government needs to put its financial house in order and that the major challenges today and for the foreseeable future are on the supply-side of the economy.'[17] Edward Kennedy and George McGovern were among the Democratic signers of that document. This performance was repeated in 1980. In fact, these documents were a hodgepodge of Republican fiscal conservatism and Democratic austerity measures together with foreshadowing of supply-side orthodoxy. But so strict a supply-side theoretician as Paul Craig Roberts wrote of these reports: 'The 1979 and 1980 JEC reports were, like the Holt and Nunn amendments of 1978, Reaganomics before Reagan.'[18] While most Democrats would now repudiate the term *supply-side,* they had, in fact, surrendered the terrain of both policy and theory to the Republicans by the end of the 1970s.

Jimmy Carter and Elite Capital

Jimmy Carter ran for president of the United States in 1976 as a political 'outsider'. Early in the primaries his cause was embraced by the leadership of the United Auto Workers and soon by other leaders in the liberal wing of the labor bureaucracy. George Meany and most of the rest of the labor leadership supported Senator Henry 'Scoop' Jackson until his defeat, but eventually labor united behind Carter. Gerald Ford was not much of an opponent and with help from the media and the Southern vote Carter came to Washington as the 'new boy on the block'.

In reality, Carter was no outsider by the time he ran for president. He had long-standing connections to the Atlanta business and banking establishment and more recent ties to the national business elite. Carter was a member of the Trilateral Commission, an organization of business and political leaders from the US, Western Europe and Asia. His administration was full of people from the Trilateral Commission, the Committee for Economic Development, the Business Council, the Brookings Institution, and other elite policy-formulating organizations, all of which had overlapping memberships and leadership bodies.[19]

The Trilateral Commission was not directly concerned with domestic labor policy in the way the Business Council and the Business Roundtable were, although it shared much of the same personnel. It saw its function as coordinating the economic policy of the advanced industrial nations of North America, Europe and Asia. Its policy was one of promoting economic integration and interdependence among these areas and, indeed, throughout the world. In a sense, the Trilateral Commission was the conscious voice of the process of corporate multinationalization and global economic integration that preceded its founding in 1973. It favored free trade, but perhaps its major concern was the free flow of investment capital around the world – including the flow of foreign capital into the US. In general, the Trilateral Commission's advocacy of unified and fluid global markets made it sympathetic to the goals of the Business Roundtable.[20]

Carter's connection to institutions such as the Trilateral Commission and the Business Roundtable did not guarantee his agreement with their views, but it did ensure a high degree of access. Carter met regularly with leaders of the Business Roundtable. Irving Shapiro of Du Pont and a member of the Roundtable, said that Carter 'is accessible. He talks. We have no trouble getting ourselves heard.' The *New York Times* said, 'In fact, big business has the ear of Jimmy Carter, Democrat, to a greater degree than was true of Richard M. Nixon and Gerald R. Ford, Republicans.'

Indeed, Carter was capable of a public deference to business leaders not usually associated with the presidency. He told a meeting of the Business Council in December 1977 that if they found anything 'that unnecessarily encroaches on your effectiveness, I hope you'll let my Cabinet officers or me know, and I'll do the best I can to correct it.... If you will let me have those recommendations, I'll do the best I can to comply with your request.'[21] What business found encroaching on its effectiveness was labor. To put it more accurately, business was able to define labor as the source of the major economic problems it believed underlay the continuing decline in the rate of profit.

If the policy direction of the Carter administration was shaped by business pressure, its precise economic thinking came largely from the Brookings Institution. Brookings Chairman Robert Roosa was a Trilateralist like Carter and a partner in the investment firm Brown Brothers Harriman & Co. In fact, almost a third of the Brookings trustees in the mid-1970s were Trilateralists. The chair of Carter's Council of Economic Advisers was Charles Schultze, a Brookings associate. The whizkid of Carter's anti-inflation efforts was Barry Bosworth, another associate at Brookings.[22]

The economists from Brookings saw the US economy's problem as one of slumping profit rates. Citing William Nordhaus's 1974 Brookings study, Barry Bosworth wrote in 1975 that 'there has been a downward trend in the rates of return on capital.' Bosworth concluded that this meant 'a need for improving investment incentives'.[23] The Council of Economic Advisers' first report in 1978 echoed this same theme. One conclusion led to the tax law of 1978 that granted massive tax cuts to business. But the analysis developed by the Brookings economists and the Council of Economic Advisers pointed beyond the need to cut taxes and directly to labor.

The Carter administration's business friends wanted to reduce labor costs, and the Council of Economic Advisers provided the arguments for doing so. Both inflation and slumping profit rates were pinned on the slower growth of productivity that unfolded after the recession of 1974–75. The answer, the council argued, was increased capital investment – specifically, an increase in the ratio of capital to labor: 'Restoring the earlier trend in the ratio of capital to labor input would make an important contribution to greater productivity growth, but such an increase will require devoting a larger share of our national output to business investment than has been characteristic of recent years.'[24]

The policy conclusion of this simple logic was to reduce the share of national income that goes to the consuming public and increase that which goes to capital. For public consumption, inflation was made the focus. Tax breaks for business, budget cutbacks on social programs, and deregulation were all sold as inflation fighters. The targeting of labor income as a cause of inflation came with the announcement of wage and price guidelines in October 1978. Carter told the nation: 'If there is one thing I have learned beyond any doubt it is that there is no single solution for inflation. We must face a time of national austerity.'[25]

The wage guidelines were monitored by the Council on Wage and Price Stability, chaired by Barry Bosworth. They were allegedly voluntary. However, the administration put the heat on unions with large visible contracts and the Council of Economic Advisers especially targeted the big pattern agreements. They wrote that 'multiyear collective bargaining agreements, which now cover over 97% of the workers in large collective bargaining units, provide pay increases that are more likely to reflect past conditions than the actual economic environment prevailing during the term of the agreement.'[26] The argument was that even if wages were not the cause of inflation, continued wage and benefit increases by the big unions perpetuated it.

In fact, labor costs in both the economy as a whole and in manufacturing had been declining as a proportion of total costs throughout the decade of the 1970s. In all industries, the share of labor costs in total sales went from 27.9% in 1970 to less than 20% by 1980. In manufacturing, labor costs as a share in the total factors of production shrank from 24.7% in 1967 to 21% in 1977.[27] The difference that union conformity with Carter's guidelines made on inflation was insignificant. Prices rose by 6.5% in 1977, 7.7% in 1978, 11.3% in 1979 and 13.5% in 1980. But federal pressure aided the employers in reducing the size of wage increases. First-year wage increases in all major contracts dropped from 10% in 1975 to 8% in 1977 and stayed below that level through 1979. In manufacturing, first-year increases fell from 9.2% in 1975 to 8.6% in 1977 and down to 8.2% in 1978 and 7.0% in 1979. The result was, of course, a drop in real wages. The average real spendable weekly earnings of a worker with three dependents fell from $93.63 in 1977 to $89.49 in 1979. For the comparable manufacturing production worker, the drop was from $110.23 in 1977 to $106.60 in 1979.[28]

Democratic administrations tend to be inconsistently antilabor. That is, while wage restraints and other policies meant to favor business have been typical of all Democratic administrations since World War Two, they have usually granted a quid pro quo, something in the way of social or economic policy that labor has requested. However, the direction of the Carter administration was consistently antilabor. Labor's sole legislative achievement under Carter was the Humphrey-Hawkins Full Employment Act of 1978. This bill, however, was amended to include an anti-inflation clause that canceled out the intent of the act. As the *Congressional Quarterly* put it: 'It was little more than a symbolic statement about Congress' desire to limit unemployment and inflation.' The wage guidelines plan came, almost like an insult, as the Ninety-Fifth Congress adjourned with labor's legislative agenda defeated. It had been evident to all that Carter, although he formally endorsed labor law reform, did not lift a finger to aid its passage. Further, in March 1978 Carter had attempted to break the strike of 160,000 coal miners by invoking the Taft-Hartley Act. [29]

The one project of the Carter years that might be construed as prolabor was the Chrysler bailout of 1979–80. The initiative, however, came from Chrysler Corporation's Lee Iacocca, and the plan that emerged from negotiations between Carter, Congress, Chrysler and the UAW was certainly to the company's liking. Under this plan, the government granted Chrysler $1.5 billion in credits in order the save the financially ailing corporation. The plan was billed by all parties as the salvation of 85,000 auto jobs. Everyone was called on to make sacrifices to save these jobs, but the workers were the only group to sacrifice anything material. In November 1979, the UAW agreed to a wage freeze at Chrysler. In January 1980, Congress imposed additional concessions, and a year later the UAW agreed to a $1.15-an-hour wage cut. In return, UAW President Doug Fraser was given a seat on Chrysler's Board of Directors. These concessions would alter the course of collective bargaining to a degree that not even the Business Roundtable or the New Right had dreamed of.[30]

The Carter years can be seen as the period of transition from the old postwar bipolar politics of Democrats (liberal) and Republicans (moderate to conservative) to a new right-of-center discourse largely shared by both parties. Not only had Democratic politicians in Congress and at the state level made a well-financed transition to the right, but the administration had provided a measure of political leadership in that direction. Carter, as a New South moderate, was a perfect candidate for the job since Sunbelt dominance played a role in this change. The business agenda was well on its way to completion before Ronald Reagan took office. Nowhere was the change more consistent than in government policy toward labor. As if to symbolize the transition, Carter's Federal Aviation Administration (FAA) began a program of harassment of air traffic controllers on the job, and in 1980 formed the Management Strike Contingency Force twelve months before the expiration of the govoernment's contract with the Professional Air Traffic Controllers Organization (PATCO). It was this Strike Force that prepared the plan that Reagan put into effect in order to break PATCO in 1981. [31]

The Carter years, of course, were also the culmination of the shift in the social balance of power that underlay these political changes. American business might be reeling from competition around the world, but in the US it was triumphant. It dumped Carter because of his incompetence and for a chance to realize the dream, now within grasp, of a Republican sweep. The rhetoric of politics would change dramatically, but the direction of economic, social, and labor policy was well established by the end of the 1970s. Labor, the poor, the minorities, women were on the outs – and business was in.

Reagan: The Line of No Resistance

The electoral coalition that brought Ronald Reagan to power in 1980 was a socially and ideologically diverse one composed of upwardly mobile urban and suburban baby boomers, disaffected blue-collar workers, newly Republicanized voters in the South and West, old-line Republicans, and evangelicals. But electorates don't set agendas or make policy. In those terms the Republican Party elite might be divided, as James McGregor Burns has pointed out, into the Market Right and the Moralistic Right. The Market Right was concerned with economic policy, while the Moralistic Right cared about abortion, school prayer, the preservation of the traditional family as they saw it, and other social matters. In spite of Reagan's rhetorical commitment to these moral issues, his administration was dominated by the Market Right. Its agenda was the business agenda left unfinished by the Carter administration.[32]

The success of the Reagan administration in carrying out this agenda was guaranteed by the power shift already apparent in US society and by the move of the Democrats away from their traditional concern with social welfare and toward the concerns of organized business. But Reagan also pursued a strategy designed to minimize opposition to his far-reaching interpretation of the business agenda. Reagan avoided messy fights by staying away from the social program of the Moralistic

Right and tended not to use legislation as the means of diminishing the welfare state and extending deregulation. The legislative battle to shift income away from the lower strata to the well-to-do and to business was limited as much as possible to the annual budget resolution and to tax legislation.

When Ronald Reagan moved rapidly in 1981 to implement supply-side policy in the budget and tax acts of that year, the Democrats simply stepped aside. As the *Washington Post* recalled, Democratic Speaker of the House 'Tip' O'Neill 'put Reagan's program on a fast track'.[33] To be sure, they made some noise about 'fairness', the last word left in their lexicon of social reform. In reality, as Elizabeth Drew documented, many Democrats used the tax debate as a 'bidding war' in which they attempted to outdo Reagan in their generosity to business and the well-to-do. What they were bidding for was PAC money, which in the 1980 election had shifted heavily to the Republicans as business saw the chance of a Republican sweep of Congress on Reagan's coattails. What they were offering was votes for Reaganomics. The leaders of the bidding war were Democrats Dan Rostenkowski of Illinois, one of the last of the old machine Democrats and at that time chairman of the House Ways and Means Committee, and Richard Gephardt of Missouri, a rising star in the constellation of neoliberals. They agreed to get further tax breaks for US independent oil operators and to corral enough Democrats to pass the Reagan tax bill in return for past contributions and with an eye to the future.[34] This prudent Democratic behavior throughout Reagan's first term earned them a big boost in PAC money through 1984.

These Democrats, of course, were only adopting the ethical norms of the businessmen who flooded Reagan's Washington. The CEOs of the Business Roundtable did not come – they had better things to do. Reagan brought in lower ranking businessmen, and occasionally businesswomen, more likely to see themselves as entrepreneurs than corporate organization types. The *Washington Post* reported that 110 of these entrepreneurs had been accused of illegal or unethical conduct since January 1981. Charles Dempsey, who had been an Environmental Protection Agency (EPA) inspector during Reagan's first term, said of the ethics of these businessmen: 'This is a businessman's administration, and these guys are used to wheeling and dealing. This administration is loaded with guys bringing the business morality to Washington, and some of them never learn....It's like they flunked a course in basic civics.'[35] More and more Democrats were flunking the same course.

The tone for Reagan's attitude toward labor was set by his handling of the PATCO strike. This strike, which began on 3 August 1981, was years in the making. Accumulated problems and grievances went unresolved by the FAA from one administration to the next. Under Carter, this history of negligence grew into an FAA management campaign of harassment against the air traffic controllers and the formation of the Management Strike Contingency Force in the summer of 1980. When the strike began, the FAA implemented the Contingency Force's plan to run air traffic without the controllers. Only four hours after the strike began, Reagan went on TV to warn that if the controllers did not return to work within forty-eight hours they will 'have forfeited their jobs and will be terminated.' Reagan stuck by this position and eventually broke both the strike and the union.[36]

Reagan's handling of the PATCO strike was clearly meant as a message to business and labor alike: that the bargaining atmosphere had changed in both the public and private sectors and that the administration's policies would aid business and undermine labor. It did not, however, signal a policy of direct intervention in collective bargaining like Carter's. The Market Right opposed this on free market grounds. The further crippling of labor would be accomplished by maintaining relatively high levels of unemployment, unraveling much of the social safety net, and by neutralizing or reversing the functions of those agencies that were created to support collective bargaining.

Unemployment rates rose during Reagan's first year as a recession unfolded, rising from 7.5% in 1981 to 9.5% for both 1982 and 1983. They dropped with the subsequent recovery, but still remained high: 7.4% in 1984 and 7.1% in 1985. Job creation under Reagan also saw an acceleration of the increase in low-paying service jobs. From 1980 through 1985, 7 million new jobs were created, all of them in the service sector. A growing number of them were part-time jobs, bringing the total number of part-time employees to 5.6 million in 1985.[37]

Reagan did not mount an all-out attack on the welfare state, but he did succeed in cutting numerous programs and reducing benefits and limiting eligibility for others important to the nation's social safety net. A simple budget cut eliminated 300,000 CETA jobs. Responsibility for welfare and unemployment insurance programs was transferred to the states, and federal grants to the states to run the programs were then reduced. This forced the states to reduce benefits, or more typically, limit eligibility. The rate at which social welfare expenditures for food stamps, AFDC, and general assistance grew was cut in half, from 14.6% in 1980 to 7.7.% in 1983. Forced to change eligibility requirements, the states dropped 1.5 million workers from the unemployment roles between 1982 and 1984. This decline was not simply a result of the recovery. The percentage of unemployed workers covered by unemployment insurance dropped from 44% in 1980 to 29% in 1984.[38]

A number of agencies important to labor, the poor, and minorities were stripped of power or cut back by administrative means. Appointments at the cabinet and subcabinet level were made with an eye to crippling the enforcement powers of such agencies as the Equal Employment Opportunity Commission, the Occupational Safety and Health Administration, and the National Labor Relations Board. Appointments were combined with budget cuts and staff reductions in agencies concerned with social justice and welfare such as Health and Human Services, Education, Housing and Urban Development, and Labor to limit their effectiveness. Real outlays for federal civil rights programs declined by 9% from 1981 to 1983.[39]

Perhaps of greatest consequence to labor, however, was the demise of the NLRB as an instrument for achieving union growth and for the redress of grievances. Reagan's first approach was to leave vacant two open seats on the board and let it become further overwhelmed as cases piled up. But in 1983 Donald Dotson was appointed chairman of the NLRB. Under Dotson's leadership the board produced in 1984 a string of decisions designed to curb labor.

The *Myers Industries, Rossmore House,* and *St. Francis Hospital* cases adversely affected the already dubious ability of the board to grant labor its statutory right to organize. Other cases limited the power of unions to protect their members' jobs. In the *Otis Elevator* case, for example, the NRLB ruled that an employer did not have to bargain over the closing of a plant. *Milwaukee Spring* gave management the right to transfer work to a nonunion facility without bargaining with the union. *Bohemia, Inc.,* established that unions had no right to information about a firm's non-union operations. *Clear Pine Moldings* allowed an employer to fire a union member for verbal conduct, even during a strike.

Dotson's NRLB also found in favor of employers more often than any previous board. An AFL-CIO study comparing the Dotson NRLB to two earlier Republican-dominated boards showed a significant difference in behavior. Whereas the two earlier boards had upheld worker unfair labor practice charges against management 86% and 85% of the time, the Dotson board ruled against management in only 55% of its decisions. In representation cases arising out of union organizing efforts, the earlier boards had upheld management 36% and 44% of the time, while the Dotson board stood with the employers in 75% of its decisions.[40]

Reagan pushed the business agenda into new territories beyond limits where most Democrats were willing to venture. Economic deregulation had been supported by leading Democrats such as Ted Kennedy, but deregulation of such social matters as civil rights, the environment and occupational health went beyond what they had been willing to accept under Carter. Reagan's perseverance in his agenda, however, did not bring a reaction from the Democrats. His overwhelming 1984 victory over the last symbol of mainstream liberalism, Walter Mondale, only convinced the Democrats to look even more to business for its money and ideas.

The Democrats thus continued to move to the right, in effect abandoning the field to the Republicans. Mondale, himself surrounded by businessmen and running on a conservative platform of fiscal responsibility, signaled that mainstream liberals, the inheritors of the New Deal, would no longer put forth a program of social reform or income redistribution. With his inglorious defeat, the initiative within the Democratic party fell to a coalition of neoliberals and conservative Sunbelt Democrats. Upon assuming office as the new chairman of the Democratic National Committee (DNC) in early 1985, former Kennedy aide Paul Kirk joined in the neoliberal chorus repudiating the 'special interests' (read labor, blacks, women), big spending, and other alleged Democratic sins. Kirk also made it clear that the last remnant of liberal reform sentiment in the party, Jesse Jackson's Rainbow Coalition, would be accorded no space in party decision-making circles and that no concessions would be made to his demands. Kirk made sure that Jackson's candidate for vice chair of the DNC, Gary Mayor Richard Hatcher, was replaced by the more pliable Roland Burris, a lackluster state politician from Illinois.[41] What was remarkable about the post–1984 syndrome in Democratic circles was the degree to which they accepted the business agenda and the Republican critique of liberalism as valid.

The business Democrats wasted no time in assuring that the rightward direction of the party would continue. On 27 November 1984, twenty of the Democratic Party's top fund-raisers met to discuss the 1988 campaign and ways to give business even more direct influence on the party's policies and candidates. A couple of days later some of the same people participated in a forum sponsored by the Coalition for a Democratic Majority, which was addressed by two leading exponents of neoliberal centrism, Arizona Governor Bruce Babbitt and Virginia Governor Charles Robb. Here the basic lines of prevailing thought among Democratic power brokers and funders was laid out. The old New Deal 'special interests' (imagined as labor, Blacks, and feminist women) had to take a backseat to the party's more important constituencies, new and old. Robb spelled out what he and many others thought the new constituencies were when he declared that the Democratic Party must 'also be a party of business leaders, doctors, pharmacists, stockbrokers, and other professionals.' He also voiced the other key point in high-level Democratic strategic thinking when he went on to ask, 'Since Southerners still want to be Democrats, why not give them a chance?' No one at the forum thought he was referring to Southern Blacks. This conception of the party's future was further elaborated by Harvard Professor Samuel Huntington, a former board member of the Coalition for a Democratic Majority, in a paper he wrote for the conservative American Enterprise Institute; it emphasized the importance of the Southern white vote and accused the 'special interests' of wrecking the Democratic Party.[42]

The drift to the right in the Democratic Party received further organizational impetus in February 1985 with the formation of two policy groups. Kirk announced the founding of the Democratic National Policy Council (DNPC) as a vehicle for charting a new course for the party – apparently an effort to co-opt the center. It didn't work. Shortly after Kirk's move, Bruce Babbitt, the governor of Arizona who had sent state troopers against the Phelps Dodge strikers in 1984, and Charles Robb announced the formation of the Democratic Leadership Council (DLC). Among the DLC leaders were Richard Gephardt (Dem.-Mo.) and Sam Nunn (Dem.-Ga.), a Dixiecrat and military hardliner. The membership of the DLC leaned heavily toward the Sunbelt states of the South and West, but included Michigan Governor James Blanchard, who had been a leading congressional organizer of the Chrysler bailout, and John Glenn (Dem.-Oh.). The DLC continued to propagandize for a center/conservative approach that would appeal to Southern whites and affluent Northern voters. Its central theme, accepted throughout the ranks of party professionals, was avoidance of any association with organized labor, minorities, feminists or other 'special interest groups' that might make these voters uncomfortable. Observing this growing direction, Jesse Jackson commented, 'There is a scheme to have the party prove its manhood to whites by showing its capacity to be unkind to Blacks.' Much the same could have been said about the party's stand toward labor. Particularly attentive to the business Democrats, Kirk sent out what he called a 'stockholders report' to the members of the Democratic Business Council in August 1985 describing his success in moving the party to the right.[43]

The party's march rightward was joined and underwritten by the Brookings Institution. Brookings, ostensibly a nonpartisan economic research and policy organization, was long headed by business Democrat Robert Roosa and had always been part of the liberal wing of the Eastern establishment. After playing a leading role in Carter's right turn, it reorganized its research programs in 1980–84 and shifted its point of view to compete more effectively with those rising stars of conservative thought, the American Enterprise Institute and the Heritage Foundation. By 1984, *Industry Week* noted that Brookings 'is sounding more like Ronald Reagan every day.'[44]

The 508-point nosedive of the Dow Jones Industrial Average on Monday, 19 October 1987 signalled the doom of Reaganomics and the collapse of the already stumbling Reagan administration. As stock markets around the world crashed in late October, the administration appeared disoriented and powerless to act. In all likelihood, it was the swift intervention of Alan Greenspan, new head of the Federal Reserve System, that prevented a total financial collapse in the days immediately following Meltdown Monday. Yet, when the Republican White House and the Democratic Congress regained a measure of balance, it was the federal budget deficit that became the target of action.[45]

Not surprisingly, the cry for drastic budget cuts arose from big business and its ideologues. *Business Week* declared: 'The Market to Washington: Wake Up', and later 'Take a knife to the budget deficit...' The *Wall Street Journal* editorialized that allowing the dollar to fall against the yen and the mark would only destabilize world financial markets further. It blamed the West Germans for presuming a tight-money strategy, but pointed to real budget cuts as the means to get cooperation from them to stabilize the dollar. A group of nearly two hundred business executives, led by former Secretary of Commerce and current banker Peter Peterson took out two-page ads in major US newspapers calling on everyone to abandon their short-term 'self-interest' and 'put everything on the table except programs for the poor' in order to cut the budget deficit.[46]

The collapse of the Reagan administration and of Reaganomics in the wake of Iranscam/Contragate and the October stock market crash did not produce a renewed New Deal consensus among Democrats or, with the exception of Jesse Jackson, a move toward populist solutions. Instead, heeding the call of business, the Democrats rushed toward a new austerity consensus. Budget reduction became the central political issue of late 1987. The first symbol of this new consensus was the Budget Summit between Reagan and the Democratic leaders of Congress. It failed, but not because the Democrats were unwilling to touch social programs. House Speaker Jim Wright and Senate Majority Leader Robert Byrd agreed to a three-month delay in cost-of-living increases for social security recipients. Virtually the entire Democratic side of Congress agreed in principle to a number of proposals for regressive sales taxes. Many congressional Republicans, for their part, broke with Reagan in accepting the idea of taxes on the entitlement programs of wealthy people.[47]

Even before the crash, the spectrum of economic thinking among the white (acceptable) Democratic contenders had been narrow and conservative. The boldest of the white candidates was generally thought to be Senator Paul Simon. Simon called for a multibillion-dollar Guaranteed Job Opportunity Program modeled after the New Deal's WPA. But consistent with the conservative tenor of the political marketplace, Simon insisted that the jobs provided by the program must be at the minimum wage or it 'will not encourage them enough to get off the government payroll.'[48] Richard Gephardt focused on trade issues and his trade retaliation bill. This won him the Smoot-Hawley label from the business press, after the protective tariff act passed in 1930. Massachusetts Governor Michael Dukakis ran on the economic record of his state, without mentioning that the relatively high employment growth in that state was based on low-paying jobs. In reality, most of the Democratic candidates had no clear programs, economic or social, to offer their traditional electorate. They thus found it opportune, in view of the money needed to run for president, to jump on the business bandwagon of budget cutting – even though some of them must have understood that this was the surest way to bring on a recession. Aside from Jackson, who was clearly bucking the direction of the party as a whole, the field reflected the business priorities of the new Democratic austerity consensus.[49] Meanwhile, the business unionists of the AFL-CIO watched these new developments, sometimes decrying them, sometimes denying their existence, but unable or unwilling to challenge the new balance of power.

7

The Collapse of Labor's Political Strategy

The election of Jimmy Carter gave the labor leadership great hope. For one thing, it ended several years of internal conflict, first over the Vietnam War and then over the candidacy of George McGovern in 1972. Unions such as the UAW and AFSCME that had opposed the war had also supported McGovern. The Federation, however, for the first time in its history did not endorse the Democratic candidate for president in 1972. With the UAW and CWA supporting Carter early in the 1976 primaries and Meany campaigning for Henry Jackson, it seemed as though this split might continue. Instead, Carter's victory brought a new unity as the leaders of most unions turned their attention to achieving their legislative agenda. With the Democrats now in control of both the presidency and Congress, labor had great hope of success.

Further, in spite of its own internal conflicts and its declining ability to organize, labor entered the Carter years with its spirit of cooperation with management intact. In 1976 Lane Kirkland joined with corporate leaders like Irving S. Shapiro of Du Pont and Reginald Jones of General Electric to form the Labor-Management Group in order to discuss such matters as productivity, the energy crisis, and tax reform. The Labor-Management Group was given semi-official status in the Carter administration. However, the good faith, in fact naivete, with which labor approached both business and the new administration was soon rewarded with a stone wall of opposition.

In 1977 Congress defeated several labor proposals for reforming the minimum wage law and raising the minimum wage. As the AFL-CIO's *Memo From COPE* said: 'If any more evidence were needed that the 2-1 Democratic majority in the U.S. House is pure illusion, it was provided by the recent votes on minimum wage.' The *Memo* argued that this was not just the 'old Dixiecrat-GOP coalition.... So, in each instance, the conservative position picked up a goodly number of Democratic votes outside the South.'[1] A year later, with most of labor's agenda defeated, Doug Fraser, then president of the United Auto Workers, repeated this theme: 'Why, with the Democrats in control of more than two-thirds in the Congress and in the executive branch, has so little progress been made toward adoption of the Democratic platform the party worked so hard to develop?'[2]

For the mainstream of business unionism, the legislative frustrations of 1977 and 1978 led simply to the conclusion that more of the same was needed. PAC contributions to congressional candidates were increased from $6.3 million in 1974 to $10.3 million in 1978 and to $20.9 million in 1982. The number of union lobbyists in Washington increased dramatically from 185 in 1978 to 287 in 1982. The results of this approach were predictably disappointing. By COPE's own measures things generally changed for the worse or didn't change at all. The proportion of COPE-endorsed candidates who won, traditionally high because COPE tended to prefer candidates with a good chance of winning, shrank from 71.3% in 1976 to 66.3% in 1978 and 59.8% in 1980. In congressional votes, the 'win-loss' ratio for COPE-backed legislation declined, although more COPE-backed bills still won than lost. The percentage of 'right' votes also declined somewhat during the last three years of the Carter administration, but remained above 50%. COPE's measurement of congressional activity, however, is not much of an indicator since it refers only to COPE's narrow legislative agenda and then only to those bills that make it to the floor of one or both houses. But even by COPE's standards, all this new money and activity clearly was not bringing commensurate results.[3]

The Stillbirth of a New Social Unionism

Among a minority of AFL-CIO union leaders, the disappointments of 1977–78 began to produce what seemed like a revival of social unionism. On 19 July 1978, Fraser resigned from the Labor-Management Group and was followed by the other labor representatives. Fraser's resignation was accompanied by an angry and unusually radical statement. In it he questioned the very basis of the 'social compact' implied in the whole postwar system of labor relations. Pointing the finger at capital, he declared: 'I believe leaders of the business community, with few exceptions, have chosen to wage a one-sided class war in this country – a war against working people, the unemployed, the poor, the minorities, the very young and the very old, and even many in the middle class of our society. The leaders of industry, commerce and finance in the United States have broken and discarded the fragile, unwritten compact previously existing during a period of growth and progress.'[4]

It was clear that Fraser's frustration stemmed not only from defeats in Congress, but from what the employers had been doing to undermine union stability for years. He singled out GM: 'General Motors Corp. is a specific case in point. GM, the largest manufacturing corporation in the world, has received responsibility, productivity and cooperation from the UAW and its members. In return, GM has given us a Southern strategy designed to set up a non-union network that threatens the hard-fought gains won by the UAW. We have given stability and have been rewarded with hostility.'[5] This was the anger of a jilted lover, but it signified the possibility of a new political direction for labor.

Fraser also attacked the political establishment as well. Careful not to characterize the Democrats as being quite as bad as the Republicans, he nonetheless charged that 'the Republican Party remains controlled by and the Democratic Party heavily influenced by business interests. The reality is that both are weak and ineffective as parties, with no visible, clear-cut ideological differences between them, because of business domination.'[6]

This did not mean a break with the Democrats. But it did lead the UAW International Executive Board to call for a conference three weeks before the 1978 election 'to consider the formation of a new alliance aimed at transforming the American political system by making it more accountable, responsible and democratic.' To do this, the UAW said, 'specific demands would be made on the Democratic Party at its coming mid-term convention next December, and efforts will be made to strengthen the party as a membership organization in which the members will have a greater voice in selecting the party's candidates.'[7] The idea seemed to be to make the Democratic Party more like the European Social Democratic parties.

This meeting was held on 17 October 1978 and included representatives of thirty unions and seventy-one other organizations representing women, minorities, farmers, environmentalists and other social activists. The response was good enough to warrant calling a convention for 15 January 1979 to form the Progressive Alliance. Its founding statement was radical, its tone militantly populist, warning the 'right-corporate alliance' that 'there are more of us than of them. More workers. More women, more minorities. More young and old. More working farmers. More middle income people who are tired of being told by the corporate elite that less is really more.' Repeating Fraser's earlier theme, the statement noted: 'Today, both the Democratic Party and the

Republican Party stand unwilling to serve as vehicles for achieving economic and social justice.' The Progressive Alliance would 'organize inside and outside the political parties, hold citizens hearings, sponsor demonstrations, underwrite independent research and publications, communicate through the media and work with all who seek to apply democratic principles of participation to our economic and political life.'[8]

The negative experience under Democratic hegemony that gave rise to the Progressive Alliance also produced a certain amount of talk about forming a labor party. In a speech to a Machinists' legislative conference only a week after the founding convention of the Progressive Alliance, George Poulin, general vice president of the Machinists, criticized the Alliance for hoping to reform the Democratic Party. He speculated that it might take a deep recession to do that. Failing that, he argued, 'then labor and the trade unions will seriously have to consider formation, in alliance with other orphaned groups, of a new third party.'[9] IAM President William Winpisinger was also vocal about a labor party. He threatened to endorse Barry Commoner, environmentalist presidential candidate of the Citizens Party in 1980, if Ted Kennedy were not nominated by the Democrats. At the same time, Tony Mazzocchi, a vice president of the Oil, Chemical and Atomic Workers, began publicly calling for a labor party. He made this a plank in his 1981 run for the presidency of the OCAW. In California, State Federation Secretary-Treasurer Jack Henning told a 1979 Labor Rally: 'The two-party system is no longer serving the economic interests of working people. Labor must consider the advantages of a separate political party.' A motion to this effect was proposed at the California Federation of Labor convention in 1980. Indeed, the idea of the Progressive Alliance itself suggested a labor party. When, at an April 1979 meeting of the UAW's Local Union Press Association, Cleveland's populist Mayor Dennis Kucinich told the audience that there was only one party in America, the probusiness 'Demipublicans', one participant asked, 'Why doesn't the Progressive Alliance run candidates?'[10]

The Progressive Alliance itself was an unwieldy letterhead organization. But a certain amount of activity at that time suggested that it might take an activist direction. In August, for example, the UAW organized a campaign that urged its members to take time off at work in order to fill out a card protesting Carter's energy policy. Originally, this was to be a brief work stoppage, but in practice few plants stopped work and the action was poorly coordinated. It was nonetheless an unusual on-the-job activity for an American union. In October the Progressive Alliance cosponsored a day of protest against oil company profiteering with the Citizens/Labor Energy Coalition (CLEC). CLEC, largely sponsored by the Machinists, was the actual organizer of the action, however.[11] But the Alliance itself seemed unable to mobilize its constituencies.

In fact, the Progressive Alliance never did much of anything. A proposal for a mass march on Washington to protest Carter's budget cuts was watered down to a routine lobbying effort. Talk of creating local chapters and recruiting members for this 'coalition of coalitions' ceased. The Alliance, said to represent 20 million Americans, provided no direction for them, nor did it have any real communication with them. It never held another national conference, and within a year of its birth it was dead. It is hard to say whether the Progressive Alliance was a sincere effort that was shelved for other, more pressing matters, or simply an outburst of pressure activity designed to impress or warn wayward Democrats.

The signs that the UAW, the leading force in the Progressive Alliance, was not really headed in a left direction were abundant. Only days after the 17 October conference, Doug Fraser and Glenn Watts (of the Communications Workers), two major leaders of the embryonic Alliance, endorsed Carter's new wage and price guidelines. Fraser moved into the UAW's 1979 negotiations with the Big Three in routine manner in spite of his verbal attack on GM in July 1978. The 30 May announcement that Chrysler would close its Dodge Main (Hamtramck Assembly) plant, cutting 3,200 jobs, brought no concerted action or plan from the International, in spite of an initially militant response from the local and widespread community support for a fight. In October 1979 Fraser, along with AFL-CIO President Lane Kirkland, signed the National Accord, an agreement to cooperate with the Carter administration's wage restraint and productivity plans in return for vague promises by the administration not to fight inflation with higher unemployment.[12] If the Progressive Alliance statement was full of radical social unionist language, the practice of the supporting unions remained firmly in the camp of business unionism. Furthermore, two events served to set these unions on a course almost diametrically opposed to that implied in the program and rhetoric of the Progressive Alliance. They thus slipped from rebellion against the Democrats back into dependence, and from confrontation with 'Corporate America', as Fraser had termed capital, to a new era of cooperation with big business.

The first was the onset of the contest for the 1980 Democratic presidential nomination, which was enough to put most of labor back into the only mode of political operation it had ever known – latching on to one or another major candidate. A major problem for the Alliance was that two of its main leaders, Fraser and Watts, backed different candidates. Watts stuck with Carter, while Fraser and the UAW went with Ted Kennedy, as did Winpisinger of the Machinists. The greater problem, of course, was that the organizers of the Progressive Alliance had proposed no political orientation for the group. Consequently, all the elements of this 'coalition of coalitions' simply reverted to habit. Formed as much out of disgust with Carter and the Congress as disappointment in capital's new hostility, the fragments of the Progressive Alliance found themselves informally united behind Carter when he won the nomination. This alliance was on Carter's terms: more austerity.

The second event that derailed the new consciousness that the Progressive Alliance seemed to symbolize was the Chrysler bailout. This bailout was more than another government giveaway. The Chrysler Corporation Loan Guarantee Act of 1979 (signed by Carter on 7 January 1980) demanded of the UAW both sacrifice to ensure the company's immediate survival and cooperation with its plan for recovery. Thus, it presented business unionism with a challenge that contradicted its momentary turn toward radical social unionism. Either the new social unionist coalition had to deepen its nascent radicalism and demand a different solution to Chrysler's problems, or it had to revert to business unionism and abandon the rhetoric of class confrontation.

The Chrysler Bailout

Modern business unionism in the United States has never developed a method of dealing with large-scale business failure. In the postwar period, companies came and went, but most of the industries in which unions were based continued to provide jobs. If Packard went under, it was probably because GM, Ford, or Chrysler beat it in the US market. But as long as the US market grew and the players were US firms producing for a domestic market, the failure of one firm probably meant more work at another – minus the tolerated annual loss of jobs due to new technology and higher productivity. Business unionists therefore didn't worry much about corporate failures.

In the automobile industry, however, the rules changed. For one thing, the number of passenger car producers dwindled to four, meaning that any failure would have a significant impact. The growing penetration of the US market by imports, particularly following the oil price increases of 1973 and the recession of 1974–75, meant that the production lost from a failure could be picked up by an overseas firm. US producers stuck with big cars, so the Japanese and others took a larger piece of the market by introducing smaller, more fuel-efficient products. By 1981 they had captured 29% of the market. This might not have mattered if the US market had continued to expand rapidly, but it didn't. The US and Canadian market shrank from 61% of total world demand for cars in 1960 to 37% in 1980. The demand for cars in North America had grown by 39% in those two decades (compared to over 400% growth in the US gross national product), but the European market had grown 188% and the Latin American market 600% in the same period.[13] This, of course, led US producers to invest abroad in order to capture a share of these fast-growing markets.

As noted earlier, new investment by US industrial firms was increasingly financed by borrowing from banks rather than by using internally generated funds. In auto, the Big Three all adopted the same growth strategy: first, in the 1950s, expansion in the large, more profitable big-car market; second, expansion abroad. GM was the leader in both strategies, with Ford a close second. Chrysler, however, was in bad shape during the 1950s. Lynn Townsend took the helm in 1958 and turned the company's fortunes around, making Chrysler profitable and competitive during the 1960s. Townsend also led Chrysler into a number of overseas ventures, buying control of Simca in France and Rootes in Britain. These ventures incurred debt, of course, and the debt grew when they proved to be unprofitable. Chrysler also ran into trouble in the domestic market, where it had also expanded capacity under Townsend. Chrysler lost money in both recession years, 1974 and 1975. Following the recession it made money again in 1976 and 1977, selling some of its foreign holdings to cover its past losses. In 1977 the new president, John Riccardo, decided to focus Chrysler production on the up-scale, large-car market. In 1978 and 1979 Chrysler lost money. Further, beginning in 1978, Chrysler had planned a $7.5 billion modernization program for which it was raising money. By mid-1979 Chrysler had a total debt of $1.5 billion and a payment schedule it could not meet. In 1979 Chrysler unveiled its high-priced New Yorker and St. Regis models, which had cost $57 million in retooling, just as OPEC announced another oil price increase. In mid-1979 the company had 80,000 cars in unsold inventory valued at $700 million.[14]

Negotiations for a bailout had begun even before the disaster of 1979. John Riccardo had been in close touch with the forty or so banks that had held Chrysler's debt since 1976. Negotiations with the Carter administration and the UAW had been under way during 1978 even before Lee Iacocca became president of the company in November 1979. Indeed, by early 1979 Chrysler had worked out a $750 million line of credit with domestic banks and another $400 million with Japanese banks. On 9 August 1979, Secretary of the Treasury G. William Miller announced that the US government would provide $750 million in loan guarantees. But the banks wanted more than federal guarantees. The *Wall Street Journal* reported on 6 August that Chrysler's banks had presented their own plan to the corporation. They wanted concessions from the union as part of a plan to reorganize Chrysler. On 9 August UAW delegates from Chrysler met in Chicago and rejected a proposed two-year wage freeze. They agreed, however, to be 'as flexible as possible' in the current talks with Chrysler. As late as November, Chrysler's banks were still keeping up the pressure and threatening to withhold further loans. In fact, the UAW leadership agreed to the freeze in contract negotiations.[15]

The final agreement was worked out in Congress in the House and Senate Banking committees and emerged as the Chrysler Loan Guarantee Act of 1979. A Loan Guarantee Board would administer the plan, but the act was specific about the sacrifice to be made by Chrysler workers – $462.2 million in wages and benefits (measured as the difference from the Big Three pattern) from the union employees, including the voluntary wage freeze in the contract, and $125 million from nonunion staff. In reality, this was only the beginning. In December 1980, the Loan Guarantee Board demanded and got an additional $1.15-an-hour cut in UAW wages. Doug Fraser in turn received a seat on Chrysler's Board of Directors. The workers got an employee stock ownership plan. All of this contrasted sharply with what Iacocca had demanded to assume the presidency of Chrysler. In addition to the same $360,000 salary Riccardo had received, Iacocca demanded $1.5 million to be paid in installments from January 1979 to June 1980. While he later made the gesture of taking no salary for a year, Iacocca had by 1985 become the second highest paid US executive, when he earned $11.4 million.[16]

The demand for wage concessions clearly came from the banking community. But in the congressional debate, two freshmen congressmen from the House Banking Committee, Paul Tsongas (Dem.-Mass.) and Richard Lugar (Rep.-Ind.), served as point men for business. This pair was indicative of the rightward political shift then occurring in Congress. Tsongas was a neoliberal and Lugar a conservative; Lugar had gotten the idea for the Chrysler bailout from the New York City bailout of a few years earlier – in many ways the model for the Chrysler plan. The New York plan had put the city in the hands of its bankers and extracted concessions from its union employees. In return, Victor Gottbaum, the head of AFSCME District Council 37, was given a seat on the board that oversaw the austerity plan. In 1979 congressional neoliberals and conservatives could agree on the virtue of labor sacrifice.[17]

An interesting aspect of the process was the involvement of Doug Fraser. Fraser had been in on talks with Vice President Mondale about getting administration and congressional backing for the bailout. The UAW's early reluctance to agree to wage and benefit concessions collapsed, and on 25 October the UAW reached an agreement with Chrysler granting $203 million in wage and benefit concessions and $100 million in deferred pension fund payments. In announcing the agreement,

Fraser noted that 'these actions make it clear that the UAW has met its responsibilities in the broad effort to save Chrysler workers' jobs and restore the company to stability.' His leadership in getting the Chrysler UAW members to ratify a wage freeze that they had rejected in August appeared to be a well-timed maneuver to convince both Carter and Congress to pass the bailout bill. Even before the vote had been taken, Fraser and UAW Vice President and Chrysler Department head Mark Stepp boarded a plane to go to Washington and meet with Mondale. Carter announced he would back the proposal for maximum loan guarantees to Chrysler. Fraser then worked with Mondale and Michigan Democratic Representative James Blanchard to rally congressional votes.[18]

By the time the bailout went into effect, the language of the UAW leadership had returned to the cooperative norms of business unionism. The talk of 'one-sided class war' disappeared. UAW Vice President Don Ephlin summed up the new attitude in the December 1980 issue of *Solidarity*, the UAW's monthly magazine: 'We know how to strike, how to fight, how to bargain. We don't have to prove those things as much any more. What we do have to prove is that we can solve problems.'[19] But the Chrysler bailout opened the gates for a flood of demands for concessions that has yet to abate. The bailout also put the UAW in a new posture – that of a partner in corporate triage and salvation. The era of labor-management cooperation had arrived. At GM and Ford the relatively moribund Quality of Work Life programs took hold. Plant closings were no longer something to be fought, but to be managed. Anticorporate rhetoric was out, enterprise unionism was in. While some labor leaders like Winpisinger continued to make anticorporate noises, the potential coalition implied – though hardly realized – in the Progressive Alliance shattered and died quietly. As if to symbolize the collapse of its previous independent, progressive direction, Fraser led the UAW back into the AFL-CIO in 1981.

The terms of the Chrysler bailout and subsequent events should have warned labor that employers were not out to cooperate but to take advantage of labor's weakness. First, demands to reopen the contract to get further concessions after the UAW had granted a wage freeze should have alerted the union at all levels that a new strategy was necessary. Second, the massive rationalization and job loss that accompanied the bailout should have signaled everyone that this nonadversarial, 'joint problem solving' approach was simply a ploy to get union cooperation in drastic reductions of the workforce. About eighteen Detroit-area plants were scheduled to close in connection with Chrysler's salvation. In the end, a few of them were saved, but most closed and by 1982 Chrysler's hourly workforce was down to 57,000 from a high in the 1970s of 100,000. Most of the closed plants were in Detroit's inner city, and a large proportion of the jobs lost were those of Black workers. Far from seeing all this as a warning, the UAW leadership adopted it as a strategy for the future.

Several organizations in Michigan proposed alternative plans or amendments to the bailout plan. The United Coalition, a large rank-and-file caucus in UAW Local 51 at Lynch Road Assembly and Mound Road Engine (both slated for closing) proposed in 1979 that government aid be tied to saving jobs and communities. This could be done through aid for research and development for retooling or conversion to new products. The Detroit Alliance for a Rational Economy (DARE), headed by lawyer and City Council member Ken Cockrel, made a similar proposal; it called on Chrysler to maintain a certain proportion of employment and investment in the city. Detroit Congressman John Conyers proposed legislation that would put six labor and community representatives on Chrysler's Board, provide training for laidoff workers, and retool Dodge Main or convert it to other products. The most radical proposal came from the Michigan Citizens Party. It proposed the creation of the Public Autoworker Corporation for Transportation (PACT), which would purchase closed plants and convert them to produce mass transit vehicles and other energy-saving devices, employing laidoff autoworkers. The PACT proposal was similar to the Steel Valley Authority idea proposed later by the Tri-State Conference on Steel and eventually endorsed by the United Steelworkers.[20]

But in 1979–81 the UAW abandoned its momentary radicalism. It sought to save Chrysler by mending fences with the Carter administration and moderate elements in Congress. From its nascent radical pressure strategy it returned to conventional lobbying. The UAW promised cooperation with management to make the bailout work. In fact, the course of UAW politics veered sharply toward the center in those years, departing not only from its new radicalism, but even from its traditional social unionist rhetoric. Cooperation with capital at the industry level and protectionism at the political level became the new UAW politics, placing it firmly in the center of AFL-CIO thinking.

Labor Reacts to Reagan

By the time Reagan took office the political agendas of both labor as a whole (labor law reform, full employment, a higher minimum wage) and of its 'left' wing had collapsed. Further, a sense of defeat pervaded labor's higher ranks as its political initiatives failed at the hands of its own political 'friends' and as the erosion of its bargaining power became evident in the wave of concessions that mounted in the months before

Reagan was sworn in. Most of Reagan's first term found labor doing the best it could to stem the tide of budget cuts. There was little the AFL-CIO could do about many of the changes pushed by the Reagan administration because he effectively avoided battle on the ground most familiar to the AFL-CIO leadership – the give-and-take of Congress. Thus, there was little to be done through the normal channels of American democracy to stem the decline of the NLRB, OSHA, and other state institutions upon which labor was heavily dependent.

In 1981 the AFL-CIO did take the fairly unusual step of calling a mass march on Washington. Solidarity Day was an impressive event. Over a quarter of a million trade unionists marched in the streets of the nation's capital. But the organizers of the march presented no program. The event was part of a plan to influence the Democrats rather than a challenge to Reagan. Frank Swaboda of the *Washington Post* reported that 'for Kirkland and the nation's trade union movement, however, the current rally appears to be a crucial part of a broader plan to return to power within the Democratic Party.' According to Swaboda, the AFL-CIO would follow this up by raising $1 million for the Democratic National Committee.[21] Subsequent Solidarity Days II, III, etc., were not marches or protests, but election day mobilizations that gave a little color to labor's usual election day routine of providing some troops for the Democratic senators and representatives who would desert labor ever more resolutely as the Reagan years unfolded. These efforts thus had little or no impact on labor's position within party circles or on the direction of Democratic politics.

In June 1980 *Business Week,* in a manifesto entitled 'The Reindustrialization of America', sparked a debate that seemed to run counter to the general drift toward market-based solutions. *Business Week* proposed that business, labor and the federal government get together to plan the salvation of US industry. The idea of a national industrial policy was promoted by a number of academics and had some business backing. A leading business proponent was investment banker Felix Rohatyn of Lazard Frères, who had been one of the major architects of the 1975 New York City bailout and organizer of the banker-dominated Municipal Assistance Corporation (known as Big MAC), which supervised city finances. Looking back on that experience from the early 1980s, Rohatyn gave his own political summation: 'The direction and philosophy of a large unit of government was fundamentally and permanently changed as a result of the involvement, some would say intrusion, of the private sector in government. In my judgement, this is a principle that is applicable to a vast array of national problems for reasons not too dissimilar to the New York City experience.... The United States today in many ways is similar to New York City in 1975.'[22]

Rohatyn even tried to convince Jimmy Carter of the idea in 1980, but with no success. Carter did lend his prestige to a revitalization of the old Labor-Management Group under a new name, the Economic Revitalization Board. When Carter left the White House, Rohatyn, who was cochair of the board along with Irving Shapiro of DuPont and Lane Kirkland, reorganized it as the Industrial Policy Study Group (IPSG). In the next couple of years it included Joshua Gottbaum, son of Victor Gottbaum and an employee of Lazard Frères, Ted Kennedy, economists Walter Heller and Lester Thurow, and a number of AFL-CIO leaders.

For some in business circles, a string of joint government-business ventures from Penn Central in 1970 to the New York City bailout in 1975–76 and the Chrysler plan of 1979 pointed toward the need for a national economic policy that could aid industries in trouble, prevent the decline of others, and address common problems such as low productivity and lack of funds for investment. Neither *Business Week* nor most of those in business who flirted with the idea saw it as state planning of the European type. Most envisioned it as a voluntary, tripartite effort that would guide government in providing needed incentives. The difference between this approach and the incentives provided by the supply-side tax policies of Reaganomics or the macropolicies of Keynesianism was that an industrial policy was coordinated and its incentives targeted by mutual agreement.

With no strategy for countering Reagan other than waiting to elect Democrats, labor jumped into the industrial policy debate in 1983. One of the first labor proposals came from the UAW. Called 'Blueprint for a Working America', it was projected as Chrysler writ large, with the addition of more labor participation and congressional review as a concession to democracy. The inspiration for the plan was no secret. The UAW's *Washington Report* wrote, 'The Chrysler comeback is what we've all been talking about – an industrial policy'. The UAW plan differed from some academic proposals in that it called for 'social accounting' as one of the criteria for decision making. The example of 'social accounting' given in the text of the 'Blueprint', however, was the Chrysler bailout.[23] The AFL-CIO unveiled its own industrial policy proposal at its fall 1983 convention. It was, in fact, the product of Rohatyn's Industrial Policy Study Group, although the Federation claimed that it had been 'prepared by the AFL-CIO and its Industrial Union Dept.' Like all such proposals it was basically an organizational flow chart with a tripartite body on top and, in this case, Rohatyn's pet idea of a new Reconstruction Finance Corporation.[24] The most original labor-sponsored proposal came from the Machinists. Published in the summer of 1983 as a book entitled *Let's Rebuild America*, the Machinists' proposal was far more detailed than most and actually made policy recommendations. It also rejected tripartism in favor of a labor-dominated board. To a greater extent than most industrial policy proposals of that time, it emphasized government control over corporate behavior. Its fiery 85-page introduction by William Winpisinger retained all the anticorporate language and style of 1979's Progressive Alliance rhetoric.[25]

Labor's hope, of course, was to provide a programmatic basis for influencing the Democrats and reversing the party's drift to the right. For a time, the idea percolated in Democratic Party circles. Felix Rohatyn introduced Walter Mondale to industrial policy. Gary Hart hired Joshua Gottbaum of the IPSG to advise him on industrial policy. It was said that Walter Mondale had taken to the idea and might use it in the 1984 campaign.[26] Industrial policy, however, never became an issue in the Democratic primaries or at the 1984 convention in San Francisco. Instead, when Mondale declared himself a candidate in 1983 he also declared himself a fiscal conservative. The discussion of industrial policy ended when the AFL-CIO announced its united endorsement of Mondale in the primaries.

Business unionism's strategy for the Reagan era had little to do with Reagan or resistance to his policies. It was a strategy solely focused on returning the Democrats to power in Washington and to maximizing labor's organizational role in the party. Following Carter's disastrous defeat in 1980, Charles Mannatt moved to improve the party's organizational operations and fund-raising capacity. As noted, he set up the Democratic Business Council to bring in greater business support. But he also made some concessions to labor. The AFL-CIO was given thirty-five automatic seats on the DNC and the NEA another nine, an unprecedented act. In return, the AFL-CIO poured money into the DNC in hopes of strengthening its influence on that body. In preparation for the election, the AFL-CIO contributed $2.5 million to the DNC, one-third of its 1983 annual budget. To present a unified face to the party, Kirkland came up with the idea of a unanimous Federation endorsement of a candidate prior to the primary, something the AFL-CIO had never done before. In January 1983 Kirkland began lining up the other members of the Executive Council in preparation for its fall meeting. When Kennedy announced he wouldn't run, resistance to a unified endorsement of Mondale disappeared.[27]

Labor's efforts in the 1984 election were probably its most energetic ever. The unions aggressively sought to elect delegates to the Democratic National Convention. Additionally, they put their phone banking, direct mail, and voter-identification/mobilization apparatus into high gear. Their political contributions totalled an all-time high of $35 million. But the results were less than impressive. In the primaries, Mondale carried the union vote by large majorities only in hard-core blue-collar areas. In

New Hampshire and Massachusetts labor gave Hart a majority. Labor's goal in the general election was to give Mondale 65% of the union household vote. It came nowhere near that goal. Union voters cast 43% of their votes for Reagan in 1980. By 1984 Reagan had demonstrated just how antilabor he really was, yet he got 46% of the union vote.[28]

This did not stop the AFL-CIO leadership from a mood the *New York Times* described as 'determined self-congratulations'. The *AFL-CIO News* saw in the election 'a voter rebellion against the Reagan recession' in spite of the fact that Reagan defeated Mondale by a far larger margin than he had Carter. Victor Gottbaum wrote in the *New York Times* just before the election that 'labor took a quantum leap forward in American politics in 1984.'[29] These glowing judgments would be modified in the light of subsequent experience, but it was remarkable that so visible a defeat could be seen as some sort of victory. In fact, labor emerged from the 1984 elections with its candidates in disgrace, less influence in Democratic ruling circles, and no viable wing of the party prepared to come to its defense.

It is worth noting that the 'historic' primary endorsement of Mondale by the Executive Council of the AFL-CIO was emblematic of another political shift that has seldom been noted. The unity achieved in that move was entirely on the terms of the center and right-wing elements of the AFL-CIO leadership. The UAW, AFSCME, Machinists and others had previously tried to bolster the most liberal wing of the Democratic Party, often represented by Kennedy. In 1984 they endorsed the party's rightward-moving center in the person of Walter Mondale. Furthermore, Kirkland now had a degree of political hegemony as chief political broker that his predecessor and mentor, George Meany, never had. A number of international union presidents continued to oppose, in predictably timid fashion, the excesses of Kirkland's far-right foreign policy initiatives. At the 1987 AFL-CIO convention they forged a back-room deal with the Kirkland forces that actually put the Federation on record against further aid to the Nicaraguan *Contras*. A primary endorsement was out of the question for the 1987–88 election cycle because of the disarray among the Democrats themselves, but on most questions the more liberal or social democratic officials have allowed Kirkland to set the tone. Dissent on the left of the labor bureaucracy was limited to a handful of leaders of small unions, such as Henry Nicholas of the Hospital Workers and Rich Trumpka of the United Mine Workers.

The reentry of the Teamsters into the AFL-CIO in 1987 portended a change in top-level Federation politics – for the worse. For Jackie Presser and the Teamster hierarchy, the threat of a federal government trusteeship that surfaced during 1987 was reason enough to run for cover in the more respectable AFL-CIO. For the group of international union leaders, which included William Wynn of the UFCW and Robert Georgine, head of the Building Trades Council, it promised the weight to challenge Kirkland's choice as successor, Thomas Donaghue, for the presidency after Kirkland's retirement. In general, however, Teamster membership means more power for those unions most associated with criminal elements and with an older craft style of business unionism. Quite possibly it means the green light to more thuggery toward oppositionists and an even more narrow approach to politics.[30]

The abandonment of industrial policy left labor with essentially a one-point political agenda for the decade – trade protection. This is not to say that labor abstained from other legislative fights. But most of what labor fought for in Congress were things it had earlier lost. In 1984, for example, labor helped pass a law supposedly prohibiting the use of Title 11 of the Federal Bankruptcy Code to break a union contract, as Wilson Foods had done in 1983. As Reagan's second term unfolded, labor was able to win a few more defensive victories. In 1985 it defeated Reagan's attempt to tax employee benefits. In 1986 labor pressure defeated an amendment to the Hobbs Act that would have made offenses committed during a strike federal crimes punishable with prison sentences. But labor's greatest hopes and efforts went into a series of legislative fights that were supposed to save US jobs through a variety of protectionist measures.[31]

Protectionism has long been favored by the AFL-CIO, but it was one of a number of goals in a broader program with a progressive appeal beyond the workers immediately affected by the legislation. Following the collapse of that broader agenda and with the conversion of unions like the UAW that had previously opposed protectionism, it and related efforts at restricting immigration became the central priority of labor's active legislative program. The narrowing of its program further crippled labor's ability to play a leading role in creating a social counterweight to Reaganism and the business agenda. Opposition to Reaganism came to mean nothing more than putting a Democrat in the White House. So far as combating the business agenda, labor disqualified itself as much as the Democrats it hoped to elect. It is almost certain that the 1988 presidential campaign will be fought squarely on the turf of the business agenda.

Labor was trapped in the PAC strategy it had adopted four decades earlier. The functions of COPE and the Legislative Department as lobbyists, of the top Executive Council members as brokers in the structure of the Democratic Party and of the Federation as a mobilizer of votes were interdependent elements of a strategy that had never been proven and in the 1970s had been ignored by more and more of the party's structures and politicians. The success of the lobbying and brokering functions was thought to depend on labor's ability to mobilize enough voters to guarantee the Democrats a national presidential majority.

At almost every level, modern business unionism has viewed political mobilization as a technical matter. First is the question of turning out the union vote by using mailings, phone banks, and other techniques. To mobilize this vote in 1984, for example, union members were told that Reagan was a threat and that Mondale stood for labor. But union members, who could hear and see Mondale for themselves, weren't persuaded. Many union members don't vote because, among other things, the candidates that labor pushes do not address the fears and uncertainties, much less the class interests, of union voters. Those who do vote cast their ballots based on considerations such as personality, racism, and disgust with the previous administration – in other words, in much the same way as other Americans.

At one level, the labor bureaucracy's inability to turn out the vast majority of union members to vote for labor's endorsed candidate should surprise no one. It is simply a function of the bureaucratic structure and practice of most unions and of the ideology of business unionism itself. Business unionism is about dollars, health plans, and pensions. It is about administering contracts and providing services. Political decisions about political, social and foreign policy issues are reserved for the labor elite (the international executive boards and the AFL-CIO Executive Council) or for ceremonial passage at infrequent international conventions. Real debate over political or social issues was suppressed by 1950 and has been discouraged ever since. Political 'education' consists of packaged leaflets, booklets, or phone calls at election time. For the average union member politics thus has little or nothing to do with the union. His or her political ideas are as likely to be shaped elsewhere by the same factors that influence other citizens.

The concept of the labor vote as the members and families of union members is, of course, a losing idea at a time when they form a shrinking proportion of the potential electorate. A labor strategy for defeating the right would at the very least require some conception of a working-class electorate. But labor's approach to this idea is again a purely technical one – voter registration. It is often argued not only by labor activists, but by political progressives, that the problem of liberal retreat is one of inadequate electoral support. The answer is said to be voter registration. This approach, however, is as fundamentally apolitical and flawed as the COPE view of how to mobilize the labor vote. In fact, between 1980 and 1984, 12 million new people registered to vote. Only 4 million of them bothered to vote, and two-thirds of them voted for Reagan in 1984. In the congressional elections they voted 49% to 39% for Republicans. It is not hard to guess who voted and who didn't. The newly registered affluent or upwardly mobile voted, hence the Republican majorities. The new working-class registrants sat it out like those before them.[32]

The low turnout of working-class voters is a function of the deeper problem of working-class alienation/exclusion from the US political process. As Walter Dean Burnham has pointed out, two-thirds of the nation's nonvoters are working-class. This sort of apathy, Burnham shows in great detail, is unknown in other Western democracies and was not characteristic of earlier periods in US history. The question of working-class participation is only marginally affected by administrative barriers to registration or other technical problems. It is a question of politics; that is, of the class content of politics. Based on both voting trends and opinion poll data over the decades, Walter Dean Burnham came to this conclusion:

> It follows that a political system with *no* organized working-class left will be marked by heavy abstentions among the lower classes; the active electorate will thus be significantly more middle-class than the population at large; and that there will be, comparatively, a tendency for the electoral market and public policy to reflect higher tolerance of unemployment and a lower tolerance of inflation than if the lower classes organized and participated.[33]

Neither PAC in its day nor COPE or the AFL-CIO today field candidates of their own. As dependent pressure groups, they select from among candidates over whom they have no control. Their two most powerful levers of influence, money and the ability to mobilize voters, are no longer as powerful as those of business in the eyes of party leaders and candidates. Candidates who might be capable of activating masses of working-class voters cannot rise high enough in the Democratic Party to affect national policy or achieve national candidate status. The politics of class conflict that such candidates would need to emphasize run counter to the social harmony themes that have characterized the Democrats for half a century. Even a figure of national prominence with a ready-made social base, such as Jesse Jackson, has not been able to alter the course of the party. Within the confines of the Democratic Party there is no way out of this dilemma and no way to reverse the decline of labor's political influence that has been under way since the early 1970s.

For labor it is a Catch-22 situation. So long as the Democrats can attract enough of the middle- and upper-income vote to appear close to victory, they will not experiment with a political discourse that threatens these groups. So long as labor cannot find candidates capable of articulating both themes of working-class partisanship and programs that convincingly promise to bring positive change to the daily lives of low-income people, it cannot mobilize the vote needed to influence the political agenda of the nation. The defeat of the various proposals for class-based third parties by the leadership of the CIO, along with the simultaneous abandonment of a social unionist perspective, has left labor defenseless in the political arena and business in charge of the agenda of both parties. Not even the organization of new workers into unions would guarantee an increased labor vote in itself. The mobilization of a broader working-class vote is a task beyond the reach of direct mail and phone banks. It would require a politicized union membership. But the depoliticized culture of US unions is a barrier to the mobilization of the membership as political activists and organizers. To overcome it, political debate and controversy within the unions would have to be legitimized once again. This idea will not appeal to today's business union leaders, much less to the politicians and professionals of the Democratic Party.

In all likelihood, a genuine shift in the balance of power in society as a whole cannot be achieved without the creation of a new, working-class political party capable of reaching far beyond the ranks of those currently in trade unions. The organization of millions of service workers could expedite that process, if the political will were present and if they were organized on the basis of a social unionism that would point toward political activism. Most likely, the launching of such a political project on a serious scale would accelerate the growth of unions as well.

8

Concessions: From a Bailout to a Tidal Wave

The wage and benefit concessions made to the Chrysler Corporation in October 1979 were pushed through by the UAW leadership as a sign of good faith to Chrysler's bankers and an incentive to Congress to pass the Chrysler Loan Guarantee Act. Certainly no one thought a six-month wage freeze, the surrender of six paid holidays, and the deferment of pension increases would solve Chrysler's financial problems. But the bankers were still hesitant about extending Chrysler's line of credit, President Carter was not yet committed to the plan, and congressmen outside the Rust Belt states were wondering how all this would look in the 1980 elections. The concession agreement was more a political act than an economic one.

The consequences of this political act, however, were profoundly economic. One of the largest, most powerful industrial unions in the US had demonstrated that wage and benefit bargaining was not a one-way street. Congress got the message right away. In January 1980 it made passage of the bill contingent on further concessions. The UAW accepted the loss of seventeen paid holidays and the continued delay of all pay raises for Chrysler's hourly workers. A year later, Lee Iacocca asked the union for an additional concessions package worth $673 million. The Federal Loan Guarantee Board backed Iacocca. These concessions involved a $1.15-an-hour wage cut as well as the loss of three more paid holidays. This put Chrysler workers about $3 an hour behind workers at Ford and GM, introducing a new economic element in Big Three bargaining. The pattern, established four decades earlier, was broken.

From the start, the UAW leadership pushed hard to sell the cuts to the members. At each stage, the UAW sent out letters to all Chrysler workers. In 1979 the letter simply said, 'An agreement that involves some sacrifices ... was necessary to get support for government assistance to save our jobs.' In 1980 the blackmail theme was more explicit: 'If the additional sacrifices are not made ... there will be no loan guarantees for Chrysler. Without the loans, Chrysler will go under and so will Chrysler jobs.' By 1981 the union had the concessions formula down pat: '... without the sacrifices, there will be no loan for Chrysler and those jobs will go under along with the company.'[1]

UAW Vice President Mark Stepp, who was in charge of selling the 1981 agreement to the Chrysler Council, tried to convince the delegates that the agreement was another one of the UAW's 'precedent-setting' breakthroughs. He claimed that Chrysler had signed a letter of agreement granting 'the right for workers to have something to say about their destiny.' What Chrysler agreed to were joint union/management committees that could discuss problems voiced by employees. Far from being some new instrument of power, they were another step toward the surrender of autonomous union power. Chrysler's letter said that employee representatives would be given the chance to 'constructively input ideas into the decision-making process prior to implementation', but went on to state that 'the Corporation cannot agree to any limitation on the responsibility for the final decision.' Chrysler described this as a 'non-adversary procedure', a concept that would go hand in hand with concessions for the next several years. Chrysler had granted the UAW nothing it did not have and, like Fraser's tour of duty on the company's Board of Directors, it all came to nothing.

In selling these setbacks at the local level, the union sometimes stated the case more bluntly. One of the cruder displays of salesmanship came from International Representative Jack Horne. He told members of Local 869, 'Those of you who don't want to take a wage cut, go out and find another job. No one's stopping you from leaving this organization.'[2] Whatever the approach, it was clear for all to see that the UAW leadership was more than willing to grant concessions and to fight hard to get the members to swallow them.

Neither this fact nor the economic logic of breaking the pattern were lost on the other automakers. A Ford spokesman told the *Detroit Free Press*, 'You can bet we're watching Chrysler's efforts with a good deal of interest. We haven't done it [ask for concessions] yet, but we'll see what happens on this go-around with Chrysler.' GM Chairman Roger Smith was even more to the point: 'You cannot have a two-tier industry.' In other words, Chrysler now had a competitive advantage. In February, *Business Week* carried an article entitled 'Pleas for Wage Relief Flood into the UAW'. In the first nine months of 1981 the UAW's Research Department assessed seventy-five requests for concessions. The union's early plea that the Chrysler case was exceptional went out the window.[3]

The pressure mounted on the UAW all through 1981, and in December the International Executive Board reversed its previous refusal to reopen the Ford and GM contracts. In February 1982 the UAW agreed to sweeping concessions at Ford. All paid personal holidays (a shorter worktime program initiated in 1976 to help create jobs) were ended. The

Watsonville: Latina strikers and their supporters confront the police.

3% annual improvement factor, first negotiated in 1948, was dropped, and three COLA and all pension increases were deferred. The deal was estimated to be worth $1 billion to Ford.[4] In April GM got the same agreement, saving $3 billion over twenty-nine months. GM executives then proposed hefty bonuses for themselves. American Motors, of course, got into the act and received $115 million in concessions similar to the Ford and GM settlements.[5]

In 1982 Ford and GM workers began opposing concessions. On 15 January 1982, 152 UAW members from thirty-seven locals met in Flint, Michigan to form Locals Opposed to Concessions (LOC). LOC adopted an alternative program to concessions, calling for a $1,500 tax credit for auto buyers, passage of the UAW-backed local content law (requiring a certain proportion of cars sold in the US to be made domestically), and a 'national inquiry into the destruction of this country's industrial base by the multinational corporations.' LOC's main activity, however, was to campaign for a rejection of any concessionary contract. Critiques of the Ford and GM proposals were widely circulated. Despite this activity, LOC leaders admitted that most UAW members were scared. Don Douglas, president of Local 594 in Pontiac, Michigan and a leader of LOC, confessed, 'Everyone realizes that all the wheels of power are rolling in that direction and they're just caught up in it.' At Ford, the International's fearmongering produced a 73% majority for ratification. At GM, where LOC was strongest, however, the agreement passed by only 52%, one of the closest Big Three ratification votes ever.[6]

The Chrysler concessions were not the first such give-backs. Companies in rubber, aerospace, meatpacking and other industries had demanded and sometimes received concessions. But the Chrysler bailout was a highly visible public event. And the UAW contracts with the Big Three were arguably the backbone of the entire pattern structure of industrial collective bargaining. If the UAW, a strong union with a reputation for militancy, could put bargaining based on company performance and competitiveness ahead of the traditional pattern, why not others?

The spread of concessionary bargaining was rapid. Following the GM settlement, the seven corporations covered by the Basic Steel Agreement asked the USW to open the contract and make concessions. This proposal was rejected by Steelworkers local union presidents in 1982. But by the end of the year, major concessions had been negotiated in airlines, meatpacking, agricultural implements, trucking, grocery, rubber, among smaller steel firms, and in public employment.[7] The years 1979 through 1982 might be termed the first round of concessionary bargaining. These were recession years and a number of the industries in which give-backs were made were experiencing financial or competitive problems. Labor, therefore played down the importance of concessions, calling it a temporary phenomenon. Academics friendly to labor also tended to dismiss the trend as an aberration. Richard Freeman and James Medoff, for example, wrote in their 1984 book *What Do Unions Do?* 'Concessions are therefore found only in industries undergoing extreme economic problems.'[8]

But employers didn't see it that way. A 1982 survey of four hundred corporate executives (from both profitable and ailing firms) by *Business Week*, revealed that 19% of them said that 'although we don't need concessions, we are taking advantage of the bargaining climate to ask for them.' Profitable firms that received concessions during the first round included GM, Kroger, Iowa Beef, Gulf Oil, Texaco, Caterpillar Tractor, and United Parcel Service. Furthermore, some of the industries involved were not declining industries like auto or steel, but growing ones like trucking, meatpacking, and even airlines. In these industries, the specific problem was the growth of a nonunion, substandard sector within an industry that had become competitive in the domestic market. The airline unions, with their history of craft, company-by-company bargaining, were unprepared for the competitive atmosphere that deregulation brought. In the case of trucking (which was also deregulated) and meatpacking, the Teamsters and United Food and Commercial Workers, respectively, adopted policies of granting concessions – piecemeal in trucking, across the board in meatpacking – which inevitably accelerated the employer drive for concessions.[9]

The second round of concessions bargaining, beginning in the economic recovery year of 1983 and going through 1985, opened with major concessions in the Basic Steel Agreement. With the companies coming back for the third time in six months, USW Vice President Joe Odercich, acting for ailing President Lloyd McBride, pushed through an early settlement (the contract wasn't due to expire until August). In February 1983 the USW granted the seven major steel firms a $1.25-an-hour wage cut, the loss of six COLA payments, reductions in vacation time, and the reduction of Sunday pay to time and a quarter. The pact was said to be worth $3 billion to the steelmakers. It specified that the wage cut would eventually be restored, but future rounds of concessions negated that part of the agreement. Phelps Dodge also took on members of the USW at its copper-mining facilities in the Southwest. This led to a long, bitter and ultimately unsuccessful strike, with the company imposing deep cuts on a nonunion workforce. The Teamsters signed the second National Master Freight Agreement to contain across-the-board concessions, including a two-tier wage scale, loss of the COLA, and concessions on production standards. The second round also saw profitable firms such as Greyhound, the three major aerospace corporations, the major oil refiners, Hormel, and growing service industries like the hotel industry demand concessions with all the insistence of Chrysler or General Motors.[10]

By the end of the second round of concessions, the nation was in its third year of economic recovery. Concessionary bargaining had crossed industry lines, and unions in some industries had made their second set of give-backs. The notion that concessions were a temporary phenomenon visited only on ailing industries and firms was no longer tenable. Indeed, a 1985 Brookings Institution study of concessions bargaining by Daniel J. B. Mitchell noted the spread of such bargaining. Constructing a table of all industries in which bargaining occurs, Mitchell showed that from a few traditional blue-collar industries in 1981, wage freezes or cuts had spread each year until in the period January 1984–June 1985 no industry had escaped some concessionary settlements.

Mitchell explicitly rejected the most common explanations: 'The table shows that wage freezes and cuts began in a narrow range of industries in 1981 and have been spreading progressively ever since. As the number of industries affected grew, the conventional explanations – deregulation, foreign competition, general economic distress – became harder to credit, and the alternative hypothesis of a demonstration effect became more difficult to reject.' Noting that distress in the auto industry is not likely to carry over to Las Vegas hotels or Disneyland, two scenes of concessions in 1984, he put the point even more explicitly: 'But the longevity of the concession movement and its spread to less-than-dire situations suggests that the initial concessions have encouraged other employers to try their luck in demanding similar settlements.'[11]

Indeed, the rapidity of the demonstration effect' as well as its ability to leap from one industry to another was apparent by January 1980, when Detroit Mayor Coleman Young, looking to his own negotiations with Detroit city workers, noted that 'we are closely examining the recent Chrysler contract, because it contains a principle which I believe we may be forced to adopt.' Detroit public employees later had to accept a two-year wage freeze.[12]

Mitchell's analysis went a step beyond noting the 'demonstration effect'. He explicitly cited the changing balance of forces between capital and labor: 'Additional evidence of a shift in the wage-setting climate is to be found in the union environment itself. Declines in union membership, reduced strike activity, changes in the political and legal balance between unions and management, shifts in management bargaining strategies, and the history of the union-nonunion wage differential all confirm a change.'[13]

A highly visible demonstration effect in combination with a deteriorating balance of power not only encouraged the spread of concessionary demands by employers, but demands for more give-backs by the same employers in subsequent contracts. Once again, Chrysler, with the backing of the federal government and the collaboration of the UAW leadership, staged the first demonstration. Employers with such varying financial conditions as the basic steel companies, Greyhound, UPS, countless trucking firms, the auto companies, and the meatpackers all came back to their unions for additional concessions.

The impact of the spread of concessions on collective bargaining agreements was immediate and continuous, creating a wage deceleration that has showed no signs of abating in the second half of the 1980s. Table 5 shows annual average first-year wage increases negotiated in new major contracts (those covering 1,000 or more workers) in the private economy for the years 1981–86. It also shows the wage changes negotiated the last time the same parties bargained – usually two or three years earlier. The annual series for manufacturing is also included, but comparable data for 'last time' settlements were not available for this category.

Table 5
Mean First-Year Wage Adjustments in Major New Contracts

Year	Number of Workers	First Year	Last Contract	All Workers in Manufacturing
1981	2.4 million	9.8%	n.a.	7.2%
1982	3.3 million	3.8%	8.5%	2.8%
1983	3.0 million	2.6%	9.3%	3.0%
1984	2.3 million	2.4%	5.9%	2.3%
1985	2.2 million	2.3%	3.9%	8.0%
1986	2.5 million	1.2%	3.5%	-1.2%

Sources: US Bureau of Labor Statistics, *News*, 27 January 1984; 24 January 1985; 27 January 1986; 27 January 1987; BLS, *Handbook of Labor Statistics*, Washington 1985, p. 332–33.

Whether the results were compared from year to year, when different groups of unions negotiated, or with the last time the same unions bargained, the downward direction was clear. It was also evident that wage concessions in manufacturing hit sooner and were more drastic. In 1986, the last year for which complete figures were available, the first actual decrease in the average for any industrial category occurred. Since the large manufacturing contracts tend to lead bargaining trends, the future was bleak for others as well.

The impact of concessions goes beyond wage rates, however. It has hit other benefits with increasing force. The Bureau of Labor Statistics publishes data on total compensation (wages and benefits) only for new contracts covering 5,000 or more workers, but this series reveals the same downward trend. The average first-year adjustment for total wages and benefits fell from 10.2% in the private nonfarm economy in 1981 to 1.1% in 1986, indicating that declines in the larger bargaining units were even greater than in the others. Cost-of-living clauses have been another major casualty of concessionary bargaining. In 1979 about 60% of all workers under major contracts (covering 1,000 workers or more) were covered by COLAs. According to the BLS's figures, only 50% of those covered by major contracts had COLAs by 1983; by 1986 the figure had fallen to 31%.[14]

In the face of worker impatience with second and third rounds of demands for concessions, the employers looked for new formulas that would induce employed workers to ratify concessionary contracts. One such device was the lump-sum or bonus payment – a one-shot amount of money that would not be folded into the wage rate, but would be large enough to produce ratification or cooperation for the moment. The effect of lump-sum payments on worker income was substantial. According to the *Wall Street Journal*, 'While many corporate executives are promoting the bonus programs as a tool to share the wealth and increase productivity, the plans clearly mean less money for most workers.' Because of the compounding effect of regular annual increases in the wage rate, lump-sum payments over the life of a contract can mean a lot less money. For example, a worker making $8.00 an hour just before a new contract would gain about $2,000 over the three-year life of the contract if his/her wage rate were increased 2% a year. A 2% annual bonus, on the other hand, would produce only $1,000 in three years.

Further, a lump-sum payment would mean that in the following bargaining round the wage 'platform' would be the same as it had been three years earlier. In both these ways, bonuses perpetuated wage deceleration and avoided cost increases in premium pay (overtime, weekends, holidays, and so on) or benefits based on wage rates. In 1984, 700,000 workers, or nearly a third of those covered in bargaining, took lump-sum payments in lieu of wage rate increases. By 1986 nearly a million workers, or 40% of the total, received such bonuses.[15]

Another device that captured capital's imagination for a period was the two-tier wage system. It allowed the employer to hire new workers at wages rates below those of current employees. Short-term 'starting rates' were not new, but the two-tier plans of the 1980s either created a permanent lower stratum of employees, at least until all the higher paid workers retired, or a prolonged wage gap between the two groups of workers. Since a two-tier system required no sacrifice from those currently employed, it was often easier to sell than a straight wage cut or freeze. Of course, it also undermined the potential solidarity of the workforce because two groups of workers were performing the same work for different pay. These schemes became popular in 1983, and 800,000 workers were covered by contracts with two-tier structures by 1984. In 1985 another 700,000 workers came under similar provisions. The largest single contract to adopt two-tier pay was the Teamsters' 1985 National Master Freight Agreement. The union that negotiated the largest number of two-tier agreements was the United Food and Commercial Workers, which signed 87 of the 261 two-tier agreements negotiated in 1983–85, most of them in the retail grocery industry. In 1986 another 200,000 workers came under contracts containing two-tier pay systems.[16]

The first round of concessions had focused on wages and benefits, but concessions on working conditions, work rules, production standards and other aspects of the workplace regime became increasingly common in the second and third rounds. No agency records such concessions, nor are they easily quantifiable. But according to Thomas Kochan, a professor at the Massachusetts Institute of Technology, 'You can go back to almost any recession and find examples of unionized companies aggressively going after work rules. But you have to go back to the Depression to find as much of it as is going on now.' A 1982 *Business Week* poll of corporate executives of unionized firms showed that 57% preferred concessions on work rules to those on wages.[17]

The significance of contract language regulating working conditions through such means as job classifications, work rules, and production standards is often seen by the public or even by unaffected groups of workers as something anachronistic or irrational. In fact, such regulations are neccessary for the functioning of most systems of production. Workers engaged in the collective production of goods or services must know what they are doing, where their responsibilities begin and end, and agree on a manageable rate of work so that the different operations are properly coordinated. The more complex the operation, the greater the need for universal rules. Otherwise, the result is simply chaos. Frederick Taylor and the 'scientific management' school recognized this principle as much as any trade union. The difference, of course, was that management wants the right to set these rules as it sees fit, while labor needs to shape the rules to protect itself.

There is no greater efficiency inherent in management's version of work regulation than labor's. Harry Braverman, David Noble, Harley Shaiken and many others have shown that management's attempts to define work rules are shaped by its need to control labor, not by any technically objective standard of efficiency. Indeed, the literature of industrial relations underlying such programs as Quality of Work Life recognizes the inevitability of management inefficiency. This is because the workers who collectively perform the complex operations of modern industry have a better understanding of what is really involved in their work than do managers who have no hands-on experience. Management attempts to increase efficiency often simply produce low-quality products or services. In the end, all forms of workplace regulation reflect a large element of subjective self-interest.[18]

From the standpoint of labor, work rules, job classifications and other methods by which the union attempts to regulate the organization, pace, and quality of work are essential and rational forms of protection. Management cannot arbitrarily load one individual or group with more tasks, combine jobs to reduce the workforce, or deprive a worker of the work he or she was hired to do. Union regulations are also important to safety. Management's disregard for safety in large-scale operations is well-known. Workers can be endangered if they are pushed to perform work they are not familiar with. The existence of clearly defined jobs also provides some choice for workers with different abilities and temperaments. It is a fact that workers often bid for jobs with no difference in pay and will even take a pay cut if the work suits them better. Finally, the existence of established rules gives the workplace union some power. Work-to-rule is, of course, an important means of asserting union power – one reason management would like to dump such rules.[19]

In general, modern industrial unionism prefered to leave the workplace regime to the control of management and its modification to the local union. Job classifications are often spelled out in national contracts for the purpose of establishing wage rates, but detailed work rules are seldom a part of national agreements. Employer demands for modifications in work rules during national negotiations usually take the form of getting the international union's permission to bargain with locals for such changes. Work-rule concessions at the plant and local union level accelerated in the second half of the 1980s, further undermining pattern bargaining and the trade union principle of common work standards.

Pattern Bargaining and Capital's Competitive Imperative

Standard wages, benefits and conditions are the economic foundation of unionism. They underwrite the solidarity of the membership by establishing an egalitarian means of determining wages and benefits in place of employer favoritism or external economic criteria. But standardization is also the objective basis for both the defense of living standards and for future improvements. In 1909 John R. Commons noted that in order for any group of workers to raise their wages above a given market level they would have to 'take wages out of competition'.[20] This meant standardizing wages throughout a particular labor market regardless of the competitive pressures on the employers.

Except for rare cases of true monopoly (for example, AT&T until very recently), all employers producing and selling the same (or substitutable) goods or services are in competition in a capitalist society. Labor, no matter how well organized, cannot eliminate the competition among employers, but it can eliminate the competition among workers. In Commons's time, most labor markets and unionized employers were local or regional. The major exceptions were coal, firearms and rail transport. The new basic industries such as steel were still nonunion. Most unions were craft unions. They attempted to 'take wages out of competition' by establishing a standard union rate and forcing employers to hire only from the union. This involved either organizing all the workers in the same craft in a given market or driving nonunion workers out of the market in one way or another. In general, only the building trades unions were successful in this effort, and their success was often based on ethnic exclusivity and racial discrimination. This craft approach to suppressing competition among workers was basic to the old business unionism of the American Federation of Labor.[21]

Industrial unionism approached the question of eliminating competition among workers in an entirely different way. Rather than working to limit the labor market or exclude potentially competitive workers, the industrial unions attempted to organize all the workers in the industry. The industrial union approach was inclusive rather than exclusive, national or even international rather than local or regional. The unions then fought to standardize wages, benefits and conditions for all the workers. Industrial unionism was egalitarian in that all workers performing similar work received the same package of wages and benefit standardized through the mechanism of pattern bargaining.

As we have seen, the origins of pattern bargaining in the US created certain potential weaknesses. For example, the major industrial patterns were introduced during World War Two in a bureaucratic fashion, leading to dependence on the federal government. Efforts were made to exclude the rank and file from direct influence over the content and direction of the patterns. The question of working conditions was left largely outside the purview of the national pattern agreements precisely to allow capital a measure of flexibility. The unions were weakened as potential protectors of the patterns through their bureaucratization and depoliticization. And, finally, the entire industrial union movement remained dependent on political forces far more influenced by capital than by labor.

Nevertheless, as long as the economy grew these patterns functioned as a means of protecting and improving the living standards of millions of workers. They provided a measure of protection not only for those directly covered by the major industrial patterns, but for workers performing similar or related work in the thousands of new plants built during the three decades following 1950 – at least those fortunate enough to be organized into unions. Workers outside of manufacturing – for example, in transportation and communications – also benefited from the first major patterns as they established their own in the 1950s and 1960s. Eventually, after the mid-1960s, even public employees were able to bargain on the basis of 'comparability', that is, the standards set in private industry for similar work. There is even evidence that union pay levels and benefits have a spillover effect on nonunion employers in the same industry.[22]

For this system of pattern bargaining to work, the major patterns must remain intact. But, as we have seen, the structure of the patterns started to deteriorate in 1948, when the major industrial unions ceased to present the same demands at the same time. Pattern bargaining then became specific to each industry. Beginning in the 1960s, nonunion sectors developed in most industries, slowly at first, then rapidly, putting increased competitive pressure on the patterns. In the 1970s import competition in some industries added to this pressure. The main effect here, however, was not to put US workers into direct wage competition with overseas workers (a situation the employers could not have imposed due to the magnitude of the wage gap) but to intensify domestic competition. The simultaneous crisis of profitability gave the employers the incentive they needed to break the 'social compact' on which US labor relations were based. The rise of a competitive, nonunion sector in one industry after another gave them the first lever. Ultimately, however, it was the cooperative posture of business unionism in accepting concessions that turned a crack in the patterns into a flood of concessions.

In October 1979 the UAW's acquiescence to concessions put Chrysler workers' wages into competition. Beneath all the language about saving jobs, the UAW leadership demonstrated its willingness to make wages, benefits and then working conditions subject to competitive bargaining. The pattern in auto was broken, and the standard that upheld worker solidarity eliminated. Naturally, the other US automakers moved to end Chrysler's advantage by reducing the pay and fringe benefits of their own workers. A degree of wage parity was reestablished in 1985, but by that time the automakers had imposed bidding between plants (in which work rules were bartered for alleged job security) and the dynamic of competition was out of control.[23]

In other industries, concessions were made on a 'pattern' basis – that is, all the firms covered by the pattern agreement were given wage relief. This was the case in meatpacking in 1982 and 1984, steel in 1983, and trucking in 1982 and again in 1985. The unions believed that this strategy would prevent the breakup of the patterns because it preserved a standard. In fact, it simply opened the door to competitive bargaining. The wage freeze granted major meatpackers by the United Food and Commercial Workers was aimed at reducing pressure on the local unions to grant concessions by giving the companies under the pattern a break in relation to the lower wages of newer nonpattern firms, union and nonunion alike. The Teamsters granted concessions to make union firms more competitive with nonunion operators. The USWA gave the seven basic steel corporations wage cuts to help them meet overseas competition. But once a union agreed to concessions in an industry with a lower pay, nonpattern sector (union or not), wages and other forms of compensation were put into competition, and the resulting centrifugal forces were hard to reverse. Smelling blood, the employers refused to limit their demands for concessions to the orderly process the unions hoped for.

If many labor leaders did not seem to grasp the economics of the situation, capital and its advisers understood it perfectly. Charles Lieberman, an economist for Shearson/American Express, explained it to *Wall Street Journal* readers: 'Unlike the major industrial economies of Europe, the US labor market is becoming progressively more competitive. This development reflects the gradual erosion of the power of labor unions as well as the impact of deregulation.'[24] With this understanding, in 1983 the Conference Board predicted the outcome of 1984 bargaining in accurate and ominous terms:

> Labor-market competition will affect bargaining...even during the recovery. Companies will be attempting to cut labor costs by hiring more part-time employees. They will press for two-tier pay systems in which new hires (or rehires) come on the payroll at far lower rates. And, finally, an abundant supply of labor makes it more possible than ever before to operate during a strike. This possibility constrains union demands. Moreover, the additional risk that the company may emerge without a union-represented work force is also a constraint on union leaders in the mid-1980s.[25]

This dark reference to scabbing was no doubt inspired by the Phelps Dodge strike that began in 1983, but competitive bargaining could be achieved by cooperative methods as well. In 1983 an internal memo by Alfred S. Warren, Jr., GM vice president for labor relations, called for a variety of competitive innovations in 1984 bargaining. For example, it advised the company to 'shift forms of compensation to gain sharing: expand profit sharing in lieu of returning AIF [the 3% annual improvement factor] and additional wage/COLA increases.' This strategy would tie worker pay to company performance. The method for winning this and similar demands was to influence the UAW leadership by providing 'opportunities for Union-management dialogue and joint problem solving' and to get the 'union to understand the competitive challenge'. The memo suggested concentrating on UAW Vice President Donald Ephlin, then head of the GM Department. The plan was to eliminate 80,000 GM workers' jobs. UAW Local 160 at the GM Tech Center obtained and published a copy of the memo, embarrassing both Ephlin and GM. Nevertheless, the cooperative spirit at GM was enough to prevent the union from getting back the 3% AIF in 1984, in effect putting more emphasis on profit sharing.[26]

Like GM, other employers participating in pattern agreements soon took the competitive logic of concessions bargaining one step further. In steel, for example, once the seven major steel companies covered by the Basic Steel Agreement received substantial concessions in 1983, the differing cost structures of each company became as much an issue to them as their common differences with foreign steel suppliers. Former Bethlehem negotiator George Moore, Jr., told *Business Week:* 'There is a revolution going on in the steel industry, and each company ought to negotiate contracts which are responsive to its own operations. As the commonality between these companies decreases, there is less reason to continue the coordinated approach [to bargaining].'[27] In fact, the pattern system in steel began unraveling in the late 1970s, when several steel fabricating firms that previously bargained 'me-too' contracts under which their workers got basic steel rates, broke out of the pattern. In 1982 Wheeling Pittsburgh got two rounds of deep concessions from its workers, breaking with the Basic Steel Agreement. Finally, in 1985 the six remaining basic steel firms announced they would no longer bargain together, and pattern bargaining in steel came to an end.

In 1986 the Steelworkers made no attempt to impose a pattern agreement or maintain anything resembling standards in wages and benefits. Instead, USW President Lynn Williams decided to bargain on the basis of individual company performance. He chose LTV, financially the weakest of the six former pattern firms, to bargain with first. His strategy was to set a ceiling on concessions, arguing that since LTV was the weakest firm, the others would have to take smaller concessions. The USW granted LTV a $3.60-an-hour cut in labor costs in March, four months before the contract expired. In the next three months, the USW negotiated agreements with National, Bethlehem, and Inland with smaller packages of concessions.

But USX, always the toughest negotiator and formerly the leader in coordinated bargaining, wanted cuts near the LTV level. USX demanded $3.30 an hour in pay reductions. Williams's strategy of making LTV a ceiling seemed to have worked in that no company asked for more. But in reality, it simply guaranteed that the other firms would demand concessions and that USX would go for the showdown it had long contemplated. In the end, USX, the strongest corporation in the industry, got $2.45 a hour in savings, larger than those of any other company except LTV. Maury Richards, a local union president at LTV who had opposed that contract in March, was right when he said: 'We exerted a downward pressure on the rest of the union; we increased the concessions the other guys had to take. LTV is one of US Steel's biggest arguments.'[28]

The National Master Freight Agreement was first negotiated by Teamster President Jimmy Hoffa in 1964 when he pulled together the union's regional contracts. It established standard wages and benefits for nearly half a million workers in 600 companies and set the terms for other national contracts, including car haulers, steel haulers, tanker drivers, and United Parcel Service workers. By the mid-1980s the NMFA covered only about half as many workers at 285 firms, and the related contracts in car hauling and at UPS no longer conformed to NMFA standards. Trucking, unlike steel, was a growing industry with no imports to worry about. After deregulation, it became a competitive industry in which the largest firms grew bigger: The ten largest firms' share of truck freight tonnage grew from 21% in 1979 to 32% in 1985. Employment levels in trucking as a whole are subject to cyclical ups and downs, but the general level of employment in the industry as a whole is at or above the level of the 1960s and 1970s. Because of intense competition, however, layoffs due to failures or cutbacks have been severe. The entry of nonunion firms is now easy, and the already large nonunion sector has grown.[29] The unraveling of pattern bargaining in trucking preceded deregulation, however. Beginning with the 1970 contract, Teamster presidents who followed Hoffa granted more and more firms concessionary 'riders', special addenda to the NMFA that granted concessions in working conditions. Thus, competitive pressures were mounting even before deregulation. After the 1982 NMFA, the union gave individual members the 'right' to make personal wage concessions in the form of 'loans'. The 1985 contract continued the fragmentation of bargaining by granting concessions in supplementary regional contracts.[30]

The centrifugal force of concessionary bargaining was nowhere more graphically demonstrated than in meatpacking. The meatpacking industry went through a series of structural changes in the 1960s and 1970s. Many old plants were closed as the companies opened new ones outside the industry's traditional centers in Chicago and Kansas City. Conglomerates bought several of the major packers, in many cases divesting them later. Meatpacking faced no serious competition from imports, nor was the industry as a whole in crisis, unlike auto or steel. But as new firms entered the industry, a substandard, competitive sector developed. Toward the end of the 1970s pressure from numerous companies, both profitable and unprofitable, began to convince UFCW local unions that they had no choice but to make concessions. One UFCW staffer said at the time: 'After Chrysler went down, we started getting hit by very aggressive moves from the companies for mid-term concessions. They were hitting the local unions and trying to turn them against the International.'[31]

In 1981 the UFCW leadership came up with the utterly remarkable idea that the best way to stem the tide of concessions being made by locals in the pork-producing sector of meatpacking was to grant a wage freeze to all the companies under the pattern agreement. In a letter to all affected meatpacking locals dated 18 December 1981, UFCW President William Wynn announced the four objectives of the union's new strategy: 1) to 'preserve and expand master agreements', 2) 'to bring lower wage operators more in line with master agreement companies', 3) to resist 'mid-term contract concessions', and 4) to 'minimize the wave of plant closings'. Predictably, Wynn's strategy achieved none of these aims.

The voluntary offer of a wage freeze put the pattern wages into active competition by granting relief to the pattern employers. Here, as elsewhere, this simply unleashed the desire of employers for a further improvement in their competitive position. The master agreement in the pork sector fragmented. Lewie Anderson, head of the UFCW's Packinghouse Committee, told the *Wall Street Journal* that in the first eighteen months of the new agreement the number of workers receiving the pattern rate of $10.69 an hour had dropped from 50,000 to 30,000. Far from creating an orderly closing of the wage gap as other firms raised wages, the industry experienced a rapid downward spiral in wages. According to US Labor Department figures, the average hourly wage in meatpacking plants went from $9.19 in January 1982, when the UFCW's voluntary 44-month wage freeze went into effect, to $7.93 in January 1985. In addition, a number of the substandard firms got further concessions during that period, fouling the union's plans to raise off-pattern wages. The hope of resisting midterm concessions by granting a major midterm concession was certainly ill-founded. In June 1983 Wilson Foods declared bankruptcy and cut wages from $10.69 an hour to $6.50. Greyhound demanded midterm concessions from workers at its Armour division and closed the plants when the workers rejected them. They were later reopened on a nonunion basis by ConAgra, which bought them from Greyhound. Swift Independent and Dubuque Packing closed plants and reopened them with wage reductions of 40% to 50%. Employment in meatpacking plants declined by almost 10,000 during this period.[32]

The 44-month agreement contained a 1984 wage reopener provision, presumably to allow the union to negotiate an increase once order was restored. The situation in the industry remained chaotic, and the companies pushed for further concessions in 1984. The UFCW did not have to reopen the contract, which didn't expire until September 1985, but it did, granting a $1.69-an-hour wage reduction to those employers still under the pattern. The basic labor rate in plants still under the pattern, mostly Hormel and Oscar Mayer plants, was $9 an hour. The new agreement called for an increase to $10 an hour in September 1985. The UFCW claimed that by 1985 concessions would be over, but it was wrong. In

Tennessee, where Oscar Mayer workers had avoided the $1.69 wage cut, the company demanded a $.69 cut in October 1985 to bring that plant's rate down to the level of the others. In Detroit, UFCW Local 26 suffered three defeats in late 1985 and early 1986. Kowalski Sausage broke the UFCW at its plant and cut wages. Hygrade workers took a cut from $10.69 to $9.50 with an additional $.80-an-hour reduction in benefits in February 1986 after a six-week strike. Thorne Apple Valley, which already paid below the pattern rate, imposed a wage freeze in February 1986 after a three-week strike.[33]

Concessionary demands continued into 1986 and 1987. The profitable Patrick Cudahy Co. demanded a third round of concessions from workers at its Cudahy, Wisconsin plant. The workers, members of UFCW Local P-40, rejected the demands by a 95% vote in January 1987 and went on strike. The company wanted cuts of $1 to $3 an hour, which would have brought wages down to $6.25 to 8.65. Cudahy was once part of the industry pattern, but was able to impose pay cuts in 1982 and 1984. On 14 December 1986 the workers at Iowa Beef Processors' flagship plant in Dakota City, Nebraska rejected a demand for a wage freeze until 1990. These workers had taken a $1.07 cut in 1983, and their rates were already below the industry pattern. IBP was also a profitable company, showing once again that the competitive imperative of capital does not apply only to ailing firms.

John Morrell, another profitable company, went for further concessions in 1986 and 1987. In 1986 it had an operating profit of $28.1 million on a net sales of $1.87 billion. Its parent corporation, United Brands, made a profit of $111.9 million in 1986. But it sought to improve its competitive position by seeking another round of wage cuts. In 1986 the UFCW stepped in to end a strike at Morrell's Arkansas City, Kansas plant and accepted a wage cut to $7.25 an hour. In 1987 Morrell forced the eight hundred members of UFCW Local 1142 at the Sioux City, Iowa plant out on strike by demanding a $1.25-an-hour pay cut from the previous $9.25 basic labor rate. Local 1142 sent roving pickets to Morrell's Sioux Falls, South Dakota plant, where Local 304A honored Local 1142's picket line.

The leaders and members of Local 304A in Sioux Falls realized that if Morrell had its way in Sioux City, the company would turn on them next. Craig Hobbs, a steward from Local 1142, put it this way: 'If [the company] shoves this down our throats, they'll be up here when they get done with us.' Indeed, while the UFCW claimed as late as November 1986 that there was a Morrell master agreement, none of the company's three major slaughtering and packing operations had the same basic labor rate, and none of them bargained at the same time.

Beginning in 1986, the UFCW did manage to win wage increases at some plants. At Swift and Armour Dial (but not the ConAgra-owned plants) wages were raised to $10 an hour in September 1986. Most Hormel and Oscar Mayer plants went to $10.25 in September 1986 and were slated to reach $10.70 in September 1988. By 1988, the best of the new contracts would recover a rate first negotiated in 1979 and implemented in 1981. Real wages would be far below the level reached at the beginning of the decade. And there was no longer an industry pattern. These contracts, which represent a tiny minority of the workers once covered by the pattern, no longer cover the same period – that is, Swift, Armour Dial, and Morrell are behind by a year and below the wage levels at Hormel and Oscar Mayer, which means that the former companies have a competitive advantage. Even within the two remaining single-company 'chain' agreements, not all of the plants at Hormel or Oscar Mayer receive the same rate. For example, workers performing slaughtering at Oscar Mayer's Perry, Iowa plant receive less than workers doing processing. These contracts were negotiated at the height of an economic recovery; given the domination of competitive rates in the industry, it is quite likely that another round of concessionary demands will emerge in the next recession.[34]

Local Unions in Competition

The competitive logic that shatters industry-wide patterns also tends to penetrate any company with duplicate operations or the ability to outsource production. Companies demanded that local unions make concessions, usually on working conditions or work rules, with the threat that if they didn't give in the work would go elsewhere. This tactic emerged in the auto industry after the Chrysler bailout. In April 1980 Ford announced it would close at least one of its six stamping plants to reduce excess capacity. Ford then asked UAW Local 420 at its Cleveland stamping plant to grant a number of work-rule and job description changes for both production and skilled workers. In this way, the Cleveland plant was given the opportunity to compete with the others to stay open. The International pushed for acceptance, and the local agreed.[35]

In the fall of 1981, Ford told workers at its Sheffield, Alabama aluminum casting plant, that it would close the plant if they did not agree to a 50% cut in wages and benefits. The casting could be done elsewhere. At the same time, Ford asked Local 182 at its Livonia, Michigan plant for a number of work-rule changes, making explicit the threat to move work away from the plant. Bill Grenham, financial secretary of the local, said: 'Management told us there were other manufacturers that want this job. They're looking to get it done for the lowest possible price.' At the same time, Ford won concessions from three Detroit-area UAW locals, awarding them work on new projects. In the case of two of the locals, Ford let it be known that it was considering sending the projects to Toyo Kogyo, a Japanese firm that is 25% Ford-owned.[36] The notion of bidding for future work then supplemented the threat of plant closings.

The UAW's Ford Council had voted not to reopen the national contract or make any concessions before its official expiration in September 1982. But Don Ephlin, then in charge of the UAW's Ford Department, announced that locals could reopen their own contracts. Further, the national agreement was renegotiated in February, seven months before its expiration. In the new agreement Ford promised not to use outsourcing to close any plants. But it retained the right to lay off workers or close departments because of outsourcing. Ford also got the lever it needed to continue forcing locals to reopen local contracts. In a letter to the UAW, Ford agreed to give locals a thirty-day notice of any 'major outsourcing action', during which time the local could 'propose any changes in work practices or any local deviations from the Collective Bargaining Agreement that might make it feasible for the company to continue to produce without being economically disadvantaged.'[37]

Bidding wars between plants thus became a regular feature of labor relations in the auto industry. As one UAW local official put it: 'The threat to close plants also helps these large corporations pressure different plants into a bid war against each other for their jobs. The corporations want to cut labor costs and the workers are giving without receiving any return value.'[38]

General Motors has accelerated the use of intraplant competition to whipsaw the UAW in recent years. GM used it to impose the Japanese-inspired 'team concept', which blurs the identity of the union and encourages workers to outproduce others doing the same work, on the Van Nuys, California assembly plant. Despite this threat, the UAW International has approved use of the team concept, which reached its ultimate expression in the Saturn contract signed with GM in 1985. Resistance to the team concept at the local level has been widespread and strong, however. In December 1985, the manager of the Van Nuys plant and the head of the union shop committee informed the workers that their plant might be closed in 1988 or 1989 if they did not accept the team concept. Their plant was in competition with GM's Norwood, Ohio plant, which also produced the Chevrolet Camaro. Resistance was still strong, but the team concept was accepted by a vote of 53%, with the proviso that it would not be implemented until the early 1990s, when the plant would produce a new car.[39]

In November 1986 GM asked UAW Local 594 in Pontiac, Michigan to reopen its contract and grant work-rule concessions. Without concessions, the company said, it would move the plant's medium-duty truck production to the Janesville, Wisconsin plant, which had already agreed to concessions. The company did not even promise to save the 2,500 Pontiac jobs involved if concessions were made. A company official told Local 594 President Don Douglas, 'We just want you to be in the race.' Local 594 refused to reopen the contract or to engage in competitive bidding with UAW members at Janesville. At that point, Governor James Blanchard intervened by sending the state's Commerce Director, Doug Ross, to pressure the union. When Douglas asked Ross why Local 594 should engage in such competitive bargaining, Ross replied: 'Everybody's doing it – [Chrysler's] Jefferson [plant], NUMMI, Janesville.' Ross further commented, 'There's obviously no solidarity within your union.' Douglas replied, 'We're trying to correct that.' Douglas believed that the UAW leadership, which was very close to the Blanchard administration, was involved in arranging Ross's visit: 'To go to the press and take on a big UAW local, Ross had to have clearance from Blanchard *and* the UAW International's endorsement.' Local 594 continued to refuse to open its contract until the national contract expired.[40]

By 1987 competitive bargaining on a local union basis was widespread. The *Wall Street Journal* noted that '12 of GM's 22 assembly plants now have "competitive" agreements, in most cases because the local unions agreed to reopen local contracts before their September 1987 expiration.' Most of the local contract changes involved reducing job classifications and changing other work rules. By 1987, Chrysler had negotiated 'modern operating agreements' at five of its remaining thirty-one plants.[41]

The trend toward competitive local bargaining on the basis of working conditions suggested that even wage bargaining might be put on a plant-by-plant basis. In these cases, the competition is not limited to plants within the same firm, but to those performing similar work in the industry, even where outsourcing is not likely. This has already occurred in meatpacking, where workers performing slaughtering in the higher wage companies are paid less than workers doing other jobs because of the existence of substandard plants in the industry. At Firestone Tire, four of the company's eight plants pay wages below the national contract, meaning, as the *Wall Street Journal* pointed out, that 'the company really doesn't have a national wage rate.'[42] Taking the collapse of pattern bargaining in steel one step further, the 1986 contract at Armco established different wage rates at most of the company's four plants. The Ashland, Kentucky plant accepted a wage freeze, two plants in Kansas City took wage and benefit cuts of $2.25 an hour, and the Baltimore plant took a $3.25-an-hour reduction.[43] In all likelihood, the Armco agreement will set a precedent for future bargaining in a number of industries that employ dual or multisourcing of their components or products.

Do Concessions Save Jobs?

The entire rationale for making concessions has been that they will, in one way or another, save jobs. This rationale has advanced from an argument for a temporary or exceptional modification of bargaining practices and contracts to a basic component of business unionist ideology for many union officials – committed as they are to shifting the union to a nonadversarial relationship with industry. However, few have put it as bluntly as UAW Vice President Don Ephlin, who announced that the role of the union in this era is to 'reverse the rapid decline of America's manufacturing industries and help restore US competitiveness where it counts, in the battle for markets and jobs.'[44] In this view, concessions, like protectionism or labor-management cooperation, are just one means to that end.

Top union leaders do not mean by such statements that they plan to save all existing jobs. Since they share the company's concern about being competitive, they accept that rationalizations, new technology and other labor-saving steps will be needed. Nevertheless, when selling a contract to the members who are worried sick about losing their jobs, this more businesslike view of saving *some* jobs by allowing the company to cut labor costs is seldom mentioned. The concessions, they argue, will save jobs. But do they?

By the mid-1980s the record indicated that the answer is no, concessions do not save jobs or plants. A study of twenty-two tire plants that made concessions between 1977 and 1981 showed that all but five of them closed anyway.[45] In 1983, the same year that it received concessions from the USW, US Steel announced plans to close one-third of its remaining steel capacity as well as various finishing and fabricating mills.[46] Chrysler, of course, closed several plants as part of the bailout operation and continued closing plants after returning to profitability.[47] In March 1987 Chrysler announced that it would buy AMC from Renault for $1 billion; in that same week, it also announced that it would close a parts plant in Indiana.[48]

In 1986 the UFCW published a list of twenty-five plants that had been closed in whole or in part after concessions had been granted and concluded that 'the evidence is overwhelming that concessions do not prevent the closing of meatpacking plants.'[49] In November 1986 General Motors announced the closing of nine plants and sections of two others. In February 1987 GM amended this by announcing a $10 billion cost-cutting effort. This would include the 'review' of additional older assemb-

ly plants. GM also stated that it would reduce the proportion of components produced in-house (now 70%) by using outsourcing – a move
that one industry analyst speculated could mean the closing or sale of
as many as twenty components plants in the near future.[50]

Seven years of concessionary bargaining did not save jobs at the industry level either. As Table 6 shows, the level of employment at the end
of 1986 had not returned to the prerecession levels of 1978 in any of the
major manufacturing industries in which concessions were widespread,
except for aircraft and trucking. Employment gains in the former are explained by Ronald Reagan's defense budget rather than by concessions.
In trucking the explanation lies in the growth of consumption (personal
and business, of domestic and imported goods) during the recovery and
that trucking is not as susceptible to labor-saving technology as most
other industries. What is indisputable is that the Teamsters' concessionary policy has not stopped the shrinkage of the number of workers
covered by the National Master Freight Agreement or the growth of a
nonunion sector.

Table 6
Production Workers by Industry (in Thousands)

Industry	12/1978	12/1982	12/1986	Change (1978-86)
Auto	832.7	491.7	652.2	-180.5
Steel	449.7	242.6	201.1	-248.6
Meatpacking	136.4	119.1	122.0	-14.4
Tires	92.8	70.2	63.7	-29.1
Oil Refining	103.2	93.7	75.6	-27.6
Chemicals	629.7	580.8	568.1	-61.6
Aircraft	307.8	296.1	339.4	+31.6
Coal Mining	213.8	158.2	138.6	-75.2
Trucking	1206.7	1055.3	1267.1	+60.4

Sources: US Bureau of Labor Statistics, *Supplement To Employment and Earnings*, vols. 1 and
2, March 1985; *Employment and Earnings*, January 1987.

One reason that concessions don't save jobs is that labor costs are seldom the cause of a corporation's or industry's financial problems. As
noted in Chapter 6, during the 1970s labor costs as a proportion of total
costs shrank in the economy as a whole and in manufacturing. On an industry-by-industry basis, the manufacturing industries listed in Table 6

saw labor costs decline or remain stable as a proportion of sales in 1976–80. Wages and benefits rose, but the cost of other industrial inputs rose faster.[51]

Business itself did not see concessions as a means of salvation. One steel industry executive told *Business Week,* 'I don't think you can get enough money out of wage cuts in the long run to save the industry.' Ernest Savoie, Ford's director of labor relations, was even more specific: 'The factors outside collective bargaining far outstrip the gains we can make in wages and benefits. We could cut labor costs in half and still be uncompetitive.'[52]

Indeed, labor costs are about 25% to 35% of total costs in most manufacturing industries where concessions have become common. Concessions to this or that firm make little real difference to a large multinational corporation. If concessions are to make a difference they must be generalized so that the entire cost structure of the economy is transformed. This was a goal that the Business Roundtable sought through legislation in the 1970s. In the 1980s, concessions and union cooperation in making other changes that reduce costs in the long run became central to capital's strategy for enhancing the overall competitiveness of the US economy. Ford's Savoie explained that what employers wanted was 'a bending of the labor cost trend line'. He went on to say that he saw the concessionary contracts of recent years as a 'transference from *we* vs. *they* to *us;* from adversarial to converging; from rigidity to flexibility; and from partisan to common interest.'[53]

Just Who Are 'We'?

The team concept, or the 'transference from *we* vs. *they* to *us*', became popular with management in the late 1970s and early 1980s for precisely the same reasons that they began to demand concessions: to involve the union in improving the competitive position of the company, the industry, and the nation in the interests of capital and at the expense of labor. Concessions relieve capital of burdens that it believes undermine its ability to increase profits. But what capital really seeks is an entire change in the rules. When it is able to rid itself of unions completely, it does so. When the union is entrenched, it looks for another way. The 'team concept' provides a permanent, institutional change in day-to-day company operations and labor relations. Concessions seek to tie worker compensation to company performance and to eliminate work rules that stand between the workers and management's will. The team approach by-passes such rules altogether. Its focus is not on wages or benefits per se, but on productivity, the exploitation of the workers' understanding of the production process, and above all the consciousness of the worker.

These sorts of programs go by various names: team concept, employee involvement, labor/management participation team, quality circles, and perhaps most commonly, quality of work life (QWL). Whatever the name, they share the purpose of getting workers to identify with company goals. Depending on the particular scheme, the union is either integrated into this process or marginalized altogether. The GM-UAW Saturn agreement of 1985 would have marginalized the union by explicitly granting work teams and various committees many of the functions usually associated with the union's shopfloor organization. The Saturn agreement was signed before the plant was built.[54] Obviously, it is more difficult to eliminate union functions where an entrenched union exists. So most QWL programs set up parallel or alternative structures that involve rank-and-file members, shopfloor union officials, and supervisors as part of the same team or group.

However, QWL programs are ultimately directed at the consciousness of the workers. They seek not simply to get union leaders to cooperate or to integrate the union, but to change how the workers perceive their own position in production and, hence, how they see unionism as well. In *Inside the Circle: A Union Guide to QWL*, Mike Parker described this process:

> Solidarity in the labor movement hinges on the concept of "we". QWL confuses and shifts the meaning of "we" in two ways. First… it encourages competition within the labor movement so that each local union sees another [local] as "they" rather than "we". Secondly, QWL works openly to include the employer as part of the worker's definition of "we". Once this shift is made, the employer has won the game, because almost everything else flows naturally from identifying with the employer.[55]

QWL programs do this by appealing to genuinely felt needs. Like concessions, they seem to offer a way to protect jobs by helping the employer. But unlike concessions they offer a positive-sounding approach. They are designed to appeal to the worker's need to be treated as an intelligent human being who understands what he or she is doing either individually or as part of a group. QWL programs promise to listen to the workers, to take their suggestions about production methods seriously, to give them 'a say'. The workers are encouraged to 'participate' in solving the company's problems. Because business unionism long ago rejected a working-class approach to enhancing workers' power on the shopfloor or in any way attempting to control destructive management policies through asserting union power in its traditional adversarial form, the field of 'worker participation' and industrial democracy was left to industrial psychologists and management theorists who gladly provided the tools to manipulate the desire of workers for recognition and power.

In reality, of course, under QWL programs as under the 'tough guy' school of labor-management relations, capital continues to command, management to manage, and supervisors to supervise. Ford's manual for its Employee Involvement Program, for example, states this explicitly: 'Managerial prerogatives: The ultimate decision, authority and responsibility is retained by management.... Supervisor role: Supervisory management still directs the tasks, however their role is changed to a participative-catalyst role.'[56]

The point of departure of QWL programs and the team concept is the language of industrial democracy and worker participation, but the goal is something quite different: acceptance by the workers of management's competitive imperative as a day-to-day guiding principle of behavior. Obviously, workers with that sort of consciousness would not see much point in 'arbitrary' union standards beyond the pension and social insurance provided for in the union contract. It is hardly surprising, then, that some of the most aggressive companies, like GM and USX, not to mention nonunion companies like IBM, are among the greatest proponents of QWL programs.

By the mid-1980s QWL programs were running into resistance because workers saw that relations in the workplace had not really changed. Management still ruled and took advice only when it paid off for the company. There was no sharing of results. Probably most crucial was that these programs, like concessions, did not stem the decline of jobs in the industries where they were most accepted. Team competition between high schools was one thing, but when your team lost in plant and departmental bidding wars, the price was your job and your future. The 'we' of yesterday dissolved once again as people saw what the real rules of the 'circle game' were.

The real nature of QWL and other fake worker participation programs is best revealed by their widespread use as a union avoidance technique. QWL programs are promoted by the Council for a Union Free Environment, a management antiunion organization, and by such union-busting consulting firms as Modern Management, Inc. An AFL-CIO study of union organizing drives conducted in 1982–83 showed that unions won only one out of twelve elections at manufacturing firms with QWL-type programs. Charles McDonald, head of the AFL-CIO organizing department, summed up this experience: 'The one company "benefit" that drastically affected union organizing drives was the quality of work life plan, particularly in manufacturing establishments.'[57]

In addition to QWL programs, there has been another important variant on the theme of institutionalized labor-management cooperation. In this strategy, management invites the union to share power in company decision making – though in fact such 'sharing' is illusory. These plans do not attempt to go around the structure of the union as QWL does, but to make the union as a whole a partner in the business. The Chrysler bailout involved some elements of this strategy by including UAW President Doug Fraser on the Board of Directors, granting the union the right to sit on joint committees which would discuss various problems, and by holding out the promise of some control through stock ownership. This experience may have played a part in shifting the thinking of the UAW leadership from its brief flirtation with anticorporate politics and the Progressive Alliance toward a new level of cooperation with industry leaders, but few would argue that any real power changed hands as a result.

A more instructive example of this approach to corporate problem solving was the 'power-sharing' scheme that emerged at Eastern Airlines as a result of years of industrial conflict. In December 1983, after years of sharp conflict and heavy-handed management under the leadership of CEO Frank Borman, Eastern Airlines reached an agreement with its three unions, the Air Line Pilots Association, the Transport Workers Union (representing flight attendants), and the Machinists. The unions granted wage concessions and the promise of a 5% increase in productivity, and in return were given one seat each on the company board and stock, which was to reach 25% of the company's total by the end of 1984. In the beginning the stock was held in trust by each union. The plan also included a QWL-type arrangement at the workplace level. Unlike most such plans, however, the Machinists also negotiated a 'contracting-in committee', which was able to bring work previously done outside the company under the Machinists' jurisdiction.

But the limits of the agreement soon became apparent. Information received by union representatives on the board was ruled confidential, the Machinists' stock trustee was replaced by a judge who declared he was using the stock in the interests of the union rather than the stockholders, and the agreed-to rewards for cost-saving suggestions were not granted. Eastern even reneged on the wage level recovery that was part of the concessionary agreement. Neither the concessions nor the innovations ended Eastern's chronic financial problems.

Most important, the unions gained no real power over company policies. P. J. Baicich and W. R. Brown, two IAM activists, assessed the reality of Eastern's Board of Directors under this setup in *Labor Notes*. Noting that IAM representative Charles Bryan pressed the union's point of view at board meetings, they wrote: 'However, a rump executive board was created which bypassed the employee representatives. Moreover, much of the information that the worker representatives did get was confidential and could not be released to the public or the union membership. Thus union representatives were as much captive as they were active on the board.'[58]

In 1986 virulently antiunion Texas Air Corporation bought Eastern. The Machinists union attempted to use its stock to prevent the takeover, but the new court-appointed stock trustee abstained on the vote on the Texas Air bid at the November 1986 stockholders meeting. As Baicich and Brown put it, 'So much for workers' power through stock ownership.'[59]

For many labor leaders, the idea of power sharing seemed to be inspired by various joint industrial decision-making schemes that had been established in Western Europe's economically strongest countries where the level of unionization was very high and labor-based Social Democratic parties frequently held political power. Here, pale imitations of these structures were applied to ailing firms by declining unions in the hope of accomplishing something like the Europeans had achieved during the height of the postwar boom. The Chrysler experiment did not evolve into an example of much of anything. The Eastern Airlines plan had largely collapsed under its own weight even before Texas Air took over and terminated it.

In spite of the disastrous effect of concessions on union bargaining power, the clear intent of QWL programs as a 'union substitute', and the complete failure of the 'power-sharing' approach to alter real power relations one iota, much of the US labor leadership continues to hold out labor-management cooperation or nonadversarial labor relations as some sort of alternative to the collapse of the old system of collective bargaining based on pattern bargaining supported by government regulation. In fact, the popularity of nonadversarial labor relations reflects the conversion of a large number of union leaders to the competitive logic of the business enterprise, a fact that has given rise to the term *enterprise unionism*. Enterprise unionism differs from company unionism in that the union involved is still controlled and administered independently of the employer. Its identity with the goals of the employer is less an ideological preference for business norms than an adaptation to the effects of intensified competition in a global economy. But in the end, it signals the decline of industrial unionism.

9

The Crisis of Industrial Unionism

Labor organization largely reflects the structure of capitalism itself at a given time. From the early organizations of artisans in colonial days to the AFL of the 1880s, craft unions reflected the structure of the American economy in its transition toward industrial capitalism. Local and regional markets gave way to a national market only by the end of the century, and new industries drew on existing craft labor for their workforces. As workers attempted to band together for protection, they too drew on existing forms of organization. As the organization of production itself changed, particularly under the influence of Frederick W. Taylor and the 'scientific management' school and as markets became national, workers sought new forms of organization. The Knights of Labor, with its mixture of craft unions, proto-industrial unions, and city-wide organizations, attempted to bring all workers under one banner with a sort of general unionism.

To be effective, unions had to have the power to impose their will on the employers. As we have seen in Chapter 8, this usually meant organizing the entire relevant labor market. Where production was based on craft methods, the organization of a craft union might be sufficient to give labor this power. Similarly, so long as local labor markets were the norm, the standards imposed by the union had only to be local in scope. But as industries and the employers that composed them became national and the importance of craft labor to the production process diminished, new forms of organization were needed to underwrite labor's power.

For most of the twentieth century, the historic direction of organized labor in the US has been toward industrial unionism. Around the turn of the century, a small number of industrial unions took shape in coal mining, metal mining in the West, and the garment industry. The famous attempt by Eugene V. Debs to form an industrial union on the railroads went down to defeat in the Pullman strike of 1894. The Industrial Workers of the World attempted to organize all workers into one big union, with affiliates organized along industrial lines. The legendary radical syndicalism of the 'Wobblies', as they were known, inspired hundreds of thousands of workers to fight for industrial organization. But the IWW failed to achieve a stable, organized base. Following World War One, William Z. Foster, then a radical syndicalist who believed in working within the mainstream of labor, led mammoth organizing drives in meatpacking and in steel. But violent resistance from the employers, racial divisions among the workers, and the cowardice and disunity of the AFL unions led to the defeat of these struggles.

Not until the CIO established stable organizations did industrial unionism become a central and influential part of the economic land-scape. The success of the CIO led to the transformation of many AFL craft unions into semi-industrial unions. During the 1930s and 1940s unions such as the Teamsters, the Machinists, the International Brother-hood of Electrical Workers, and the Carpenters aggressively organized factory workers on an industrial basis. For many unions, particularly those in the building trades, the industrially organized members re-mained a second-class jurisdiction in a craft union. However, some unions like the Teamsters and Machinists came to resemble the in-dustrial unions of the CIO. By the 1960s public employee unions such as the AFT and AFSCME organized beyond their original craft bases and also came to resemble industrial organizations. Other craft unions took conscious steps toward becoming industrial unions when they merged with other unions in the same industry. The merger of several craft or-ganizations to form the United Transportation Union in 1969 was a step toward industrial unionism on the railroads. The formation of the American Postal Workers Union in 1971 was a similar step in the post-al service.

The AFL-CIO did not pressure competing unions to merge, however, and its official policy specifically avoided favoring industrial over craft organization. Nevertheless, such mergers did occur – for example, the 1968 merger of the Amalgamated Meat Cutters and the United Packing-house Workers. Indeed, even though the merged union had agreed not to make craft versus industrial unionism an issue, it seemed that in-dustrial unionism had carried the day. The only well-organized in-dustries that maintained craft organizational and bargaining practices by the end of the 1970s were the building trades, the railroads, and the airlines. In the later two cases, the craft structure of bargaining had vir-tually been written into the Federal Railway Labor Act, which deter-mined the rules for representation in both those industries. Industrial

Phelps Dodge strikers: a pro forma corporate campaign failed to draw the line against the corporate offensive.

unionism seemed the irreversible wave of the future.

But the vast changes in the structure of the economy that accelerated in the 1970s and 1980s not only weakened unionism in general, but also created serious problems for the future of industrial unionism. The match of union and employer that had been a feature of pattern bargaining, for example, changed with the rise of conglomerates and as companies changed hands. These changes fundamentally affected corporations' view of their comparative position. Finally, the very policies through which many unions attempted to stem or reverse their membership decline contributed to the weakening of industrial unionism. This did not mean a return to craft unionism. What began to emerge by the mid-1980s was a formless type of general unionism that conformed more to the business union bureaucracy's desire for mere organizational survival than to any economic strategy or industrial rationale. It was an organizational response that failed to address the basic questions of power that underlay the crisis of unionism.

From Industrial Unionism to General Unionism

Because of the changes in industry and ownership structures, union mergers seem the logical counterpart to corporate behavior, while organizing drives are obviously on the agenda. But the organizing and merger policies of a growing number of unions for the past decade have created organizations that have less and less relationship to their original industrial jurisdictions and none in particular to the new shape of industry. Seeking to expand their financial and staff resources, their influence in the AFL-CIO nationally and at the state and local levels, and their political clout, many unions organize or absorb groups of workers in industries with little or no economic connection to the union's current membership. These unions are thus increasingly changing from industrial unions to general unions. They have become multijurisdictional organizations bargaining in several industries without significant strength in any but – perhaps – their original jurisdiction. In some cases this policy of random growth actually increases disunity within an industry.

Many large unions have attempted to maintain their size or even grow by absorbing any group of workers that seems organizable. Chief among these are the Teamsters, the Service Employees International Union, the Communications Workers, the United Food and Commercial Workers, and the United Auto Workers, but most unions pick up new members whenever they can. The primary target of most of their organizing efforts is the state and local public sector. Often, several unions compete to organize the same group of public workers. Such was the case in the highly destructive 1985–86 fight between AFSCME, CWA, the National Union of Hospital and Health Care Workers, and the Teamsters over various groups of Ohio state employees.[1] Much of this is not really new organizing at all, but the absorption of an existing public employees' association.

The result of this focus on public workers and their associations is not industrial unionism in state and local employment, but the institutionalization of fragmented bargaining in a growing number of states and cities. From the standpoint of industrial unionism, it would have made more sense for the AFL-CIO to establish AFSCME as the industrial union in that jurisdiction and to have launched a major national organizing drive in the 1960s when public workers were joining unions and the momentum of the civil rights movement promised a powerful alliance. Instead, AFSCME was largely left to its own devices, and other unions entered this relatively easy field of organizing. Some of the locals of other unions, such as CWA in New Jersey and SEIU in Massachusetts have turned out to be more imaginative and militant than AFSCME. In fact, AFSCME has lost bargaining groups to other unions from time to time because its day-to-day practices fell far short of its generally progressive posture. Nevertheless, the result of the multiunion race to recruit public workers has been labor disunity in many bargaining situations.

In the 1980s this fragmentation was one factor in the decline of the percentage of organized public workers and the same sort of concessionary bargaining that swept the private sector. The proportion of state and local workers belonging to unions reached its height in 1975, when 50% were organized. By 1982 only 45.7% were organized as the number of state and local employees in unions dropped by nearly half a million. The bulk of this drop came after 1980.[2] The 1975–76 turning point is probably related to the concessionary posture taken by AFSCME in the New York City bailout crisis of those years – in effect, the Chrysler of the public sector. Thus, the focus on getting public workers into private sector unions has not stemmed a decline in unionization. This irony is explained by the fact that many 'organizing drives' simply absorb existing associations. Thus, the growth of SEIU, AFSCME, and CWA does not change the total number of organized workers, it simply changes their affiliation.

The actual number of workers newly organized annually by AFL-CIO unions in both public and private sectors is small. According to the AFL-CIO's organizing department, AFL-CIO unions organized about 80,000 workers a year in the mid-1980s. They were also losing about 20,000 a year through decertification elections, leaving a net gain of about 60,000. Even when unions cooperate in organizing drives, such as the joint

UFCW/SEIU drive at Beverly and the multiunion effort at Blue Cross/Blue Shield, their efforts lack an industrial or jurisdictional rationale. For example, the nine unions involved in the Blue Cross drive, which targets 28,000 clerical workers in twenty cities included the Steelworkers, the Electrical Workers (IUE), UFCW, CWA, and AFSCME (in a rare move outside the public sector). Over 3,000 Blue Cross clerical workers in Michigan are already represented by the UAW.[3] Thus, if the campaign is successful, these clerical workers will be represented by a bewildering variety of unions under a patchwork of local contracts rather than a national contract signed by one union with the perspective of organizing insurance workers. The workers involved will have no means of common action or communication. They will be in minority jurisdictions, and their needs will have low priority in unions with no particular expertise or base in their industry.

The distorting effect of random organizing on industrial unionism is probably secondary to that of the union merger movement of the past decade or so. The AFL-CIO once regarded mergers cautiously, but union mergers are now its preferred strategy for ensuring survival and/or growth in difficult times. The AFL-CIO's 1985 report *The Changing Situation of Workers and Their Unions* devotes more space to the question of mergers than to any other question. It notes that due to membership losses about fifty AFL-CIO affiliates had less than 50,000 members and another thirty had under 100,000. These unions often have the least ability to grow, according to the report. Mergers are the logical solution.[4] Kevin Kistler, an AFL-CIO regional director, put it frankly for the *Wall Street Journal:* 'It's a hell of a lot quicker and cheaper to add members through a merger than it is to organize new members.'[5]

The Federation's official approach to mergers is sensible enough. The statement in *The Changing Situation of Workers and Their Unions* sums it up clearly:

> Accordingly, both active AFL-CIO encouragement of mergers and guidelines as to appropriate and inappropriate mergers deserve a high priority. For example, mergers are more likely to be effective if the partners share a community of interest either because of a substantial overlap in the industries in which their members work, or because a substantial portion of their members work in industries that are vertically integrated, or because a substantial portion of their members work for a common, conglomerate employer.[6]

Although the Federation became aggressive about mergers, it was considerably less insistent that affiliates follow these guidelines. A brief look at trends in union mergers shows a drift away from any industrial community of interest.

There were ninety-two national union mergers in the US between

1955 and 1984. Mergers occurred at an accelerating rate over the years. Thus, of these ninety-two mergers, forty-one took place between 1975 and 1984, and twenty-four occurred between 1980 and 1984. Through the mid-1970s, the vast majority of these mergers made some sort of industrial or craft sense in that the unions involved had clearly met the Federation's criteria. In the second half of the 1970s, however, mergers became increasingly random, reflecting the tendency of unions like SEIU, UAW, UFCW, CWA, and others to pick up smaller unions regardless of jurisdiction. Some examples include merger of the Mailers Union into the International Typographical Union, the merging of the Distributive Workers of America (District 65) with the UAW, the Jewelry Workers with SEIU, the Barbers and Beauticians and the Insurance Workers with the UFCW, the Brick and Clay Workers with the Aluminum Workers, and the Production, Service and Sales Union with the Hotel Employees and Restaurant Employees. Including the absorption of public employee associations by private sector unions, fully fifteen out of thirty mergers conducted in 1979–84 pointed in the direction of general unionism rather than industrial unionism. Almost all of the mergers since 1984 have been of the general union type.[7]

Some mergers come technically close to the AFL-CIO's official guidelines because they involve overlapping jurisdictions, but in reality they contribute to the trend away from industrial unionism. The UFCW is a good example, having been created in 1979 by merger of the Amalgamated Meat Cutters and the Retail Clerks International Union. The Retail Clerks' main base was among grocery store clerks, while the Meat Cutters represented grocery store butchers, so there was an industrial overlap in the retail grocery business. Further, the bargaining practices of both retail clerks and butchers in grocery were similar in that wages were locally and regionally determined rather than based on an industry-wide standard.

The Amalgamated Meat Cutters, however, had been the result of a 1968 merger with the United Packinghouse Workers. Both unions represented packinghouse workers, and the Amalgamated that merged with the Retail Clerks in 1979 had come a long way from its craft origins among retail butchers. It had organized packing and processing plants as these opened in areas away from the traditional strength of the UPW. In terms of bargaining traditions, the Amalgamated after the 1968 merger was split between local craft bargaining and craft structures and many of the traditions of industrial unionism that it inherited in meatpacking, including national pattern bargaining. The Retail Clerks Union, though no longer restricted to clerks, still conducted its bargaining on a local market (low-wage, and sometimes sweetheart) basis in the tradition of craft unionism. The 1979 merger, in spite of an overlap in the grocery business, produced a multijurisdictional union with conflicting traditions and methods of bargaining. In the UFCW, packinghouse workers, who had composed about 40% of the Amalgamated Meat Cutters, accounted for only 10% of the UFCW. As the number of organized packinghouse workers dropped in the 1980s from 117,000 in 1979 to 88,000 in 1984, their proportion of UFCW membership declined further to about 8%. Politically, the UFCW was dominated by officials from the Retail Clerks who had no experience in conducting pattern bargaining for an industrial union or determining national contract strategy.[8]

The packinghouse contracts inherited by the UFCW were a tiny portion of the approximately 20,000 contracts administered by that union. The ability of rank-and-file meatpackers or their local union leaders to influence such an organization was greatly reduced. Because of the dual nature of the Amalgamated, the older style of local market bargaining on a semi-craft basis dominated the experience and thinking of the leadership of the UFCW at all levels. While no one would admit it, the 1981 strategy of concessionary bargaining looked more like the sort of competitive bargaining the Retail Clerks had used in local labor markets for decades than like the national master contract bargaining once prevalent in meatpacking.

The UFCW merger carried its tendency toward general unionism further than many by proposing to merge local unions as well. Between 1979 and the end of 1984 some 2,100 locals had merged to form 660 locals, and the process was to continue until the end of the decade, according to UFCW spokesman Allen Zack. The rationale for merging locals of workers in diverse industries was purely administrative and financial.[9] In practice, this meant merging packinghouse locals into much larger locals of retail clerks, insurance employees, barbers and whoever else the UFCW had picked up. Thus, packinghouse workers no longer had a political structure of their own above the plant stewards' organization. The merged locals were inevitably dominated by the officials and the concerns of retail clerks. This was another step toward suffocating the industrial traditions in meatpacking and left the packinghouse workers a tiny, voiceless minorities in giant locals.[10]

Like most multijurisdictional unions, the UFCW had national committees or departments to oversee the day-to-day business of the various industries or crafts. Thus, the National Packing Committee was formed after the merger; it was headed by UFCW Vice President Lewie Anderson. Additionally, there were company-wide 'chain' committees at the larger companies. The UFCW liked to claim that these committees were autonomous, but they clearly did nothing not approved by President William Wynn. The letter announcing the 1981 concessionary strategy to locals containing packinghouse workers, for example, went out over

Wynn's signature, and the policy it contained was clearly developed by the UFCW's top leaders.

The ability of packinghouse members to influence such strategic decisions was further diminished as the Packing Committee and company chain committees became decreasingly representative of meatpacking. The Packing Committee, like the company chain committees, was composed of officials from local unions that contained meatpacking members. Because many locals had been merged, a large number of these officials were from the retail grocery section, since they dominated these new general union locals. The influence of packinghouse workers and even of the few former packinghouse officials in the hierarchy like Lewie Anderson, was further diminished by the power of the UFCW Regions over locals. The Regions were run by directors appointed by President Wynn and were loyal to that wing of the top leadership. In the conflicts rumored among top leaders, the meatpackers almost always lost. Submerged in locals they didn't control, increasingly denied direct representation on the Packing Committee, their only form of national communication, the packinghouse workers became a fragmented minority with declining influence. By mid-1987 rumors were circulating that Wynn was displeased with Packinghouse Director Lewie Anderson's handling of a number of strikes that dragged on in 1987 (IBP in Dakota City, Nebraska; Cudahy in Cudahy, Wisconsin; John Morrell in Sioux City, Iowa) and planned to fire or demote him. The bargaining for meatpacking plants would be turned over to the UFCW's regional directors, ending all pretense of bargaining on an industrial basis in meatpacking.[11]

In general, mergers of unions diminish democratic practices and remove the membership even further from any influence over union affairs. Gary Chaison described this process in his comprehensive study of union mergers from 1890 to 1984:

> When there is a high degree of integration in either an amalgamation or absorption, more powerful and centralized governing structures tend to emerge. These can reduce membership participation because of the large committees and meetings, the creation of additional layers of government between top officers and the membership, and the increased time and money needed to run for higher level office. Also staff specialists, rather than member volunteers, might begin to play a greater role in decision making within the union.

In other words, previously bureaucratic unions become even more so. Not surprisingly, the salaries of the top officials tend to rise as well.[12]

Longtime advocate of union reform Herman Benson took note of this problem in the July 1987 issue of *Union Democracy Review*. Noting the trend toward diversified membership, he wrote:

> When members of each union shared common experiences, they readily un-
> derstood their common grievances and common aspirations. Meatpackers
> had their own Packinghouse Workers union. Seamen were divided into
> several unions; but in each, seamen were dominant. Now packinghouse
> workers are an atomized minority engulfed in a general food and retail union.
> Of the 25,000 members of the National Maritime Union, only 10,000 are un-
> licensed deep sea sailors, once the main base of the union. Opposition can-
> didates for office in the NMU find it hard to reach the shoreside members of
> their own union who work in factories.[13]

The more disparate and dispersed the separate pieces, the more un-
controllable becomes the national officialdom and its full-time staff,
which remains the only coherent centralizing force in a sprawling institution. As it becomes increasingly difficult for a diversified membership to exercise their hypothetical sovereign right to control their union,
the need becomes more urgent to strengthen the institutions and practices that make for democratic government in unions.

In the case of mergers that involve a union in new industries, increased bureaucratization is not just the result of more and bigger committees. Multijurisdictional organizations are necessarily multiagenda
organizations as well. That is, they must deal with the specific problems
of workers in diverse industries with different economic contours and
problems. Meetings of merged locals must deal with more subjects or
suppress the discussion of some. Union conventions become more ceremonial as the actual amount of business grows. Bureaucratic norms increase because it becomes convenient to leave more things to staff experts, limit the scope of discussion or of bargaining, or to insulate
seemingly complex decisions from the growing number of pressure
groups in the union.

The inherent difficulty of maintaining bureaucratic control over a
greater number of jurisdictions has also led to what might be termed the
'Teamsterization' of the American labor movement. That is, increasingly heavy-handed methods of direct control replace normal bureaucratic
procedures when 'trouble' pops up within the membership. Previously
'clean' unions turn more to direct and even violent means of control. A
recent example was the fate of the New Directions reform caucus based
in Region 5 of the UAW. When Jerry Tucker announced that he would
oppose the UAW Administration caucus's candidate for director of
Region 5, he was summarily fired from his job as assistant regional director for breaking caucus discipline. Tucker lost his election at the 1986
UAW convention by less than two-tenths of a vote (324.416 to 324.577).
Protestations at the convention were met with the intimidation of

delegates by International reps and various pro-administration officials. A subsequent investigation revealed irregularities in the case of some pro-administration delegates. Herman Benson, protesting the departure from democratic norms, described the response of the UAW leadership: 'The sad fact in Region 5 is that the leadership's main response has been to circle the wagons in defense of the power structure. According to recent reports, overzealous guardians of the official stockade in St. Louis have physically harassed active Tucker supporters.'[14] Not only were Tucker's supporters attacked and beaten, but Administration supporters used racial slurs against Black members of the New Directions caucus. In spite of protests sent to UAW President Owen Bieber, none of the officers involved in the violence were reprimanded.[15]

Another sign of increased heavy-handedness in union affairs has been the rise in the number of trusteeships. All international and national unions have some provision for placing locals in trusteeship – supposedly only in cases of financial problems or election fraud. In the past, dictatorially run unions like the Teamsters or the pre-1972 United Mine Workers used trusteeships as a means of political control. Most industrial unions had sufficiently effective political machines and bureaucratic procedures to make trusteeships unnecessary. But the expansion of jurisdictions and hence problems has tested the political and procedural skills and energy of the top officials of these increasingly multijurisdictional unions. The shortcut of trusteeship becomes a growing temptation.

The UFCW first turned to trusteeships to stem the tide of local concessions at the end of the 1970s. More recently, trusteeship has been used to quell opposition to the unwritten policies of the central leadership. The trusteeship of Local P-9 in the midst of its strike at Hormel's Austin, Minnesota plant was imposed to quell resistance to concessions. The UFCW also put a British Columbia local into trusteeship for allegedly organizing workers outside its jurisdiction. Local 2000, which had been a Meatcutters local prior to the 1979 merger, was invaded by armed UFCW reps from the US for the crime of organizing grocery clerks. This incident was part of a larger struggle between the UFCW's two Canadian regions. Region 18 had been the Amalgamated Meatcutters' region before the merger, while Region 19 came from the Retail Clerks. The leaders of Region 18 were generally critical of UFCW President William Wynn's approach to concessions. Along with the British Columbia trusteeship, Wynn unilaterally appointed a new regional director. This in turn led the Newfoundland Fishermen to withdraw from the UFCW. Earle McCurdy, secretary-treasurer of the Newfoundland Fishermen's local told the US publication *Labor Notes* that there were basic differences in union philosophy between his members and the leaders of the

UFCW: 'The UFCW sees trade unionism as a business. We see trade unionism as a democratic people's organization.'[16]

Trusteeships appeared in other multijurisdictional unions in 1986–87. The Hotel Employees and Restaurant Employees Union placed in trusteeship a Los Angeles local in which candidates critical of the union leadership were involved. The SEIU placed Local 250 in the San Francisco Bay Area under trusteeship after taking over the direction of a strike at Kaiser-Permanente, a large health maintenance organization. The SEIU cut off strike benefits and ended the strike in December 1986. International union officials never left the offices of Local 250 and in January 1987 it was officially placed in trusteeship.[17]

General unionism also weakens the union's ability to resist concessions and maintain standard wages, benefits and conditions. In dealing with more employers with diverse problems it becomes easier to take the line of least resistance. Today that approach leads to fragmented, competitive bargaining. In the case of merged unions or those that grow by picking up public employee associations, different habits and styles of bargaining are incorporated into various levels of leadership and the likelihood of a coherent response to employer pressure is diminished.

The experience of the UFCW illustrates this point. In this case, the combination of a multi-industry membership and a craft tradition of local bargaining reenforced each other and led away from genuine industrial unionism regardless of the economic rationale for the merger. The UFCW came to represent insurance workers, barbers, workers in food-processing plants other than meatpacking, and retail workers in a number of different branches of retail trade, in addition to retail grocery and meatpacking workers. Many of the other groups the UCFW has picked up or organized since 1980 have traditionally bargained on a local or regional basis. For example, the UFCW represents workers in some of Campbell Soup's processing plants but does not bargain there on a chain or pattern basis.

The retail grocery business has long been dominated by national or superregional chains. Yet neither the Retail Clerks nor the UFCW has ever attempted to impose national standards, let alone national contracts, on these chains in spite of the extensive whipsawing practiced by the major employers. Instead, the UFCW has generally taken a cooperative line in the grocery industry and has participated in a Joint Labor Management Committee along with the Teamsters since 1974. By 1986 the situation had gotten so bad that union appointed a new director of collective bargaining, William Olwell. Olwell made a few noises about a new militancy but has indicated that the UFCW's approach will continue to be fragmented bargaining. In May 1986 he told *Supermarket News:* 'We don't have a national picture as to what we want. We can't say we want 12% across the board for each year of the contract, in all areas of the country. It doesn't work that way. We have to look at each local situation.'[18] Olwell was speaking of the grocery negotiations of 1986, but it was clear that this view increasingly dominated UFCW practice.

In spite of gaining 64,000 members through mergers since 1980, the UFCW has continued to decline in size. While not stopping the UFCW's shrinkage, this method of organizing has contributed to the decline of industrial unionism by creating a multi-industry union and by accepting or even promoting a local-labor-market, plant-by-plant system of bargaining. The trend toward general unionism among unions with a craft tradition of bargaining (such as UFCW and SEIU) converges all too well with the fragmentation of industrial pattern bargaining among former industrial unions (such as the UAW, CWA, USW, IBT, IUE and HERE) that are moving toward general unionism in their own way.

Defenders of this approach frequently argue that it is better to see a group of workers organized into a general union, or a union in another industry, than to see them go unorganized – a point that is certainly correct. Similarly, it is unreasonable and unrealistic to expect a shrinking union like the ITU to stick it out alone. The union that might make the most industrial sense to merge with may not offer the best deal. Or there may be a history of rivalry that makes merger seem impossible. But there is no need to assume that hospital workers in a particular place could only have been organized by the SEIU and never by 1199, or that the insurance workers had no place to go but the UFCW. There is nothing in the structure of the economy that commands the UAW to organize university employees rather than the thousands of unorganized workers employed by the auto industry's parts suppliers, or the Teamsters to recruit public employees rather than nonunion truckers. The growing nonunion sectors of most major industries attest to the choices available. In fact, these situations are typical products of a labor movement that has lost its bearings and has no strategic outlook.

A consequence and/or cause of this lack of direction is that decisions are made solely on the basis of narrow, bureaucratic considerations. That is, the desire of one union's leadership to organize a particular group of workers is seldom based on strategic considerations or even the belief that it has enough economic clout in a given industry to set a standard of any sort. Random organizing promises to improve the workers' situation for the moment, but offers no guidance for achieving further advances or even for holding on to past gains in an era of crisis and change. It is a nickel-and-dime business unionism which sees unions as service organizations and bargaining 'strength' as a question of internal organizational resources.

The leadership, therefore, gives priority to the financial considerations that underlie this service approach. Such a service organization achieves financial growth primarily by recruiting members. What they do or where they fit into the economy is secondary. In its more sophisticated manifestation, this view emphasizes that labor gains will really come through political action (electing Democrats) and legislation (plant closing laws, labor law reform, industrial policy, or protectionism). Politics, legislation and elections, however, are likewise reduced to questions of financial and organizational resources, and little notice is taken of the fact that labor's political position has become ever more tenuous in spite of the growing use of labor money and technology in politics.

By 1987 the practice of American business unionism emphasized preserving organizational strength through general unionism and accepting the competitive imperative of the employers in bargaining. In a handful of cases, this resulted in larger organizations with less bargaining power. More typically, it produced unions that declined in both size and power. In either case, it has left the US labor movement with no clear line of advance.

The New Proletarians

The shift from industrial employment to private service sector employment reflects the growth of new industries on a scale that equals the rise of mass production industry after the turn of the century. By far the greatest challenge facing unionism today is the organization of these new or expanded industries. However, business unionism treats them as though they were a passing phenomenon or an amorphous mass of employees requiring no special organizations. No new industrial unions have been launched or contemplated in the growing service industries. Unions with a base in sectors such as retail trade have sought growth in other areas. The AFL-CIO has often attempted to save traditional industries through concessions, QWL programs, protectionism, or industrial policy schemes. But even if such devices could save basic industry in the US, they will not stop the shift toward service work.

The long-term trend of capitalism toward increased service employment is inherent in capitalism's need to bring every form of human endeavor under the control of capital and the rule of profit. But at different stages of development the specific sort of services brought into the marketplace has varied with the contours of the economy. The accelerated growth of low-paying service jobs in the last two decades has been a result of two specific developments: the expansion of the administrative bureaucracy of US corporations in their function as world headquarters for multinational operations, and the continued subordination to large units of capital of services once performed by individuals or small businesses.

In the decade of the 1970s, 13.4 million of the 19.6 million new jobs created, or 68%, were in the private service sector. In the first half of the 1980s, all of the new jobs created (that is, all net job growth) were in service industries, while goods-producing industries lost jobs in absolute numbers. Thus, from 1960 to 1985, the proportion of jobs in the goods-producing sector of the economy fell from 38% to 26%. These figures underplay the shift from industrial production work to non-goods-producing functions because they do not include the rise of nonproduction jobs in the manufacturing sector. Nonproduction jobs as a proportion of employment in manufacturing firms rose from 16.4% in 1947 to 28.2% in 1977.[19]

A great deal of this shift, in the economy as a whole and within manufacturing, can be explained by the growth of US corporations and their position as multinationals. As bureaucracies commanding billions of dollars in income and assets that direct operations all over the world, they have created a demand for a wide variety of technical, professional and administrative personnel on a scale equal to many governments. In addition to those they employ directly as part of their headquarters function, US multinationals draw on a vast number of smaller firms for various kinds of services.

In occupational terms, the proportion of managerial, professional, technical, sales, and administrative support employees in the civilian labor force (excluding teachers, nurses, and retail sales clerks) rose from 38% in 1970 to 43% in 1980. The number of employees in administrative support work alone grew by 4.4 million in those years. The number of executive managers and administrators nearly doubled to over 10 million. 'Business services' became an industrial classification by itself. In 1958 business services employed only 656,000 people. By 1970 it employed 1.7 million. By 1980 that figure had grown to 2.4 million and by 1984 to 3.6 million. What defines business services as an industry is not the provision of any particular service, but the fact that they serve other businesses. Not surprisingly, the fastest growing categories within business services are computer and data processing services, which grew by 250% from 1974 to 1984. Between 1984 and 1995, business services are expected to produce another 2.6 million jobs.[20] For all practical purposes, these 3.6 million employees work for the nation's corporations as professionals, clerical workers (full-time and temporary), computer programmers and operators, designers, artists, maintenance personnel, etc. If we add these employees to the approximately 14.5 million nonproduction and supervisory workers in private business, we get about 19 million people who directly serve the bureaucratic functions of Corporate America.

While a large percentage of the employees who support these global headquarters functions are poorly paid clerical workers, the growing number of highly paid administrative, executive, technical and professional people directly and indirectly associated with this function has created a new, affluent upper-middle class. It includes all kinds of professionals such as lawyers, architects, engineers, accountants, and others whose services depend on corporate-generated demand. The expansion of financial services in the epoch of the arbitrageur is an obvious example. More spectacular than the numerical growth of this group has been the rise in their incomes. For example, while the proportion of non-production employees in manufacturing grew by 72% from 1947 to 1977, the overall annual cost of corporate bureaucracy rose by 1200% in the same period.[21] The result has been a growth in the proportion of affluent families; families making over $41,000 a year composed 15% of the population in 1978 but 18% in 1982. Much of this affluence reflects the increase in the number of families with two working members, but the increase in discretionary income is no less real. Eighteen percent of the civilian population in 1982 was, after all, more than 41 million people and the $41,000 figure was the bottom cutoff not an average.[22]

The growth in low-paying service and sales jobs is in fact partly a function of the growth of this affluent middle class. Put simply, affluent Yuppies are the consumers of many of these services, which are no longer organized as personal or domestic services, but businesses in themselves. In 1981 *Business Week* argued that this phenomenon was creating not only a bipolar income structure but bipolar markets as well. One market for the affluent, described by *Business Week* as a 'vast market for luxury products and services, from travel and designer clothes, to posh restaurants, home computers, and fancy sports cars.' *Business Week* expected this market to be large enough to sustain the growth of low-paid service and retail jobs. At the low end of the income scale is another market characterized by K-Marts selling low-priced, often imported products to low-income families. This market, too, employs large numbers of low-paid workers.[23]

In *Prisoners of the American Dream* Mike Davis points out that the growth of upscale markets and their low-paying service jobs spell bad news for America's traditional mass production industries, and none more than the auto industry. Yuppies buy Audis, Honda Accords, and BMWs, not Chevies or Fords. Low-paid service workers don't buy new cars, domestic or foreign. Using AFL-CIO figures for 1960–75, Davis shows that the middle-income strata, the traditional upper working- and middle-class market for mass production industry in the US declined, while both the higher- and lower-income strata grew. The study cited above shows that the trend revealed in the AFL-CIO figures continued into the 1980s. From 1978 to 1982 the number of families making less than $17,000 rose from 30% to 40% of total households; these families contained 92 million people. Included in this downwardly mobile group were those below the official poverty line. They rose as a percentage of the population from 11.5% to 15%, or 34.5 million people. The traditional middle-income strata shrank from 55% of the population to 42%. Thus, the decline in good-paying industrial jobs was also linked to the changing consumer preferences of the affluent, on the one hand, and the limitations on consumption by the burgeoning working poor, on the other.[24]

The growth of low-wage jobs throughout the economy accelerated in the 1980s. A study done for the Joint Economic Committee of Congress in 1986 showed that whereas during the 1970s one out of five new wage earners found work at the low-end of the wage scale (jobs paying less than $7,000 in 1984 dollars), since 1979 60% have gone to work for less than $7,000 a year. Conversely, net new employment in both the middle and upper wage and salary levels declined from the period 1973–79 to 1979–84.[25] In other words, the working class as a whole is becoming poorer.

This trend also means, of course, that there is a vast army of low-paid, unorganized workers with no hope of a better job or higher income on the basis of current and foreseeable economic trends. It should be evident that among the tens of millions outside of unions who face deteriorating living standards are many who represent labor's best hope for redressing the eroding balance of forces in US society. Yet, just as the AFL chiefs of craft unionism viewed the new industrial workers of the 1920s and early 1930s as unorganizable riffraff, so today's business unionists appear to regard the mass of poor and near poor working people as beyond the reach of trade unionism. These bureaucrats look instead to the much smaller pool of professional workers who more nearly resemble themselves.

Service Workers and the Public Sector Experience

In examining the relative decline of unionism in the US, the AFL-CIO Committee of the Evolution of Work looked at the current union membership to determine what it might do about the unorganized. In its second report, *The Changing Situation of Workers and Their Unions*, issued in February 1985, the committee discovered that current union members are 'better educated than the general population', that '39 percent have either had some college or completed a college degree', that 'union households are typically middle class', and that 'union members are much more likely (58 percent) then the general population (34 percent) to see their work as "a career, not just a job"'.[26] Lane Kirkland, writing elsewhere, has made explicit who he thinks the base of organized labor is and should be: 'Unions affiliated with the AFL-CIO have a higher proportion of members with college degrees than the population at large, and we also have a higher proportion of members with graduate degrees. As the composition of our membership shows, trade unionists are nothing more – and nothing less – than the American middle class and those who aspire to it.'[27] The average union member, it is imagined, looks somewhat like the average business union bureaucrat, but with half the income. The desirable unorganized worker is thus presumed to look like the average union member, only with less income.

This comforting view is probably best explained by looking at those areas in which unions have been successful in the last decade or two. Most of the net union growth since the 1960s has been in white-collar work, shifting the composition of organized labor toward white-collar members. In the 1950s blue-collar workers composed about 80% of union members. By 1980 they were only slightly more than half. The number of union members grew by over 4 million from the end of the 1950s to 1980. The number of blue-collar workers in unions fell by almost 3 million, meaning that union growth was the result of some 7 million white-collar workers coming under union coverage.[28]

Public sector workers accounted for a very large part of that growth. From 1953 to 1976, the high point of public employee organization, over 5 million public workers were added to union roles, bringing the total to almost 6 million. The public sector as a whole went from a union density of 11.6% in 1953 to 35% in 1980, a higher proportion than manufacturing, mining, or construction. Among state and local public workers, the percentage of union members was even higher, rising to 50% by 1975.[29]

It is also true that while the majority of unionized public workers are blue-collar or low-paid service or clerical workers, a much larger percentage of public sector professionals are unionized than those in the private sector. Whereas in the private sector only 5.2% of managerial and professional employees were in unions in 1984, 38.1% of those occupations in the public sector were unionized. Of technical, sales and administrative employees, 8% in the private sector were unionized compared to 30.2% in public employment.[30] Teachers alone counted for over 2 million of the 6 million organized public workers. By 1976, 1.8 million were members of the National Education Association, while another 400,000 belonged to the American Federation of Teachers.[31] Thus, public sector unionism has a more professional cast to it, a fact that reinforces the AFL-CIO's view of the desirable union member as middle class.

The organization of public sector professionals was, of course, an important gain for organized labor. But it was a gain that could not be repeated in the private sector to the same extent. For one thing, the professions involved are different, as are many of the administrative functions. A very large proportion of the professionals employed at the federal, state, and local levels of government are associated with functions of the welfare state. Directly or indirectly, these professional workers are in public and social services involving human welfare – the majority of them in education, health, and public welfare. In 1960, 59% of state and local employees worked in these categories, and in 1980 the figure was 63%.[32]

Further, the professions involved are more collective and social in character than most of those in the private sector: teachers, nurses, and social workers versus lawyers, accountants, engineers, and executives. The vast majority of professionals in the private sector are concerned, directly or indirectly, with profit maximization. Publicly employed professionals thus have a stake in the welfare state and tend to have a more liberal outlook, while professionals employed by private corporations tend to share management's view of the world. In short, the organizing possibilities among private sector professionals are far more limited than among public employees. The major exceptions are likely to be professionals working in privately operated social, educational, and health services.

The organizable among unorganized private sector workers are to be found among lower paid and probably less educated workers who do not see their work as a career but as the dead-end jobs they really are. These workers are employed throughout the economy: about 12 million nonunion production or nonsupervisory workers in the private goods-producing sector. This is because the loss of union jobs in industry has been faster than the destruction of jobs generally. For example, while the net decline in manufacturing jobs from 1980 to 1984 was 800,000, the loss of union jobs was 1.4 million. This loss was greatest in durable goods manufacturing; 500,000 jobs were lost but the decline in union jobs was 1 million. Although the service sector as a whole gained about 5 million jobs, led by business services and health services, 700,000 union jobs were lost. This sector included a total of about 50 million jobs in 1984, of which a little over 5 million (or 10%) were unionized.[33] A constantly growing proportion of these nonunion jobs is thus likely to be low-wage and no-benefit in nature.

The organizing success among low-paid public sector service workers from 1965 to 1975 also pointed to the possibility of organizing private sector service workers. While a large number of professionals were organized, the majority of unionized public employees were low-paid un-skilled or semiskilled workers. The 1968 organizing campaigns and strikes of sanitation workers in Memphis and hospital workers in Charleston showed that it was possible to organize such workers. By the mid-1970s, 48.1% of public sanitation workers and 42% of public hospital employees were organized.[34]

Another factor indicating that private service workers are also susceptible to organization is the similar social composition of these two groups. Women compose 48% of public sector employment. In the private sector, women compose 60% of both service (as narrowly defined by the Bureau of Labor Statistics) and financial service employees. In retail trade, women are 50% of the workforce. The Bureau of Labor Statistics does not publish such direct industry figures for Black workers, but a much higher proportion of both Black men and women work in the public sector than is true of whites. Occupationally, Blacks form a higher than average concentration in such private and public service jobs as clerical, food service, health service, maintenance, public transportation, social work, and recreational activities.[35]

The success of many public employee organizing drives has been based on the recognition of the importance of women and minority workers in the public sector workforce. Unions such as AFSCME and 1199 consciously pursued a strategy of alliance with the civil rights movement in the 1960s, as the examples of both Memphis and Charleston show. In the 1970s and 1980s, these same unions, along with SEIU, attempted to capture the spirit of the women's movement in their approach to organizing.[36] In this way, these unions adopted a modern social unionism that made their organizing efforts more effective.

Organizing among public service workers also necessitated a rise in militant tactics and strikes. Strikes among public workers were mostly illegal. In the early 1960s, before the explosion of organizing, the number of public worker strikes fluctuated between twenty-eight and thirty-six a year, with the number of days lost to strikes running between 15,300 and 79,100 a year. In the second half of the 1960s, however, the number of strikes rose steadily to over 400 in 1970, with 2.4 million days lost. The results in wages and benefits were also significant. In the first generation of public employee bargaining during 1960–75, public employee wages and benefits rose up to or beyond the level of those performing comparable work in the private sector.[37]

Changes were necessary in these unions if they were to adopt more militant tactics and social unionist ideas, however. The old leaders of AFSCME and the SEIU, for example, were quite conservative and generally opposed to militant tactics. Before Jerry Wurf became president of AFSCME in 1964, that union opposed strikes by public employees and relied almost exclusively on lobbying to win wage increases. Wurf had to lead a bitter struggle to replace AFSCME President Arnold Zander and his administration. The concept of a public employee organization as a pressure group in state or local government changed to one of an industrial union engaging in collective bargaining and resorting to traditional labor tactics when necessary.[38] During these same years, the SEIU went from being a craft union of building service workers to a more socially conscious union willing to organize almost anyone. The NEA was transformed from a professional association of educators (including administrators) to an aggressive collective bargaining agent for primary and secondary school teachers. Simultaneously, many state employee associations began to act more like trade unions. Without this shift in orientation, the organization of public workers would have been unlikely. For the most part, the changes simply brought these organizations into line with the collective bargaining practices of the more liberal of the contemporary industrial unions prior to their period of decline. The organization of private sector service workers will require even greater changes, given the decline of unionism and its turn in the 1980s to nonadversarial practices, but the public sector experience of the 1960s and 1970s is evidence that the task is not impossible.

Industrial Unionism and Organizing the Unorganized

Very little new organizing among the unorganized has occurred in either the public or private sector for the past decade. The unions that have grown in recent years have done so by recruiting among people who more or less match Kirkland's vision of the middle-class trade unionist. The largest single group of workers to join AFL-CIO unions during the 1980s were members of public employee associations or unions absorbed by unions such as AFSCME, SEIU, and the CWA. They accounted for over 200,000 new AFL-CIO members between 1980 and 1984.[39]

Indeed, some unions have accomplished most of their growth through absorbing smaller unions. AFSCME, for example, derived over half of its growth from 1975 to 1984 through absorbing associations (259,200 out of 506,800 new members).[40] The SEIU, however, presents the most extreme example of this practice. In 1980 SEIU President George Hardy reported that 'in the past ten years our "reach-out" program has resulted in 22 affiliations by independent or other AFL-CIO unions.' These mergers added 230,000 members to the SEIU from 1971 to 1985. From 1980 to 1984 virtually all of SEIU's growth came from four mergers (really acquisitions): the International Jewelry Workers (1980), the

Oregon State Employees Association (1980), the National Association of Government Workers (1982), and the California State Employees Association (1984).[41]

Recent successes in new organizing have also centered on public employees or university clerical workers, such as those at Yale, Columbia, Boston University, and elsewhere. The content of these organizing drives has differed enormously. The fight over Ohio State University employees in 1986 was a bitter contest between AFL-CIO unions, in which AFSCME, the winning union, played down the adversarial elements of unionism.[42] The organizing drives at the universities, on the other hand, were militant and creative in their approach to a mostly female clerical workforce. Most of these successes were conducted by unions with other major jurisdictions. Similar organizing efforts at hospitals and other service employers by many of the same unions have failed. A facetious critic of this approach to growth might ask, 'What does labor do when it runs out of state employee associations to merge with and large, urban universities to organize?'

The relative success with state and university employees in recent years is explained in part by the fact that these are noncompetitive sectors of the economy. The fight to organize them may be very difficult, as at Yale, but the bargaining unit is a noncompetitive entity unto itself. To gain power over the Board of Trustees of Yale or Columbia does not really require an industrial union approach. Students will not leave for Harvard because it pays its clerical workers less. Nor will the benefactors of such institutions switch their loyalty because of a clerical strike. The university will not move its campus to Taiwan or contract out to the state university system. The state of Ohio cannot send its clerical work to Pennsylvania or treat its ill in West Virginia institutions. Higher productivity by Illinois state employees will not put Indiana out of business.

So long as 'the relevant workers', as labor economist Charles Craypo calls them, are all organized and the unions (if there is more than one) at the university or state bargaining unit are united in their goals, they possess as much potential bargaining power as they are likely to get regardless of what international or national union they belong to. Thus, these kinds of workers look for the union that offers the best deal, the most resources, or whose message most conforms to their own current consciousness. Naturally, it would help if a union could establish a pattern nationally, but such a pattern would not have great economic significance for workers in noncompetitive situations.

To be sure, public workers and those in nonprofit, noncompetitive areas face a variety of pressures. Taxpayers or university benefactors, including powerful foundations and governments wielding big grants, often bring significant pressure on administrators to contain labor costs.

The administrators can point to workers at similar institutions accepting less pay for the same work, just as the unions can argue the reverse. Such institutions can use scabs in the event of a strike. In some instances, contracting work out to the private sector creates a competitive situation. Where genuine competition exists, as between the US Postal Service and UPS or in a growing number of local sanitation services, the organization of all the relevant workers becomes as necessary as in private industry. Nevertheless, with these exceptions, the bargaining position of the vast majority of workers in public and nonprofit institutions is fundamentally different from that of workers in private industry. Thus, for the workers involved, the question of affiliation with a union in the same 'industry' is secondary. The claims of the union to be able to shift the balance of forces with this single employer are grounded in reality. To put it another way, wages do not need to be taken out of competition, because the employer is not under the pressure of market competition.

The vast majority of unorganized workers, however, do produce goods or services in competitive markets. This is as true of industries that do not face serious overseas competition, such as meatpacking or trucking, as it is of auto, steel, tires or garment. It is equally true of retail and wholesale trade workers, whether what they distribute is made domestically or abroad. Such workers greatly outnumber those in noncompetitive situations. Excluding the instructional staff, there are about 1.3 million public and private university employees in the US, fewer workers than are employed by department stores alone. In state and local employment, there remained about 5 million unorganized workers, slightly over half the total. Some of these are administrators and many are scattered in small (potential) bargaining units. This is a significant number of workers, of course, and they should be organized. But their numbers pale in comparison to the nearly 15 million nonsupervisory retail workers, who are only 9% organized, or the 4.5 million nonsupervisory workers in wholesale trade, who are somewhat more unionized. These figures do not include an additional 18 million nonsupervisory workers in 'services', as defined by the Bureau of Labor Statistics, or the 4.2 million nonsupervisory employees in finance, who are almost totally unorganized.[43]

For the low-paid workers in the competitive private sector, however, the organization of a few workplaces here or there will not alter the balance of forces between capital and labor. Every bit as much as their counterparts in auto or steel, workers in these industries must be organized on an industrial basis to have any significant bargaining power. Further, bargaining must be based on an industry-wide standard to translate this power into significant and long-term effects on wages, benefits or conditions of work. Thus, although much of the workforce of the large grocery chains belongs to the UFCW and the Teamsters, the employers have been able to whipsaw these unions for years because bargaining is local or regional. The same competitive forces undermine the success of organizing drives.

Unions lose about half the workplaces where they win NLRB elections because the employer is able to thwart the bargaining process. Having a foothold among only a few of the employers in an industry, or worse still, only a few operations of one employer, leaves the union with little bargaining power. Employer resistance becomes even greater when they see themselves losing competitive advantage to unorganized businesses. The threat that the business will go under or the plant will be closed if it loses its competitive position is a credible one for unskilled workers in today's high unemployment economy. For workers, the sense of isolation is discouraging in the face of such resistance, which is why the new union often collapses after a couple of years of frustrated bargaining. One reason why it is hard to organize a high-tech plant in Silicon Valley or Boston's Route 128 is that almost none of the industry is organized. Employers are always willing to explain the economics of this situation in the form of a threat to close the plant or move the work. The workers, who are likely to number only a few hundred at most, do not see thousands of their colleagues joining them in this effort.

The success of the CIO in the 1930s (or currently of industrial workers in South Africa and Brazil, under far more adverse circumstances than exist in the US), was rooted in the breadth of its organizing drives. Entire industries were organized within the space of a few years and contracts were won in an even shorter time span. Companies found it difficult to make credible threats based on the loss of competitive advantage when all or most of the employers were being forced to increase pay and benefits. The near simultaneity and comprehensiveness of the growth of unionism in these industries created a sense of motion and power that allowed workers to overcome employer resistance and stick out economic downturns.

Much of the service sector has come to resemble more and more the traditional areas of union strength in goods-producing industry. As service work has increasingly come under the reign of capital and subject to demands of profitability, it has become subject to more of the organizational norms of capitalist enterprise: increasing concentration of capital in ownership, growing concentrations of employment, greater application of technology, intensified division of labor often involving deskilling or deprofessionalizing, and downward pressure on labor costs. All of these trends make the service sector more and more susceptible to unionization.

A good example is the hospital sector of the healthcare industry. If transportation, utilities and communications – all of which are heavily blue collar – are excluded from the private service sector, healthcare workers composed almost 30% of the total of nonsupervisory service workers in 1984. Over two-thirds of all healthcare employees worked in hospitals. From 1970 to 1983 hospital expenditures rose from $25.6 billion to $136.3 billion. The number of hospitals and hospital beds declined somewhat, but employment in hospitals rose from 2.5 million to 3.7 million in the same period. On average, the size of the hospital as a workplace grew from 357 employees in 1970 to 537 in 1983, much larger than the average factory. The workforce overwhelmingly comprised low-paid workers or collectivized professionals. Of the 3.1 million hospital employees in 1976, 2.1 million were aides, orderlies, or housekeeping workers. Nurses accounted for over 750,000. Doctors, however, numbered only 54,231, while other professionals and skilled workers 'made up only a small proportion of the total hospital workforce.' Seventy-six percent of the workforce was female and 18.9% were Black or other minorities. Unionization of hospital workers was already greater than that of most service-producing workers (excluding transportation, utilities, and communication), having risen from about 9% in the late 1960s to 20% by 1977.[44]

Private healthcare is unusual in that it some of it is noncompetitive, while the competitive sector is divided between locally competitive services and a newer national competitive sector. The latter consists of investor-owned, for-profit chains that accounted for 38% of all hospital beds in 1983.[45] The entrance of such firms makes the older, local, bargaining approach increasingly untenable and the fragmented state of existing unions intolerable. Obviously, an attempt to realign organized private sector hospital workers into one union would confront massive bureaucratic resistance from unions such as SEIU, the Teamsters, and others that have organized hospitals, making such a proposal impractical so long as bureaucratic business unionism rules these organizations. But the economic logic of such a move and its obvious appeal to workers in that industry seems clear enough.

In a growing number of service industries, the concentration of capital ownership is quite high in spite of the large number of firms in the industry. This often means that a relatively small number of large companies employ a significant portion of the workforce. In wholesale and retail trade, the 198 firms worth over $250 million in assets accounted for 37% of all the assets in the industry. Retail trade employed 15.5 million people in about 1.5 million establishments in 1983. But about 3.5 million of these, or nearly a quarter, worked for the 50 largest firms. The US Department of Commerce's *Industrial Outlook* for 1986 confirmed that larger firms were increasing their share of the total market. Of those 1.8 million workers who worked in department stores, almost 1 million were employed by Sears, J. C. Penney and K-Mart alone. Similarly, the top 100 commercial banks employed half the 1.6 million banking workforce.[46] Thus, the number of large firms that would have to be organized to establish a strong foothold in a number of service industries is relatively small, suggesting that the organization of service workers is a manageable task.

Neither the AFL-CIO, its affiliates, nor the Teamsters have attempted to conduct a national organizing drive in an unorganized industry. Except for the United Mine Workers and the Amalgamated Clothing and Textile Workers, no industrial union has even attempted a large-scale effort to organize the unorganized in its own traditional industry. And such efforts are at best episodic and involve only a few locations. As noted earlier, unions put less money per worker into organizing now than in the past. The section on organizing in the AFL-CIO's *The Changing Situation of Workers and Their Unions* does not even mention the question of an industry-wide approach to reaching the unorganized.[47] Yet it does not take much imagination to envision campaigns that could be launched by certain unions with help from the Federation as a whole.

For the UFCW, one obvious course would be to organize the employees in the major national retail (nongrocery) chains like K-Mart, Sears, and J. C. Penney on a national basis, establishing a pattern goal in the industry. Significant organization in any one of them would provide a power base in that industry. Labor costs in retail trade (excluding food) run only about 15% to 16% of total costs and have not increased in years, so there is clearly room for improvement.[48] Further, the power relationship between the workers, their union, and the employer would be clearly focused. Like most firms in the retail and service sectors, these employers face no foreign competition.

The insurance industry is also dominated by large national firms with the ability to pay. The carriers employ 835,000 nonsupervisory employees (not including brokers, agencies, etc.).[49] The AFL-CIO-coordinated campaign to organize Blue Cross would probably have a better chance if it were coupled with simultaneous drives at other major health insurance firms and if it were directed at creating an industrial union for insurance workers. There are union footholds in this industry, and workers from unionized firms could play a large role in organizing those at other big companies.

The problem of conglomeration, which exists in many service industries, can be addressed by supplementing industrial organization with coordinated bargaining, corporation-wide steward's councils, and other tactics that have been developed to deal with multi-industry employers. The greater the extent of union organization, the more powerful the various levers that labor has over conglomerates. John L. Lewis understood this fact of industrial life. As part of launching the CIO, Lewis's Mine Workers poured huge financial and human resources into organizing the steelworkers. This was not philanthropy. Some of the steel corporations, like US Steel, were among the most powerful employers in coal mining as well as steel. Lewis reasoned that a unionized steel industry would help protect his union's position in the coalfields. While neither Lewis nor the Steelworkers ever really used the leverage implied in such organization, it is obvious that this approach could be the key to regaining some of the power lost to unions through conglomeration.

10

Other Voices

As the decline of labor and the loss of union power became evident, new voices arose in the second half of the 1970s and in the 1980s to question, contest, and oppose the complacency of the business union bureaucracy and its turn toward nonadversarialism and concessions. Recession and the disastrous effects of restructuring in some industries precluded a resurgence of the wildcat strike movements of the late 1960s and early 1970s. The new forces for change in the unions concentrated on internal union affairs, either as opposition or pressure groups, or on the development of methods of struggle designed to meet the challenges of a changing industrial world. What arose was not really one movement with a common set of grievances and goals, but a series of movements within various unions.

The new activism of this period took shape when labor was on the defensive and often before the contours of the crisis were clear to those involved. In the earliest stages, most of the activists in these new movements or organizations saw their problems as particular to themselves, but a number of factors tended to change this consciousness over time. One was the presence, for the first time since the 1930s, of a significant number of politically aware activists with some background in or connection to the political left and social movements of the 1960s and early 1970s. The role of these leftists should not be exaggerated, however. Often they played a catalytic role and, as the shape of the crisis became clearer, provided elements of an analysis of trends and events for the far larger number of activists with no such political background. And leftists sometimes had a destructive effect by attempting to impose inappropriate or untimely agendas on movements. By the early 1980s, however, many activists in the labor-based left had reached a maturity that allowed them to play a positive role in pointing out new directions for a labor movement in crisis. The vast majority of the new activists and dissidents in the unions, however, were not leftists or veterans of the movements of the 1960s. They learned many of the lessons of such social movements, but largely through their own experience.

While many of these movements died or had little visible impact, they all contributed to the development of a new layer of union activists, often working-class 'baby boomers', who by the mid-1980s had important roles in thousands of local unions, both as local officers and rank-and-file members. Still, neither this experience nor the generational factor guaranteed a programmatic consensus on the conduct of unionism that all of these new activists and leaders shared. But the permanence of concessionary bargaining and the turn of so many top union leaders to open collaboration with capital set in motion a convergence of these various movements. In the second half of the 1980s, a common set of values and precepts about what a union should be began to take place. The first form of this new consciousness might be described as solidarity consciousness: the realization that few struggles could be won without significant or even large-scale support from other sections of the labor movement. The second phase was the growing perception that the old rules of business unionism didn't work and that a new direction for labor was needed.

Resistance to the nonadversarial direction of much of the business unionist leadership began before the magnitude or nature of the crisis of labor was clear to all involved. The union rebels of the 1970s often saw the leadership abandon the more effective methods of the past and retreat in the face of management aggression. The solution, then, was to get rid of the leadership and to make changes in union structure that would guarantee rank-and-file input into future decision-making and minimize the tendency of leaders to accommodate the employers. The thinking of many of these union reformers was shaped by the experience of the Miners for Democracy and other rebel movements of the late 1960s and early 1970s (see Chapter 4). In some cases, dissident candidates succeeded in replacing more conservative incumbents, although in most they did not. Yet these movements did have an important impact on events in the unions and industries in which they worked. The ability of the activists in these movements to survive and continue to be effective or to join with the new movements of the mid-1980s depended a lot on the importance the movement had placed on leadership development, rank-and-file involvement, and permanent organization. Illustrating this point were the two leading – and contrasting – rebel movements that began in the 1970s, the reform movements in the Teamsters and Steelworkers.

Jerry Tucker of the UAW's New Directions caucus speaks at TDU's 1987 convention.

Reformers in Steel

Formal nonadversary labor relations came early to the basic steel industry. In 1971 USW President I. W. Abel negotiated a contract that included joint union/management productivity committees at the plant level. In 1973 he went further and agreed to the Experimental Negotiating Agreement (ENA), under which the union agreed not to use the strike in national bargaining in return for a $150 bonus for each worker, a quarterly cost-of-living adjustment as a floor for 1974 bargaining, and the right to settle negotiation disputes in arbitration. The rationale he offered for accepting the productivity committees and the ENA was that the industry was under growing pressure from imports and that it had to raise productivity and avoid costly strikes.[1]

The steel industry did indeed have problems. Like other US industries, its return on invested capital had slumped since the 1960s, falling from 12.5% in 1966 to 7.1% in 1976. In addition, the severe 1974–75 recession affected steel production even more than previous recessions had. Steel employment dropped from 513,600 production workers in

1969 to 431,300 in 1977.

However, the argument that imports are the problem was specious in the 1970s. Imports had made gains during the 1960s and by 1968 accounted for 16.3% of US consumption of steel products. Import levels fluctuated along with US production levels, but in 1977 imports had only 17.5% of the market. US steel production was on average higher than in the 1950s or 1960s. In 1977 production was about the same it had been in 1968, over 82,000 lost jobs earlier. Moreover, domestic steel prices more than doubled during the 1970s, while labor costs fell as a proportion of total costs in the second half of the decade.[2] For the steel corporations the crisis was a function of global overcapacity in steel, on the one hand, and a falling rate of profit rooted in the capital-intensive nature of the industry. For steelworkers, the crisis meant lost jobs, stagnant or declining real incomes, and an increasing number of plant closings.

The negotiation of the 1974 contract under the terms of the ENA coincided with the election of Ed Sadlowski as director of District 31, the USW's largest district, based in the heart of the industry in the Chicago-Gary area. Sadlowski was an avowed reformer who beat Sam Evett, candidate of the entrenched machine of Joseph Germano, when the Department of Labor supervised a new election because the regular 1973 election had been stolen. Opposition candidates in other USW districts did well, but did not win. These elections clearly showed that there was militant sentiment for change throughout basic steel; and in a few places like District 31, Youngstown, and the iron ore range the reformers controlled important locals.[3]

Before 1977, the structure of the steel industry looked much as it had for decades. The same companies dominated and diversification was still marginal. The crisis of the industry didn't involve many plant closings in those years, but rather the shutting down of departments or in-mill operations and their replacement with more efficient ones that would produce more, not less. From the mill floor it was easy to see that it was not declining production (due to imports or any other cause) that was costing jobs, but the companies' efforts to combine jobs, to intensify 'discipline' as a means of increasing productivity, and to replace older facilities with newer technology. The union allowed these developments because Abel and his successor Lloyd McBride accepted the business union notion that the well-being of the union as an institution depended on the profitability of the company.

The rebellion against these conditions in steel began as a reform movement within the union. The nature of steel production makes the sort of shopfloor conflict associated with auto and many other industries problematic. The scale of production is mammoth, the workforce more spread out, and the integration of the process less apparent. Also, workers cannot stop a blast furnace in the same way they can an assembly line or a flow of parts. Solutions to major problems usually require the attention of the union, at least at the local level; and many require intervention by the International. To change things in the mills, workers felt, the approach of the union had to be changed first.

The reformers proposed to end the ENA, mobilize the International to challenge harassment, and gain the right to ratify their contract, which they did not have. They saw the ENA and the International's timidity as the keys to the union's weakness in dealing with the steel giants, and the election of a new leadership and the right to ratify as the rank-and-file's instruments to fight back. The Steelworkers, like the Mine Workers, elected top union officers by national referendum, making it easier for the reformers to attempt a direct run for power.

With a secure base in the largest district in the union, District 31, where Ed Sadlowski had been elected director in 1974, leaders of dissident locals and caucuses came together to form Steelworkers Fight Back in 1975. Originally, the idea was to form a national network of oppositionists to pressure for their demands. But the decision was made to run Sadlowski for USW president, and Fight Back became the campaign organization. Fight Back was an ill-organized venture. It had no formal membership and was run mainly out of District 31's offices by a small group of leaders. It soon gained widespread support, but never developed a way for its supporters to participate beyond promoting the Sadlowski campaign from the summer of 1976 through the election in February 1977.

Fight Back was further weakened as an organization by Sadlowski's tendency to rely on those USW staffers who supported him – in effect, substituting their ability to reach the members for any attempt to bring these members into Fight Back. Three of the four Fight Back candidates for International office were staffers. It was also decided to limit the number of candidates by running only for the top International positions and not running Fight Back candidates for District director outside of District 31, where Jim Balanoff ran to replace Sadlowski. This decision restricted the potential for developing district-level organization outside District 31.[4]

The 1976–77 campaign had a crusading spirit to it in spite of its organizational shortcomings. The focus of the campaign was on issues like ENA, opposition to a dues increase, and the right to ratify. Further, Sadlowski had been fairly outspoken on broader social questions, such as the war in Vietnam and civil rights, but played down the question of affirmative action in spite of the fact that it was still a hot issue in 1976–77 due to Black dissatisfaction with the 1974 affirmative action consent decree agreed to by the union, companies, and the federal government.

In the end, Sadlowski got 249,281 votes – 43.1% – to Lloyd McBride's 328,861. In locals with over 1,000 members, which were mostly basic steel locals, Sadlowski received a 51.9% majority of the vote.[5]

The vote pointed to a weakness in Fight Back's program and strategy. Its program was really based on the concerns of workers in basic steel. But they were no longer a majority of the USW's members. The percentage of members in primary metals industries fell from 52.4% in 1969 to 40.9% in 1980, and these figures included workers in copper and aluminum as a result of mergers that had occurred in the 1940s. The USW also had members in nonbasic steel fabrication (13.3%), mining (8.2%), transportation equipment (6.0%), and a variety of other unrelated jurisdictions where Sadlowski's message was lost. Thus, Fight Back had the difficulty of mounting an opposition in a multijurisdictional union, a problem that today's dissidents increasingly face.[6]

Sadlowski's electoral defeat was not the end of the reform movement, however; it continued to be a force in several districts and at the International level for some time. Indeed, in the 1979 local union elections throughout the USW, the reformers held their previous positions and made some important gains. These included the election of Ron Weisen as president at the Homestead Local 1397 in Pittsburgh and Alice Peurala as president of Local 65 at the Chicago South Works of US Steel.[7] But as a movement in basic steel with no strategy for reaching the other constituencies in the USW, Fight Back inevitably faced decline and fragmentation. Fight Back might, in fact, have developed such a strategy and a broader leadership to carry it out if it hadn't ceased to exist as an organization after the 1977 election. Much like the Miners for Democracy before it, only with a smaller organized base, Fight Back just disappeared. With no organizational framework within which to discuss strategy, train new leaders, or recruit in other jurisdictions, the reform movement remained confined to basic steel – and that industry was on the verge of a precipitous decline.

Domestic steel production plummeted sharply following 1979. During and after the 1980–82 recession the steel corporations carried out drastic rationalizations. Even before the recession, plant closings had swept the industry, and basic steel employment plunged from 449,700 production workers in December 1978 to 242,600 in December 1982. The recovery skipped steelworkers; employment rose to 260,600 production workers in late 1984, but plunged again, this time to 201,100 at the end of 1986. Moreover, during the same period the industry's leading employers intensified their efforts to diversify.[8]

The reformers continued to organize around the same issues that the Sadlowski campaign had emphasized. In November 1979 a meeting of about forty representatives gathered at Homestead Local 1397 to plan a campaign for the right to ratify directed at the Basic Industry Conference meeting in December and more generally at the 1980 basic steel negotiations.[9] To those affected, the campaign made sense and had a great appeal, but again the reformers scarcely took note of the other constituencies in the union. A further irony accompanied the continued emphasis on the right to ratify. The USW leadership finally granted it just when basic steel bargaining fell to pieces, and in fact used ratification to gain approval for deep concessions from a demoralized membership.

As individuals, many of the activist leaders were well aware of the changes in the industry. There were fights against plant closings, and some of the leaders of the reform forces played a leading role in them. Notable was the formation of the Save Our Valley drive led by the Youngstown-based Ecumenical Coalition to Save the Mahoning Valley. This campaign included leaders from Youngstown steel locals like Ed Mann and John Barbero, long-time reformers and militant unionists.[10] Eventually, similar campaigns developed in the Pittsburgh area as steel reformers joined to organize groups like the Mon Valley Unemployed Committee (MVOC) and the Tri-State Conference on Steel.[11] Some of the proposals for preventing plant closings that came from these organizations were raised on the floor of the 1980 USW convention. USW President Lloyd McBride's only response was, 'How can we force a company under our present government and free enterprise system to stay in business when they don't want to?'[12]

In 1980 basic steel bargaining itself took a turn that the reform forces were slow to respond to. The ENA was discontinued because the companies didn't want to be held to arbitration anymore and at least some, like US Steel, envisioned the day when a showdown would come. In 1980 the USW and the basic steel companies also agreed to 'labor/management participation teams [LMPTs]', their version of quality of worklife programs. By this time, it was clear that the old rules were changing fast. The reform forces were unable to respond in a united, coherent manner. There was no organized opposition to the LMPT plan above the local level. In fact, the reformers didn't even have a unified position on the 1980 contract. For example, District 31 Director Jim Balanoff in his role as a member of the Basic Steel Conference voted to approve it.

In 1981 five reform candidates for district director ran as an alliance in an attempt to give some coherence to the reform forces. However, their program was virtually unchanged and didn't address the question of plant closings or the concerns of nonsteel jurisdictions. Further, the level of organization within the districts remained weak or nonexistent in all but a few locals. Partly as a result of these factors, only one reform candidate, Dave Patterson of Canada, won. Jim Balanoff lost his directorship to Jack Parton; Joe Samargia lost in the iron ore range, Ron Weisen lost to the incumbent, and Marvin Weinstock lost in a three-way race. Balanoff's defeat was a major setback and the other elections disappointments. Balanoff acknowledged the problem of weak organization in the decline of the movement he had helped to spawn. In 1981 he wrote: 'Our mistake in '77 was that Steelworkers Fight Back didn't stay alive. You need an organization. I don't think the losses would have occurred if Fight Back had stayed alive.'[13]

In spite of their organizational weaknesses, the reform forces continued to exist as a network of local union leaders through the mid-1980s. When McBride moved to reopen the basic steel agreement in 1982 to grant the companies concessions, these leaders played an important role in getting the Basic Steel Industry Conference (comprising 400 local leaders) to reject the idea, unanimously in July and by a vote of 231-141 in November. Nevertheless, in January 1983 the companies came back for concessions, and McBride pushed once again for acceptance. On 28 February, the local union presidents voted 196 to 63 to accept virtually the same package they had rejected in November.[14] Even with an organization, of course, it might have been impossible to get the local presidents to oppose concessions indefinitely with the industry still in a slide and with no membership ratification rights.

The disarray of the reform forces became unavoidably apparent in the months before the special election called for March 1984 to replace McBride (who had died in November 1983). The election was scheduled for 29 March 1984. A 19 November meeting of about sixty reformers in Hammond, Indiana choose Local 1397 President Ron Weisen as their presidential candidate, while the USW leadership named interim President and Canadian Director Lynn Williams as its candidate. Then, a couple of weeks later, USW Treasurer Frank McKee announced his candidacy. McKee adopted some of the reformers' favorite demands: the right to ratify contracts; opposition to further concessions; and direct involvement of local presidents in negotiating the basic steel agreement. Many once associated with the reform trend went over to McKee as a more realistic candidate. Joe Samargia, long a militant oppositionist, described their mood: 'The rebels are looking for a win. They need a win.' McKee was much better known than Weisen outside the Pittsburgh area and the reform movement. His ability to split the reform opposition left Weisen unable to get enough local union nominations to make the race. With the reformers split and without a candidate, McKee then shifted the emphasis of his campaign from the reform program to the fact that Williams was a Canadian. He even attacked Canadian steel imports and put himself forward as the 'All American Steelworker'. Without an organization or their own candidate, the reformers were powerless to influence the direction of the campaign. In the end, Williams beat McKee with 59% of the total vote, 53% in the US and 92% in Canada.[15]

In addition to the lack of organization and the continued concentration on basic steel, Philip Nyden cites a 'lag in social movement adapability' as a major factor in the decline of the reform movement in steel. There is no doubt that the reformers faced a difficult situation by the early 1980s. Things had changed rapidly since Ed Sadlowski first became director of District 31 in 1974. By the mid-1980s the companies could make a convincing case for their economic troubles, and the rise of imports gave both industry and union leaders something to blame that a reform opposition could not easily deal with and that helped divide opinion among the ranks. Nyden suggests that the movement was unable to adapt its strategy and organizational tactics to the changes in the industry and workforce. This tendency to lag behind changes in the objective situation can be the result of early successes. That is, as long as a reform movement seems to be growing within its traditional constituency there is a tendency not to make additional outreach efforts or to broaden the program, particularly when these steps might defuse the movement's appeal to its original base. In general, the reform movement in steel opted for quick electoral victories. Its early successes at the local level prompted this approach and probably helped divert its leaders' attention from the problems taking shape.

It was possible to see the movement as still advancing through the 1981 district director campaign – though not after the results. However, Balanoff was probably right in identifying the failure to make Fight Back an organization after the 1977 election as the turning point. Real organization provides the kind of forum for assessing new developments and reassessing old strategies. It is, in effect, the neccessary (though not sufficient) framework for dealing with the problem of lags in consciousness and movement adaptability. It may, of course, have been that ultimately the devastation of the steel industry was too deep and too rapid for any sort of opposition movement based in the industry to sustain itself through the period of restructuring. But a developed organization capable of reaching out to new constituencies and grappling with a changing economic atmosphere would have had a far better chance of living to fight another day.

Teamsters for a Democratic Union

The reform movements that arose in the Teamsters union in the 1970s were shaped by forces that tended to push them in the direction of organization. Primary among these was the fact that the Teamsters differed sharply from the CIO industrial unions in manufacturing. The Teamsters had been a decentralized craft union of local drivers and helpers until the 1930s. Bargaining was strictly local, and interstate trucking was not fully organized on an industrial basis until well into the 1940s. Even then, master contracts were regional in nature and not uniform. As a whole the industry itself was not really national until the development of the Interstate Highway System in the 1950s. Jimmy Hoffa took control of the Teamsters at the right moment to begin centralization of bargaining. To do so, he moved to centralize the union itself and to put greater and greater power in the hands of the general president. Neither the old craft structure nor the new centralized organization created by Hoffa offered routine channels for democratic expression above the local level.

The leadership institutions that Hoffa shaped also lacked the legitimacy typical of most industrial unions, where open corruption was the exception. Hoffa did not just build a more centralized bureaucratic union, he created an alliance with organized crime and other Teamster leaders tied to it. At the same time, the methods by which the succession of union leaders who followed Hoffa to the Teamster presidency and then to prison lacked the political character and sophistication of those routinely employed by most other union leaders. The rebellion in the Teamsters thus took a very different course from the one in steel.[16]

Dissident Teamsters did not have the option of running a candidate for international president, unlike the Steelworkers Fight Back movement. 'Elections' in the Teamsters occurred at highly rigged national conventions. The vast majority of delegates were local union officials who were automatically delegates under the IBT's constitution. Highly dependent on the International for the successful prosecution of grievances, few were willing to dissent in public. Furthermore, many Teamster locals were run much like the International itself, and dissent was violently suppressed. Finally, while workers covered by most of the major Teamster contracts had the right to vote on their contracts, the rule requiring a two-thirds vote to defeat a settlement negated any real right to ratify. The need to reform this union was greater than most, but the channels for pursuing reform were few.[17] Dissident Teamster movements therefore tended to be direct action movements when they moved beyond the local level. The 1970 wildcats and the brief appearance of TURF in their wake were examples of this tendency.

Rank-and-file workers in the US trucking industry also faced a very different set of circumstances than those in steel or other industries. Until 1980 trucking was a regulated industry within no possibility of foreign competition. In addition, it was a growing industry. The freight tonnage carried by Class I and II regulated firms rose by about 80% from 1967 to

1978. Employment in the industry grew well into the 1980s. The changes in the trucking industry that occurred under regulation and accelerated after deregulation involved the growth of a small number of national trucking firms that increasingly dominated the industry and set a more aggressive tone in labor relations. The growth of a small number of firms into truly national trucking systems gradually changed the balance of forces that had existed between the Teamster's union under Jimmy Hoffa and the employers generally. The National Master Freight Agreement crafted by Hoffa was barely in place when he went off to prison in 1967. Under the leadership of Frank Fitzsimmons, who replaced Hoffa, this national contract began unraveling long before deregulation occurred.[18]

Trucking serves US industry. Its customers are, for the most part, industrial corporations. It is also a labor-intensive industry with labor costs constituting about 60% of operating expenses. Thus, in the view of the commanding heights of American capital, the growth of trucking labor costs accomplished by the NMFA through the 1960s and into the 1970s was a matter of concern. Trucking figured into the Business Roundtable's political agenda in the 1970s in the form of the campaign for deregulation, which it believed would contain labor costs through intensified competition. But even before deregulation became law, corporate pressure on trucking firms to contain costs grew as the falling rate of profit in basic industry became more apparent. In addition, the proportion of freight handled by union workers declined by an estimated 20% to 25% from 1967 to 1977. With deregulation, all of these centrifugal forces intensified the pressures on the union. The nonunion sector played much the same role in trucking that overseas competition, capital flight, and out-sourcing played in manufacturing.[19]

Under Frank Fitzsimmons, the system of master agreements began to come apart as the union granted more and more special riders in different regions or sectors of the industry and as it cut local deals that undermined work standards. In reaction, dissident Teamsters around the country established contact in 1975 and began to talk about an organized campaign around the 1976 contract. The initial network included veterans of earlier struggles, such as the 1970 wildcat, TURF, PROD (the Professional Drivers Council, a group concerned with safety issues founded by Ralph Nader associate Arthur Fox), and a number of local rebels such as those in Local 208 in Los Angeles, Local 407 in Cleveland, and Local 299 in Detroit. A few had political experience in the social movements of the 1960s and held a socialist view of what militant industrial unionism should be like. In the fall of 1975, this network took a step toward organization:

So about 40 Teamsters from 15 cities decided to do something about it, gathered in a Chicago hotel, and launched Teamsters for a Decent Contract (TDC). They returned home to distribute across the country some 100,000 copies of a leaflet demanding a decent contract. They organized protest demonstrations at trucking companies and union halls. The slogan they adopted was: READY TO STRIKE.[20]

TDC set up a national center in Cleveland and published a national newspaper called *Convoy*. TDC was more a national network than a real organization, but it brought activists around the country into a common campaign and, at the same time, helped to generate organized activity around local issues. Although its slogan was 'Ready to Strike', TDC could never have led or coordinated a national strike in 1976. But its constant pressure activities, its ability to get information out to the members – often before the union did – and the visibility afforded Teamster activity of any kind in the wake of Hoffa's 1975 disappearance gave it an impact beyond its numbers and fragile organization. Thus, in 1976 Fitzsimmons felt compelled to call the first official national strike of freight workers, probably in the hope of heading off a repeat of the 1970 wildcats. After a couple of days, Fitzsimmons came back with an offer from the employers that was better than his initial proposal. With this in hand, and the near certainty that the two-thirds rule would prevent a rejection, he called off the strike. In Detroit, where TDC had considerable support, a wildcat continued briefly until the TDC leaders, seeing that it could not be spread to other areas, called it off.[21]

The leaders of TDC saw freight as the strategic power base in the union, but from the start they also realized the need to reach out to other jurisdictions. Although TDC was primarily organized around the NMFA, it also intervened in the 1976 carhauler and UPS contracts. Carhaulers in Cincinnati, Flint, and Detroit wildcatted against their settlement. They sought TDC's help and became one of TDU's strongest bases of support over the years. UPS workers conducted their own contract campaign through an organization closely associated with TDC called UPSurge. UPSurge adopted the 'Ready to Strike' slogan and when it became apparent that Fitzsimmons would sell them out, UPS workers in the Central States Conference wildcatted. UPSurge disappeared after the contract fight, but UPS workers became an important part of TDU through the efforts of TDC leaders.

The TDC's ability to influence the course of bargaining in freight, and to a lesser extent at UPS, revealed both its potential to affect events and the weaknesses that had plagued its own campaign as well as the work of TURF before it. The potential convinced the leaders of TDC to form a permanent opposition organization and reform movement within the

IBT that could grow through intervention in both local and national contract struggles. In September 1976, two hundred Teamsters attended a convention that founded Teamsters for a Democratic Union as a permanent organization. *Convoy* became TDU's national paper, and local TDU chapters were encouraged to put out local papers or newsletters. In addition to organizing contract campaigns, TDU helped local groups put out newsletters, organized bylaw reform campaigns to make the local unions more democratic, and provided advice and support for workplace struggles around the country.[22]

To overcome the weaknesses that had crippled previous opposition movements, TDU put heavy emphasis on leadership development from the start. Although TDU's annual conventions accomplished a great deal of business in setting the direction for TDU nationally, they were also educational events drawing on experts of all kinds and activists from other unions with experiences relevant to the Teamsters. Through its Teamster Rank & File Educational & Legal Defense Foundation, TDU developed a series of manuals for organizers, stewards, and members. Its legal rights handbook for Teamsters remains unique in its thoroughness. It also published pamphlets and newsletters analyzing the conditions in various Teamster jurisdictions to aid contract and other campaigns. Additionally, both the TDU's International Steering Committee and the many local chapter steering committees became important focuses for leadership training and development.[23]

TDU also paid close attention to changes in the industry. In 1978, for example, *Convoy* documented the growth of nonunion trucking and warned of the consequences. In subsequent years, it also analyzed the likely consequences of deregulation, the growth of the large national carriers at the expense of smaller ones, and other changes in the economy of the industry.[24] One of the opening paragraphs of the *Steward's Manual*, for example, states:

> Today's unions are faced with new challenges: runaway shops, mergers, buy-outs, concessions contracts, widespread use of casual workers in the freight industry who never get seniority, de-certification, productivity standards, double breasting (one nonunion company set up alongside a union company which owns both operations), quality of work life programs (a scheme which takes away the adversarial relationship with the company), union busting, and bankruptcies as the trucking industry consolidates into larger and larger companies.[25]

From the start, TDU attempted to strengthen its base in various Teamster jurisdictions by providing channels through which different groups of Teamsters could deal with their employers and at the same time function as part of a united reform movement. For example, TDU set up committees for UPS workers, carhaulers, steelhaulers, company-wide networks at some of the bigger trucking firms, and a cannery workers' network. These committees allowed TDU to intervene effectively in scores of contract fights and to grow through its ability to organize and support real struggles. In both 1976 and 1979, for example, the TDU carhaulers organized contract committees. In 1979 the Carhauler Contract Committee organized a majority to vote against an inadequate contract, although Fitzsimmons was able to impose it anyway by invoking the two-thirds rule. After 1979 the Carhaulers Coordinating Committee became a permanent part of TDU. TDU also organized the Steel Haulers Organizing Committee (SHOC) to pull together all steelhaulers, including those in the Fraternal Order of Steelhaulers (FASH) who were trying to bolt the union. SHOC was able to spread and coordinate a wildcat strike that began in eastern Ohio. This strike forced the International back to the bargaining table and produced an improved contract. Through these struggles and campaigns TDU grew from a few hundred activists in 1976 to an organization of several thousand in the 1980s.[26]

TDU took another step in strengthening the Teamster reform movement when it merged with PROD in 1979, increasing both its membership and the range of activities in which it engaged. In particular, PROD brought to TDU a Washington office and experience in legislative matters. TDU, for example, was then able to lobby and agitate against deregulation, while at the same time pointing out the faults of the old system of regulation. The newspapers of the two groups were merged to become *Convoy Dispatch* and page three of each issue became the 'Washington Watch', which kept TDU members abreast of legal and legislative developments affecting them and the broader labor movement. In December 1982 TDU capped a long PROD-initiated legislative campaign with victory when Congress passed a law protecting the jobs of 'whistle blowers', employees who refused to drive or operate unsafe equipment.[27]

Over the years, TDU has had growing success in establishing a base among some of the Teamsters' nontrucking jurisdictions. Probably the most important has been among the largely Chicana and Mexicana workers in California's food processing industry. TDU became an active presence in Watsonville, California–based Local 912 in the early 1980s, when it campaigned for bilingual union meetings. While the TDU chapter was always small, it was able to provide a vision of what a union could be and to help organize the victorious 1986–87 strike at Watsonville Canning. And because it was a national organization, TDU also made it difficult for Teamster President Jackie Presser to crush Local 912 or put it into trusteeship, which he threatened to do. In fact, in the midst of the year-and-a-half strike, TDU ran two candidates for office, José Lopez for president and Joe Fahey for recording secretary and business representative. Lopez came in second in a field of four and Fahey won.[28]

Following deregulation in 1980 and the onset of the recession, Teamsters, like other workers, were forced on the defensive and confronted with wave after wave of demands for concessions. TDU's contract campaigns reflected this change in climate as it became the leading force in the fight against concessions in trucking, grocery, and food processing. This focus on the struggle against concessions helped TDU to grow and to begin to define the terms of debate within the union in spite of its relatively small size in comparison to the IBT's total membership. For example, in 1983 Jackie Presser, who had just become president of the union, attempted to push through a relief rider (contract amendment) to the NMFA that would have created a two-tier wage system in freight. TDU started a countercampaign early and was able to help organize an overwhelming rejection vote of 94,086 to 13,082. In this campaign TDU worked along with non-TDU local officers who had been won to opposition on this issue. Since 1983 TDU has kept the IBT leadership on the defensive on the issue of two-tier plans and has succeeded in defining two-tier wages as a disaster to effective unionism. TDU continued its campaign against the two-tier system in 1985; in response, Presser denied that the contract contained any such provisions because the 30% gap between new hires and current workers would close in three years. Ultimately, the contract was ratified by a narrow margin, indicating widespread opposition to even a modified two-tier system.[29]

In 1986 TDU launched a campaign for the right to vote for the union's top officers. By the time of the IBT convention in May, TDU had thousands of signatures on a petition which it presented to the delegates. The TDU-sponsored resolution on the right to vote, like its other motions, was defeated as expected because of the rigged nature of Teamster conventions. But TDU continued this fight by taking the issue to the courts later that year. This campaign gained national prominence in June 1987, when the US Department of Justice announced that it was considering placing the entire Teamsters union in trusteeship under the provisions of Racketeer Influenced and Corrupt Organizations (RICO) Act. TDU immediately countered by opposing government takeover of the union and demanding instead a referendum election for the top officers of the IBT. TDU argued that a government takeover could not rid the Teamsters of mob influence because it would leave intact the election system that had perpetuated corrupt leadership for: only membership control could clean up the union. To butress its case, TDU pointed to the Department of Labor–supervised election in the United Mine Workers that had brought the MFD to office in 1972. The government's course of action remained in doubt in late 1987.[30]

In 1986–87 two of TDU's legal and pressure campaigns bore fruit. TDU led the fight against drug testing as Jackie Presser tried to impose rules that would have made such testing virtually mandatory. TDU distributed educational materials for the Teamster membership in freight and took the issue to court. In a similar lawsuit, TDU was successful in banning drug testing for carhaulers. In December 1986, after intense pressure, TDU succeeded in getting the National Highway Traffic Safety Administration to ban the use of Jifflox, an unsafe coupling devise used on eighteen-wheel tractor-trailers.[31]

Local union elections were also an important focus of TDU activity in many areas. Most of its early attempts to win local office were unsuccessful, but TDU began to have increasing electoral success as the 1980s unfolded. In November 1983 *Readers Digest* reported that 'TDU members have won executive board positions in locals in 17 states, representing more than 125,000 Teamsters.'[32] Some of the candidates who won office were part of broader reform slates supported by a local TDU chapter and inevitably a few of those elected proved unreliable. But over time, TDU's electoral practice produced more solid results. In 1985 TDU member Linda Gregg won the top office of Local 435 in Denver, Colorado. Then, in December 1986, TDU candidates took control of New York City Local 138, after the president had beaten one of the TDUers in public. By the late 1980s there were countless TDU stewards, and TDUers sat on the executive boards of about forty US locals.[33]

Most TDU leaders understood that in order to have the forces to gain widespread local power, a much higher level of class struggle throughout US industry is necessary. Teamster reform cannot exist in isolation from the conditions and consciousness of the rest of the working class. However, with its emphasis on direct intervention on the issues, its ability to broaden the scope of issues, its growth in new constituencies, and its consistent efforts to train and broaden leadership, TDU is in a position to give direction and coherence to a rising level of struggle. Unlike reform attempts in other unions, TDU provided an organized context for new activists. When events create a larger pool of activists, TDU will be able to provide them with a vehicle for effective, united action on a larger scale.

Union Reformers and the Impulse for Broader Change

In the 1980s, challenges to incumbent administrations representing substantially different and broader approaches to unionism occurred in a number of internationals. Possibly the most visible of these was Ed

Asner's campaign for president of the Screen Actors Guild. Asner, best known for his TV role as Lou Grant, was in fact a political progressive with a developed sense of militant social unionism. In 1981 Asner ran and won as a member of the Caucus of Artists for Merger (CAM), a group formed out of an unsatisfactory settlement of the 1980 actors strike. Central to CAM's program for the union was merger with the Screen Extras Guild, a move that would strongly benefit the lowest paid artists in the industry, and eventually merger with AFTRA, a move that would unite all video media artists. In spite of pressure from the union's right wing, led by Charleton Heston, Asner remained a militant and an outspoken critic of the Reagan administration's (and AFL-CIO's) Central America policies.[34]

Another oppositionist to win was Rich Trumpka, who challenged and defeated Sam Church for the presidency of the United Mine Workers. Trumpka was an unusual candidate for UMWA office. He was a working coal miner who had earned a law degree in his spare time. His program did not call for a simple return to traditional miner militancy, but for rebuilding the structure of the union and organizing nonunion coal production, which by the early 1980s accounted for over half of national coal tonnage. A number of top AFL-CIO figures, including Lane Kirkland and William Wynn, openly supported Church, who represented the last of the old guard in the UMWA and had come to power in 1979 in the vacuum left by the collapse of the old MFD leadership during and after the 1978 miners strike. Church, who had no program for the union, red-baited Trumpka for alleged association with leftists. Nevertheless, Trumpka defeated Church with 68% of the vote in November 1982. In 1984 Trumpka succeeded in negotiating a nonconcessionary contract, using the threat of a selective strike – rather than the UMWA's traditional no-contract, no-work policy. The one major company that refused to sign the master agreement, A. T. Massey, was struck – a story that will be told later. While more cautious than Asner, Trumpka also represented something new – a leader willing to combine political with economic issues. He led the formation of the labor-based Shell Boycott against apartheid in South Africa and, in the second half of the 1980s began talking about the need for a new independent political force in the US.[35]

In 1981 Tony Mazzocchi, former vice president of the Oil, Chemical and Atomic Workers, challenged incumbent Robert Goss for the presidency of that union. During the campaign, Mazzocchi argued that the traditional strike weapon was ineffective in a highly automated, continuous process industry like oil refining, OCAW's primary jurisdiction. He stressed instead that broader alliances, new tactics, and a new approach to politics were needed. And, unlike any other candidate, Mazzocchi called for the formation of a labor party in the US.

Because of his strong record on health and safety in the industries covered by OCAW he was a popular candidate and succeeded in building a strong network of supporters around the country. Nevertheless, he lost to Goss by just over 3,000 votes – 69,090 to 72,856. Some of his supporters attributed his defeat to the disaffiliation of the 20,000-member Canadian district, where Mazzocchi was popular, two years earlier. Although Mazzocchi remained popular among activists in the OCAW, the leadership was eventually able to isolate his activity to District 8 on the East Coast. Mazzocchi, however, has continued to be active on health, safety and environmental issues and to campaign for the idea of a labor party throughout the 1980s.[36]

The only other oppositionist to challenge an incumbent president and do well in the 1980s was Dave Daniels, who ran very well against Moe Biller in 1984 and 1986 for president of the American Postal Workers Union (APWU). Like the USW and the UMWA, the APWU has a national referendum vote for its top officers. Outside the few unions that have national referendum votes, it is very difficult to mount a challenge for an international union office. Even though Mazzocchi had been a vice president of the OCAW, his supporters had to do a great deal of grassroots organizing to run a credible convention campaign. Since most unions elect their top officials at conventions, most reform efforts in the 1980s began at the local or regional level. Among some of the most important of these were the successful 1983 challenge by John Glasel for president of 17,000-member Local 802 of the American Federation of Musicians in New York City in 1983; Georgianna Johnson's ousting of Doris Turner as president of 70,000-member Local 1199, also in New York City, in 1986; Delene Reed's victorious campaign for president of the Detroit Metro Area Local of the APWU in 1986; and the sweep of militants in Local 201 of the IUE at GE's Lynn, Massachusetts operations in 1985.

Perhaps the most encouraging development of the late 1980s was the formation of the New Directions caucus in Region 5 of the UAW. Along with important local victories for the opposition forces in the UAW, such as those by Pete Kelly in Local 160, Carole Travis in Local 719, and Bill Parker in Local 1700, the growth of New Directions represented the first serious challenge to the UAW leadership since the late 1960s. New Directions grew out of a series of innovative in-plant struggles organized by Assistant Regional Director Jerry Tucker. Called 'running the plant backward', these campaigns revived some old tactics such as the slowdown and created an atmosphere involving the rank and file in collective action on the job. First tried at Moog Electronics in 1983, this strategy allowed the contract to expire. With the contract's no-strike clause inoperative, the 'concerted activity' of the workers was now protected by the National Labor Relations Act. Of course, the company fired workers anyway, but in the end the union got their jobs back. This strategy proved effective against aggressive management in a number of plants in Region 5.

Tucker developed a strong base in many locals throughout UAW Region 5, which covers Missouri, Arkansas, Louisiana, Kansas and the Southwest. As noted in Chapter 9, he challenged incumbent Regional Director Ken Worley at the 1986 UAW convention and came within a fraction of a vote of winning. Defeat at the Anaheim convention did not stop Tucker or the New Directions caucus, however. Victor Reuther lent his support to Tucker's legal appeal to overturn the elections. In summer 1987, New Directions increased its strength in Region 5 as its candidates swept the local union elections.

The New Directions movement was also a key part of the developing opposition to the nonadversarial labor relations schemes being pushed by more and more companies. At the UAW's April 1987 Bargaining Convention, New Directions joined with militants from other areas to attack the Saturn agreement and demand an end to the whipsawing described in Chapter 8.

As the leader of New Directions, Tucker represented something more than an 'out' bureaucrat turned renegade. He advocated a turn away from the conventional business unionism of the UAW. For one thing, New Directions was an organized caucus and not simply a network built around one personality. Tucker often argued against depending on his candidacy as a panacea and continued to emphasize direct action and grass-roots organization. At a region-wide meeting of New Directions on 20 June 1987, Tucker told the one hundred participants, many of them newly elected local officers, to 'educate and provide accountability to their membership, and continue to advocate democratic debate, solidarity, and unionism with a higher purpose.' Tucker's rejection of business unionism was even more explicit. He told a meeting of the Labor Solidarity Network of Greater New York that 'business unionism, the ritual dance of sitting around a hotel room, talking to corporate counterparts, devoids you of a real sense of solidarity.'[37]

To be sure, reformers and oppositionists suffered setbacks as well, though seldom as serious as in steel. In 1987, the militants in the leadership of IUE Local 201 lost badly in the local elections. Similarly, Michael Shulman, the sole oppositionist to break through machine control of United Federation of Teachers in New York City, was unseated as vice president in April 1987.[38] These two cases illustrated, in different circumstances, the difficulty that isolated oppositionists or militants face in office. Management frequently takes a harder line with militant leaders than it did with those more willing to cooperate with company priorities. Management's hope is to discredit the militants by making life worse on the job. If the new union leaders are unable to change the balance of forces (by mobilizing the members using innovative tactics, and/or making alliances with other social forces) and deliver on their promises, they often go the way of the incumbents they defeated. Indeed, the regular turnover of local officials in many unions who are unable to win any real improvement in conditions has been a factor contributing to the membership apathy that defeats the militants who are unable to break through it.

During the 1980s, the impulse to find ways to change conditions fundamentally often led union reformers into projects beyond ordinary union activity – at least as defined by business unionism. Thus, faced by the ravages of a devastated industry, for example, many who had been involved in the Steelworkers reform movement of the 1970s and early 1980s searched for ways to alleviate the hardships brought on by plant closings and layoffs. By 1982 Steelworkers locals had begun setting up food banks to aid the jobless. By mid-1983 there were about 225 local USW food banks in western Pennsylvania alone. In 1982 steelworker activists in Baltimore and Pittsburgh took the lead in founding organizations of the unemployed open to all jobless workers. In Baltimore, the United Committee of Unemployed People (UCUP) led a successful campaign for a state-sponsored thirteen-week extension of unemployment benefits that would provide income for some 10,000 workers excluded from an extension of federal unemployment benefits. In the Pittsburgh area, where the devastation of the steel industry was most acute, local union activists organized the Mon Valley Unemployed Committee, which led a campaign for a moratorium on home mortgage foreclosures with considerable success throughout 1982 and 1983. MVUC also organized a demonstration of 5,000 people to 'greet' Ronald Reagan when he visited Pittsburgh in April 1983. In June 1983, MVUC hosted the first national conference of organizations of the unemployed in Erie, Pennsylvania. At this conference the National Unemployed Network was formed, the first national organization of the unemployed since the 1930s. While this movement did not become a mass phenomenon like that the 1930s, many of its organizations survived into the late 1980s – and were well in place for the next recession.[39]

The crisis that hit industries like steel and auto particularly hard also began to breed an economic radicalism unusual in the US. Often taking the form of an alliance between local unions or labor activists and church groups, a number of campaigns took shape in the 1980s that challenged the right of capital to destroy the lives of workers and their communities by closing plants in the name of profitability.

From 1980 through 1982, GM closed five of its six California plants, leaving open only its Van Nuys plant near Los Angeles. Sensing that they would be next, members and officials of UAW Local 645 at Van Nuys in 1982 formed the Campaign to Keep Van Nuys Open along with church leaders in the area. The campaign began with job actions, rallies and marches; its central tactic was a threatened boycott of GM products in the Los Angeles market if GM closed the plant. In 1984, continued confrontations and the threatened boycott succeeded in keeping the plant open. As noted earlier, the company was able to impose the 'team concept' on the plant as the price for keeping it open. Although the leaders of the campaign opposed the 'team concept', the fear of unemployment among the members was too great to overcome despite five years of success in preventing the closure.[40]

The most distinctive organization to come out of the crisis in steel was the Tri-State Conference on Steel. Founded in 1981, Tri-State was a coalition of union, community and church activists in eastern Ohio and western Pennsylvania. Tri-State was unique in that it went beyond pressure tactics to prevent the closing of plants to formulate a broader approach to the crisis of the industry. It projected the formation of a Steel Valley Authority (SVA), an autonomous public agency controlled by communities and unions in the Tri-State area (Pennsylvania, Ohio and West Virginia) with the power to buy mills and plants that private industry refused to run. In the plan the plants would become public property and their rehabilitation would be funded with public money. The SVA would attempt to work out purchasing arrangements with the states, which would use some of the steel for infrastructure projects.

The corporations rejected the idea, of course. Tri-State learned through the bitter and unsuccessful fight to stop the closing of US Steel's Dorothy Six blast furnace at its Duquesne mill that the corporations did not want a public competitor in the market and preferred to close (in this case, demolish) a plant rather than sell it. In response, Tri-State advocated using the right of eminent domain to force corporations to sell plants to SVA.

The experience with Dorothy Six at Duquesne gave momentum to the actual formation of the Steel Valley Authority in western Pennsylvania. In 1985 nine towns in the Pittsburgh area agreed to join the SVA and in 1986, the State of Pennsylvania incorporated it. The formula for applying eminent domain and/or purchasing a closed plant, however, was a modification of the earlier public ownership concept borrowed from the Tennessee Valley Authority. The new SVA board called for one-third public ownership, one-third private ownership, and one-third worker ownership through an Employee Stock Ownership Plan (ESOP). But even this compromise formula was hard to implement because the SVA had no public money. This fact led the Tri-State Committee to intensify its regional organizing efforts in 1986, understanding that a much stronger movement for economic change would be needed to make projects like SVA a reality.[41]

The SVA concept was something new in postwar labor activism, introducing the ideas of public ownership and economic planning with a grass-roots perspective. Unlike the abstract industrial policy proposals that had appeared in labor circles in 1983, the SVA was conceived by local union activists and fought for in an active and aggressive manner. Many of them had experience in the reform movement in the USW. Their strategy was mobilization and grass-roots organization – something they had learned in the union. Though they had few resources and faced the active hostility of capital, they nonetheless moved the basically conservative political leaders of several communities to make SVA a reality – albeit an imperfect one.

As in all such reform efforts, of course, the reality of SVA reflected the existing balance of forces in the area. The politicians who formed the majority of SVA's board were not flaming socialists out to seize private industry. Indeed, although some of the labor activists in this small movement are socialists, the Tri-State Conference on Steel has steered clear of any political label. It casts its economic radicalism in the mold of American pragmatism rather than ideological politics – a strategy that is both the strength and the weakness of the project. Further, without an independent political vehicle to shape the politics of the town councils that dominate the board of SVA, the movement has had to make concessions to capital and become dependent on the very banks it has fought for years.

However, these efforts by union activists to confront the broader economic problems that shaped the context in which their unions existed was a progressive and important development. Organizing the unemployed, fighting plant closings, and projecting the notion of public ownership and economic planning are all radical steps for most US unionists and those they ally themselves with. But clearly the problems facing workers in this epoch of crisis, restructuring, and internationalization of the economy cannot be addressed solely in terms of union democracy and militancy. They require a political approach. Efforts such as the Tri-State Conference, MVUC, UCUP, the Campaign to Keep Van Nuys Open, or the Oakland, California– based Plant Closure Project are all important steps toward a more political rank-and-file labor movement.

Like all such movements in the US, however, these fights to limit capital's mobility and prerogatives run up against the fact that US politics is a capitalist monopoly; that is, the two major parties are both dominated by capital. In Britain, where the left wing of the Labour Party was able to dominate the Greater London Council, experiments with local planning and development similar to those advocated by Tri-State could be implemented more fully because of the politics of the Greater London Council – until the Thatcher government succeeded in abolishing it. But in the US, radical pressure campaigns face the barrier of the Democratic Party's fundamental commitment to capital. A movement that at best can only pressure the two parties of capital must fight on capital's terrain.

Building Communications across Union/Industry Lines

A major problem of union reform efforts is parochialism. This parochialism is, of course, in part a product of the norms of business unionism. If unionism is nothing more than collective bargaining over wages and benefits there is no need for regular cross-union communications at the rank-and-file level. Business unionism thus fostered an 'insider-outsider' mentality in union politics. The leaders of the Steelworkers went farther than most when they made it unconstitutional for a candidate for top union office to take outside contributions, including those from members or officers of other unions.[42] In fact, the notion that union affairs should be sealed off from the rest of the world is a feature of business unionism. Like so many aspects of contemporary unionism, this 'insider-outsider' doctrine has its origins in a legitimate concern: in this case, the protection of union affairs from the influence of the employer and the government. In practice, however, modern business unionism has long accepted a blurring of such lines in relationship to government, on which it has been heavily dependent, and even in relation to the employers in an era of nonadversarial labor relations. This insularity, however, is preserved as a means of maintaining business unionist consciousness among lower level officials and the rank and file. In reality, the 'insider-outsider' doctrine applies only to the members and to dissident officials. As we have seen, top union officers from different internationals do not hesitate to support one another against opponents.

While top union officials have ready communications with one another and with their own membership, union activists and local union officials are isolated from one another by both the structure of the unions and the reality of day-to-day working-class life. To begin with, most working-class activity is local and sectoral in nature. In the period of economic growth that followed World War Two and lasted until the late 1960s, strikes remained economic in nature and were waged against specific employers. Even the significant rise of strike activity in the late 1960s remained confined within industry or employer lines. Lacking regular communications, the militants of the 1960s and 1970s were unable to learn from one another or to see the changing economic situation in broader class/power terms. As a result, most of the strike and reform movements of the late 1960s and early 1970s disappeared without a trace. Activists later in the 1970s began to see the limitations of such insularity.

At the most practical level, the union insurgents of the 1970s tended to seek help from outside their own union primarily as a means of redressing the near monopoly of resources possessed by the incumbents. Miners for Democracy, Steelworkers Fight Back, Teamsters for a Democratic Union and many other opposition movements sought the help of members of other unions, family members, outside lawyers, and external sources of financial aid. But the insurgents felt a need for cross-union contact that eventually went beyond the practical questions of resources to those of the information and analysis that could be supplied by experts and by the experiences of other movements. Obviously, the official labor media, designed as it is to perpetuate business union ideas and the careers of top officials, is not suited to these purposes. Thus, unofficial labor publications and educational projects began to proliferate to meet this need. Among the most important of the national alternative labor media of the 1980s were the *Union Democracy Review*, *Labor Notes*, *Labor Research Review*, and *American Labor*. Foremost among the independent labor education projects was the New York-based Institute for Labor Education and Research, later renamed the Labor Institute, and some of the projects of Workers Education Local 189 (an independent labor educators group expelled from the American Federation of Teachers in the early 1970s for supporting Dave Selden against Albert Shanker in the 1973 election for president of that union).

A precursor of many of the publications of the 1980s was *Union Democracy Review*. Edited by long-time union reform advocate Herman Benson, *Union Democracy Review* originated in the early 1960s when it was called *Union Democracy in Action*. *UDR* is primarily concerned with the formal democratic rights of union members, holding up the UAW's Public Review Board as its model for the protection of members' rights. It is the publication of the Association for Union Democracy (AUD), whose major supporters include labor attorney Joseph Raugh and former UAW Vice President and founder Victor Reuther. Since 1972, AUD has supported MFD, Steelworkers Fight Back, and TDU, as well as many smaller movements. In 1979 it held its first national conference on union democracy in Detroit and published a handbook entitled *Democratic Rights of Union Members: A Guide to Internal Union Democracy*. During the

1980s AUD also held a series of regional conferences.

In general, AUD avoided confrontation with the leadership of the more liberal industrial unions, but by the late 1980s, developments such as the Saturn agreement and the UAW's harsh response to reformers Jerry Tucker and Carole Travis brought Victor Reuther and the AUD into closer association with the opposition in the UAW. In fact, AUD's concerns seemed to broaden as the *UDR* commented on a variety of economic and social questions. For example, AUD sponsored a conference on women in the unions in 1986.[43]

Two other projects that attempted to provide analysis and new ideas for union activists without antagonizing top officials were the American Labor Education Center (ALEC), which published *American Labor*, and the Labor Institute. *American Labor*, which came out every other month in a newsletter format, usually devoted each issue to a particular topic such as corporate campaigns or in-plant strategies. At other times, an issue would simply provide educational material on a specific topic.[44] The Labor Institute, which was closely associated with Tony Mazzocchi, developed similar educational materials, including the 1982 book *What's Wrong with the US Economy*, but it also conducted innovative, practical classes for local unions.

In the late 1980s the Institute took on a more activist orientation as it involved itself directly in the campaign to keep open the Freehold, New Jersey 3M plant. The institute and OCAW Local 8-760 decided on a strategy different from those typical of plant-closing fights. They demanded that if 3M refused to keep the plant open, it should provide a permanent income to the displaced workers, allowing them to advance their education or seek training. The Institute produced studies showing that 3M could well afford such a program. The campaign achieved some fame when rock star Bruce Springsteen, who was from Freehold and who wrote a song about plant closings there called 'Hometown', signed a public appeal calling on 3M not to close the plant. Probably even more significant, however, was the strike by 3M workers in South Africa in support of the Freehold workers. Led by Amon Msane, this strike set a new high in active international solidarity and led to a US tour by Msane and OCAW Local 8-760 President Stanley Fischer in 1986. When Msane was arrested upon his return to South Africa, Local 8-760 and the Institute launched a campaign that freed him. The cross-union networks of the Institute and other new projects helped spread the campaign rapidly.[45]

The *Labor Research Review*, which was published by the Midwest Center for Labor Research (MCLR), came out of the contacts between a number of academics and activists in the Steelworkers reform movement in the Chicago-Gary area. The MCLR provided research on a variety of issues not generally available from the USW. Overtime, MCLR expanded its concerns and began publication of the *Labor Research Review*. The *Review* provided in depth analysis of issues effecting labor, including the development of campaigns such as that waged by the Tri-State Conference on Steel. Like *American Labor*, it covered new tactics but its approach was more analytical and more open to debate. The *Review* was directed at union activists, but clearly at a more select and sophisticated layer of activists than many of the other alternative publications targeted. It filled a need for well-researched material that was not coming from either most official labor education programs or from the unions. In the second half of the 1980s, MCLR devoted much of its energy to plant closings in the Chicago-Gary area, developing what it called an 'Early Warning System' for detecting future plant closings.[46]

The most openly oppositional of the alternative publications was *Labor Notes*. Founded in 1979 to serve as a means of communication among insurgents in different unions, *Labor Notes* was openly critical of the functioning of the labor bureaucracy and supportive of union reformers. The bulk of each monthly issue has been news and analysis of major events and trends. For example, in 1979 it warned that pattern bargaining was in trouble and since then has followed its decline along with the development of concessionary bargaining. A major theme of *Labor Notes* articles was opposition to nonadversarial approaches in the labor movement. Although its point of view on questions like concessions and labor/management cooperation was clear, it has always featured debate and controversy. In addition to the monthly newsletter, *Labor Notes* has published several books and pamphlets on key issues. The most popular of these have been *Stopping Sexual Harassment* by Elissa Clark (1982), *Concessions and How to Beat Them* by Jane Slaughter (1983), and *Inside the Circle: A Union Guide to QWL* by Mike Parker (1986).

The cross-union perspective of *Labor Notes* was strengthened by the four national conferences it held in 1981, 1982, 1984, and 1986. The conferences, which attracted from five hundred participants in 1981 to eight hundred in 1986, were educational in format and included up to forty workshops and panels. The conferences brought together activists, dissidents, and insurgents in order to build a national network that could help define the issues and debates taking form in an embattled labor movement. For example, the exploratory meeting that led to the formation of the National Unemployed Network was held at the 1982 *Labor Notes* conference. Like TDU conventions, *Labor Notes* conferences were designed to be training grounds where activists could participate in the debates of the day.

Labor Notes also attempted to rekindle the spirit of social unionism in its publications and events by dealing with issues such as racism, sexism, and internationalism. Conferences not only featured workshops on various aspects of these questions, but included caucus meetings for Blacks, women, and, in 1986, Latinos. The 1984 Black Caucus meetings produced the Black Rank and File exchange, an ongoing organization of Black unionists based in Detroit. Its international coverage tended to expand as the new labor movements in South Africa, Brazil, the Philippines, Mexico and El Salvador grew in importance. Indeed, *Labor Notes* deepened its ties with the union movements in these countries by bringing representatives from their leading unions to speak at its 1986 conference.[47]

All these projects and publications were organized and staffed by people with a background in labor who regarded themselves as socialists. All were directed primarily at activists who were not socialists. From different angles, most of these efforts attempted to re-create the bridge between leftist intellectuals and ideas and working-class activists that had been destroyed by the end of the 1940s. That interaction had been a key element in the creation of the CIO and in the generally progressive and militant direction it took in its early years. During the 1980s the interaction between militants and socialists of various kinds began to be reconstructed through these various nonsectarian channels. While this interaction remained confined to a relatively small layer of union activists, it was, along with the increased presence of socialists and leftists in the unions, a significant development. It was not simply that the leftists provided the ideas for the activists to carry out, but that the activists were training themselves in analytical and political skills that had been largely missing at the grass-roots level in the 1950s and 1960s and only marginally present in the 1970s. The business union bureaucracy's monopoly on information and analysis was being broken and their views of the world challenged by a new generation of leaders and activists with access to independent sources of information and training. This work has laid the basis for developing an alternative view of what unions can be.

11

The Black Working Class Since
the 1960s

The experience of the Black working class has always been shaped by the two worlds in which it exists: Black America and working-class America. As a section of the US working class, Black workers, like other workers, are defined by their relationship to capital. With only the rarest of exceptions, however, capital in the US is owned by white people who participate in and, when it is convenient, encourage the racism of the society as a whole. Thus, while the owners of capital as a social class have never had any regard for the needs of any section of the working class, their attitude toward Black workers has always been unique – from the days when they attempted to use Black workers as strikebreakers and Henry Ford's effort to create a dependent Black workforce, through the decades of 'last hired, first fired', and even into the era of affirmative action. In this respect, the experience of Black workers, even as workers, is different from that of the white majority of the working class.

Black workers also exist as part of Black America, a geographically dispersed nation within a nation. The separateness of Blacks in the US is historically rooted in the experience of slavery, but perpetuated in the subsequent social transformations and migrations of the majority of Blacks: the post–Civil War experience of rural Southern peonage, and the rise of ghettoization throughout the urban centers of the US. This last phase, beginning roughly around World War One, has involved the integration of the majority of the Black community into the working class. But this class integration has not been accompanied by a broader integration in society as a whole. An article in the *Detroit News*, for example, concluded: 'For most whites and blacks, racial integration stops when the workday ends.'[1] This was not a statement about the South in the

1950s or Detroit during World War Two, but a description of life in 1987 Detroit, a city with a Black majority, large Black middle and working classes, and a Black mayor. While the invisibility of Black people in American mainstream culture has begun to break down, racial segregation has remained the norm in housing, education, and daily social life decades after the last Jim Crow law was struck from the books.

As a part of this separate Black America, Black workers and trade unionists share in its particular social crisis. A key aspect of this crisis has been the return and rise of racially motivated violence against Blacks and minorities outside the South. The rise of such violence can be traced to the late 1970s, but it has continued throughout the mid- and late 1980s. The brutal beating of three Black youths by a gang of whites wielding baseball bats that took place in Howard Beach in the Borough of Queens in New York, caught the public's attention. But the Howard Beach attack was preceeded by a string of other such attacks throughout 1986.[2] According to Manning Marable, the roots of this rise of racist violence lie in the convergence of the general state of race relations with an economic crisis 'that increasingly pits the petty bourgeoisie, working class, and permanently unemployed of different ethnic groups against each other over increasingly scarce resources.' But Marable also sees the current mode of Black political activity as a problem, noting that a factor in the boldness of whites in their attacks lies in 'the absence of a powerful, democratic and progressive movement by Blacks which challenges racism in the streets as well as the courts.'[3] This absence has conditioned all Black efforts in the 1970s and 1980s.

The economic contours of the crisis of Black America are an extreme and distorted version of the economic polarization described in Chapter 1. On the one hand, a small, politically dependent new middle class has developed in the many major cities that have had Black administrations. On the other, a far larger phenomenon of the last couple of decades has been the growth of the Black 'underclass', a more or less permanently unemployed mass composed mainly of the most recent generations of the Black urban poor. An indication of the growth of this underclass is the doubling of the unemployment rate for Black teenagers from 24.7% before 1969 to about 50% in the 1980s.[4] Between these two social phenomenon is the Black working class. To a greater degree than the working class as a whole, this section of both the US working class and the Black community has seen its income and job status decline in recent years. In particular, the gains made by Black workers in public and industrial employment in the 1960s have been halted and have begun to erode.

The Fight for Affirmative Action

The economic forces behind this decline have been discussed earlier. They are the related phenomena of industrial migration from city to suburb or countryside; the general decline of industrial employment due to technology, capital flight, and foreign competition; the end of public sector employment growth; and wage deceleration. As a result of these forces, urban Black workers have lost many of the better paying industrial jobs they gained during the 1960s, as well as the option of moving into decent paying public jobs. In response they have been forced to take lower paying jobs or face prolonged unemployment.

A factor in this process has been the seniority system embodied in most union contracts. This meant that when recession, closure, or relocation hit, those with the least seniority were the first to go. Since in many cases Blacks (or women or Latinos) had only recently been hired when the big recession of 1974 began, they were out of the industry. This process was repeated and deepened in the 1980–83 recession. But it also occurred in declining industries such as steel even during periods of recovery. Seniority also governs promotion in most unionized industries, and promotion to better jobs often means promotion to more secure jobs.

Not surprisingly, the major issue among Black trade unionists in the 1970s was affirmative action in both hiring and promotion. Nowhere was this fight sharper than in the steel industry. In May 1971 a group of five Black steelworkers at Bethlehem Steel's Sparrows Point complex in Baltimore filed suit against Bethlehem and the United Steelworkers for racial discrimination. It had been known for years that Bethlehem maintained, with union agreement, separate seniority lines within departments. Since the Blacks at Sparrows Point were concentrated in the worst departments, promotion to better jobs was virtually impossible. In the heat of the civil rights era of the 1960s, George Mercer, one of the five members of USW Local 2610 to file suit, had gotten the Equal Employment Opportunity Commission (EEOC) to impose his promotion to crane operator on the company and the union. But the company, again with union complicity, continued to pay him at the laborers' rate. This led to a Labor Department decree later that year granting 1,600 Black workers a financial settlement for past discrimination. Nevertheless, Blacks were generally dissatisfied with the decree, since it left the question of seniority unresolved. After three more years of pressure, the Labor Department and the union negotiated a consent decree that led to modification of the seniority system.[5]

The white backlash to attacks on the seniority system was immediate. Brian Weber, a white worker at a Kaiser Aluminum plant in Louisiana, filed suit charging 'reverse discrimination'. Weber had failed to get a craft job because Blacks with less seniority had been advanced under the terms of a similar consent decree negotiated by the USW at Kaiser. Since it had negotiated the decree, the USW (and the company) opposed Weber. The case was dismissed by the US Supreme Court in 1979. The Weber case was the industrial analogue of the Bakke case; Allan Bakke had sued the University of California after he was bypassed for admission to medical school in favor of Black students. Though the Bakke case was ostensibly not a labor issue, Albert Shanker, president of the AFT and a public opponent of affirmative action quotas, threw his weight behind Bakke. The AFL-CIO remained silent on the Bakke case, although a writer for the *New Republic* maintained that 'most of the unions of the Federation hierarchy line up with Albert Shanker and Allen Bakke.'[6]

Similar, though less publicized, fights went on in the auto industry as well. In 1973, for example, Black workers at GM's Detroit Diesel Allison plant in Indianapolis filed suit against the company and the UAW for violating Title VII of the Civil Rights Act by denying Blacks entrance to skilled trades jobs. In fact, this was but one of 1,335 Title VII charges filed with the EEOC against the UAW during 1964–73. Although the number of Black workers in the UAW had increased by the end of this period, the UAW leadership continued to resist affirmative action. The decline of Black self-organization within the UAW in the 1970s limited the effectiveness of the fight for affirmative action there, and the skilled trades in auto remained a nearly all-white enclave throughout the 1970s and 1980s.[7]

The 1983 agreement reached between the EEOC and General Motors was indicative of the problems of implementing affirmative action in the 1980s. GM agreed to a $42.5 million program to redress the effects of previous discrimination. As part of the settlement, $4 million in back pay would go to those individuals who had filed EEOC suits. Another $15 million was earmarked for grants to college and technical schools. The rest went to various training programs, all of which were designed for white-collar employees or for advancement into supervisory or executive positions. The skilled trades jobs were left untouched and the vast majority of Blacks in GM blue-collar jobs were unaffected.[8]

The Reagan administration also made a number of moves to undermine or cripple affirmative action programs. Some progress had been made since affirmative action programs for government contractors with more than 50 employees had been mandated by Executive Order 11246 in 1965. An EEOC study of 34,000 firms showed that minority employment among government contractors had grown from 12% in 1967 to 19% in 1983. (However, the general employment trends of this period indicate that even this progress may have been concentrated in

Jim West

Michigan Blue Cross workers and their families walk the picket line in 1987 in a successful fight against concessions.

low-paying jobs.) In 1985 the Reagan administration began talk of undermining this program by raising the employee level to 250. The principle of affirmative action in hiring was upheld by the Supreme Court in 1986, but in the meantime a great deal of damage had been done.[9]

One of the biggest setbacks in affirmative action occurred in 1984 when the Supreme Court ruled that affirmative action in layoffs was valid only when a seniority system could be proved to have been based on the intent to discriminate. This ruling, which came in a case involving Memphis fire fighters, confirmed the last-hired, first-fired principle that had victimized Blacks for generations. In 1981 Black fire fighters had won a court decision requiring the Fire Department to maintain the existing percentage of Black employees during layoffs in that year. The city and the fire fighters union appealed the ruling, and it was eventually overturned. The AFL-CIO supported the Supreme Court's ruling, while UAW attorney Leonard Page was quoted as saying he was 'pleasantly surprised.'[10] Opposed by both the Reagan administration and the leaderships of most unions, Black workers were in a poor position to sustain such gains as they had made.

In general, the political and trade union activities of Black workers in the 1970s and 1980s were conditioned by the demise of the mass movements of the 1960s. Whereas the dynamics of the civil rights movement of the 1960s had tended to activate every section of the Black community from the middle-class leadership to the underclass, the frustration, repression, and exhaustion of Black activism in the early 1970s led to different, more conventional types of pressure or service activity. Douglas Glasgow, a sociologist who has studied the movements of the Black underclass in Los Angeles in the 1960s and 1970s, noted the change on the streets when he returned to Watts in 1975, ten years after the Watts rebellion. Various social service institutions were still present, Glasgow reported:

> Notably missing, however, were the social activists flooding the streets and the many mobile offices set up in the sixties for emergency responses to the community's needs. In the mid seventies, the arena of social protest has been relocated. Now they were found in political caucuses; the publications of small inner-city research firms, which pointed out the worsening condition of need among Blacks; and the papers delivered at conferences by Black educators, sociologists, social workers, psychologists, and other professionals who examined the special problems of those confined to the ghetto. Solutions were sought through trade-offs between different segments of society and through negotiated settlements.[11]

The grass-roots organizations of the poor, such as the Sons of Watts, the Black Panther Party, and many welfare clients organizations had disappeared or been institutionalized as part of a service network. Similarly, the organizations of Black rank-and-file industrial workers, from the Steelworkers for Justice at Bethlehem's Sparrows Point plant in the early 1960s to the League of Revolutionary Black Workers in Detroit in the late 1960s, had disappeared. The activities of the 1970s, from the growth of electoral action within the Democratic Party framework to attempts to redress the effects of past discrimination in industry through legal action, lent themselves to implementation by professionals and middle-class influence brokers.

In addition, the economic climate that followed the 1974–75 recession made direct action appear unviable in most instances, whether in industry or in the streets. With the Civil Rights Act of 1964 and the Voting Rights Act of 1965 in place, much of the activity of both Black trade unionists and the major civil rights organizations turned toward the more conventional channels of the US political system to enforce or defend the gains that had been made. The affirmative action campaigns, for example, were largely limited to legal action by small groups of workers or to traditional advocacy organizations like the NAACP. Like most active workers, Black unionists turned toward pressure and reform activity within their unions.

Black Union Reform in the 1970s and 1980s

Frustrated by the lack of progress within the labor movement and the conservative stance of the AFL-CIO leadership, a group of Black union officials issued a call in 1972 for a convention to form the Coalition of Black Trade Unionists (CBTU). The CBTU's founding conference drew 1,200 Black union officials and rank and filers. Although the convention put considerable emphasis on the presidential campaign of George McGovern, its organizers projected CBTU as a permanent Black pressure group within the unions. They vowed to fight for Black equality on the job and within the structures of organized labor. Indeed, the mere formation of CBTU was somewhat of an affront to the white labor bureaucracy, which continued to tout the A. Philip Randolph Institute as the legitimate organization of Black unionists. Clearly, the leaders who formed CBTU felt the need for something independent of their white colleagues. A second national conference, which drew about 1,400 delegates, was held in 1973 to formally make CBTU a permanent organization. [12]

A major concern of the CBTU was the development of Black leadership within the union hierarchy. The number of Black officials had remained small in spite of the efforts of Randolph and others in the 1960s and the growth in the number of Black union members during those years in both basic industry and public employment. However, resistance to real change by the white leadership of the AFL-CIO and its affiliates, as well as by the Teamsters, blocked the CBTU's efforts. Ten years after its creation, only one of the AFL-CIO's affiliates had a Black president, while the thirty-five member AFL-CIO Executive Council had only two Black members. In 1982 William Lucy, then secretary-treasurer of AFSCME and president of CBTU, assessed the progress of Blacks in labor's officialdom: 'There is more participation in the intermediate levels than there was, say, ten years ago.... There've been some breakthroughs into vice-presidential positions in international unions. Each one has their one this or two that. But the leadership levels are not nearly reflective of participation by minorities as is the workforce.'[13]

Lucy was himself a victim of the persistence of racism in the unions. When Jerry Wurf died in 1981, Lucy was a leading contender for the presidency of AFSCME. He was defeated, however, by Gerald McEntee, who was head of AFSCME in Pennsylvania. Most people believed that the major factor arguing for McEntee's succession was race.

Along with the actions of the rank-and-file Black workers who initiated the countless EEOC suits during the 1970s, the CBTU played a role in moving labor from open, official opposition to affirmative action to its acceptance where the government had already mandated it, as in steel or the telephone industry. But neither CBTU nor the other Black advocacy organizations had the strength to force labor to fight for affirmative action. Talk of coalitions between labor and the civil rights (and women's) organizations was widespread toward the end of the 1970s, but even this little progress collapsed as the economy began another nosedive in 1980 and industrial restructuring accelerated throughout the rest of the decade. CBTU remained a large organization during the 1980s. Its conventions continued to draw over 1,000 delegates and to pass some of the most progressive resolutions to be found in labor circles. But it never became the active presence that the NALC had been for a few years in the late 1950s and early 1960s.

CBTU was limited by the context in which it functioned: the lack of a mass movement in the Black community and the anomalous position of the Black trade union bureaucrat. Randolph and the NALC rode the crest of a powerful and growing movement. The civil rights struggle gave them both the authority and the backbone to assert an independence from the white labor bureaucracy that was not apparent among the leaders of NALC before or after those years. CBTU's leaders were sincere in their attempt to found an effective pressure group, but they took their step just at the moment that the self-activity of Black workers, either as civil rights activists or militant unionists, had subsided. As high-ranking union officials themselves, the major founders of the CBTU, who included Lucy, Amalgamated Meatcutters Vice President Charles Hayes, UAW Vice President Nelson Jack Edwards, and District 65 President Cleveland Robinson, were unlikely to take any steps that would provoke a serious confrontation with the white leaders of the AFL-CIO without mass pressure from below.

Moreover, the position of today's few ranking Black labor officials is a contradictory one that tends to separate them from precisely the Black rank-and-file base they need to make a project like CBTU work. As responsible officials of their union, they work daily, within the constrained atmosphere of the bureaucracy, with the very white leaders on whom they need to exert pressure. Thus, their efforts are compromised – whether to create more openings for Blacks within the hierarchy of their own union or to force the union leadership to confront the racism among white members by fighting for affirmative action. It was therefore unlikely that they would take the lead in an effort to mobilize the Black ranks to pressure the white leaders. Rather, these Black officials have themselves needed pressure to move. But this pressure has not been forthcoming during the 1970s or 1980s. Furthermore, the pressure not to confront the white labor bureaucracy is reinforced by the desire of most Black community leaders to seek legislative alliances with them. Although most Black leaders harbor a deep and well-founded distrust of white labor leaders, they see them as one of their few allies. As a part of the Black leadership, Black labor officials must share the concerns of other Black leaders. Thus the pressure to maintain peace with white labor officialdom comes from two sources that are more present in the daily lives of most full-time Black labor officials than the Black rank and file. One of the most telling results of this dual pressure was the CBTU's endorsement of Walter Mondale rather than Jesse Jackson in the 1984 Democratic primary and convention fights.[14] Lacking an organized rank-and-file counterforce, the Black labor leaders who founded and ran CBTU followed both the white labor bureaucracy and most of the Black leadership into the Mondale camp.

The economic pressures on the Black working class, however, have been even greater than those on the class as a whole. Black workers who belong to unions have thus had an even sharper interest in making those unions effective instruments of resistance to employer aggression. Not surprisingly, Black workers have played a key role in all of the major union reform movements of the 1970s and 1980s – even where their numbers were small, as in the United Mine Workers. Blacks were important in the Steelworkers reform movement and are a large part of the leadership and base of the New Directions movement in Region 5 of the UAW. Blacks were also part of the leadership of dissident movements among Greyhound drivers and Philadelphia public transit workers in the Amalgamated Transit Union and among New York City Transit Authority workers in the Transport Workers Union. But in addition to playing a role in mixed or predominantly white movements, Black workers have also led primarily Black-based reform movements in a number of unions in the 1980s.

Jackson, Electoral Politics, and the Black Working Class

Electoral action as the major form of Black political activity in the 1970s and 1980s has often been portrayed as a natural extension of the civil rights movement of the 1960s. In its earliest thrust it had a radical spirit that embodied the militancy and even the Black nationalism of the late 1960s. The first Black mayors, Kenneth Gibson of Newark and Richard Hatcher of Gary, often spoke in nationalist terms. There was considerable talk about breaking with the Democrats and forming an all-Black party. In March 1972 a national Black political convention, called by Hatcher and others, attracted over 3,000 participants. It passed a 'Black Agenda' and founded the National Black Political Assembly, which was seen by many as a preparty formation. But the talk of independence soon died, and many of the leaders of the Assembly turned to the McGovern campaign. The Assembly later collapsed as a significant organization.[15] Electoral action grew, however, as the central means of advancing the interests of the Black middle classes and leadership strata. As the Democrats moved to the right in the years following the overwhelming defeat of McGovern, continued reliance on the Democratic Party as the context for Black political action became a conservatizing influence throughout the 1970s and well into the 1980s.

At one level, Black electoral action within the two-party system appeared successful. The number of Black elected officials in the US rose from 1,472 in 1970 to 5,654 in 1985. But this fourfold growth in representation did not represent much of a change in the power of Blacks in the US. The vast majority of these officials (4,953 in 1985) were city, county or school board officials, who, outside a few large cities, have little power to improve the conditions of their Black constituents. These Black elected officials were also concentrated in the South – 3,801 of the total in 1985. The highest levels achieved by Blacks were in state legislatures and the US Congress, where Blacks accounted for only 407 out of 7,926 legislators in 1985.[16]

Probably the most significant permanent aspect of Black electoral action was the election of Black mayors in a number of the largest cities, beginning with the election of Richard Hatcher in Gary, Indiana in 1967 and culminating with the election of Harold Washington as mayor of Chicago in 1983. By the mid-1980s, such major urban centers as Detroit, Philadelphia, Chicago, Gary, Newark, Atlanta, and Los Angeles had Black administrations.[17] Nevertheless, they often presided over decaying cities with declining tax and industrial bases and were powerless to stop or even slow the increase of poverty and hopelessness in the predominately Black inner cities. The perception that the majority of a new generation of Black people had no hope for decent employment grew during the 1980s.

Federal support for urban programs began to decline under Carter and all but dried up under Reagan, and the new Black administrations simply did not have the resources to address the problems of the ghettoes. Increasingly, the only available resources came on the terms of capital – tax rebates for the few jobs they created in the cities and favors in exploiting the potentially profitable areas of the city, usually downtown. The more conservative Black mayors, such as Wilson Goode of Philadelphia and Thomas Bradley of Los Angeles, readily accepted the priorities of capital. Black mayors with radical or movement backgrounds, such as Hatcher in Gary, Coleman Young in Detroit, and Andrew Young in Atlanta, made their peace with local capital just like their more conservative counterparts. Reluctantly or enthusiastically, they succumbed to the ubiquitous downtown development schemes that left Black neighborhoods without the resources to stem blight or unemployment. Neighborhood development, in Coleman Young's Detroit or Harold Washington's Chicago, came to mean little more than contracts for what remained of Black business. The jobs and income generated by this approach have been minuscule in relation to the problems that Blacks face and tend to flow into the hands of capital or to accrue to professionals or small businesses. [18]

So far as working-class and poor Blacks are concerned, the major achievement of the new Black city administrations has been a moderation of police violence against Blacks. While no city has changed the fundamental role of the police as guardians of private property, they have ended some of the abuse of police power – largely by increasing the number of Black police officers and administrators. Police violence played an important part in the election of some of the first Black mayors, notably Coleman Young and Richard Hatcher. Their elections were followed by bitter fights to increase the number of Black police officers, abolish officially approved programs of extreme violence against Blacks such as STRESS in Detroit, and create some objective standards to guide the use of violence. Although these efforts had some impact, a University of California sociologist surveying violence against minorities could still report in 1987 that 'there are very few communities of color where police brutality is not already an issue.'[19]

Black administrations have also played a role in changing the social structure of the Black community in many cities. While the rise of Black employment in the lower, more working-class jobs in the local public sector preceded the appearance of most Black mayors, Black administrations did provide employment for educated Blacks in higher-paying city professional and administrative jobs previously held by whites.[20] In cities like Detroit, Gary, and others where Blacks held office for a considerable period, this produced a significant new middle class dependent on the political administration and, hence, on the national power structure of the Democratic Party (the potential source of more funds) and on locally based capital. This new social grouping differs from the old Black petty bourgeoisie in that it does not depend on the Black consumer market but on city politics. As a political creation, it participates in political affairs with far greater frequency than either the working class or the underclass. It also participates in the broader leadership of the Black community along with the traditional petty bourgeoisie, the older professional groups, and the Black labor leadership. Its importance in these circles has increased because small business has declined in the Black community through ruin or replacement by white-owned chain stores.[21]

The most salient fact is that the new middle class depends on Black incumbency for its existence. Since few whites vote for these Black mayors, the unity of the Black vote is essential in most cases to guarantee reelection. As a result, the new Black middle class views as dangerous any attempt to create a more radical force in the Black community or among Black workers, particularly if it threatens to split the Black vote in a municipal election. The Black administration accepts the priorities of capital and the national Democratic Party, the new middle class supports the administration, and the Black labor leaders feel constrained to function within this consensus. Following the same course, the Black working class also supports the Black administration because it fears the white alternative, but it has little to say about policy so long as it remains disorganized.

The role of organized labor in the elections of many of the Black mayors, particularly the earlier ones, tended to follow a pattern. The white leaders of the major unions in the city, whether from industrial or craft unions, tended to support the white candidate, while Black officials supported the Black candidate. Prior to 1973, when Sadlowski and the reformers captured District 31 of the Steelworkers, District Director Joe Germano had been a supporter of the white machine in Gary. The USW thus officially supported Hatcher's white opponent. Black steelworkers, however, were an important component of the vote that gave Hatcher the election. Only after the reformers, who included Black and white leaders, took over District 31 did the Steelworkers in the Chicago and Gary areas back Black candidates. The same pattern was repeated in the 1973 election of Coleman Young as mayor of Detroit. Black autoworkers and the heavily Black UAW locals in Detroit supported Young, but the top regional and International UAW leadership backed a white liberal in the primaries. Following Young's election, when it became apparent he would join the coalition of capital and labor leadership that guided economic development, the UAW routinely backed Young.[22]

The behavior of the white labor leadership in these situations was largely a function of their previous accommodation to the racism of most of their white members. Since the 1940s attempts to confront racism in the ranks had been rare in even the most liberal of unions. Since their own incumbency usually depended on the support of the white majority of union members or at least on the white local leaders who attended conventions, most white labor bureaucrats hesitated to confront the consciousness of their white members in the primaries. In the general election, where the alternative would have been to support a Republican, their institutional ties to the Democratic Party superceded their concerns about their members and they backed Black Democrats. This was what happened in the 1983 campaign of Harold Washington in Chicago. In the primaries, white labor leaders, with notable exceptions like USW reformer Jim Balanoff, tended to side with the old white machine candidates, but in the general election, the alternative was to back an openly racist, antilabor Republican, and many white labor leaders supported Washington. However, these leaders were unable to carry large numbers of white union voters into the Washington campaigns in 1983 and again in 1987.[23]

The irony of the 1970s and 1980s was that the power of the Black community as a whole declined precisely as more Blacks became officeholders in urban America. This was evident from the priorities of the Carter administration. In 1977, for example, Maryland's Black Congressman Parren Mitchell, NAACP Director Benjamin Hooks, Urban League Director Vernon Jordan and Operation PUSH Director Rev. Jesse Jackson jointly charged the Carter administration with 'callous neglect' of Black America.[24] To a large extent, the Black leadership, including its trade union officials, was paralyzed by its responsibility to administer the crisis of most major cities and by its increased dependence on the national political and economic (white) power structures. In a sense, the Black leader was in the same political fix as the labor official: both depended on the Democratic Party for legislation that could alleviate the deteriorating economic conditions of their base. But their influence within that party visibly declined as the balance of class forces in US politics changed in the 1970s and 1980s.

The combination of declining political influence, demoralization among the masses (largely a function of 'underclass' growth and high unemployment), and leadership paralysis pointed toward disaster as the Reagan years unfolded. Aware of this, sections of the Black leadership (in particular, the civil rights 'leadership family', mostly former associates of Martin Luther King, Jr.) began to discuss how to break this deadly cycle of defeat. Their answer was to call for a march on

Washington on the twentieth anniversary of the 1963 March for Jobs and Justice. Their hope was to rekindle a movement that could put Black concerns back on the nation's agenda. The organizers of the march, who included Coretta Scott King and Black Congressman Walter Fauntroy (a coordinator of the 1963 march), made every effort to create a broad coalition to build the event. Although the march received considerable support from Black and progressive labor leaders and activists, the AFL-CIO leadership was hostile to it. Kirkland, in fact, called on AFL-CIO unions to put their efforts into building Labor Day events to take place a week after the Washington march – an action meant to diminish labor participation. Bayard Rustin of the A. Philip Randolph Institute attacked it in a letter to Coretta King. On the other hand, progressive unions with large Black memberships, including District 65 of the UAW, AFSCME, and 1199, supported the march. About 300,000 people attended – more than in 1963.[25] But 1983 was not 1963. The march did not take place in the context of an ongoing movement in the streets. Its message was essentially to continue the electoral trend that had become the de facto strategy of the Black leadership. As a one-shot event it could not have changed the balance of forces that continued to work to the disadvantage of Black America.

Jesse Jackson, the controversial leader of Operation PUSH in Chicago, had another idea. He put himself forward as a candidate for president of the United States in the 1984 Democratic primaries. Sensing the frustration in the Black community and the paralysis of its leadership, Jackson took this step largely on his own initiative. In fact, most of the Black leadership family opposed the idea. Most Black mayors and congressmen opposed it as well. But the politically active base of the community responded positively. Although a part of the Black leadership family, Jackson was not an officeholder or a member of the dependent middle class. He had his own base in Operation PUSH and nationally among the Black clergy, of which he was a member.

Jackson, of course, had no hope of winning in 1984. His strategy was to demonstrate the importance of the Black vote to the Democrats, enlarge that vote both through vigorous registration efforts and through the increased voter participation a Black candidate could anticipate, and force Black issues back on the agenda of the party. Jackson did not call for a break with the Democratic Party, and there was never any question that he and his supporters would back whomever the Democrats nominated. Rather, he called for an electoral demonstration that he hoped would force the party to renegotiate the terms of dependency.

The bulk of the Black leadership endorsed Mondale, so Jackson's Rainbow Coalition took on the character of a rebellion of the base against an elite that for years had failed to provide real leadership. But the base that rebelled was not exactly the most downtrodden sector of the Black community. Since the Rainbow Coalition was not really a grass-roots organization, Jackson's main campaign mobilization came from the Black churches, implying that much of his voting base was among the more stable Black working class as well as the middle classes. In New York state Jackson gained 87% to 89% of the Black vote, but he also received a third of the votes of all union members, a figure which had to include the votes of a fair number of Latino and white unionists as well as Black workers.[26] In all the primaries, Jackson carried a large majority in all sections of the Black community. Yet in nine of the thirteen primaries covered by the CBS News/*New York Times* 1984 Election Survey, Jackson did better among higher income voters than among the poor. Further, among those who were elected as Jackson delegates to the Democratic Convention the majority appeared to be solidly middle class. For example, 58% of the Jackson delegates earned $35,000 or more a year, compared with 63% of the Mondale delegates and 56% of the Hart delegates. Twenty-six percent of Jackson's delegates earned $50,000 or more a year, compared with 31% of Mondale's and 29% of Hart's.[27] The plebian electoral rebellion of 1984 had been commandeered by the Black representatives of the Black elite classes.

This phenomenon was not peculiar to the Jackson campaign or the Rainbow Coalition. For example, a large majority of all the Black delegates at the 1984 Democratic Convention were from middle- or upper-income groups. Only 17% of the Black delegates made under $25,000 a year; 37% earned $25,000 to $50,000; 34%, $50,000 to $100,000; and 7% made $100,000 or more. As a group the Black delegates to the 1984 Democratic Convention were better educated than the white convention delegates – 73% of the Black delegates had a college degree, compared to 60% of their white counterparts, while 55% had graduate or professional degrees.[28] Black political scientist Manning Marable has noted that, in general, 'The central fact about Black political culture from 1865 to 1985 is that only a small segment of the Afro-American social fraction, the petty bourgeoisie, has dominated the electoral machinery and patronage positions that regulate Black life and perpetuate the exploitation of Black labor.'[29]

This phenomenon is more of a reflection of the class character of politics in the US than of the social structure of the Black community, in which the petty bourgeoisie and middle classes are a small minority. In spite of the importance of working-class voters in most urban areas or even of the role played by unions in voter mobilization and policy brokering, the petty bourgeois domination of the day-to-day affairs of party politics is true of US urban politics in general. In his study of politics in Gary and the rise of Richard Hatcher, Edward Greer argues,

'...in reality the urban machines have neither served the working class nor stood above class interests. Rather, the urban ethnic machines have been a political instrument of the petty bourgeoisie. Both the ideology and the policy of the machine reflect this character.'[30]

Greer goes on to show that the petty bourgeois machine is itself necessarily subordinate to the interests and demands of big business. In the case of Gary, totally dominated by the steel industry, the subordination of small business and its allies to big business is highly visible. In cities with a more diverse business structure this relationship is more complex, but in any case it is the starting point of all US politics and those of the Democratic Party, which dominates most urban industrial areas, in particular. The development of media politics and flood of corporate PAC money in the last two decades has increased the dependence of the Democratic Party on big business in national politics, but the domination of the party begins at the local level in the link between big business and the petty bourgeois operatives of the party's grass-roots machinery. As Greer points out, this link has a natural ideological aspect and a predictably individualist outcome. He writes, 'As with small businesses generally, the ideology of the machine bosses 'rests upon their identification with business as such.' Thus, machines prefer to buy off their opponents individually rather than make substantive policy concessions to them.'[31]

This does not mean, of course, that the precise politics of all machines are the same. Because of the persistence of institutional racism, the Black and white petty bourgeoisie and middle classes have a different relationship to capital and to American society in general. The Black middle classes are likely to hold more progressive political and economic views than their white counterparts. Thus, when the links between business and a new Black city administration are still weak, the more radical Black leaders tend to push for policies to benefit the Black community and, when necessary, to resist big business demands for a time. Hatcher was a clear case of this tendency. But these leaders remain within the system and lack a truly independent political force (since they also depend on the national Democratic Party for resources and their political futures). They inevitably succumb and accept the urban priorities of big business as the framework for their economic policies. Such resources as go to the Black community accrue to middle-class individuals rather than taking the form of overall community development or massive job programs. The new machines, of course, are different from the classic white ethnic machines. The nature of the patronage involved is somewhat different, for example. Rather than using graft, city contracts are in most cases shifted from white to Black businesses through perfectly legal affirmative action programs. The jobs filled by Blacks in the administrative hierarchy and higher paying professional civil service slots are made available largely by getting rid of (unofficial) racial barriers rather than through direct patronage of the old sort. The effect, however, is basically the same. The Blacks who fill the majority of jobs or are awarded city contracts are drawn from the literate middle classes. The lives of the Black working class and underclass continues to deteriorate.

Jesse Jackson operates within this context, but has a somewhat different relationship to it than most Black electoral activists. Before his 1984 candidacy, Jackson was not particularly involved in electoral politics beyond the occasional endorsement of a candidate. In ideology and in practice, Jackson accepted the petty bourgeois concept of community development as fully as anyone. He was an outspoken advocate of Black capitalism and the major activity of Operation PUSH was getting contracts and franchises for Black entrepreneurs and positions in corporate hierarchies for educated Blacks. Jackson dealt with white capital as a pressure force, often using tactics of the civil rights era, and with Black businessmen and professionals as an advocate. The theory behind PUSH and other Black capitalist projects is that growing Black businesses will create jobs in the Black community. It is quite possible for a person like Jackson to sustain sincere compassion for the Black poor, while primarily orienting his politics toward the petty bourgeoisie. PUSH, of course, had its origins in Operation Breadbasket, the campaign organized by Martin Luther King, Jr., in 1965. It was thus a precursor of King's later and more radical Poor People's Campaign. Not surprisingly, PUSH took a more conservative direction in the 1970s as the notion of self-help replaced that of mass struggle. Nevertheless, Jackson's relationship to white capital and the political power structure of Chicago was more akin to that of the old Black petty bourgeoisie, which depended on the Black market and not on white capital. Indeed, Jackson's primary support network was the Black clergy, the core and almost sole intact sector of the traditional Black petty bourgeoisie.[32]

This relative social independence, combined with the fact that the Democratic Party hierarchy made no effort to co-opt him, explain Jackson's apparent political radicalization during and after the 1984 campaign. That is, Jackson began his campaign with the notion that a demonstration of the independent significance of the Black vote would be sufficient to get some concessions from the Democratic Party's white leadership. In the context of this approach, neither a labor program nor an orientation toward labor were particularly important. But the 1984 Democratic Convention showed that the Party leadership and its middle class and labor supporters were not impressed by Jackson's quite credible showing among Blacks. They made no concessions to Jackson's demands for reforms in the party's rules.[33]

The general election revealed two things that the Democratic politicos already believed: that the vast majority of Blacks who voted backed the Democratic candidate in spite of the humiliation of Jackson, and that Black voter participation continued to lag behind that of whites despite all the registration efforts and appeals from the Black leadership. That is, the Black working class and Black poor might turn out in larger than usual numbers to back a candidate like Jackson or Harold Washington, but this did not carry over to a routine election in which two white candidates confronted one another. In this respect, a large portion of the Black working class joined the majority of the white working class in the 'party of the nonvoters'. This confirmed the belief of the Democratic leadership that electoral politics in the US had become the terrain of primarily a middle-class electorate in which middle-class candidates, funded by business money, reflected business ideology and middle-class concerns.

All of this seems to have further radicalized the programmatic side of Jackson's post-1984 campaigning. To a greater degree than in the 1984 primaries, Jackson has attempted to give the Rainbow Coalition a more radical/populist programmatic content. He has appeared at various strike support rallies, from Watsonville, California to Austin, Minnesota; backed embattled farmers in the Midwest; and courted white as well as Black labor leaders. The lack of any clear labor favorite among the remaining Democratic presidential contenders in 1987 precluded the sort of unanimous primary endorsement made by the AFL-CIO in 1983 – 84. The only white union president to endorse Jackson in 1988 was Kenneth Blaylock of the American Federation of Government Employees, but the splintering of the labor bureaucracy in the 1988 primaries freed Black labor leaders to support Jackson. Jackson got almost unanimous backing from Black labor officials and considerable support among both white and Black unionists at lower levels. In fact, exit polls showed Jackson getting 35% of the union household vote on 'Super Tuesday', which included primary elections in sixteen states and caucuses in four others. In the Michigan caucuses, Jackson upset both the UAW's implied support for Richard Gephardt and Detroit Mayor Coleman Young's endorsement of Dukakis by taking 55% of the vote. These vote totals obviously included some significant degree of white working-class support.

Furthermore, the disarray of the Democratic Party in 1986–87 probably created a greater opening for a pressure campaign in 1988 than was possible four years earlier. Divisions in the labor bureaucracy in the 1988 primaries freed Black labor leaders to support Jackson. In 1987–88 Jackson also got the backing of many of the Black community and political leaders who had refused to support him in 1984. This was partly because none of the front-running white candidates were noted for their connections with the Black community or their concern with Black issues. After the Michigan caucuses on 25 March, Jackson temporarily became the front-runner with both the greatest number of delegates and the largest popular vote.

Although Jackson did not mute his populist message, he began to act more like a mainstream candidate. He was no longer running as a rebel against the party. Higher expectations, for example, of federal appointments for several Blacks in a Democratic administration, also required a more 'responsible' posture in Democratic Party affairs. The more real the possibility of a renegotiation of the terms of Black dependence within the Democratic Party coalition, the greater the need to moderate the oppositional content of the campaign. In this situation, there was only a remote likelihood of the Rainbow Coalition actually becoming a grass-roots mass organization rather than the narrow, top-down affair it was until well into 1987. Such a mass organization would alienate both the Black leadership, which would see it as a competitor to the traditional Black advocacy groups, and to the Democratic power brokers, who would view it as an embarrassing reversion to the 'interest group' image they had so studiously tried to distance themselves from. In fact, the Rainbow Coalition was stripped of its resources and put on the back burner.

While Jackson's 1988 campaign was still financially threadbare compared to those of his opponents, it was more firmly rooted in elements of the Democratic Party elite. California's Black political boss, State Assemblyman Willie Brown, was prominent in the Jackson campaign, as were other Black political power brokers such as real estate magnate Joel Ferguson in Michigan. In Detroit, Jackson was meeting with a small group of individuals dominated by local Black entrepreneurs like millionaire auto dealer Mel Farr. Fundraising, which had played little role in the 1984 campaign, was a higher priority in 1988. Jackson also allied himself with a few white Democratic leaders, including Bert Lance, Jimmy Carter, and Felix Rohatyn, who functioned as advisers.[34]

Although still radical in tone, the 1988 campaign took on the characteristics of the brokering operations once typical of COPE and labor's other political projects, a direction that would have little to offer working-class and poor Blacks. For one thing, this orientation would certainly reinforce the role of the articulate middle-class elements at the expense of the involvement of working-class or poor Blacks. A COPE-style operation calls for skilled professionals who can deal with well-healed power brokers. The terrain of Democratic Party brokering and fundraising is not conducive to plebeian rebellion. As I argued earlier, the COPE strategy has a built-in trajectory towards failure. It operates in a milieu (the Democratic Party) in which the rules of behavior are determined by capital and enforced by its upper-middle-class minions. As the political representative of a mass working-class organization, COPE is supposed to carry the implied power of organized labor. But as a seeker of influence in elite political circles it can never call its base to action in any way more radical than election day mobilizations and episodic, one-shot demonstrations. A Rainbow Coalition of this type would be caught in the same trap. And its credibility as a mass force would be considerably less than COPE's because, unlike the unions, it does not have a mass membership base.

The alternative to this direction was a break with the Democratic Party. Indeed, numerous activists saw this as the future of the Rainbow. A January 1986 poll conducted by the *Washington Post* showed that 66% of the Blacks interviewed favored a second Jackson run for the presidency in 1988, while 53% of all those interviewed believed Jackson could go on to run as an independent. A small number of labor leaders had begun calling for some sort of break with the Democrats. Henry Nicholas, president of the National Union of Health Care Workers, told the 1985 convention of the Farm Labor Organizing Committee that labor might have to take the lead in forming a 'new political entity'. UMWA President Rich Trumpka told the 1985 convention of the Newspaper Guild that 'all of us in the labor movement must consider that we are not going to establish a government of the people in this country as long as we remain so closely tied to the Democratic Party.'[35] These statements, of course, were not clear calls for a new party, but they reflected the high level of dissatisfaction with the Democratic Party.

By the late 1980s, the Black working class faced the same political dilemma as organized labor. The leaderships of both sought ways to move the Democratic Party back to a more liberal stance on the issues that most concerned them. Labor's tactics were far more conventional than Jesse Jackson's and, in 1984, had conflicted with them. But as unconventional as the Jackson campaign of 1987 – 88 might be in its political positions, it pointed toward an institutionalization of political dependence similar to that created by the CIO in 1943 when it established PAC. Since Jackson could not conceivably win the Democratic nomination, the forces he represented would remain imprisoned in the Democratic context as an organized pressure group unable to take the one action that might actually force the Democrats to make serious concessions – the withdrawal of the Black vote. For all its rhetorical radicalism, the Jackson campaign seemed headed toward a strategy that had failed labor and the Black community for nearly half a century. A political break with the Democrats led by Jackson in 1988 could have alterd the US political landscape in a way that had not occurred since the Populist movement of the 1890s. This would be particularly true if he could carry a significant number of the white workers and farmers he had supported in 1985 – 86. In that event, an independent campaign would have a class character pointing toward a fundamental realignment of US politics along class lines that would provide a way out of the cycle of pressure and accommodation that characterizes working-class and Black politics within the Democratic Party and, by extension, within society as a whole. But given the forces that Jackson relied on and the orientation he seemed to be pursuing, such a break was extremely unlikely.

Disillusionment with the effectiveness of pressure tactics in the Democratic Party had led much of the Black leadership to return to the Black capitalist solutions that the Jackson campaign had seemed to transcend. Previously radical Black mayors like Marion Berry of Washington, D.C. and Richard Hatcher called for less dependence on government programs. The Black leadership family set up the US Investment Company in 1985 to 'provide funds for Black businesses, along with expert managerial guidance.' In the same year, the Black Leadership Roundtable, a coalition of three hundred organizations, established a $200,000 'national Black capital fund' to promote Black business 'whereby we become the employers of our own people'.[36]

If the limitations imposed on the Rainbow Coalition and Jackson campaigns of 1983–84 and 1987–88 by its Democratic Party context left no clear road forward for the Black working class or Black labor, the return of Black capitalism presented a roadblock. The Black capitalism of the 1980s was typified by franchise operations of white-controlled retail or fast-food chains. The new petty bourgeoisie it created was financed by the minimum-wage labor of Black youth and would resist unionization. As a source of employment in the Black community, it promised primarily short-term, high-turnover jobs that are hard to organize by conventional means. And as a source of income for the Black underclass, Black capitalism cannot compete with the underground economy.

Further, the new Black petty bourgeoisie, like the new political middle class, is dependent on parts of the national white power structure. Its politics are likely to remain limited to the cycle of pressure and accommodation represented alternatively by the Jackson campaigns in the Democratic Party and the return of Black capitalist ideas. The combined weight of these two new class elements along with the stagnation of the Black working class and growth of the underclass spelled a negative balance of class forces in Black political affairs. Black workers remained the largest section of the community, but they were not yet organized to provide a more consistently progressive political lead than any of the middle-class elements. Obviously, the organization of the unorganized in the service industries and low-wage goods-producing industries where the Black working class is concentrated would be an enormous step toward fulfilling the potential of Black working-class leadership in the struggle against oppression. Not only could such organizing diminish the overrepresentation of the middle classes in Black politics, but it would strengthen the organized position of Blacks within American society in general. As we have seen, Black workers are far more predisposed to join unions than their white counterparts. Indeed, in some of the few important organizing efforts in recent years, such as at Cannon Mills in North Carolina, Black workers played a leading role in organizing within the plants. This potential is the greatest hope for both the Black community and organized labor in the years to come.

12

Other Social Movements in the US Working Class

In addition to the massive gap between Black and white, the working class in the United States is crisscrossed by social, racial, national and sexual differences reflecting the distinct forms of oppression that affect these groups beyond the shared experience of working-class life. As with Black people, movements have arisen among other national minorities, of which Latinos are numerically the most important in the working class, and among women. What began to develop in the second half of the 1980s among organized workers would be inexplicable without reference to the experience of Latinos and women within the US working class.

Related to the question of the multinational character of the US working class as well as to the globalization of the economy is the question of internationalism. No labor movement in the world has a more sordid history of xenophobic attitudes toward the working classes of other nations than that of the United States. Rooted in the imperial status of the United States and in the racism that has permeated American life since its beginnings, the anti-internationalism of US labor has become a debilitating feature of its inability to respond to the realities of an altered world economy.

Fortunately, the policies that reflect American labor's insularity have been challenged in recent years, and some initial experiments in practical internationalism have taken place. An understanding of the nature of these social and political developments within labor since the 1960s is essential for any analysis of what has taken shape in the 1980s and of the future of organized labor in the US.

The Working Women's Movement

Throughout the postwar era women became more and more a permanent part of the workforce. While the civilian labor force participation rate of men actually declined from 86.4% in 1950 to 76.7% in 1986, that of women rose steadily from 33.9% in 1950 to 55.4% in 1986. Women increased their proportion of the civilian labor force of workers over twenty years of age from 26.7% in 1950 to 41.2% in 1986.[1] Over 80% of women workers are employed in the service sector. In retail trade, finance, services, and government, women constitute about half or more of the workforce. But even in manufacturing the proportion of women rose from 26% in 1960 to 31% in 1980. In spite of the recession of 1980–82, women composed 32% of the manufacturing workforce in 1983.[2]

The rapid expansion of the female labor force did not translate into greater unionization among women workers. The percentage of employed women belonging to labor organizations actually fell from 18% in 1970 to 13.8% in 1984.[3] This trend followed that for labor as a whole, but it also reflected the great increase of women workers in unorganized service industries. Nevertheless, as a result of the growing presence of women in both manufacturing and public employment, women grew as a proportion of union members from 23% in 1973 to 30% in 1980. Indeed, the highest percentages of organized women in 1980 were found in education (33%), public administration (23.4%), and manufacturing (22.2%).[4]

Both as workers and as union members, women face unique problems beyond those experienced by their male counterparts. The income of women remained fixed at about 59% of that earned by men doing the same or comparable work. While most industrial union contracts mandate the same wage level for the same job, wage discrimination against women can be maintained by discriminatory job descriptions and by the de facto exclusion of women from the more skilled jobs. Also, the typical benefits package was oriented toward the needs of male workers with nonworking wives and did not meet such needs as daycare. Beyond the traditional concerns of collective bargaining were other women's concerns that were hard for a male-dominated union structure to comprehend or deal with effectively, such as sexual harassment on the job.

The emergence of a mass women's movement and the rebirth of feminism in the late 1960s had particular impacts on organized labor. Like the Black civil rights movement of a few years earlier, the women's movement altered America's political and social agenda. Its impact on working-class women, however, was complicated by the class nature of the movement. The women's movement of the 1960s and 1970s was based primarily among educated middle-class women. As feminist

Guardian/Bob Sanders

FLOC members and supporters picket Campbell's headquarters as part of their successful corporate campaign.

thought and organization developed in the late 1970s and into the 1980s, it turned even more to an individualist brand of feminism more concerned with the individual advancement of professional women within business, academia and the arts. A more working-class-oriented socialist-feminism grew as a trend within the women's movement, but it remained too small to affect the movement's public image.

Opinion polls taken in the 1970s routinely showed that working-class and poor women did not identify with the women's movement as they saw it. But numerous studies also showed that the consciousness of many working women was affected by the issues and concerns voiced by the women's movement. The phrase, 'I'm not women's libber, but...' appeared frequently in surveys as the preamble to a list of grievances voiced by women in almost all industries and occupations.[5] Furthermore, explicitly feminist concerns such as the need for child care, affirmative action, pay equity (or comparable pay) and the Equal Rights Amendment became the common coin of women union activists in the 1970s and 1980s. Perhaps most important of all, the existence of a visible women's movement capable of winning concrete legislative and social goals helped to break down the sense of powerlessness women are socialized to feel in male-dominated institutions.

Organized labor was and remains dominated by men in spite of the large numbers of women who belong to unions. With the sole exception of the National Education Association, which has a slight female majority on its executive board, not even those unions with large proportions of women members reflect that fact in their leadership institutions. In 1978 the proportion of women among top union officers was small even where women were the majority of members. For example, the ILGWU had an 80% female membership, but only 7% of the officers and board members were women. For the ACTWU, the same proportions were 66% and 15%; SEIU, 50% and 15%; CWA, 51% and 0%; AFSCME, 40% and 3%; UFCW, 39% and 3%; AFT, 60% and 25%; the Teamsters, 25% and 0%. In 1980 the AFL-CIO put the first women, ACTWU Vice President Joyce Miller, on its 34-seat Executive Council.[6]

The lack of women in union leadership positions was a symptom of business unionism's view of itself as a movement of male breadwinners. Organized labor had long embraced the 'family wage' concept which saw men as heads of families responsible for the economic support of the entire family. A corollary to this conception was that women did not need as much money since they were not breadwinners. Pay equity between men and women was only a concern for business unionism where men and women held exactly the same job. The segregation of the workforce into male and female jobs, which often underlay pay inequities in any given firm or industry, was not the concern of business unionism. Benefits packages also reflected the notion of the male as breadwinner.

But reality had changed. Households headed by women without spouses rose from 9.3% in 1950 to 16.2% in 1985. The percentage of married women (whose husbands were present) who worked increased from 23.8% in 1950 to 54.2% in 1985.[7] In 1986, when TWA Chairman Carl Icahn told striking members of the Independent Federation of Flight Attendants that they could afford wage cuts because they were not breadwinners, they responded by asking Icahn (rhetorically) just who was going to feed them. Reality conflicted with the old idea of the male breadwinner, and union women, directly or indirectly inspired by the women's movement, began to work to change things.

In the early and mid-1970s a working women's movement began to emerge. From the start it was a diverse movement comprising many organizations. Most of them were local in nature, and none spoke for the movement as a whole. The working women's movement never really came together as a nationally visible movement to the same extent that the larger women's movement did. It did not develop a recognized group of national representatives. A large part of its activity was conducted in conferences. For example, in October 1979 the first conference on sexual harassment on the job was held in Detroit. It was organized by the Michigan Task Force on Sexual Harassment, a group that included people from universities and public agencies as well as unions. In the same year, a smaller conference was held in New York City concerning reproductive rights in the workplace.[8] By the mid-1980s educational conferences for union women were being organized by various unions, indicating that the movement was getting somewhere.

The first organization of women trade unionists to combine the concerns of feminism with traditional labor issues was the California-based Union WAGE (Union Women's Alliance to Gain Equality), founded in 1971 by Ann Draper, director of the Amalgamated Clothing Workers Western District union label department, and Jean Maddox, president of Local 29 of the Office Employees International Union. Draper and Maddox hatched the idea of a working women's organization at a conference of the National Organization of Women (NOW) in that year. Union WAGE soon grew to be a significant organization in California. The Union WAGE program contained what would become many of the demands of the working women's movement of the 1970s and 1980s: equal pay for equal work (now known as pay equity), affirmative action, employer- and government-supported child care, greater female participation in union leadership, and the organization of unorganized women workers. One of the positions that made WAGE unique, however, was its stand on the ERA and protective legislation.

When WAGE was founded, the campaign for the ERA was already under way in California. Many experienced women unionists feared that the ERA alone would lead to the destruction of much of the protective legislation developed at the state level over several decades. This legislation covered only women, and WAGE called for a labor ERA that would extend existing protective legislation to cover men. They were quite successful in getting many California women's organizations and unions to support their position. Even NOW joined the WAGE campaign for the extension of protective legislation. In 1973 the WAGE campaign secured the passage of legislation requiring the state to extend to men a number of protections, including limitations on hours, premium overtime pay, and required rest and meal periods. The bill was signed by then Governor Ronald Reagan.

With the formation of the Coalition of Union Women (CLUW) in 1974, the future existence of WAGE came into question. The organization divided over whether to join CLUW or expand WAGE beyond its base in the San Francisco Bay Area. WAGE continued to exist until 1982 because many of its activists felt that it was more independent of the male labor bureaucracy than CLUW. But the existence of CLUW as a national organization with a similar set of concerns made the survival of WAGE difficult.[9]

The most visible organization of this movement was the Coalition of Labor Union Women. Three thousand trade union women attended the founding convention in Chicago, and by 1980 it had 12,000 members. CLUW embraced the program that would become the common set of goals for most of the working women's movement: daycare, affirmative action, comparable worth. But CLUW was an organization of union officials. From the start it reflected that fact in its major goal: the advancement of women in the trade union bureaucracy. In 1980 it launched an eighteen-month project called The Empowerment of Union Women. The focus of CLUW was well described in a 1980 press release for the project: 'The major function of the project is the development of a handbook for union women, which will offer political skills training and action strategies for advancing within the labor movement hierarchy, as well as leadership training and educational resources for organized women.'[10]

CLUW's focus on the advancement of individual women within the labor hierarchy paralleled that of the middle-class women's movement as it developed in the late 1970s. This orientation made it useful for the women officials who composed most of its membership, but reduced its relevance to most working women. CLUW's advocacy of such issues as affirmative action probably helped to legitimate it within labor, but CLUW itself could not become the organization of the working women's movement. Its one foray into organizing the unorganized, the 1982 Baltimore/Washington Women's Organizing Campaign, jointly sponsored with the AFL-CIO's Industrial Union Department, was abandoned as a failure in 1984.[11] CLUW's unwillingness to confront the labor bureaucracy, in which it had situated itself, made it unsuitable as an organization for ordinary union women to advance their collective demands.

A 1979 questionnaire circulated by *Labor Notes* among its readers revealed that 'signs of militancy and organization among working women come from two distinct areas – those women workers who are least typical and those who are most typical.' Among the least typical it included women who had gotten jobs in industries such as auto, steel, construction and mining.[12] A number of support organizations grew out of the increase in the numbers of women in nontraditional jobs. Women working in construction formed Hard Hatted Women in Pittsburgh and Cleveland and Women in Skilled Trades in Detroit as mutual support organizations. Women who had gone into the coal mines were aided by the Coal Employment Project, which held a number of national conferences. Its first one, in June 1979, was attended by about sixty women miners and another sixty supporters.[13] The Coal Employment Project continued to function into the second half of the 1980s even though the industry remained in a long slump.

The working women's movement was also evident in industrial unions like the UAW and the USW. The auto industry had long employed significant numbers of women in production work. Furthermore, as a result of pressure from women UAW members in the 1940s, the UAW was one of the few unions to have a national Women's Department, as well as women's committees at the local union level. Thus, in the UAW the movement appeared more as a revitalization of existing structures than as a novel or distinct movement. One dimension of this was the proliferation of women's conferences that dealt with real issues. Rather than the passive events union conferences had often become, these conferences provided a chance for women to share experiences and build self-confidence. Sometimes this found its way back to the local union women's committee, which then took on a new vitality.

In the steel industry, an influx of women in the mid-1970s into production and skilled jobs changed the sexual balance in many plants and departments. However, the USW had no history of addressing women's issues in even the limited way that the UAW had. Furthermore, during the late 1970s, when the working women's movement began to take shape in the industry, its leadership tended to be associated with the reform forces in the union. Thus, in the nation's two major concentrations of steel production, Chicago-Gary and Pittsburgh, the working women's movement had to found its own organizational expressions. In the Pittsburgh area, women new to the mills organized Women of Steel, primarily as a support group. In USW District 31, a stronghold of the union reform movement, a district-wide women's caucus was organized in the late 1970s. The caucus got the district, then headed by reform leader Jim Balanoff, to sponsor annual women's conferences beginning in 1978. These conferences addressed such issues as maternity and health on the job, daycare, women's organizing, and procedures concerning existing civil rights laws.[14] In both steel and auto, the movement succeeded in bringing women into the leadership of the local unions at the level of shop organization and committee structure. In one sense, however, these advances undermined the separate identity of the women's movement in those unions.

In the UAW, where the women's movement existed within official structures, this change was less noticeable. But in the USW, it tended to lead to the decline of the women's organizations. And the deep slump in the steel industry in the 1980s led to layoffs of most of the women in the movement. A 1985 video, *Women of Steel*, documented the changes in self-confidence and consciousness that their experience in steel had brought about and what happened to some of those women after they lost their jobs. Although out of the industry, one of the women had become an activist in the Mon Valley Unemployed Committee.[15] Indeed, among the women who chose to work in nontraditional jobs and industries in the 1970s, the ideas of the larger women's movement had a significant impact, even if the source of the ideas was not always acknowledged.

The typical women worker of the 1970s and 1980s wasn't a steelworker or coal miner, but a clerical worker. Thirty-five percent of employed women in 1979 worked in office clerical jobs, while another 7% worked in retail sales. Outside of the public sector and some industrial corporations where the clerical staff joined the production workers' union (like the UAW at Chrysler), few clerical workers are organized. More than anything else, this reflects the fact that most unions have ignored industries or corporations with a predominately female workforce. Union leaders have presumed that women clerical workers are not interested or capable of organizing into unions, much less of running their own.[16]

Activists from the women's movement began to challenge those assumptions in the early 1970s. The best known such effort was 9 to 5, which started in Boston in 1973. But similar groups existed in other cities, such as Working Women in Cleveland and Women Employed in Baltimore. The feminists who started these projects did not set out to unionize clerical workers. They attempted rather to use some of the techniques of the women's movement, such as consciousness-raising groups, to give clerical workers a sense of worth and the self-confidence to take the next steps. These were typically small actions to put pressure on employers. Out of this organizing a few viable groups emerged around the country, and in 1977 they joined together to from a national 9 to 5.[17] In 1979 eleven groups merged to form Working Women, National Association of Office Workers, still known as 9 to 5.[18]

Local chapters used a variety of pressure tactics to win gains for groups they had helped to organize, from mass demonstrations, lawsuits, and corporate campaigns to calling in government agencies. Sometimes, the mere activity of the organizing drive brought results in the form of pay increases, as in Boston. One 9 to 5 organizer described the results of this first period: 'From 1974 till 1980, however, the combination of one-time actions on employers and year-long corporate campaigns and legal suits resulted in impressive victories – promotions and back-pay awards, job posting and grievance procedures, raises and childcare programs. Equally important, members changed their ideas about the possibility of change, their relationship to employers and government, and the value of organization.'[19]

An ambiguous attitude toward unions characterized this first period. Boston 9 to 5 had been chartered as a local of SEIU in 1975, but national

Working Women was independent. In 1981 the SEIU set up a national District 925, drawing its staff from 9 to 5. District 925 would be run 'by women and for women', promised SEIU President John Sweeney. District 925 represented 4,000 workers by 1984 and claimed about 6,000 by the end of 1986. At the same time 9 to 5, National Association of Office Workers continues as a separate, but allied organization with twenty-five city-wide chapters and 12,000 members outside of the SEIU or any other union. It has continued its tradition of issue-oriented campaigns with a national campaign on the dangers of VDT work. But the two organizations overlap. Karen Nussbaum, who heads 9 to 5 from its national office in Cleveland, is also president of District 925, which is run out of SEIU headquarters in Washington. The relationship is unique and experimental.[20]

The strength of the 9 to 5 experience, in and out of the SEIU, is that it has attempted to organize a group of workers by speaking directly to their specific needs and by involving them from the start in the process of building the organization through manageable actions. In the case of 9 to 5, the first task was 'to build identity rather than collective bargaining units.'[21] But identity could lead to the solidity of union organization, as District 925 hoped to show. The successes of District 925 have, with the major exception of the Syracuse, New York drive at Equitable Life Assurance, been in the public sector. The challenge of applying the methods of 9 to 5 to the private/competitive sector remains ahead.

From the longer term view of the successful organization of clerical workers as a mass phenomenon, the very strength of the 9 to 5 approach, presents a problem. It is an occupational approach to organization. Clerical workers are spread throughout a variety of industries and do not dominate any industry's workforce. How is the strength that comes from collective identity and a sense of self-worth to be translated into real bargaining strength? As the 9 to 5 organizer above noted elsewhere, victories became harder to secure through pressure tactics once the element of surprise was gone. Then you need real power. In an industry such as insurance, the clerical staff may well have sufficient power, at least if it is organized on a national scale.

Ultimately, the problem is not conceptual. Just as 9 to 5 was able to overlap its staff and ideas with efforts by SEIU to organize public sector clericals and now Blue Cross employees in Ohio, so the 9 to 5 approach could be put into the context of an industrial union approach to national organizing. In the Equitable Life and Blue Cross campaigns, 9 to 5's techniques showed their effectiveness in convincing women workers of the need to organize. The need to link their organization with those of other workers in the same companies and industries in order to gain maximum leverage over the employer could easily be an extension of these advances in organization. The major question in this case would be the same as that faced by linking up with the SEIU – the ability of the women workers to run their own affairs and to get genuine support for their efforts from other sections of the union. The barrier is not anything that 9 to 5 or its unique approach to organizing an important group of workers represents. It is the self-interest of the business unionist bureaucracy, which for the moment expresses itself by seeking duespayers anywhere they can be found rather than thinking through power relations and trade union strategy.

The impact of the working women's movement as well as that of the more visible middle-class feminist organizations of the 1970s and 1980s is difficult to measure. The gains seem clearest at the level of national politics, where it is usually easier for union leaders to support specially controversial issues. Since 1973, the AFL-CIO has supported the ERA and joined in coalitions with the National Organization of Women and the Women's Political Caucus in lobbying and legislative campaigns around women's issues, much in the same way many unions have supported civil rights legislation. But changes are less apparent in day-to-day union practice.

In a small number of unions (AFSCME, SEIU, and HERE, for example), an explicitly feminist issue such as pay equity has actually been made a bargaining issue. Many unions have accepted the idea that sexual harassment on the job is a grievable issue. For a time, reproductive rights on the job became a recognized health and safety issue in some places. On the other hand, the gains made by women through affirmative action in steel were not defended by the USW when the layoffs of the 1980s all but wiped out employment of women in the industry. Furthermore, the collective bargaining practice of most unions continued in the mold of business unionism. Women's issues such as child care seldom became part of the bargaining agenda. As the labor leadership retreated in the face of growing employer aggression and as concessions and nonadversarial labor relations monopolized the bargaining agenda, women's issues, like the concerns of minority workers, were usually swept aside.

Yet these issues remain a part of the culture of most industrial and public sector unions in a way they were not before the advent of the women's movement. They continue to be most actionable in the noncompetitive sectors (public employment and university clerical staffs, for example) that employ large numbers of women. It is increasingly clear that they can play a role in successful organizing where women are a large part of the workforce. It seems almost certain that significant advances in unionization among women workers in the private sector will again help make women's issues central to large parts of organized labor and to help revive a working women's movement throughout the working class.

The Internationalization of the US Working Class

In one sense, the US working class has always been a multinational one. Since the emergence of an industrial working class in the mid-nineteenth century, its ethnic and racial composition has changed from generation to generation. But the majority of the new immigrants who entered the bottom ranks of labor were white Europeans who rapidly assimilated American culture. The great dividing line within the class was always racial. As Blacks moved from the farm to industry in the twentieth century they were not allowed to integrate like other distinct groups in spite of their status as Americans, and after abolition, as citizens by right. White racism preceded the formation of the industrial working class and was carried into the new working class by the whites who first composed it. As both Mike Davis and Herbert Hill have suggested, racism was a unifying factor among white workers. American trade unionism was affected by this racism from the beginning in spite of episodic efforts to overcome it, as with the National Labor Union of the 1860s and the Knights of Labor in the 1880s.

While the roots of America's particularly virulent tradition of racism lie in the institution of slavery, white racism has never limited its prejudice to Black Americans. Herbert Hill notes that the almost universal endorsement of the Chinese Exclusion Act of 1882 by organized labor helped set the tone of racial exclusion at the moment that modern trade unionism was taking shape in the US. It turned the 'anti-coolie' agitation on the West Coast in the 1870s into a national position of organized labor. In fact, the craft unions that would join together to form the precursor of the AFL in 1883 vigorously lobbied for the act – but so did the Knights of Labor. The fusion of the anti-Asian sentiment with traditional anti-Black racism reinforced the notion of white superiority. No one put it more crudely than Samuel Gompers himself when he wrote in the *American Federationist* in September 1905: 'Caucasian civilization will serve notice that its uplifting process is not to be interfered with in any way.... The Caucasians are not going to let their standard of living be destroyed by negroes, Chinamen, Japs or any others.'[22] There is a discomforting continuity between Gompers's view of how to defend the living standards of white craft unionists and the anti-Japanese (and, hence, anti-Asian) sentiment that accompanies the protectionist 'Buy American' stance of the industrial unions in the 1980s. As in the past, business unionism's knee-jerk response to the new waves of immigration that have occurred in the last two decades is to seek their exclusion from the workforce.

Political and economic events throughout the world have once again forced large numbers of people to seek a new life or at least employment in the US, still viewed as the richest country in the world. War and turmoil in the wake of the Vietnam War have brought new groups of Asians. Political and economic crisis in Central America have led hundreds of thousands of Central Americans to seek refuge. And a serious deepening of Mexico's economic problems in the 1970s has accelerated the traditional flow of Mexican workers not only into the Southwest, but into many other parts of the country. (An irony of virtually all the new immigration into the US in recent years is that the underlying political and economic forces that have sent people here were usually the result, direct or indirect, of US policy in the area.) In terms of both magnitude and spread within the US, it is the migration across the Mexican border that has had the greatest impact.

The US has had a significant Latino population ever since it seized a third of Mexico's territory in 1848 and the island of Puerto Rico in the 1890s. But until World War Two it remained confined to a few regions. The large-scale immigration across the Mexican border, from Puerto Rico to parts of the East Coast mainland, and the growing immigration from other Latin American nations in the 1970s and 1980s changed that. The US Bureau of the Census estimated that there were about 17 million people of Hispanic origin in the US in 1984, of whom 14.6 million were US citizens and 2.4 were 'aliens'. This figure did not include the 3 million Puerto Ricans living in Puerto Rico who are US citizens. The 2.4 million Latino noncitizens are supposed to include all 'illegals' in the country. Most estimates of the undocumented Latino population put it at closer to 7 million. Taken together, the Latino population of the US was around 24 million or more by the mid-1980s – about 10% of the total population.[23]

According to official figures, the number of Latino workers in the civilian labor force grew by about 50% from 1975 to 1983, reaching over 6 million workers. These were divided almost evenly between men and women.[24] But again, the figures grossly underestimate the number of undocumented workers. Whatever the precise figures, it is clear that Latinos constitute a large and growing section of the US working class. Latinos can be found working in most industries, but like other minorities they are concentrated in low-wage manufacturing, service, and retail jobs, and they are a majority of the nation's migrant agricultural labor force. Recent immigrants and undocumented workers tend to fill the lowest paying entry jobs, with large concentrations in hotels and restaurants, retail food stores, and food processing factories.[25]

The official position of the AFL-CIO after World War Two was not very different from that of labor in the 1880s. It sought to exclude foreign labor through federal legislation. In the 1950s the AFL-CIO raised the cry of 'too many Mexicans taking jobs from Americans' on the eve of Operation Wetback, a massive sweep by federal and local law enforcement agencies and the armed forces that rounded up over 1 million Mexicans in 1954. In 1982, the Federation supported the punitive Simpson-Mazzoli bill, which was designed to eliminate undocumented workers by fining the employers who hire them. This legislation would have accelerated the raids that the Immigration and Naturalization Service (INS or *La Migra* to Latino workers) already makes on communities and workplaces. It would have made employers hesitant to hire any worker of Latin American, Caribbean or Asian heritage for fear of fines and disruptions in production due to INS raids or investigations. At the last minute, under pressure from Latino labor and community leaders, the AFL-CIO withdrew official support for the Simpson-Mazzoli bill. Its stated objections, however, were not to the major provisions of the bill, but to its 'guest worker' program, which would have allowed foreign workers temporary access to the US labor market.[26]

A growing number of AFL-CIO unions with large Latino memberships have taken a different attitude from that of the Federation leadership. The ILGWU, ACTWU, UAW, and some others have aggressively sought to organize Latino and Asian workers, including undocumented workers. The garment industry has a strong concentration of Latinas and Asian women around the country. Much of this production is organized on a sweatshop (or even homework) basis by employers who feel free to push around workers who can't speak English and who may be undocumented. Thus, the ACTWU and ILGWU have had a strong stake in organizing these workers. Additionally, local unions with large Latino memberships often seek to protect them even if their international supports AFL-CIO policy. They have opposed INS raids and attempted to provide arrested workers with legal and other forms of help. This progressive approach to the problem is most apparent in cities or areas where much of the available workforce for entry work in garment shops or other small-scale manufacturing is Latino or Asian. Most union leaders, however, prefer to exclude foreign workers rather than organize them.

Latino workers tend to favor unionization in spite of the indifference of many unions and the difficulties that employers and the INS present in organizing Latinos and especially undocumented workers. In 1984 Latinos accounted for about 6% of the union members in the US,[27] and Latinos are thus the second largest minority group in organized labor. However, this fact is scarcely reflected in the composition of union leadership or even in the treatment accorded Latino members.

An example is the International Ladies' Garment Workers Union (ILGWU). Founded in 1900, mainly by Jewish immigrant workers, the union had become largely Latino, Black and Asian by the 1950s. The leadership of the ILGWU, however, continued to be primarily Jewish men from the most skilled jobs. As early as the late 1950s, this led to protests from the growing number of Puerto Rican and Black workers. In 1957 and again in 1958, Puerto Rican and Black workers organized demonstrations at the ILGWU's headquarters in New York to protest sweetheart contracts. Throughout the 1960s a bitter fight raged between the ILGWU leadership and the NAACP, which charged the union with discrimination against minority workers in the skilled trades. In the 1970s Puerto Rican, Black and Asian members began protesting other discriminatory policies, and often organized local caucuses to challenge the leadership. For example, minority members in the 15,000 member Knitgoods Local 155 united to organize the Rank and File Committee in 1971. In the late 1970s, Puerto Rican, Black and Asian members initiated a protest of discrimination in the ILGWU's East River Cooperative Village. A lawsuit was filed in 1977 charging that only whites were allowed housing in this union-owned housing project. In 1983 the campaign staged a mass demonstration at the union's headquarters demanding that the housing be opened to Latino, Asian and Black members. A court settlement was reached in 1986, but then thrown out when the ILGWU objected to the court-awarded attorney's fees.[28]

The language barrier is one of the major problems faced by immigrant workers. When the business of the union is conducted solely in English it is impossible for Latino and Asian members who do not understand English to know what is going on or to participate. In Local 2 of the Hotel and Restaurant Employees in San Francisco, this problem led to the formation of a Latino caucus in 1980. Over two-thirds of Local 2's 17,000 members are Latino, Asian or Black. Latinos, mostly Mexican immigrant workers, account for 25% of the membership. In 1980 Latino members of Local 2 organized Latinos Unidos to support a hotel strike. They asked that meetings be bilingual and that the informational flyers and proposed contract be translated into Spanish. After the strike, Latinos Unidos demanded that the new contract be published in Spanish. The leadership of Local 2 simply ignored their demands, so the caucus published its own summary of the new contract, as well as regular bulletins dealing with the problems of Latino workers. In response Local 2's leaders finally made some concessions. They hired a Spanish-speaking organizer, translated the contract into Spanish, and held regular meetings in Spanish at which members were free to air problems. Latinos Unidos eventually fell apart because many of its functions were taken on by the local. But a consequence was that the Spanish meetings soon became purely informational in character and attendance dropped off. The lesson drawn by many Latino members was that there was a distinct role for Latinos Unidos to play; in 1986 there was talk of reviving it.[29]

In Teamsters Local 912, the development of a Latino caucus intersected with the growth of TDU, the broader reform movement in the Teamsters. Local 912 had about 7,000 members in canneries in California's Salinas Valley. Most of these workers were Mexican women. The union had an entrenched Anglo leadership and conducted all its business in English, effectively excluding the vast majority of members who didn't speak English or didn't speak it well. The TDU chapter in Local 912 organized a pressure campaign for local elections. There had been only two elections since the local's founding in 1952, and Richard King had headed the local ever since. A specifically Latino caucus, called Caucus Latino Rebelde, was allied with TDU in the election contest. The King leadership scheduled the election at a time when production was slow and most Mexican workers returned to visit their families in Mexico. There were numerous other irregularities, and King beat the TDU slate. But Local 912 remained the site of opposition organization, and another election was held in 1986, during the hard-fought strike at Watsonville Canning. King was encouraged not to run again by the Teamsters international, and Business Representative Sergio Lopez, a fairly popular Latino, ran. TDU did not run a full slate, but its candidate for recording secretary won. The groundwork laid by TDU and Caucus Latino Rebelde was a factor in the strong organization of the Watsonville strike: it was no longer possible to intimidate the Latino membership of Local 912.[30]

Latino workers have also organized new unions and been among the first to use new outreach techniques. The best known, of course, is the long struggle of the United Farm Workers in California. Beginning in the 1960s, UFW leader Cesar Chavez used both strikes and a highly visible national boycott of grapes and lettuce to bring unionism to California agribusiness. In the late 1970s the organization of farmworkers spread as new organizations appeared around the country. In the Southwest new organizations such as the Texas Farm Workers and the Arizona Farm Workers Union (AFWU) began as spin-offs of the UFW. In Ohio and Michigan, the Farm Labor Organizing Committee (FLOC) developed a new approach to bargaining involving not only the farmers who employed migrant labor but the corporations to whom they contracted their crops. In New Jersey and Pennsylvania, Puerto Rican and other Latino farmworkers have been organizing the Comité de Organizadores de Trabajadores Agricola (COTA). COTA has won recognition from the state of New Jersey as a legitimate union and has organized a number of farms in both states. As with the UFW, all of these new farmworker organizations have sought and received help from both labor and community organizations.

In preparation for a strike at a ranch employing three hundred workers, many of them undocumented, the Arizona Farm Workers Union set up the Maricopa County Organizing Project (MCOP) in early 1977. To deal with the undocumented workers, MCOP exposed and publicly 'tried' *coyotes* (who act as labor contractors to bring Mexican workers to US ranches or other jobs) known for taking large amounts of wages in return for their services. MCOP activists also went to Mexico and visited the homes of undocumented migrants who worked in the county. MCOP thus built support on both sides of the border. They also threatened *coyotes* with legal action if they tried to bring in scabs during the strike. Then AFWU led a 24-day strike at Goldmar, Inc., which resulted in the first labor contract signed with undocumented workers. In 1979 the AFWU won contracts requiring the employer to contribute ten cents an hour per worker to the Farmworker Economic Development Fund, which financed municipal improvement projects in the towns in Mexico from which many of the workers came.[31]

One of the most innovative approaches to farmworker organizing in the US has been that of the Farm Labor Organizing Committee. FLOC began organizing in the tomato fields of northwestern Ohio in the late 1960s. In the summer of 1968 it called a successful strike, winning contracts at twenty-two farms. But the following season, many of these tomato farms switched to other crops. The farmers in the region contracted their annual crop to food processing corporations, particularly Campbell's and Libby's. These corporations control the prices since the contract is signed before growing season. FLOC reasoned that to win, it had to force the canneries to be a party to bargaining. FLOC leader Baldemar Velasquez described the situation:

> The canneries agree, before the tomato season begins, to pay the growers so much per ton, thereby predetermining the price that the growers can pay the workers.... It's a no win system for the worker. If he asks the grower for a raise, the grower tells him that the cannery must pay the grower more before any such raise can occur. If the worker strikes solely the grower for a pay raise, there will be a repeat of what happened in 1968.[32]

FLOC's strategy became to win a three-party contract. To build support among farmworkers, FLOC sponsored health clinics and helped workers with other social problems they faced. In 1978 FLOC was strong enough to initiate a strike of about 2,000 farmworkers in Ohio. To force the major canneries to bargain, FLOC initiated a national boycott of

Campbell's products in 1979.[33] In late 1984, Ray Rogers and Ed Allen of Corporate Campaigns, Inc., donated their services to help the union develop its boycott into a full corporate campaign. This campaign was mounted against the Philadelphia National Bank and Prudential Insurance, both of which were financial backers of Campbell's. By this time, FLOC had extended its organizing into the cucumber fields of Michigan, where growers contracted with Campbell's subsidiary Vlasic. The strategy began to pay off in 1985 as Campbell's moved closer to an agreement. The company tentatively agreed to a commission composed of representatives of FLOC and the growers and chaired by former Secretary of Labor John T. Dunlop. This commission would establish and oversee procedures for union recognition. As a contract victory came within reach, the 1985 FLOC convention voted to explore affiliation with the United Farm Workers. On 18 February 1986, FLOC signed a three-way contract with Campbell's and thirty-two Ohio and Michigan growers.[34] FLOC had won because of its willingness to go beyond ordinary business union methods. Its boycott of Campbell's was actively opposed by the UFCW and never endorsed by the AFL-CIO. But FLOC sought and received much help from labor's grass roots as well as from church groups and political activists. Its democratic form of unionism and its strategic and tactical creativity were a model of how unions can begin to deal with the complex relations between different sectors of capital using both membership mobilization and 'outside' support.

Latino workers played a prominent role in the growing resistance to intensified employer aggression in the 1980s. Like so many struggles in the 1980s, some of these would be lost, like the long strike by Chicano copper miners against Phelps Dodge from 1983 through a successful company-organized decertification election (in which only scabs could vote) in 1985. One of the most important strikes against concessions was that at Watsonville Canning, mentioned earlier. At Watsonville, one thousand workers, mostly Latina women, held out for eighteen months without one defection from their ranks, beat a company attempt to decertify the union, forced a corrupt leadership out of office, and finally won a partial, but important, victory. As with the farmworkers, the Watsonville strikers employed a number of innovative tactics. In Boston, hotel workers, who were largely Latino, Asian, and Portuguese immigrants, beat back concessionary demands in 1985, once again employing tactics that pointed beyond the routine and ineffective methods of US business unionism.[35] By the mid-1980s, Latino workers, both citizens and immigrants, along with other groups of immigrant workers, were playing a significant role in militant resistance, the reintroduction of rank-and-file unionism, and in the development and implementation of new tactics and ideas. Far from 'undermining' the living standards of

US labor, they were among those on the frontline fighting to defend them.

Labor and US Foreign Policy

International labor solidarity has always had a peculiar meaning for American business unionism. Since the days of Samuel Gompers and the old AFL through most of the postwar era, the labor internationalism of most US unions and their bureaucracies has involved an explicit alliance with US capital. The credo of business unionism that job security and higher wages depend on the well-being of the employers has been extended into international affairs in two ways. The first is support for US foreign policy, which invariably sees business success abroad as an aspect of the general health of the economy. The second takes the form of involvement in both international labor organizations and the internal affairs of the unions of other nations in ways guided by the priorities of US foreign policy.

Thus, during the Spanish-American War in 1898 the AFL supported US intervention in and seizure of Puerto Rico and the Philippines and the imposition of unfavorable trade relations on Cuba. It extended the notion of US hegemony in the Western hemisphere when in 1918 it formed the Pan-American Federation of Labor to further the priorities of US capital within Latin American unions. In 1927 the AFL gave this effort concrete expression when it supported the US occupation of Nicaragua – the event that led to the rise of the Somoza family dictatorship.[36]

This tradition was rekindled after World War Two when the AFL set up the Free Trade Union Committee to intervene in the European labor movement in hopes of reducing the influence of Communist-led unions. The major CIO unions did not fully embrace capital's foreign policy priorities until the early 1960s, when the American Institute for Free Labor Development (AIFLD) was formed. AIFLD was created as an adjunct of the Alliance for Progress, the Kennedy administration's program for advancing both economic dependence and development in Latin America. AIFLD was to help shape Latin American labor leaders in the mold of US business unionism.[37]

The alliance of labor with capital could hardly have been more explicit. AIFLD included on its board of directors not only top labor leaders but business figures like Nelson Rockefeller and J. Peter Grace, who was chairman of the AIFLD Board until 1980. Its 1962 launch was funded by the Agency for International Development (AID) and W. R. Grace, ITT, Exxon, Shell, Kennecott, Anaconda, American Smelting and Refining,

IBM, Koppers, Gillett and eighty-five other corporations active in Latin America.[38] No one expressed the business unionist/corporate purpose of AIFLD more articulately than Peter Grace himself: 'AIFLD urges cooperation between labor and management and an end to class struggle. It teaches workers to help increase their company's business and to improve productivity so that they gain more from expanding business.'[39]

In fact, AIFLD did more than train Latin American union officials in the routines of contract unionism. It intervened in the affairs of unions in the area and played a role in the execution of US foreign policy. Most notorious in its earliest years was its role in the military coup in Brazil that overthrew the elected populist regime of João Goulart in 1964 and established one of the most systematically brutal dictatorships in Latin American history. At the time AIFLD Executive Director William Doherty bragged that AIFLD graduates 'were so active [in the Brazilian coup] that they became intimately involved in some of the clandestine operations of the revolution before it took place.'[40] It was soon clear that the CIA had played a major role in the coup and that AIFLD worked closely with them. Victor Reuther, who was international affairs director of the UAW, protested the role of AIFLD and its liaison with the CIA. But the Brazilian affair was only the first of many of AIFLD's involvements in coups and US military and political interventions against elected governments that it regarded as too left wing. These included interventions in the Dominican Republic in 1965 and Chile in 1973.

AIFLD's activities were not limited to these rather dramatic interventions. Throughout the 1970s and 1980s AIFLD worked in Central America to create a docile labor movement that accepted the priorities of capital in the region. Sometimes this effort went to absurd lengths, as with Juan Alfaro, leader of the AIFLD-backed Confederation of Unions United of Guatemala, who explained in a 1986 interview that his federation's union for agricultural workers preferred to organize small farmers rather than plantation workers 'because there's no boss to confront.'[41] More typically, its favored unions are used to bolster those regimes in Central America on which American capital shines its grace or to oppose those of which it disapproves. To accomplish this it does not rely so much on training as on money. Adrian Esquino, a leader of the AIFLD-created UPD in El Salvador, explained to the *Wall Street Journal* that AIFLD had stopped funding his union because it didn't follow the line: 'AIFLD is a disaster for workers. AIFLD says if you do what we want, we'll give you money. The institute buys union leaders.'[42]

In the 1960s the AFL-CIO International Affairs Department headed by Irving Brown generalized this approach to other areas of the world. It established the African American Labor Center (AALC) in 1964 and the Asian American Free Labor Institute (AAFLI) in 1968. AAFLI's first job was to attempt to establish unions in South Vietnam and to direct an AID land reform program that was supposed to be central to winning the war. AAFLI also helped to found the Trade Union Congress of the Philippines in 1975 with the cooperation of the Marcos government. Like so many creations of the AFL-CIO's version of international solidarity, the TUCP is a small federation with only a few thousand members. Its main function seems to be to combat the much larger labor federation, KMU (Kilusang Mayo Uno), on the grounds that the KMU is influenced by communists.[43]

The role of the African American Labor Center in South Africa since the growth of the new unions in that country also illustrates the largely negative approach of the AFL-CIO to labor movements in the Third World. In spite of the growth of the industrial union movement that produced first the Federation of South African Trade Unions and then, in 1986 through merger with several other unions, the Congress of South African Trade Unions (COSATU), AALC channeled money only to local unions or those national unions it considered politically safe. It also promised money to several unions if they stayed out of COSATU. The political question involved was between those unions, such as COSATU and its affiliates, that advocate disinvestment by US corporations operating in South Africa and those that are at least silent on the question. In line with its staunch defense of US business interests at home, the AFL-CIO opposes disinvestment as a tactic in the fight against apartheid in South Africa.

One of the most dramatic instances of the AFL-CIO's willingness to splinter foreign labor movements was the intervention of AIFLD in El Salvador in 1984–87. AIFLD had actually created some unions and peasant organizations of considerable size in El Salvador in the late 1970s. These were united in the Unidad Popular Democratica (UPD) in 1980, largely to counter the rise of more left-wing mass organizations and unions in the same period. The enormous repression that began in 1981 forced most unions and mass organizations underground or destroyed them altogether. As a favored child of US foreign policy, the UPD was allowed to function by the Salvadoran military, although right-wing death squads murdered two AIFLD agents and a Salvadoran working with the land reform program that helped give UPD much of its mass peasant base. As US policy turned toward the creation of a civilian government to give the war effort a democratic facade, the UPD became important in mobilizing support for centrist politicians, notably Christian Democrats; the group played a key role in the 1984 election of José Napoleón Duarte as president of El Salvador. Duarte promised certain economic reforms in return for UPD's active support. When he failed to deliver on any of them, the UPD became openly critical of Duarte. At that point, AIFLD withdrew its financial support from the UPD and moved to create an alternative based on a tiny labor federation (the CTD) whose leaders were associated with the far right. AIFLD also attempted to remove union officials from their positions unilaterally. Most of the UPD unions joined with the more left-wing labor groups to form the UNTS (Unidad Nacional de Trabajadores Salvadoreños) a broad united front of labor and peasant organizations opposed to the policies of the Duarte administration and its US sponsors. AIFLD attempted to disrupt the UNTS well into 1987 by bribing various UPD leaders. In response, one of the demands of the UNTS on the Duarte government was a call to expel AIFLD from El Salvador.[44]

All of these maneuvers, from the Philippines to Central America and South Africa, were conducted in the name of AFL-CIO policy in the context of the aggressively interventionist policy of the Reagan administration. The deepening US involvement in the intensification and prolongation of the war in El Salvador, the growing controversy over US aid to the Nicaraguan *Contras*, and the explosion of the struggle against apartheid in South Africa all brought both US foreign policy and the role of the AFL-CIO into sharper focus in the 1980s. Just as public opinion over Reagan's policies was divided, so was opinion within the unions. For those labor leaders who opposed not only Reagan's domestic policies, but his foreign policy as well, the alignment of AFL-CIO and Reagan on foreign policy became a growing embarrassment.

In 1981 the twenty-four top union officials, most of them presidents, formed the National Labor Committee in Support of Democracy and Human Rights in El Salvador. The committee's main purpose to was oppose the Reagan/AFL-CIO policy in Central America. Seven labor leaders, including Jack Sheinkman, secretary-treasurer of the Amalgamated Clothing and Textile Workers, and William Lucy, secretary-treasurer of AFSCME, traveled to El Salvador in June 1983 to investigate the situation there for the National Labor Committee. They recommended that US military aid be withheld until human rights violations ceased and the murder of the AIFLD workers was fully investigated. They also concluded that the upcoming 1984 presidential elections 'offered no solution to El Salvador's ongoing conflict.'[45]

At the October 1983 Convention of the AFL-CIO, officials associated with the National Labor Committee put their position forth for the first time in a challenge to the AIFLD position, although no direct attack on AIFLD was made. Because many of the presidents on the National Labor Committee represent sizable industrial unions and command large votes they were able to force Kirkland and the pro-AIFLD forces to retreat. To avoid a highly visible floor fight, Kirkland and his supporters

agreed to a number of amendments, including ones calling for limitations on US military aid until the human rights situation in El Salvador
improved. Reagan's certification of progress on human rights in El Salvador was rejected by the convention. This was somewhat of a
breakthrough in that open conflict over foreign policy issues has rarely
surfaced at federation conventions.[46]

The fight emerged again at the 1985 AFL-CIO convention. Like that
of 1983, it followed a visit by several AFL-CIO leaders to El Salvador,
where they saw the real consequences of US policy and AIFLD intervention in the unions. This time the debate surfaced on the convention floor.
Winpisinger of the Machinists, Kenneth Blaylock of the AFGE, and Ed
Asner of the Screen Actors Guild spoke forcefully against AFL-CIO support for Reagan's policy. Winpisinger also publicly attacked AIFLD. The
openness of the debate helped to publicize the split within the house of
labor over Central America and over US foreign policy in general. Like
the 1983 fight, however, this struggle also ended in a compromise.[47]

These convention victories unfortunately had no real impact on the
conduct of the AFL-CIO's International Affairs Department or its offspring AIFLD, AALC, and AAFLI, which remained controlled and
protected by the office of Lane Kirkland. This insulation from any
semblance of democratic control or accountability was made possible by
a hierarchy of organizations funded primarily by the US government.
Before 1983, the operations of AIFLD, AALC, and AAFLI were overseen
by the Federation's International Affairs Department, which had been
headed by Irving Brown since the end of World War Two. To further insulate their overseas adventures from the influence of dissenting unions,
Kirkland, Brown and others cooperated with the Reagan administration
in the creation of the National Endowment for Democracy (NED), which
Congress chartered. NED includes both Kirkland and Shanker on its
board, along with Secretary of Labor William Brock, antilabor Senator
Orin Hatch, Henry Kissinger, and other business and political leaders.
With a budget of $18 million in 1984 and $18.5 million in 1985, NED channeled $11.5 million in government funds to the AFL-CIO's Free Trade
Union Institute, which was created for this purpose. The institute then
dispensed this money to AIFLD, AALC, AAFLI, and to the Force
Ouvrière in France. Nowhere in this process do even the presidents of
the unions affiliated with the AFL-CIO have the opportunity to alter or
stop this flow of funds.[48]

One of the strangest aspects of this semicovert operation is that much
of it is administered by members of a small political sect, the Social
Democrats-USA (SDUSA). Probably very few union members in the US
have ever heard of this group. Though it is rumored to have fewer than
a hundred members, it is one of two US organizations affiliated with the

Socialist International (the other being the Democratic Socialists of America). However, there is nothing socialist about the politics of this group but its name. It is mildly liberal on domestic questions and aggressively hawkish on foreign affairs. Its highest ranking public member is Albert Shanker, president of the AFT. Bayard Rustin, who until his recent death headed the AFL-CIO's A. Philip Randolph Institute, was a well-known member. But members of SDUSA are most pervasive in the Federation's foreign policy establishment. Following the flow of funds downward, we see that Shanker sits with Kirkland on the Board of Directors of the NED. The president of NED is Carl Gershman, former executive director of SDUSA. The major recipient of NED funds is the Free Trade Union Institute, whose director, Eugenia Kemble, is also a member of SDUSA. The head of the International Affairs Department of the AFL-CIO, which has set policy for AIFLD, AALC and AAFLI, since Irving Brown's retirement in 1986, is Tom Kahn, another member of SDUSA. Kahn was for years an assistant to George Meany and then to Kirkland. None of these people was elected to office in the foreign affairs bureaucracy. It might seem strange that business unionists, who are generally quite paranoid about left-wing takeovers in other labor movements, would invest this little-known 'socialist' group with control of their international operations. In fact, the political training that many SDUSA members received in their more radical youths serves them well to spot and maneuver against genuine socialists and revolutionary nationalists, as well as communists, in Third World unions.

The debate over the Federation's foreign policy was far beyond the reach of even most union officials, let alone the rank and file. But opposition to US policy in Central America and the Caribbean (particularly the invasion of Grenada), its de facto support of the apartheid regime in South Africa, and its continued support of dictatorial regimes that ban or persecute unions has run deeper than the split in the top leadership. Labor activities in support of the fight against apartheid became widespread in the mid-1980s. AFL-CIO policy, of course, opposed apartheid, and in 1984–85 AFL-CIO leaders joined others in civil disobedience at the South African embassy in Washington. But opposition to apartheid was also pursued at the grass-roots level. The New York Labor Committee against Apartheid, composed of local union leaders and activists in that city, was one example.[49] Black workers in particular took up the issue of South Africa in a variety of ways, and apartheid became an issue in numerous strikes throughout 1985–87 as links were made to the activities of multinational employers in South Africa. Year after year, thousands of unionists joined the large peace and anti-intervention demonstrations organized by broad coalitions that included a growing number of unions.

The question of official union endorsement of mass demonstrations against US intervention in Central America became a hot issue in 1987, as Kirkland and his allies, acting in the name of AFL-CIO policy, aggressively pressured union leaders to withdraw endorsements or, failing that, minimize their efforts. At the February 1987 meeting of the AFL-CIO Executive Council, Kirkland stated that he viewed endorsement of the April 25th Mobilization for Peace, Jobs and Justice in Central America and South Africa to be outside the boundaries of AFL-CIO policy. Shanker added his two cents by accusing eight Executive Council members and sixteen additional labor leaders of being dupes of outside forces. In addition, a letter was sent to all affiliates from Bricklayers' President John Joyce reiterating Shanker's charge. Shanker went so far as to put an ad in the *New York Times* denouncing the demonstration and its labor endorsers. A counter ad by Stanley Hill, the executive director of AFSCME District Council 37, blasted Shanker, saying that union members had heard 'the same infuriating cliches and innuendoes in the days before Dr. Martin Luther King's legendary March on Washington in 1963.' In spite of Kirkland and Shanker's efforts, labor participation in the 25 April March was large and visible. Arriving in car caravans, buses and trains an estimated 30,000 to 50,000 unionists joined church and peace activists to march on the Capitol. Ed Asner, Kenneth Blaylock, and Henry Nicholas of the Hospital Workers addressed the rally. Asner sparred no words in his attack on Kirkland's attempt to stifle labor support for the demonstration: 'It is hard to believe the AFL-CIO's rhetoric about free speech abroad in the face of their abysmal regard for free speech at home.'[50]

The break in the ranks at the top and the growth of opposition to the traditionally hawkish foreign policy of American business unionism was a consequence of many trends. But of particular importance were the changes in the investment policies of US capital that were now undermining the living standards of more and more American workers. Overseas investment by many US industrial corporations in the 1950s and 1960s had been directed primarily toward production for overseas markets. It did not affect domestic employment, and since it kept the corporation's profits high it increased the ability of the unions to negotiate better contracts over the years without major confrontations. Under these circumstances, US workers actually benefited from the export of capital. Union leaders, informed of this pattern by their research departments, were keenly aware of the bargaining flexibility given them by extra profits earned in overseas markets.

All of this began to change gradually in the 1960s and more rapidly in the 1970s and 1980s. Corporations in industries such as clothing and textiles began producing abroad for the US market. Others, such as lumber and copper, imported raw materials previously produced in the US. Finally, a growing number of industries began to construct internationally integrated production systems, exporting much of the work previously done in the US. The development of the world car in the auto industry in the early 1980s was a clear example of this trend. The products of all of this overseas investment in production flowed into the US economy not as imports from foreign firms for the consumer market, but as components of products produced in the US by US firms and directed toward the US market, which meant that this form of investment cost American jobs. The plant-closing tidal wave of the 1980s was partly a function of this new direction in investment. A striking example of the meaning of this trend for US workers came in late 1986 when GM announced it would close nine US plants and build twelve new ones in Mexico, bringing its Mexican total to twenty-nine plants. The first announcement was highly public and came only a year before GM bargained a new contract with the UAW, while the second was quietly circulated among investors.[51] But most UAW activists were acutely aware of these decisions.

The change in the direction and purpose of industrial investment altered the relationship of labor to capital. What had been a boon to business unionism was now a source of unemployment, demands for concessions and resistance to unionization. The declining number and proportion of industrial jobs was, in large part, a function of this type of investment. The link between the employer's success overseas and the workers' well-being had been broken. Since the protection of overseas investment has always been a major consideration in US foreign policy, the objective interest of American workers in supporting that policy was weakened. Indeed, the support that the US traditionally gave to governments that helped maximize the return on investment by keeping labor cheap through the suppression of unions and worker-based political movements now worked against the immediate interests of most American industrial workers. While this change was no guarantee of a shift in the political awareness of US workers, it provided the basis for such a change as the various movements against US foreign policy began to address organized labor in the 1980s.

Both Central America and South Africa provided living demonstrations of the new foreign policy dynamics. US firms invested in both areas. Central America had in particular become one of the areas of the world producing both final products and component products for US corporations. South Africa, while less important as an offshore platform for the US market, was a major area of investment for scores of multinationals. In both cases, US foreign policy had nurtured regimes that kept labor cheap by means of repression. In both areas, new labor movements had arisen demanding major improvements in living standards and opposing the governments that rested on US tolerance, investment and/or aid. Often employed by the same corporation, the US worker could perceive the rebellion of his or her overseas coworker as a welcome opportunity to reduce the competitive gap that encouraged the flow of capital overseas. Strong unions in Third World offshore production centers were to be fostered, not splintered in the manner of the AFL-CIO's version of international solidarity.

US Workers in the Global Corporation

The AFL-CIO tends to reduce the problems of international production and economic integration to those of trade. In this perception, American workers are pitted against foreign workers and the solution is thought to lie in trade policy. In fact, the impact of direct imports from foreign-owned firms is considerably less than that of the export of capital and the subsequent foreign sourcing of components for products completed and sold in the US. A 1984 study by Bennett Harrison, Barry Bluestone, and Lucy Gorham showed this form of outsourcing to be a far greater cause of job loss than the imports of final products in ten of the fifteen industries they studied. The difference in the effects of these two causes was usually quite substantial. In auto, for example, 106,800 jobs were lost to outsourcing compared with 62,600 to import competition. In primary metals, 95,900 jobs were lost to outsourcing and 49,200 to imports. In chemicals, it was 99,100 to 5,800, and in rubber, 12,300 compared with 3,600.[52] This reflects the change from nation-to-nation trade to intracorporate transfers as the major conduit of capital. Charles H. Smith, a former head of the US Chamber of Commerce, noted this change in the late 1970s:

> Trade-oriented balance-of-payments accounting itself fails to measure in any meaningful way the new international relations that are developing. The United Nations, for example, estimates that the production totals of foreign affiliates of MNCs reached approximately $330 billion in 1971, somewhat larger than the $310 billion total for exports of all market economies. Yet the current accounting system fails to consider the new conditions under which international production has surpassed trade as the main vehicle of international economic exchange.[53]

If trade, the traditional mode of international economic relations, tends to pit workers in different countries against one another, international production brings them into a new, integrated relationship. A report on the globalization of the electronics industry by the North

American Congress on Latin America described this process in the late 1970s:

> Since the early 1960s production has taken a new turn, becoming increasingly internationalized in many industries. The structure which underlies this development is what one observer has called the "globally integrated manufacturing system". A single firm now integrates workers around the globe into one coordinated production system which reflects an international division of labor.[54]

Harley Shaiken takes this development one step farther by pointing out that this international integration of production also separates the interest of the worker from that of the well-being of the corporation:

> As globalization increases, there is a less direct relation between the financial fortunes of a manufacturing firm and the well-being of workers in any country in which it operates. In the United States, for example, a corporation's sales could be rising and its profits robust but the search for lower costs and even greater profits leads to production being transferred somewhere else.[55]

Thus workers are drawn together across national lines by the same employer and made part of an integrated system of production. This process, made possible largely by technology, repeats on a world scale the same process that brought industrial workers together on a national scale with the growth of mass production industry in the nineteenth century. The same forces that make such a historic shift possible for capital – rapid improvements in communications and transportation – have also created the potential for increased international cooperation among workers.

Even sections of the business union bureaucracy have come to recognize this potential. In 1966, for example, the International Metal Workers Federation (IMF), an international federation of unions in the auto, steel and machine tool industries, set up the World Automotive Councils (WACs) in GM, Ford, Chrysler, and Volkswagen. In later years, WACs were extended to British Leyland, Renault, Citroën, Toyota, Nissan and Volvo. At times, the WACs provided information and a measure of solidarity for strikes in various countries, but for the most part they remained little more than information clearing houses accessible only to the top levels of their national affiliates. Similarly, the traditional International Trade Secretariats (ITSs), like the IMF, are captives of the bureaucracies of their national affiliates. Notable exceptions to their inaction were the two campaigns waged by the International Union of Food and Allied Workers Associations (IUF) in support of the Guatemalan Coca-Cola workers in 1980 and again in 1984. Worldwide pressure was applied to Coca-Cola to force its Guatemalan franchise to settle with the striking Coke workers.[56]

Beginning in the late 1970s, networks of shop-level union activists in a number of multinationals and industries began to take shape. One of the first networks originated with Third World workers in the sugar industry. In 1977 representatives of unions from twelve countries met in Trinidad to form the International Commission for Coordination of Solidarity among Sugar Workers (ICCSASW). The ICCSASW has grown steadily over the years. In 1983 its second world meeting, held in Toronto, Canada, drew representatives from twenty nations; the 1987 conference, held in the Dominican Republic, was attended by representatives from thirty sugar-producing countries. This international network is one of the most organizationally advanced and has a permanent office in Toronto, an international steering committee, and two regular newsletters. The ICCSASW has conducted a number of international solidarity campaigns, notably on behalf of the Brazilian sugar workers union FETAPE and the National Federation of Sugar Workers in the Philippines. Like most of the international grass-roots networks that have formed, ICCSASW attempts to provide a global picture of the structure and changes characterizing its industry. In addition to the normal problems presented by the powerful multinationals that dominate this industry, sugar-producing nations tend to be monocultural so that when sugar prices drop the entire nation in affected. Thus, most of the unions represented in the ICCSASW call for crop diversification and land reform in their programs. This emphasis makes ICCSASW more political in its outlook than most of the international networks in other industries. This degree of political involvement is typical of Third World labor movements in general. Referring to the fight for crop diversification, Reginald McQuaid, the executive director of ICCSASW, commented that 'this requires a great deal of political action and pressure. Unions in the Third World see themselves as part of a broader process of political and economic transformation than appears to be the case in the US.'[57]

More typically, international networks in manufacturing have tended to start in Europe, where the multinationals have built integrated production systems across national boundaries. In the auto industry, where such international integration was highly developed in Europe by the late 1970s, shop stewards' organizations in the various countries began seeking out contacts throughout their industry as the effects of multinationalization on their bargaining power became apparent. These autoworkers were aided by a network of economic research groups concerned about the impact of internationalization on unions. By 1978, the Transnationals Information Exchange (TIE), a network of forty research and activist labor groups was formed with headquarters in Amsterdam. TIE was responsible for forming three international working groups, in auto, information technology, and agribusiness.

In 1979, TIE began to hold face-to-face meetings of workers with an international meeting of autoworkers. Attendance at this conference was limited to European workers. Its second autoworkers conference, in 1983, also included delegates from the US, Malaysia, Brazil and Japan. This meeting called for the organization of a worldwide network within General Motors, a project that was realized in a September 1984 conference of GM workers. Autoworkers from thirteen countries in Europe, North America, Latin America and Asia were able to compare notes and analyze GM's international strategy. QWL was cited as something GM was attempting to implement globally. There was also discussion of how to carry out international solidarity actions. The Brazilians proposed that everyone be informed of possible strikes in advance. In 1986, a second worldwide GM workers conference was held in Britain, hosted by the GM Conveners' (chief stewards) Committee and the Transport and General Workers Union. This conference drew twice as many delegates as the first one, more from Latin America and, for the first time, a delegate from South Africa. This conference adopted a set of common goals, including campaigns for a shorter workweek and the elimination of overtime, direct links between plants producing the same product, opposition to the integration of new plants into the GM system unless they have acceptable wages and conditions, and an effort to coordinate contract bargaining dates.[58]

In 1984 Ford workers took a similar step. Hosted by the British Ford Conveners Committee, delegates from Ford plants in sixteen countries met in Liverpool, England. Three earlier meetings had been limited to Europeans, but this conference included delegates from Brazil, Malaysia, South Africa, Australia, New Zealand, the United States and Japan. Their discussions were similar to those held by the GM workers in 1983 and 1986. The Europeans, who were accustomed to working together, proposed a permanent international committee to coordinate activities and information. Many Third World delegates saw this step as impractical, but an information network was set up with the British to be in charge.[59]

The movement for grass-roots international cooperation among autoworkers received another boost in March 1987 when the Brazil autoworkers union, the major Brazilian labor federation CUT (United Workers Confederation) and TIE cosponsored a worldwide autoworkers meeting in Saõ Paulo, Brazil. Workers from sixteen countries attended, though delegates from South Africa were prevented from attending by the South African government. Again the emphasis was on the exchange of information about corporate and industry strategies and about ways to combat them. Protectionism was discussed at length, and the delegates agreed that protectionist measures by the developed nations pitted workers in the industry against one another. As with previous conferences, the major outcome was an intensification of the communications network among autoworkers around the world.[60]

While none of the autoworkers' networks has much structure beyond communications, their mere existence can make a difference. In 1986–87, the GM network was able to prevent the company from defeating the resistance of Irish workers to GM's demands for new, flexible work rules. The Irish workers rejected the idea, and GM locked them out – certain that it could get the work done in other European plants. The company tried to give the work to its Bedford plant in England, which was scheduled to close. The English workers could have used the work, but the GM network informed the union that it was scab work and the English union refused it. GM shifted the work to an outside contractor in West Germany, which employed some Irish scabs and German students. When informed by the GM network that this was scab work, West German GM workers met with the student union and the factory's works council and informed management it would not do the job.[61]

Since 1982, IBM workers in the US have been trying to reinforce their own efforts to unionize IBM in the US by making international contacts. In that year, the US-based IBM Workers United (IBMWU) met with members of the IBM Japan Union in Montreal to exchange information. They decided to hold an international meeting in 1984, at which the IBM Workers International Solidarity (IBMWIS) was formed. The IBMWIS is unusual among the international networks in that it includes both union and nonunion groups. In the US it includes both the IBMWU, which does not have bargaining status and the Black Workers Alliance, a group fighting IBM's racially discriminatory personnel practices. The IBMWIS met again in 1985 and in 1987. Between these two world meetings, the CWA in the US and the International Metal Workers Federation, the International Federation of Commercial, Clerical, and Technical Employees (FIET, its initials in French) and the Postal and Telephone Workers International (PTTI), all International Trade Secretariats (ITSs) affiliated to the International Confederation of Free Trade Unions, announced plans for a worldwide organizing drive. It is likely that this decision was influenced by the growth of IBMWIS. A meeting in early 1987, organized by the IMF, FIET, and PTTI, drew a hundred delegates from twenty-five countries. These were union officials rather than IBM workers. At its third conference in April 1987, the IBMWIS agreed to cooperate with the CWA and the three ITSs, but to continue its approach of worker-to-worker meetings and communication.[62]

The developing grass-roots international networks have obvious strengths and weaknesses. Their strengths include the direct communication among plant-level organizations, the freedom from the bureaucratic protocol that in many cases limits the ability of the ITSs to act, and their ability to circumvent the political divisions that have led to the creation of different (and hostile) international federations – the ICFTU, which is largely social democratic; the World Federation of Trade Unions (WFTU), which is Communist; and the World Confederation of Labor, which is Catholic and generally centrist in political outlook. These political divisions do not correspond to the investment patterns of the multinationals. The grass-roots networks draw on unionists at the plant level regardless of the international affiliation of their national union.

The weaknesses of these international networks are also apparent. They command few resources and therefore have difficulty maintaining communications. The *GM Workers Voice*, which was launched after the 1983 GM Workers International Conference, has come out only a few times. While the networks have taken some solidarity actions, they are not really powerful enough to impose anything like internationally coordinated bargaining, which is usually one of their goals. This is because some of the delegates and plant-level organizations are at odds with their union leadership. This is particularly true of the US delegates, who have tended to be dissidents in relationship to their international union, even when they control their locals. While the unions in many countries have been supportive of the networks, most US unions and some those in Europe have been hostile. The UAW, for example, discouraged US autoworkers from attending the 1986 GM meeting. In some cases this hostility stems from the inclusion of rival, Communist-led unions in Europe.

For all their weaknesses, however, the grass-roots international networks, along with growing opposition to the AFL-CIO's support of US foreign policy, represent a significant step toward a genuine labor internationalism among US union activists. Further, they represent a practical means for dealing with the divide-and-conquer strategies of the multinationals. In the longer view, as today's dissidents rise in their unions and begin the difficult transformation from business unionism to militant social unionism, they will gain the resources to give this practical internationalism the force it lacks today.

To these efforts should be added the numerous US-based solidarity efforts and campaigns of the last several years. These include grass-roots labor support for Polish Solidarity in the early 1980s and for the new unions in South Africa in the middle and late 1980s. There have also been numerous worker-to-worker labor delegations to Central America, the Philippines, Mexico, Europe and other parts of the world; countless pressure campaigns to defend imprisoned and victimized unionists in various Third World countries, including South Africa; and fund-raising to support struggling unions in other nations, such as the 19 September Garment Workers Union in Mexico. While the forces engaged in these various forms of international solidarity are still small in relation to organized labor as a whole, their message has growing credibility and urgency in an era of global economic integration.

13

If Not Here, Where?
If Not Now, When?
If Not Us, Who?

The erosion and then collapse of most of the institutions that characterized industrial unionism appeared more as a surrender than a battle.
The level of resistance in the first few years of concessionary bargaining
was remarkably low. During the recession of the early 1980s, a majority
of union members feared for their jobs and felt compelled to accept setbacks they viewed as temporary. Strike statistics indicate that most
unions and their members preferred to grant contract concessions rather
than strike. The number of strikes and of strikers plunged to record lows
for the postwar era: before 1980, the number of strikes had never been
lower than 200, but in 1980 it fell to 187 and continued downward to an
all-time low of 54 in 1985. In 1986, with several big strikes such as those
at USX, AT&T, two regional telephone operating companies, ALCOA
and National Can, the number rose to only 69. The number of strikers
followed the same pattern. The number of 'days idled by strikes', as the
Department of Labor likes to put it, fell but remained near or above the
level of the late 1950s and early 1960s. Those who did choose to strike or
who were forced into it by their employer had to strike longer with no
guarantee of victory.[1]

The reluctance to strike was no doubt reinforced by the fact that most
strikes ended with concessions anyway, and a few ended in serious
defeat. PATCO, a relative newcomer to organized labor, was broken by
the Reagan administration. The copper miners at Phelps Dodge, long
known for their militancy and the radical legacy of the old Mine, Mill
and Smelter Workers, lost their union and their jobs to scabs after two

years on strike. For many, the PATCO and Phelps Dodge experiences indicated that the price of resistance had become too high. When the Reagan administration put into effect the plan developed by the FAA's Management Strike Contingency Force, bringing in military air traffic controllers until permanent scabs could be trained, the AFL-CIO chided PATCO leaders for acting brashly and not consulting Federation leaders about the wisdom of such a strike – a theme that Lane Kirkland would repeat in the strikes of TWA flight attendants and Hormel packinghouse workers in 1985–86.[2]

A handful of unions, however, tried to come to PATCO's aid. The CWA pledged $1 million and the American Postal Workers Union set up a fund for PATCO. Individual unionists joined PATCO's lines and a few rallies were organized around the country. In some ways, the support for PATCO was reminiscent of the sort of support extended to the United Mine Workers in their hard-fought 1977–78 strike, when the CWA and Steelworkers each donated $1 million and the UAW pledged $2 million. But PATCO's situation was more desperate and more than money was needed. The miners had not been replaced, and President Carter's imposition of Taft-Hartley was totally ineffective. Without regard for air safety the government had fired and replaced PATCO members on a permanent basis. The kind of decisive action that airline mechanics and pilots might have taken by recognizing PATCO picket lines was beyond the imagination of business unionism. It was also beyond the ability of individual militants. The AFL-CIO leadership made no attempt to apply political pressure, and did not even accord PATCO symbolic support by granting it recognition at the Federation's September 1981 Solidarity Day march in Washington.[3]

The defeat of the copper miners in Phelps Dodge's Arizona and Texas mines was a less visible event, but one that seemed to indicate that even as strong a union as the United Steelworkers could be defeated in an industry with a militant history. In 1983 Phelps Dodge joined the growing bandwagon of firms that no longer felt they could afford to be part of an industry-wide wage and benefits pattern. The company refused to sign the pattern agreement along with other copper firms and demanded sizable concessions. In response, a coalition of thirteen unions representing the workers at Phelps Dodge's mining facilities, with the United Steelworkers as the largest union in the lead, struck in July 1983 against concessions. For the first year, the strike was conducted as a normal withholding of labor. When the company introduced scabs in July 1984, the miners mounted a militant defense of their jobs with mass picketing. Arizona Governor Bruce Babbitt sent in the state police to protect the scabs. When the police attacked the strikers there was considerable violence: strikers were beaten and arrested. The USW International

Jim Guyette of UFCW Local P-9 speaks at the 1986 convention of Teamsters for a Democratic Union.

leadership made it clear that it wanted no more violence or conflict with the authorities. The strike was to be conducted within the limits of business unionism.

With the strike a year old and with scabs on the job, the company organized a decertification election, in which the strikers were barred from voting by law. Predictably, the union lost. The USW fought the results of the election in the courts and lost there as well. In September 1984 the USW announced that the thirteen unions were launching a coordinated corporate campaign against Phelps Dodge and threatened to withdraw funds from Phelps Dodge's major sources of credit, notably Chase Manhattan and Manufacturers Hanover banks. In October the USW did withdraw $10.8 million from Chase and a few months later Albert Shanker, president of the AFT, announced he would withdraw a sizable portion of the New York State Teachers Retirement Fund from Manufacturers Hanover. However, almost immediately he denied this was meant to pressure Phelps Dodge and reneged on the withdrawal. The USW's campaign seemed to have no place to go and no clear goal. Decertification was an accomplished fact, and it is difficult to imagine how pressuring the banks could affect it. For the next several months the USW then ran what might best be called an imitation solidarity campaign, holding some rallies and launching a token corporate campaign. This campaign was soon silently dropped.[4]

In the search for successful strategies and tactics, the corporate campaign came into increasing use in the 1980s. The term itself came from Ray Rogers, who developed the idea in the Amalgamated Clothing Workers strikes at Farah in the early 1970s and J. P. Stevens in the late 1970s. The techniques involved a combination of tactics such as consumer boycotts, legal appeals, attempts to broaden the issues from simple labor relations to moral or social matters, and pressure on interlocking sectors of the business and financial community in hopes of isolating the offending employer. According to Charles Perry, one of the first academics to study corporate campaigns, a central feature of the corporate campaign is 'conflict escalation'. In particular, the corporate campaign 'seeks to define or redefine the issue in dispute so as to draw the sympathy and support of the general public and special interest groups.'[5] But it is also, as Rogers insists, an effort to 'place workers and their unions on the offensive and put *real power* on their side of the bargaining table.' The power Rogers refers to is the ability of the union to use its own influence over bank accounts, insurance policies and pension funds to pressure financial institutions into breaking ranks with the targeted employer, as was done at J. P. Stevens.[6]

The Stevens campaign, like the Farah campaign before it, had considerable success in gaining broad labor, church and public support. A central feature was public mobilization. In these campaigns, like the United Farm Workers grape and lettuce boycotts of the 1960s, the corporations were successfully cast as corporate lawbreakers and ruthless exploiters. In each, the union bureaucracy lent effective support and the organization's apparatus was key in reaching out to potential allies. Also, these campaigns occurred at a time when a section of the labor leadership appeared to be moving toward a more anticorporate posture following the defeat of labor law reform in 1978. Concessionary bargaining and union-busting were as yet rare and the faddish concern with 'jointness' and nonadversarial schemes were a couple of years down the road. Further, these were campaigns waged against corporate 'lawbreakers', who, it was imagined, were the exception not the rule. The tactics were new and the element of surprise was an additional factor in labor's favor.

Like any tactic, corporate campaigns can be done well or poorly, aggressively or routinely. Because most of them attempt to broaden the issues and take the high ground, this strategy tends to point beyond the normal conduct of business unionism. Conversely, however, run by business unionists as a pro forma exercise in public relations corporate campaigns can lack the power to mobilize the union's ranks or active support in the community. The USW's campaign at Phelps Dodge not only started after the defeat of the unions was already a fact, but it never went beyond the stage of a threat. Similarly, the corporate campaign against Louisiana Pacific conducted for the United Brotherhood of Carpenters by the Kamber Group (consultants close to Robert Georgine, head of the AFL-CIO Building Trades Department), began in December 1983, months after the strikers had been replaced by scabs. Moreover, although most of L-P's products are bought by construction firms with no interest in supporting a union, the UBC launched a consumer boycott. The campaign was not designed to mobilize any active forces and never really became visible. In the end, most of the UBC's L-P plants were decertified and the union was beaten.[7]

The implementation of many of the corporate campaigns of the early 1980s seemed tentative and formalistic, embodying the business unionist's ambiguous attitude toward the new situation. On the one hand, they vaguely recognized that the rules of the game had changed and they needed 'new ideas', like those discussed in *The Changing Situation of Workers and Their Unions,* and in a subsequent guide to corporate campaigns put out by the AFL-CIO's Industrial Union Department, *Developing New Tactics: Winning with Coordinated Corporate Campaigns,* in 1985.[8] On the other hand, they constantly pulled their punches when such campaigns were launched. Thus, some such as the ones at Louisiana-Pacific and Phelps Dodge simply flopped. Others such as Litton and Beverly concluded with procedural agreements that left most substantive issues unresolved. Still others, such as the OCAW campaign against BASF, saw episodic actions (a rally with Jesse Jackson at the struck plant in Louisiana in April 1986, a sit-in at BASF's US headquarters in New Jersey in May 1987, and another large rally at the plant in June), but lacked the consistency and public visibility to force a resolution.

A more aggressive approach to corporate campaigns was taken by

Ray Rogers, Ed Allen and others at Corporate Campaign, Inc. The CCI concept moved beyond the pro forma implementation of the financial leverage aspects of corporate campaigns toward greater emphasis on the mobilization of the union's rank and file as the leading force. In one of its guides to corporate campaigning, CCI wrote:

Labor organizations must activate and empower the rank and file. Most unions offer little encouragement for serious rank and file involvement either in contract negotiations or in a strike or lockout. Leading up to and during contract negotiations there is much to do to prepare a support network for union members and their families in the event of a strike; to prepare a broad campaign of outreach and coalition building; and to maximize pressure on management.[9]

The purpose of mobilizing the rank and file was not simply to prepare for a strike, but to act as the main force to organize support from diverse social groups – especially those that, like unions in the 1980s, found themselves under economic and political attack. Primary among these groups were other unionists at the local union level, small farmers and farm organizations, Black community and civil rights leaders, and activists in the peace and anti-intervention (in Central America) movements. Church groups and leaders sympathetic to these causes were also asked to join an ongoing coalition.

CCI did not necessarily initiate all of the coalition building, which usually has to be done by the embattled union itself, but it increasingly incorporated this work into its campaigns in the second half of the 1980s. This general approach was used by CCI and the unions with which it worked in the campaigns for FLOC (mentioned earlier), UFCW Local P-9 (discussed later), and most recently with the Association of Professional Flight Attendants, which represents flight attendants at American Airlines. In the latter campaign, the APFA contacted CCI in early 1987 to help construct a long-term campaign that could help prevent the sort of setback experienced by the flight attendants at TWA in 1986. Aspects of the corporate campaign approach would show up in a number of strikes where rank-and-file mobilization played a key part in winning. In the Boston hotel strike mentioned earlier, for example, a highly mobilized membership directed some of its most militant activity prior to contract expiration at the insurance companies that were the main owners of the hotels. Similarly, in the strike at Watsonville Canning the ranks frequently turned their actions toward the Wells Fargo Bank, to which their employer was in debt. Both of these strikes also involved considerable mobilization of support from other unions and social movements.[10]

The Development of Solidarity Consciousness

Increasingly, those who felt that they had no choice but to fight looked to new tactics and, even more important, to the active solidarity of other unions at the grass-roots level. Learning from defeats as well as victories (whole or partial), a growing number of concerned unionists questioned the go-it-alone approach of business unionism and the unwillingness of the international unions to grant more than financial or token aid and turned to each other for help for the first time in decades. As solidarity actions increased, a solidarity consciousness appeared among an active minority. It was ignored or bitterly resisted by the business union bureaucracies, but events brought it to the fore in a growing number of struggles and in the debates about the future of unionism that germinated among activists at the rank-and-file and local union levels.

This solidarity consciousness was not class consciousness in the traditional Marxist sense. That is, it did not necessarily mean that the workers and activists who recognized the need for greater labor solidarity and social outreach drew any systematic philosophical or analytical conclusions about the struggle of classes for political power. Because of the blatant attempts by employers to weaken or destroy unions, the fact of conflicting social power was certainly an element of the developing solidarity consciousness among union activists. But the instinctual drive to mobilize support among others experiencing social duress (such as farmers or minorities) was as often expressed in populist terms as in class terms: corporate America versus working America. Further, for many of those involved in such struggles, like Black or Latino workers, the roots of solidarity were national or ethnic as much as class in nature.

What was most important about the new forms of consciousness of the 1980s, however, was that they represented a development away from the utterly fragmented, 'interest group' self-conception that long dominated and distorted the social perceptions of much of the US working class. The thrust toward unity across occupational, racial, national, and sexual lines beyond one's immediate workplace represented a qualitative step forward in social consciousness for tens of thousands of activists. It also opened a greater historical possibility of a more general awakening among working-class people because these activists represented a new generation of working-class leadership. Like most advances in consciousness, this new perception grew from experience, often beginning as nothing more than the simple cry for help.

One of the first strikes to shape solidarity consciousness on a national scale was the Greyhound strike of late 1983, which occurred after four years of concessions at Greyhound and at the beginning of an economic recovery. The Greyhound Corporation, the diversified parent of

Greyhound Bus Lines, was a profitable company and a highly visible institution. Dan La Botz, writing in *Labor Notes*, noted this fact: 'Greyhound is a part of American life, from the big city bus station to the small town terminal. The driver in the blue uniform, the silver bus, the red, white and blue insignia, "the hound". While there are only 12,700 Amalgamated Transit Union members employed by Greyhound, they are found from one end of the country to another – right down on Main Street.'[11]

Greyhound demanded deep cuts in wages and benefits and it prepared to run the buses with scabs, accepting thousands of applications from unemployed workers desperate for jobs. When Greyhound announced it would run its buses with 'replacement' drivers on 17 November 1983, members and officials from other unions began showing up at the familiar downtown bus station to show their support for the strikers in Detroit, Toledo, Cleveland, Youngstown, Atlanta, Newark, San Francisco, Philadelphia and many other cities. In some cases, the reinforced picket lines numbered in the hundreds. In Philadelphia and Boston, hundreds of unionists stopped the buses for a day or two. Rallies, picket lines, and fund-raising events occurred until the strike ended on 20 December. This support came from local unions and in some cases city central labor councils rather than from the internationals.[12]

Nevertheless, this community support was not enough to win the strike. After more than a month, Greyhound workers accepted a modified package of concessions. But the union was not broken. And in some places, unionists who had been frustrated with the limited response of city central labor councils began to organize permanent, multiunion base solidarity committees. The Toledo Area Solidarity Committee (TASC) and the Boston-based Massachusetts Labor Support Project were two such efforts. The activists had seen that the support for Greyhound had been organized at the last minute and had been too weak to defeat a large corporation like Greyhound. But the idea had been planted around the country.

The next event that helped shape solidarity consciousness for many was not a national strike or one that would ordinarily have had much visibility. On 2 May 1984, four hundred workers at A. P. Parts, a small auto parts plant in Toledo, Ohio struck against demands for concessions. A. P. was a small firm in a troubled industry. The workers were members of the UAW, the union that had opened the concessions floodgates in the first place. The company swore it would continue production with scabs. According to usual expectations, this strike would have been defeated without anyone noticing. The Toledo Area Solidarity Committee tried to help the A. P. Parts strikers, and the word of their plight spread. TASC brought some unionists to the picket lines and held a successful food collection at area plants. These actions helped make the strike visible to other unionists.

On 21 May the leadership of UAW Local 14, which represented workers at AMC/Jeep and other plants as well as A. P. Parts, called a plant gate rally on short notice. Something happened that no one had dreamed of. With only two hours to organize, three thousand workers showed up in the early morning to help stop the scabs. They fought the police and stopped the scabs for a time. A horrified UAW leadership in Detroit put a stop to further mass pickets, but support for the A. P. Parts strikers in the form of money and mass food caravans helped them stay out for nine months. They did not beat all the concessions, but under their new contract they returned to prestrike wages and benefits. Most important, the scabs were removed from the plant.[13]

A different dimension of solidarity consciousness was illustrated in the strike of the United Mine Workers against A. T. Massey that began in October 1984. Like so many other struggles in the 1980s, it began with a company trying to break a traditional master agreement. In September 1984, the UMWA had settled its national contract with the BCOA without a strike. Massey, however, refused to sign the agreement, claiming that it was not really one company and that its various mines were independent firms. In fact, Massey was itself jointly owned by two giant multinationals, Fluor Corporation and Royal Dutch Shell. As the strike unfolded, the miners attempted to stop the movement of Massey coal through nonviolent mass actions. On a number of occasions reinforcements came from nearby mines and steel mills as the word got out. But the company proved able to move coal and to withstand even militant action by virtue of the resources of its multinational parents.

To broaden the struggle and to match the power behind Massey, the UMWA attempted to make the Massey strike a national issue by exposing the operations of both Fluor and Shell in South Africa. The fight against apartheid in South Africa had already received broad church and labor support in the US, and the union took the novel step of hiring a former member of the National Union of Miners in South Africa to run a campaign against Shell. This became a national boycott of Shell and was eventually endorsed by the AFL-CIO. The Shell campaign also brought the UMWA support from the Black community and national civil rights leaders. In December 1985 the NLRB declared Massey to be one company and ordered it to bargain with the UMWA. Union President Rich Trumpka called the strike off, but the Shell boycott, still run out of the UMWA headquarters in Washington, continued. The combination of direct mass action, approved by the union leadership so long as it remained nonviolent, and a national campaign linked to the struggle against apartheid in South Africa allowed the UMWA to take the moral high ground and gave it the ability to pressure the government and the company.[14] The linking of corporate aggression by a firm in the US with its activities in South Africa has become a theme in other strikes. This, in turn, has helped to develop a greater international awareness among US labor activists.

If the Massey strike and Shell boycott had produced partial victories, the Wheeling Pittsburgh strike of 1985 was in a very real sense a rehearsal for the 1986–87 defeats in the steel industry. Wheeling Pittsburgh, the seventh largest firm in the industry, had broken out of the big steel pattern in 1982 when it won two rounds of concessions from the United Steelworkers. In April 1985 Wheeling Pittsburgh filed for protection under Chapter 11 of the Federal Bankruptcy Code, a tactic previously used by Wilson Foods and Continental Airlines. In July a federal bankruptcy judge granted W-P the right to void its labor contract and impose unilateral changes in wages, benefits and work rules. Shortly thereafter, 8,200 W-P workers went on strike to preserve their working conditions and their union contract. The implications of this struggle were clear: the basic steel contract covering five major firms would expire in August 1986 and the outcome of the fight at Wheeling Pittsburgh would influence what would happen then. John Tirpak, vice president of USW Local 1223 at the Yorkville, Ohio plant defined what was at stake: 'Everyone in the labor movement in basic steel will be watching us. And everyone in the industry – the Rodericks, the Trautleins, LTV – will be watching [W-P chairman] Dennis Carney and his company. This is one time where no one can come along with that old phrase, "nobody wins a strike". Someone is going to win and someone is going to lose this one.'[15] Although the sentiment to strike was overwhelming, not everyone was convinced that the union could win. But the workers seemed to be willing to take a stand in any event. One worker told the socialist paper *In These Times:* 'This is it. If we go down, the company goes down with us.' Another added: 'This is the Alamo of the steel industry.'[16]

The USW International, which led the bargaining with Wheeling Pittsburg, sanctioned a simple withdrawl of labor and left it at that. The local unions at W-P's nine mills were largely isolated from one another outside of negotiations, and the International took no special steps to secure victory. No corporate campaign was mounted. No pressure was applied to the various government agencies overseeing the company's reorganization under Chapter 11. No attempt was made to build a broad coalition to support the strike.

Support did come from other local unions. Many USW activists who had been involved in the reform movement of the 1970s sensed that something more was needed. In District 31 in northwest Indiana and parts of Chicago, plant gate collections were begun, and $3,000 was raised in the first morning. Bus loads of supporters from District 31 and other local unions still run by reformers also joined the picket lines and sent help in various forms. But the weakened reform forces could not tip the balance in favor of the W-P workers or force the International to do more than sanction the strike.

After three months, the USW settled for a comprehensive package of concessions in October 1985. Because the concessions were not as deep as those originally demanded by the company, many felt the strike had been justified. The *Wall Street Journal,* on the other hand, observed that the outcome 'is going to have a lot of other companies licking their chops.' USW President Lynn Williams tried to deny that the strike had been a setback: 'Nobody should be looking at Wheeling Pittsburgh as a benchmark. It is in a completely different situation than US Steel.'[17] The outcome of steel bargaining in 1986–87 indicated that the *Journal* was right and that the logic of concessions would continue to depress wages, benefits and conditions until workers somewhere were able to draw the line.

The Wheeling Pittsburgh workers had, of course, tried to do just that. But the conventional nature of the strike, the lack of broad support from the rest of labor, and ultimately pressure from the International to settle rather than have a long confrontation on its hands as negotiations opened in 1986 prevented the workers from drawing the line successfully. Conventional militance at the local level could not thwart management's demands. The International controlled the channels of communication between locals, making broader solidarity difficult even among steelworkers. For activists who watched this attempt to draw the line at a bankrupt firm, the role of the International pointed to the limits of dependence on traditional internal union channels. The isolation of the W-P workers provided yet another reason for them to seek broader support.

Among a growing number of labor activists, mostly at the grass-roots level, the experiences of the first half of the 1980s provided a series of lessons to be drawn upon in the attempt to develop new strategies for labor. The first lesson seemed to be the need for broader support within the ranks of labor, not only in one's own union, but across the old lines of craft, company and industry; across those of race, sex or nationality; and into communities facing similar and related attacks. Probably few activists drew all these lessons at once or thoroughly integrated them. But it seemed clear that as the second half of the 1980s approached, something new was abroad in the ranks of labor. Two prolonged struggles provided a clear testing of both the limits of the business union bureaucracy and the new tactics and consciousness developing at the grass roots: the strike of one thousand members of Teamsters Local 912 against Watsonville Canning in California and that by members of UFCW Local P-9 against Hormel's flagship plant in Austin, Minnesota.

P-9 Proud

The strike by Local P-9 of the UFCW at the Austin Hormel plant, which lasted from 17 August 1985 until a UFCW trusteeship was upheld in court in June 1986, was one of the most visible and controversial labor struggles of the 1980s. The organization, tactics, and methods employed by the leaders, members, and families of Local P-9 in the prolonged struggle (of which the strike itself was only a small part) pointed beyond the norms of business unionism. In doing so, they inspired tens of thousands of union activists and infuriated hundreds of high-level labor officials. As a result, P-9 and its fight have been debated throughout the labor movement and on the left as well. It was one of those events that force people to take sides and that bring into sharp relief fundamental questions about the future of organized labor. Although the strike was defeated by the combined efforts of the company, the International, the State of Minnesota, and the court system, the ideas, organizations, and directions that emerged from that struggle remain in force today. A full account of the P-9 strike is beyond the scope of this book, but a detailed description is justified by the watershed nature of this struggle.

On 9 August 1982, the George A. Hormel Company opened its new 'flagship' plant in the prairie town of Austin, Minnesota. This plant replaced Hormel's original Austin plant. The workers who entered the new plant that day were covered by three agreements between UFCW Local P-9 and Hormel. The agreement from the old plant still stood. Additionally, there was a 1978 transitional agreement guaranteeing that Hormel would build its new plant in Austin in return for concessions, including a no-strike clause. Finally, the Austin workers were covered by the January 1982 concessionary agreement described in Chapter 8. Although many P-9ers were critical of that contract, they had ratified it in the belief that there would be no wage reductions during the life of the agreement, which would expire in August 1985: UFCW Vice President and Packinghouse Division head Lewie Anderson had told them so at a union meeting in January.

The web of old and new agreements created two problems for P-9ers. The first emerged as work commenced in the new plant. Production speeds were 20% faster than in the old plant, and safety conditions were terrible from the start. Many of the older workers took their pensions and left. By the end of 1983, two-thirds of the plant's 1,750 production

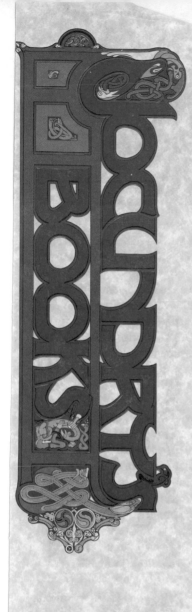

:e the new plant opened. Dissatisfaction was
3 P-9 elected a new president, Jim Guyette.
-9 Executive Board since 1980 and had op-
: late 1970s.[18]

:am that took shape between 1980 and 1985
s approach to the concessions trend sweep-
to fight it. Many of the new P-9 leaders, such
it Pete Winkels, Financial Secretary Kathy
ynn Huston, were baby-boomers. Some, like
to work in the old plant in the politically tur-
uck and Huston, entered only after the new
: in a period of industrial crisis and increased
The cooperative approach of the old P-9
1 the 1980s, and the UFCW's bureaucratic at-
ough retreat ran counter to the democratic
P' indicates that it was a local of the old CIO
<ers) and the common sense of people who
ed rationalizations to defend their actions.
icessions, the P-9ers tried first to move their
ustrations of that process led them in new

iel chain in the spring and summer of 1984,
k against further concessions. Along with
essfully argued for unity among the entire
:d a program that, had it been carried out by
1 the first step to halting concessions and en-
ry. But the chain resolutions, which included
ons, were ignored by the UFCW leadership.
ie resolutions were being passed, Anderson
tions between Local 431 and Hormel's Ot-
tte protested this action in three letters to
'ynn. Guyette argued against breaking chain
l concessions would 'destroy our chain and
:less, the Ottumwa agreement approved by
wage cut from $10.69 to $8.75 and an expira-
ing Ottumwa out of step with the rest of the
a decision of the UFCW leadership to allow
ract in September 1984, rather than waiting
for it to expire a year later. P-9 opposed this move as well.[20]

At a July 1984 meeting of the locals in the Hormel chain, Lewie Anderson treated the reopening of the contract as an accomplished fact and
talked of a chain-wide strike if Hormel insisted on a cut to $8.75 or less
at its other plants. It was already clear, however, that the UFCW intended

to accept a wage reduction as part of its strategy to make the major unionized packers more competitive with firms like IBP. Anderson's talk of a strike was meant to put Guyette on the spot by demanding that he guarantee that P-9 join a strike in September. Guyette pointed out that P-9 was under a no-strike clause from the 1978 agreement and that his local had not taken a strike vote. Guyette said that he would check the legality of strike participation, take a strike vote, and that P-9 would do whatever it could to support a strike. But the whole talk of striking was a ploy by Anderson to isolate P-9 because of its opposition to concessions. This incident became the basis for the charge by the UFCW leadership that P-9 'broke ranks with the chain during negotiations'.[21]

The charge, which would be circulated throughout the entire labor movement as part of the UFCW leadership's attack on P-9, was bogus on two counts. First, the Hormel chain was largely a fiction. As Guyette later pointed out in court testimony: 'The fact is that the Chain had never engaged in joint bargaining, had never entered into a single master agreement, had no by-laws or constitution, and had not and could not under the UFCW Constitution (except in rare circumstances) hold a single Chain-wide vote. Thus, "breaking with the Chain" was simply a euphemism for voting against the International's position.'[22]

In fact, the UFCW International had no problem with breaking chain unity in May when it allowed Ottumwa to negotiate and sign a substandard contract. Rather, the chain was a device for control by the International. It met only when Lewie Anderson called its meetings and discussed only the points proposed by him. In fact, P-9 was excluded from the September 1984 chain meeting because of its opposition to Wynn and Anderson's policy.

Second, in 1984 the UFCW leadership fully intended to reopen the Hormel contracts and grant the company another round of concessions. Like its proposal for a wage freeze in 1982, the International's willingness to take a cut in 1984 was meant to restore stability in the industry through an orderly retreat that would close the wage gap between the old major packers and their new, nonunion competitors. This was what Guyette and P-9 saw through and opposed when the local voted not to accept the $1.69 wage cut proposed by the International in September 1984 and accepted by the other Hormel locals. In fact, the logic behind P-9's decision to fight Hormel was far more sophisticated than the UFCW's strategy of preemptive concessions. According to Guyette, 'If the newest plant in the industry takes a cut in wages, then the other plants are going to say they can't compete. If concessions are going to stop, then they are going to have to stop at the most profitable company with the newest plant.'[23] The slogan, 'If not here, where? If not now, when? If not us, who?' that appeared on P-9 T-shirts expressed this strategic understanding.

Hormel imposed a cut from $10.69 to $8.25 in October 1984, invoking the 1982 contract's 'me-too' clause. The 'me-too' clause had been sold to P-9 in 1982 as a way to maintain standard wages. At that time, Anderson had said the clause contained language preventing a reduction in wages. In 1984, it turned out that there was no such language, and the cuts were upheld in arbitration. The International did not raise a finger to oppose the cuts, although they clearly threw the Hormel chain into chaos. P-9 prepared to fight.[24]

With the International unwilling to help and contract expiration less than a year away, Local P-9 set about to organize itself for a long fight and sought assistance elsewhere. But even before this moment, P-9's experience had been different than most: the members had already been involved in all of the decisions about the chain and the fight to come. Thus, by October 1984 they were ready to take two unusual steps. First, some of the wives of P-9 members formed the Austin United Support Group. Run mostly by wives, it would evolve a level and breadth of activity seldom seen in labor struggles since the 1930s. No ordinary 'ladies auxiliary' (though they set up a strike kitchen and distributed canned goods to needy families), the group organized some of the most creative solidarity programs seen in decades. They established the Emergency Fund to give short-term help to those with special and pressing financial problems. Even more innovative was the Adopt-A-P-9-Family Fund, a vehicle through which local unions or other supporting organizations and individuals could make regular monthly contributions to a specific family. In turn the family would write to their supporters to keep them informed of events in Austin. These two programs brought a financial stability once the strike began that is rare in such struggles. To keep morale up at Christmas time, they organized Santa's Workshop to make toys for the strikers' children. Through these and other activities, the United Support Group involved hundreds of people. During the strike it met nightly, with over a hundred people attending – usually different individuals each night. Long after the UFCW had ended the strike and seized the Austin Labor Center, it continued to attract hundreds of volunteers and maintain its financial support programs.[25]

The second unusual step was the hiring of Corporate Campaign, Inc., to conduct a pressure campaign against Hormel. Initially, Guyette didn't set out to have a corporate campaign; rather he first looked for a public relations firm to help publicize P-9's fight. When he read about Ray Rogers and CCI in *Business Week* he figured he had found the right 'PR' outfit. In his first phone call, Rogers informed Guyette he was not in public relations and explained just what a corporate campaign was. The P-9 membership voted to have Rogers come to Austin and give a presentation about what he could do for them. Before Rogers came, however, P-9 asked UFCW President Wynn if the International would hire Rogers and CCI to conduct a campaign for P-9. Wynn said he would consider it, but sent a telegram to Rogers warning him to do nothing without the permission of Lewie Anderson. On 20 December, Wynn announced that the UFCW would not hire CCI. But P-9 members had been impressed with Rogers's presentation in October, and in January they voted to assess themselves $3 per member per week to hire CCI.

The campaign organized by Rogers and Allen was meant to bring maximum pressure on Hormel prior to expiration of the contract in August. It began by targeting the First Bank System, a regional bank with strong ties to Hormel. The literature linked the packinghouse workers' fight with the plight of farmers who saw First Bank foreclose on them and on their neighbors. To put the campaign into effect, the entire membership of P-9 was mobilized as an outreach force. P-9ers went door to door in Austin distributing 12,000 copies of the local's newspaper, *The Unionist*. They also traveled to other Hormel plants to build direct contact with the workers there. The first few months of the campaign were a crucial factor in building the constant state of mobilization and participation of the P-9 members just as the formation of the United Support Group was key to the activation of the P-9 families. Although the P-9 Executive Board and membership continued to make the decisions about the direction of the struggle, Rogers and Allen became an integral part of the leadership of a campaign that eventually became national in scale.[26]

Unlike any previous corporate campaign organized by CCI, this one had to contend with active opposition from the local's international union. Long before the strike became a national issue, the UFCW leadership attacked both P-9 and CCI. Like P-9 itself, CCI had to answer the growing flood of public attacks that came from the UFCW headquarters or from Region 13 in Minnesota. Nevertheless, the main feature of CCI's role in Austin was mobilization and outreach. A group of P-9ers later summarized what the P-9/CCI campaign became and what it accomplished:

> Working together, New York City–based Corporate Campaign, Inc. (CCI) and the members of P-9 have achieved a great deal since January 1985. They have focused national media attention on the problems facing all packinghouse workers; broken down the barriers to communication that existed between workers at the many Hormel and FDL food plants; distributed well-researched literature dealing with the issues of give-backs and workplace health and safety to over 500,000 homes across the Midwest; mobilized support for P-9's fight from over 3,000 unions and other organizations in every state in the country; generated legal assistance to fight for the

workers' Constitutional rights and to defend them against the legal attacks of
Hormel, the government and the UFCW leadership; and kept the P-9 rank
and file moving as a constructive, non-violent force, rather than leaving them
idle, isolated and frustrated.[27]

The interaction of CCI, P-9, and the United Support Group created an
effective support infrastructure unusual for a local union at any time in
US labor history. Within Austin, long a company town, everyone con-
nected to P-9 was organized. Beyond the local and the United Support
Group, the P-9 retirees (known as the 'fiery retirees') became an active
force. Austin youth organized P-9: The Future Generation among high
school students. Nationally, CCI and the United Support Group raised
over $1 million for the Adopt-A-P-9-Family Fund, the Emergency and
Hardship Fund, and the Legal and Defense Fund. With the members of
P-9 hitting the road and sometimes even becoming permanent organizers in cities from coast to coast, they built a national support movement for the strike that began on 17 August 1985. Few such solidarity
campaigns can claim to have received support from nearly 3,000 local
unions, central labor bodies, or internationals since the United Farm
Workers' grape and lettuce boycotts of the 1960s. Most major cities had
a labor-based P-9 support committee by early 1986.[28]

This momentum and the general growth of solidarity consciousness
also led to the formation of the National Rank and File Against Concessions (NRFAC) in December 1985, which took on P-9 as its first project.
About 500 people attended the founding (and as it turned out, final) conference of NRFAC, indicating real sentiment for organized solidarity.
NRFAC played a role in launching support work in a number of cities.
But it failed to grow into a genuine national organization because of the
heavy-handed manner in which some of its initial organizers attempted
to control it. Most local P-9 support committees were independent
groups of union officials and activists. A number of the public leaders
of NRFAC appeared to back away from P-9 later in 1986, and the organization quietly ceased to be a force by the end of the year.

As the strike unfolded and the public attacks by the UFCW intensified
and were joined by the intervention of the Minnesota National Guard
and a series of legal attacks by Hormel, the fighting force created in Austin and known simply as P-9 reached out for new allies. CCI discovered
that Hormel had operating agreements with firms in South Africa. This
fact was used to contact Black communities around the country, an-
tiapartheid groups and activists, and even the African National Congress, which sent speakers to a number of P-9 support rallies both in Austin and across the country. In the spring of 1986, the P-9ers expressed
their new understanding of and solidarity with the struggle in South

Africa in a mural painted on the side of the Austin Labor Center. At the center of the mural was a woman packinghouse worker swinging a giant meat cleaver at the head of a serpent representing corporate greed. Below, farmers and workers marched behind banners reading 'All for One and One for All', 'Families Fight Back', and 'Intn'l Labor Solidarity: Abolish Apartheid'. The mural was dedicated to Nelson Mandela.[29]

Both the level of organized, democratic mobilization and the need to reach out beyond even organized labor had a profound effect on the consciousness of many of the participants. In speeches given in Austin in October 1986 and later at the November 1986 *Labor Notes* Conference 'New Directions for Labor' various P-9ers and United Support Group activists described how their understanding of the world had changed. At a rally in Austin, Vickie Guyette told how she had learned about the destructive force of racial prejudice and how her life had been changed by what she had learned in the course of the struggle. At the *Labor Notes* conference, Barb Collette said that before the strike her main interests were clothes and ceramic figurines. Now she saw herself as a human being with a consuming desire for justice. P-9 speakers, whether in Austin, Detroit, or New York expressed not only the idea of a new solidarity within the US labor movement, but their feelings of solidarity with workers in Central America, the Philippines, South Africa, and Europe who their travels and organizing efforts had brought them into contact with.[30]

The P-9ers and their families did not start out as labor reformers or radicals. Indeed, Guyette insisted at a March meeting in Detroit that there was nothing radical about what they were fighting for, just common sense for working people everywhere. Nevertheless, the consciousness of hundreds of people in Austin was transformed and, what may be most important in understanding the meaning of P-9 for the future of American labor, embodied into a network of Austin-based organizations that refuse to disappear. Not even the trusteeship and the termination of the strike, with the strikers left out of work, killed this consciousness and organization. Unlike the aftermath of most lost strikes, the leadership did not disintegrate or return to 'normal life'. A sizable body of working-class leaders was created in Austin of a sort that is all too rare in the US labor movement. Although defeated in conventional terms, they had created a kind of unionism that is different from and opposed to the standard norms of American business unionism. Rank-and-file democracy and activism, family and community mobilization, tactical creativity, solidarity extended to every corner of organized labor, and outreach to other embattled and oppressed groups in US society became the norms and methods of this bold step toward rank-and-file social unionism. These ideas were contagious.

The business unionist bureaucracy was quick to recognize the challenge to its concept of unionism implied in the P-9 struggle. P-9 as a local of 1,500 or so members was of course not an organizational threat to either the UFCW or the AFL-CIO leadership in any immediate sense. But the ideas that P-9 put forth and the spark it ignited in others infuriated the vast majority of officials at the international union and Federation levels. The attacks by the UFCW leadership on P-9 began long before the strike. In one sense, they went back to 1980 when the newly merged International attempted to impose its program of local mergers on P-9, demanding it merge with another local in another town.

Resistance to this plan by P-9 led to an early clash between Jim Guyette and Lewie Anderson, just appointed head of the UFCW's Packinghouse Division. Guyette led the opposition from the floor, and the merger proposal was defeated. According to Guyette, Anderson concluded the clash by telling the P-9 membership, 'You'll live to regret the day you turned this merger down.'[31] This clash and most of the moves against P-9 in the first few months of the strike had an 'in-house' character. For example, during 1985 the charge of 'breaking with the chain' was circulated within the UFCW. In October 1985, the International detailed its case against P-9 in a mimeographed 'Position Paper on Local P-9/Hormel, Austin Situation'. On 5 November 1985, Wynn indicated that he would approve roving pickets if Hormel didn't modify its bargaining stand, but on 17 December, with no change in Hormel's position, announced that he would not sanction such pickets. These moves were sleazy enough, but not much different from the maneuvering of many international union leaderships against rebel locals or strikes they fear will become serious confrontations. All of this changed in January 1986 when the UFCW publicly opposed the strike it had sanctioned a few months earlier in August and moved against the leaders of P-9.[32]

For many Americans, P-9 became a reality on 21 January when national television showed the Minnesota National Guard fighting strikers in order to allow scabs into the Austin plant. For almost as many Americans, the UFCW's opposition to this strike became public when Lewie Anderson appeared, along with Guyette and Labor Secretary Brock, on Ted Koppel's 'Nightline' show on 24 January to denounce Guyette, P-9, and the strike. This step was unprecedented: A top official of an international union attacking a leader of a sanctioned strike on national television. In February, the UFCW began to circulate an updated version of a written attack previously sent around the UFCW. Published as the February 1986 issue of the union's *Leadership Update*, this document attacked every aspect of the P-9 strike, the corporate campaign, and P-9's leadership in highly polemical terms. It was, from the start, circulated throughout the labor movement right down to the local level. It went to great lengths to discredit Ray Rogers, to prove that P-9 had broken with the chain, and to convince other union leaders that the UFCW's strategy for containing concessions in meatpacking was a success.[33]

The publication of this widely circulated polemic was timed for the February meeting of the AFL-CIO Executive Council: Wynn and the rest of the UFCW top leadership took the unique step of making their fight with one of their locals a matter for the entire Federation. A statement by the Executive Council endorsed the UFCW leadership's position by agreeing to circulate 'to all affiliates and its state and local central labor bodies a detailed analysis of the strike prepared by the UFCW.'[34] This 'analysis' was, of course, the February *Leadership Update*.

The literary attack on P-9 was carried to the politically progressive wing of the labor movement and to the political left, which played an important role in many places in organizing support for P-9. Bill Montross, a UFCW staffer with a leftist background, wrote a shorter version of the UFCW attack on P-9 for publications that reach progressive trade unionists and other social movement activists, notably the *Guardian, In These Times,* and *Labor Notes*. Probably the most effective attack on P-9 was authored by Lance Compa, a lawyer for the United Electrical Workers. Compa had a good reputation in progressive circles as a critic of labor-management cooperation, which he had termed 'enterprise unionism' in various articles for *The Nation* and other left publications. Compa's document was circulated in mimeographed form not only by himself, but by Lewie Anderson and the UFCW. However, Compa avoided the polemical tone of the UFCW document and couched his critique of P-9 in terms of a broader defense of industrial unionism. He characterized P-9's alleged break with the Hormel chain and its fight to preserve its previous wage rate as 'enterprise unionism'. Compa, in fact, used Guyette's quote about the newest plant in the most profitable company as being the place to draw the line on competitive bargaining as evidence of enterprise unionism. He argued that P-9's attempt to defend its higher wage went against the practice of taking wages out of competition. The argument was bogus, of course. Higher wages are simply not competitive with lower ones. Defense of the higher standard is often the very basis of successful pattern bargaining, of taking wages out of competition. While Compa did manage to thwart an attempt to get the National Lawyers Guild (an organization of progressive lawyers) to support P-9, most of the political left sided with the strike in spite of the UFCW-inspired attacks to the contrary. Whether expressed in the almost hysterical tone of the UFCW's document or the more measured tones of the Montross and Compa pieces, these arguments did not ring as true as a course for labor as the phenomenon that began in Austin.[35]

The successful introduction of scabs by late January changed the balance of forces in the strike. Before this, P-9 was in a good position by virtue of the importance of the Austin plant, which was scheduled to produce 50% of Hormel's products when fully functioning. While the scab workforce was never enough to bring production to much more than a third of capacity, the company also moved some of its operations to FDL plants with which it had a joint operating agreement. In view of these changes, some P-9 supporters privately argued that they should cut their losses and go back to work. In fact, P-9 did modify its bargaining position, but refused to return to work unless Hormel guaranteed to rehire by seniority. Hormel refused to make any compromises and the strike continued. P-9 countered the company's intransigence and the UFCW's back-stabbing by calling for a boycott of Hormel products on 26 January and the next day sending roving pickets to various Hormel plants. The pickets went without the permission of the International but with prior agreement with the shop-based organization at those plants. Most of the workers at the Fremont, Nebraska and Ottumwa, Iowa plants honored the picket line. Although their contracts contained clauses that allowed this, five hundred workers in Ottumwa and fifty in Fremont were fired. Hormel announced it would close its Ottumwa hog-slaughtering operation permanently. The UFCW International did nothing to save the jobs or defend the fired workers.[36]

In spite of the altered balance of forces, the strike was by no means lost in January. Indeed, both local actions and national support accelerated at this point. In February, the P-9 Future Generation led a walkout of Austin high school students. Support rallies and fund-raisers around the country multiplied. Large rallies were held in Detroit, New York, and San Francisco. There were more car caravans carrying food to Austin from unions in Minnesota and Wisconsin. On 13 March the UFCW International Executive Board withdrew sanction from the Austin strike. The P-9 membership voted to continue the strike and boycott on 16 March. On 12 April some five thousand P-9 supporters from all over the US attended a rally in Austin jointly organized by P-9 and NRFAC. The next day, Jesse Jackson addressed the strikers. But on 14 April the next step in the actual destruction of the strike was taken by the UFCW International when it held a closed hearing that launched the trusteeship process. P-9 was able to resist the implementation of the trusteeship for nearly two months, but in June the International seized the Austin Labor Center and the records and funds of Local P-9. Seizure of the center also meant the closing of the many operations run by the United Support Group. True to its creative nature, however, the Support Group moved into a new headquarters down the street.[37]

The UFCW did not simply put Local P-9 into trusteeship. It launched a campaign to destroy all the organizations and programs set up during the previous year and a half and to demoralize the leaders and activists of P-9 and the United Support Group. Donations to P-9 or the Adopt-A-P-9-Family were diverted to Region 13 of the UFCW, where close to $1.5 million was put to use by the UFCW to make up for lost dues from P-9. For a while, the trustees succeeded in commandeering Guyette's personal mail. Later in the year, in an effort to erase the history of what happened in Austin, the UFCW trustees personally attempted to sandblast the mural off the Austin Labor Center. No union sandblasters in the area would take the job, so UFCW staffers had to do it themselves. Former strikers were banned from all 'P-9' meetings. The official local was now based on the scabs in the plant. In October 1986 the UFCW sent all former strikers 'withdrawal cards' terminating their union membership until or unless they were rehired by Hormel.[38]

In September 1986, the UFCW signed agreements at six Hormel plants that would raise the basic labor rate to $10.70 by September 1988 – one cent above the rate negotiated in 1979, implemented in 1981, frozen in 1982, and cut in 1984. Aside from the money, the grievance, seniority, and safety provisions of the Austin contract were mostly those Hormel had unilaterally imposed in 1984. Former strikers were placed on a 'preferential hiring list', but in fact it appeared that Hormel would continue to do its slaughtering outside of Austin rather than rehire the strikers. Possibly the most novel clause in the contract was the one that banned anyone in the plant or on the list from supporting the boycott of Hormel products. Several former strikers were later removed from the list for allegedly having boycott stickers on their cars or attending events where the boycott was advocated. And unlike the other five contracts, which were three years in length, the Austin contract was four years long, again putting Austin out of step with what was left of the Hormel chain.[39]

But the P-9ers did not disband or surrender. Instead, they pursued a number of tactics in the fight to regain their jobs. The United Support Group continued its various support programs, still involving hundreds of people in its activities and publishing a national newsletter for P-9 supporters. Indeed, a large rally of hundreds of P-9ers and out-of-town supporters was held in October 1986 to celebrate the second anniversary of the United Support Group. This was followed by a benefit concert in Minneapolis that raised $15,000 and two large food caravans from the Twin Cities bearing over $15,000 worth of food.

On 14 March 1987 over seven hundred people marched and rallied in Austin to 'turn up the heat on Hormel'. The rally was organized to rekindle the boycott of Hormel products, which became the central pressure technique. The rally not only focused on Hormel, but expressed the broader themes that had come to characterize P-9 support events around the country. Dr. Fred Dube of the African National Congress told the audience something many already felt: 'Once you learn how to fight and join with others who are fighting, you find your true self and fight for a greater glory.' Business Agent Pete Winkels picked up on this idea: 'It doesn't matter if we live in South Africa, Central America, Poland, Austin or Cudahy, we all have a common fight for justice.' While the Hormel boycott was the central project, the rally also plugged the April 25th march in Washington for Peace, Jobs and Justice in Central America and South Africa – to which P-9 sent a delegation.[40]

The most controversial action following the announcement of trusteeship was the attempt by some P-9ers to 'recertify' the 'Original P-9' by petitioning for an NLRB decertification election. The first petition was rejected due to the similarity of the names (P-9 and 'Original P-9'), but a new petition was filed under the name North American Meatpackers Union (NAMPU). The NAMPU advocates also took their message to other UFCW packinghouse locals that had been sympathetic during the strike. The election in Austin was indefinitely postponed through a series of devices, depriving NAMPU of a clear base from which to organize. NAMPU posed itself as a long-term alternative to the UFCW; that is, an industrial union of packinghouse workers that would fight to reestablish the militant, democratic and social unionist traditions of the old United Packinghouse Workers.[41]

Given the widespread dissatisfaction with the UFCW by many packinghouse members, officers and even locals, this was not a completely farfetched idea. The merger, after all, was still fairly recent and its implementation was turning out worse and worse as Packinghouse locals were submerged into former Retail Clerks locals, the master contracts rendered meaningless and the bargaining strategy of the UFCW exposed as a failure. But without a base in a few plants and without cross-local organization within the UFCW, the balance of forces was too unequal for NAMPU to hope for any quick victories.

The controversy around NAMPU, however, was not based on any assessment of its near-term viability. It was around the idea of dual unionism. There are few terms in the lexicon of US business unionism more negative than 'dual unionism'. Indeed, the term throws fear into the hearts of many progressive trade unionists and the hardest of political leftists. In fact, 'dual unionism' has been a phrase used by conservative business unionists against more radical forms of unionism from the days of Samuel Gompers's campaign against the Industrial Workers of the World to the AFL's fight to stifle the CIO. And, as we have seen, there are few industries today that do not have two or more unions operating simultaneously with the blessings of the AFL-CIO Executive Council.

But some P-9 supporters were put off by NAMPU's 'dual unionism'. A few, notably some of the leaders of the National Rank and File Against Concessions who had played a significant role in building early support for the strike, dropped or played down P-9.

P-9 never put all its eggs in the NAMPU basket. In fact, there was something like a strict division of labor between those who were NAMPU spokespeople and those who spoke as P-9ers. Most of the former P-9 Executive Board members, such a Guyette, Lynn Huston, Kathy Buck, and Pete Winkels, maintained a P-9 identity and did not speak publicly for NAMPU. This is not to say that the P-9ers opposed the NAMPU effort or were not sympathetic. Rather they seem to have had a conscious strategy to pursue two courses in regard to the UFCW. One was NAMPU, the other was to continue to fight for reinstatement of workers in the plant, to challenge the trusteeship in court, and to main-tain full UFCW membership.

In the spring of 1987, this 'two-tier' strategy was given a national dimension with the decision to hold a Midwest Rank-and-File Packin-ghouse Workers Conference on the weekend of 2-3 May. The conference was attended by NAMPU, P-9ers, representatives from twelve UFCW locals, including P-40 (then on strike against Cudahy), and some workers from unorganized plants. Greetings were sent by three Canadian UFCW locals currently at odds with the International. The conference passed a Packinghouse Workers Bill of Rights that stated the new network's goal as 'one united democratic union of all Packinghouse workers'. The Bill of Rights was to be distributed to meatpacking plants and a network of activists from all plants, regardless of what union they belonged to (the Teamsters have several packing plants). The network would encourage the organization of unorganized plants, work within the UFCW to max-imize the effectiveness of its Packinghouse Division, while NAMPU would be free to pursue its petitions in Austin and at another plant in Texas where it had filed for representation in the summer of 1987. The strategy was explicitly a long-term one. The conference elected a con-tinuations committee to oversee the distribution of the Bill of Rights and to help build an international (US and Canadian) network. Whatever the fate of this particular project, it is clear that the UFCW is in for serious internal problems in its meatpacking division if it cannot reverse the situation that industry.[42]

The significance of P-9 goes beyond meatpacking and beyond the results of the Austin strike, however. The organization and conscious-ness that developed in Austin was a unique and very advanced example of working-class self-organization. The stability of the cluster of or-ganizations and projects that developed around P-9 before the strike not only prevented atomization when the strike was defeated, but was the basis for the most aggressive national and even international solidarity campaign in recent years. It was conducted without the resources of a large international – indeed, it was opposed by those resources – and without any previous experience in this type of organization or campaign.

The elements of the P-9/United Support Group/CCI infrastructure built in Austin and the aggressive solidarity campaign launched from it are a model of what unionism can be. Generalizing these norms of participation and mobilization throughout the American labor movement would be a significant step toward altering the deteriorating balance of class forces in the US. P-9 gave tens of thousands of labor activists something more important than a successful strike: it gave them a vision of what working-class people are capable of doing and the kind of unionism they can create.

Watsonville

The eighteen-month strike of one thousand frozen-food workers against Watsonville Canning illustrated another important dimension of the embryonic new unionism taking shape in the midst of labor's crisis. This was the national, as well as class, consciousness of the Watsonville strikers. The vast majority of these strikers were women – Latinas, Chicanas and Mexicanas. Most did not speak English. They were members of Teamsters Local 912, which was run by a largely Anglo and conservative leadership when the strike began. They did not control their own local, as did the P-9ers. They were also outcasts in the town of Watsonville, which in spite of a majority Latino population had an all-Anglo city council and administration. As striker Cuca Lomeli put it in an interview with the journal *Forward*, 'Among ourselves, among the working class, it is being shown that another one of the injustices here in the U.S. is that Chicanos and Latinos have always been discriminated against. And the same is happening here with the City Council and the politicians. They don't support us.'[43] Also Anglo were the employers at the many food processing plants in Watsonville and the agribusiness giants of California's Salinas Valley, which provided the vegetables for freezing and canning. A consequence of Anglo domination and discrimination was a unity in the Chicano-Mexicano community of the area forged in years of resistance and mutual support. This would be a powerful component contributing to the unity of the strike itself.[44]

The origin of the Watsonville canning strike followed a pattern that had become standard by the mid-1980s. The Teamsters had established a measure of pattern bargaining in this highly competitive industry, so that all the unionized plants paid pretty much the same rates. The wages were not high by US standards; production workers at Watsonville Canning made $6.66 before the strike. But they were generally above what Latino workers made as farm laborers, domestic servants, or service workers. In the fall of 1985, the owners of Watsonville Canning and Richard Shaw, Inc., announced they could no longer afford the $6.66 rate and demanded a cut to $4.25 a hour, along with cuts in benefits. The Local 912 leadership was totally unprepared to handle this situation. The president of the local was a friend of the president of Watsonville Canning, and the leadership of the Teamsters international union was hardly adverse to concessions.[45]

The workers at Watsonville and Shaw saw their living standard threatened – a common starting point for action in most fights against concessions. But the Watsonville workers also came to understand that the welfare of all the cannery workers in the area would be threatened if they gave in without a fight. Toward the end of the strike but before victory was in sight, striker Lydia Lerma told *Forward:* 'If we don't continue to fight and if they don't pay us what we want, then other canneries will not continue to pay what the workers are getting right now. Rather they will pay what Watsonville pays. And if we accept the $5.05 Watsonville is offering, then all the canneries will want to pay the same.'[46]

Working with the small chapter of Teamsters for a Democratic Union in Local 912, the members mounted a pressure campaign and got the local to call a strike against both companies on 9 September 1985. Most 'experts' would have judged this a losing strike a 'suicide mission', as Wynn had called the P-9 strike. But the strikers had a number of things going for them. First was the closeness of the Chicano-Mexicano community and workforce: workers in the nonstruck canneries regularly contributed to the strike from the start. Second was the existence of TDU, both in the local and nationally. While the strikers would soon set up their own organizations, a strike committee and a strike support committee, the existence of an active TDU chapter in Local 912 provided an organized focal point from which to start. In the long run, the most important aspect of TDU was its existence as an experienced organization throughout the Teamsters union in the US and Canada. TDU, as we have seen, had conducted scores of campaigns, many quite successful, within the union and many of the industries covered by it. While the Teamsters did threaten trusteeship and withdrawal of strike benefits time and again, the existence of TDU was a major factor in preventing them from doing so. TDU publicized the Watsonville strike, helped raise money for it, and provided a 'watchdog' function that neutralized the International leadership.[47]

Although Watsonville did not receive as much national attention as P-9 (perhaps because Jackie Presser did not denounce the strikers on television), Local 912 received much support from organized labor in Northern California. On 6 October, less than a month into the strike, TDU helped to organize a march and rally of three thousand people in Watsonville. On 3 November the Strikers' Committee called another rally, drawing three thousand people again. In March 1986, four thousand strikers and supporters heard Jesse Jackson address yet another mass rally in Watsonville, this one organized to commemorate International Women's Day as well as support the strike. These rallies drew on the labor movement in the San Francisco Bay Area. Although support came from Anglo and Asian workers as well, the most consistent support came from largely Chicano unions such as the UFW, Local 2 of the Hotel and Restaurant Employees, and the nonstriking members of Local 912.[48]

One of the most remarkable facts about the Watsonville strike is that not one of the workers from the plant scabbed during the entire strike. Scabs were brought in from the outside. But defiant picket lines, other forms of harassment, and a remarkable level of self-organization discouraged many of them. Watsonville Canning's owner, Mort Console, tried to use the scabs to decertify Local 912 in August 1986. He hired hundreds of scabs, but the strikers outmobilized him. Sending people and messages as far as Mexico and Texas to bring back strikers who had returned home looking for work or family support, they were able to get 914 of the original 1,000 strikers to vote to keep Local 912, against the votes of 848 scabs.[49]

The situation changed somewhat for the better in December 1986, when Local 912 held elections. As mentioned in an earlier chapter, a new team of leaders headed by Sergio Lopez replaced the discredited leadership of Richard King. Lopez was more willing to work with the strikers, albeit inconsistently. Also, Joe Fahey, one of TDU's two candidates, won both secretary-treasurer and business agent slots. Although Fahey was a UPS employee, he had been an ardent and active supporter of the strike since the beginning. The overall balance of forces in the local thus improved considerably.

As the strike moved into 1987, Watsonville Canning moved closer to bankruptcy. One aspect of the strikers' strategy since the start had been to apply pressure on Wells Fargo Bank, Watsonville Canning's main creditor. The idea had been proposed by UFW President Cesar Chavez back in November 1985. In May 1986 the Teamsters convention had voted to pressure Wells Fargo and any prospective buyer for the plant. In fact, the Teamsters did very little. But the resolution gave the strikers the legitimacy to begin campaigning for Northern California unions and labor bodies to threaten a withdrawal of funds if Watsonville didn't settle on decent terms.

Only weeks after the strikers launched this new phase of their own corporate campaign, Wells Fargo declared Watsonville Canning to be bankrupt. A new owner, grower Gill Davis, who was owed $5 million by Watsonville and whose vegetables were rotting because of the strike, made an offer to the Teamsters. The Teamster official jumped at it and attempted to get it approved at a hastily called meeting. But because most of the seasonal workers were not there, those present voted to postpone the ratification vote. Teamsters Joint Council 7 declared that the strike was over. It wasn't.

Again, the strikers organized to turn out as many people as possible and to demand dropping the clause stating that all rehired workers would be treated as new employees, losing many benefits. Hundreds of strikers and their supporters surrounded the plant to stop anyone from returning to work. No one crossed the line. The Teamster officials returned to the bargaining table and the lost benefits were returned. A mass meeting of strikers approved the new contract on 11 March 1987. The Strikers Committee led a mass victory march past the plant and down Watsonville's Main Street.[50]

The Watsonville strike was not a complete victory. In the end the strikers settled for the $5.85 an hour that the Shaw workers had taken in February 1986.[51] But, like the P-9ers, they had created a new type of organization (in this case the Strikers Committee and the support committee), tried out new tactics (the corporate campaign), and used their pride in their national identity *(La Raza)* to maintain unity and win support throughout the region. They had also proved that multiunion solidarity efforts make a difference and that the existence of a national opposition organization (TDU) within their union helped to neutralize a conservative and corrupt international union officialdom. In all of these aspects, the Watsonville strike was another major contributor to a new vision of unionism.

14

The Remaking of the American Working Class

We are living in the midst of changes of historic proportions. Not the least of these is the vast transformation of capitalism itself. Capitalism has now engulfed a majority of the globe, even reaching back into the postcapitalist, bureaucratic (Communist) societies of Eastern Europe and Asia. Further, it has developed from a system of national economies linked primarily through trade to a more integrated one of multinational corporations and global capital markets. International economic integration has in turn brought a cataclysmic increase in international competition. In the course of this competition, new centers of capital have proliferated and their geographic distribution has shifted somewhat from North America and Europe to Asia. Increasingly, all of these centers of capital have been drawn into a crisis of profitability that began in the West nearly two decades ago. The intersection of crisis, internationalization, and competition has brought growing pressure on the working classes of all the industrial centers from North America to Brazil, from Europe to South Africa, from Japan to South Korea.

Operating now from a nearly global platform, capital has attempted to advance its own competitive position by forcing every national working class to compete with the others. Using the leverage of this international competition, it has sought to promote similar competition on the domestic front. A 1986 study published by the International Metal Workers Federation took note of this trend:

> The pressures of intense competition, the major restructuring going forward in great metal industries like steel, autos and machinery, and the impact of the new technological revolution have combined to fragment many of the bar-

gaining structures that had been in place during the three decades following World War II. In virtually all of the Western European nations and most of North America, in recent years, there has been a clear tendency for much of collective bargaining to shift down from industry-wide, and even inter-industry levels, toward the enterprise and the plant.[1]

Nowhere, however, has the devolution of collective bargaining from a national/industrial level to the firm and workplace been carried as far as in the US. As I noted in Chapter 1 and discussed further in Chapter 8, the collapse of pattern bargaining in the US has been nearly complete: competitive bargaining has been imposed not only between workers in different companies, but down to the level of the workplace within the same corporation. This has not yet occurred to nearly the same extent in Canada or in European nations with traditions of national bargaining, despite the fact that their economies are also dominated by large multi-nationals.

Indeed, the contrasting experience of labor in the two highly in-tegrated economies of Canada and the US shows that the decline of unionism in the US is not simply or even primarily due to changes in economic structure. In Canada, union membership grew from 3,396,000 in 1980 to 3,730,000 in 1986. While the proportion of union members in the nonagricultural workforce varied a little from year to year, it re-mained 37.7% in 1986, slightly above its 1980 level of 37.6%.[2] As Table 7 shows, union density has consistently been higher in Canada than in the United States.

Table 7
Union Membership as a Percentage of Employed Workers, 1984

	Canada	United States
Manufacturing	45.0	26.0
Construction	38.8	23.5
Mining	32.8	17.7
Transportation	54.9	37.3
Services	38.1	7.3
Retail Trade	12.4	7.8
Government	66.6	35.8
Clerical Workers	30.2	14.0
Women	31.9	14.0

Source: Pradeep Kumar, 'Organized Labour in Canada and the United States: Similarities and Differences'. *Queen's Papers in Industrial Relations*. Kingston, Ontario 1987, Tables 1 and 2.

International solidarity: workers from South Africa, Mexico, El Salvador, the Philippines and Brazil at Labor Notes' 1986 New Directions Conference.

Part of the explanation lies in the very different balance of class forces in the politics of most of Europe and Canada. The existence of large working-class parties, whether in or out of office, gives the working class an organized presence in the political arena that American workers lack. This means that, although capital still rules, the balance of social forces is somewhat different than in the US and the openings for welfare state reforms greater. Thus, the social legislation in place when the employers' offensive accelerated in the 1970s provided a comprehensive social safety net (broader unemployment coverage, training programs, and national health care) and other protections (such as planned rather than arbitrary restructuring) lacking in the US. To be sure, business-backed conservative parties in many of these countries have emulated Reaganism to deploy the power of the state on the side of capital in both legislative and industrial struggles, but the working-class parties have helped to moderate the march of privatization, deregulation, and cutbacks in social services.

The existence of parties based on class lines has also created a higher level of both organization and class awareness of political questions. The Labor, Socialist, Social Democratic and Communist parties of Western Europe and the labor-based New Democratic Party of Canada all provide a measure of direct working-class representation in the political arena that is missing in the US. This is the major reason why voter participation is much higher in Europe and Canada than in the US.[3]

Another aspect of this difference in the political balance of class forces is that workers and/or unions in the various labor-based parties of

Europe and Canada do not have to deal directly with capital inside their own parties. Direct worker representation in Europe or Canada is typically diminished by the central role of both the trade union and party bureaucracies, who moderate their program in the face of capital's continued dominance in the economy – one reason why these parties tend to abandon their socialist promises when in office. But capital does not fund these parties and is not accorded a place in their decision-making structures. Like all working-class organizations, they must ultimately deal with capital, but they do so from an organizationally (and financially) independent position. In contrast, US labor faces not only the usual problems of party bureaucracy or electoral timidity, but the additional fact of having to negotiate and mediate its interests and demands through the petty bourgeois apparatus of the Democratic Party (from the ward-level club to the Democratic National Committee) and the less tangible, but more dominant presence of capital itself within the structure and behind the scenes of the party's operations. As a result, the balance of class forces in the US has changed not only in the political arena itself, as it has tended to do in Europe and Canada as well, but within the party through which labor has attempted to express its interests. By the end of the 1970s, organized labor in the US had been marginalized within its 'own' party, virtually eliminating any opposition role the Democrats might have played during the Reagan years.

The other major reason why capital has been far more successful in imposing competitive norms in collective bargaining has been the nature of American business unionism. As I argued in Chapters 2 and 3, business unionism was flawed at birth. Bureaucracy and the suppression of political debate and conflict within the unions have trained subsequent generations of union leaders in administration and routine rather than in confrontation and tactical flexibility. They have also disarmed the membership by depriving them of organizational and political skills and even of the motivation to participate in union affairs on a regular basis.

The narrow focus of modern business unionism on wages and benefits negotiated in the private sector has had two negative consequences. First, the abandonment of workplace control to management weakened most unions at their most basic level of organization – on the job. Second, the narrow focus on wages and benefits signaled the desertion of a broader social outlook which could have been the basis for both new organizing and for firmer political alliances with various oppressed groups. Finally, the 1948 retreat in pattern bargaining from the multi-industry level to the industry level began the entropy in the entire structure of bargaining that left the unions' defenses weak when the employers attacked in earnest. In combination with the bureaucratic structure of bargaining in general, this made US labor's basic line of defense a highly fragile one. The era of concessions and competitive bargaining that followed the collapse of pattern bargaining in turn lessened the attraction of the unions to the unorganized.

The consequence has been the forced march of the American working class toward pauperization. The nearly decade-long wage deceleration, permanently high levels of unemployment, and the growing proportion of low-wage jobs have created a bleak future for nearly all sections of the working class. While minority and women workers suffer a disproportionate part of this poverty, it is also the case that those white male sections of the class previously insulated from poverty are experiencing it in increasing numbers. It is even clearer that without a reversal of current trends the majority of the newest generations of the working class will feel the impact of poverty throughout their ranks. This situation will not reverse itself (without massive intervention from below) as capitalism goes through the business cycle. Rather, it is a long-term trend imposed by capital through concessions from higher paid workers, opposition to social programs to alleviate unemployment or existing poverty, and resistance to unionism in labor-intensive service industries. While the global economic pressures leading capital to adopt these policies are real and beyond the power of even the strongest unions to reverse, the actions and policies themselves are not immutable.

In the long run, the ability of the working class in the US to alter the deteriorating balance of political forces will depend on its ability to create a variety of mass movements and organizations capable of forcing concessions from capital. While no degree of working-class organization can change the fundamental social structure of capitalism or erase the laws of political economy, mass, combative organization can affect social policy. In the US, this means massive new organization of the organized and unorganized through a new social/industrial unionism, on the one hand, and a new, independent political strategy for the working class, on the other. However, developments of such historic dimensions will not come from the business union leadership.

From the Recomposition to the Remaking of the US Working Class

Most of the discussion of the changing composition of the working class in labor and academic circles is limited to empirical observations about the industrial, occupational and economic changes in the civilian labor force. Using the industrial definitions of the US Bureau of Labor Statistics, the shift in employment from manufacturing to the service sector is noted. In occupational terms, this change is recorded as a movement from blue-collar to white-collar work. This is presumed by some to be a move away from manual labor to clerical or technical work, from the factory to the office. From this rather vague picture it is possible to conclude that the labor force is becoming a more genteel, refined, and educated one.

For some, such as the French post-Marxist André Gorz, the trend away from goods-producing employment in the US and other developed capitalist nations toward service sector jobs is proof that North America and Europe have entered a postindustrial epoch. In most versions of this view, technology is said to have rendered the human input into the production of goods a thing of the past. The numerical decline of the traditional industrial working class is equated with the disappearance of the working class altogether. In this view, the working class is inadvertently defined by the type of product it produces, rather than by its relationship to capital.

However, the working class cannot be understood simply by the products it makes or services it performs. Rather, it is a complex, constantly evolving social formation. In objective terms, its existence as a class is defined by its relationship to capital, not by occupation or industrial status. Moreover, as a social class, it includes not only its jobholders, but those who grow up in its homes and those who retire from the labor force to grow old; in its ranks are those who work at home and raise its children, and those whom it hires to run its unions. It is a web of individuals, families, organizations, and communities, some of which are hostile to each other at one level or another, but who are tied together by a common relationship to an alien economic/social force – capital. Far from disappearing, as some argue, the working class has grown even as it has changed.

As I discussed in Chapter 9, the new sections of the working class in the service industries are employed by increasingly concentrated groups of capital which subjugate them to new technology and to deskilled, routine work processes under conditions more and more like those of industrial workers. The pay and benefits of these service workers place them in the lower ranks of the working class. These workers are themselves witnesses to and particpants in the changes in the terms of employment, and the natural leaders among them will surely seek ways to improve these terms.

In this vein, British historian E. P. Thompson in his epochal work, *The Making of the English Working Class*, explains that he uses the seemingly awkward word *making* to denote that the shaping of the English working class was not simply an event to be recorded, but a process in which the working class itself participated: 'The working class did not arise like the sun at an appointed time. It was present at its own making.' Thompson argues against views that the working class, as it was being created, was simply a collection of 'passive victims' or 'a labor force, as migrants, or as the data for statistical series.' He stresses that analyses that rest on such assumptions 'tend to obscure the agency of working people, the degree to which they contributed, by conscious efforts, to the making of history.'[4]

Like the English working class, its American counterpart has actively participated in its own development. As its occupational, industrial, ethnic, racial, cultural and economic compositions have changed as a result of the direction of capitalist investment at various points in history, it has inevitably reacted with varying forms of organization. One aspect of this has been the key role that immigrant workers (from Europe, Asia and Latin America) and later migrant workers (for example, Blacks moving from the South to the North) played in the formation of trade unions from the 1870s through the birth of the CIO and down to today with the formation of farmworkers' unions. In many cases, workers were able to transform traditionally low-wage industries into relatively higher paying, more secure sources of employment.

The experimental nature of the role of the working class as an agent of history can be seen in the variety of organizations it has formed: the eclectic mixture of craft, general and industrial unionism that characterized the Knights of Labor in the 1880s; the rise of AFL craft unionism, which quadrupled its membership from 1897 to 1903; the attempts to organize everyone from textile workers to cowboys by the Industrial Workers of the World; the campaign to organize mass industry through the amalgamation of craft unions in the early 1920s; and the rise of the CIO in the 1930s and 1940s. The active response of working people to economic change has included not only trade unions but both consumers' and producers' cooperatives, state-level farmer-labor parties, and even a mass socialist party (in the years before World War One). All of these efforts, those that succeeded and those that failed, have influenced subsequent working-class movements as well as the events of the day.[5]

In these attempts to match the power and organization of capital, the working class has never moved all at once. Since no social class is a monolith, examples of lockstep action by any social class are rare. Mass movements based on one or another class are less rare, but are still exceptional. Moreover, while these mass movements (the CIO, the civil rights movement, the women's movement) appear as instant social explosions to most people, they are inevitably a consequence of the convergence of fragmented efforts that preceded them. No movement is spontaneous from the vantage point of those who struggle in its prehistory to build and nurture it, only from that of those who record it after the fact.

Over the past decade, the majority of the working class appears to have remained passive in the face of new trends that are difficult to comprehend and even more difficult to resist without sufficient and suitable organization. In fact, working people have actively responded to events in the ways most obvious and available to them. As earlier chapters have shown, some groups have responded in collective ways: from creative struggles against concessions to the organization of farmworkers. Others, following the individualist traditions of American culture, have migrated from declining Rust Belt industries in the Midwest and Northeast southward and westward in search of employment. One consequence of this migration is the spread of workers with union experience to primarily nonunion areas and industries – a development that could prove crucial to future unionization. On an even larger scale, the migration of Latino workers from their homelands through the Southwest and into the northern parts of the US has been one of the most massive human migrations in American history. The impact of this migration on working-class organization has already become visible from new farmworker unions like FLOC and COTA to the long strike in Watsonville. Thus, migrations that begin as a random collection of individual decisions by working-class people and their families, often viewed as passive events to be charted statistically, affect the structure of the working class and, at times, underlay collective action. In their origins, such migrations reflect the human desire to seek the line of least resistance to survival, but in their consequences they often shape much of the future course of class struggle.

Those sections of the working class that have responded through collective struggle in the past ten to fifteen years have been in the minority. Nevertheless, I have emphasized their actions in earlier chapters because they have affected events, trained thousands of leaders and activists, influenced working-class consciousness, and because they potentially prefigure the kinds of actions that can influence the future. In other words, they have been the active minority that always precedes greater developments. At moments, even in relatively quiescent times, they have commanded mass followings. At other times, they have been separated from that following by the isolating effects of defeat. And, since most of these movements have lacked permanent organization, it is difficult to measure or track their impact on other workers. But the experience of the few organizations that have survived the last ten years suggests a pattern.

Organized working-class groups outside the stabilizing institutions of modern business unionism (notably the dues checkoff and the union shop), such as TDU or FLOC prior to its first contracts in 1986, reveal an organizational rhythm of turnover, growth, and leadership development. In this pattern, growth is not linear; early members may drop away for a time or even permanently. In the case of FLOC, for example, the membership tended to stabilize as more of the migrants who compose the workforce settled in towns near the fields. In TDU, all but the hard core of a chapter has sometimes dropped out of active membership as the particular struggles that brought people into TDU subsided, whether through victory or defeat; but TDU has retained the capacity to recruit and expand as new struggles arise elsewhere. In both cases, a key to long-term organizational stability has been the development, over time, of an activist and leadership core both locally and nationally. This latter development cannot be created overnight – it takes time, effort and the growth of trust within the core. But once it has been created, a working-class organization of some durability has been established and a larger pool of workers beyond its formal membership has been influenced by its ideas. In times of focused struggle, such as a contract fight, this periphery has often become active again. [6]

In different, usually less organized ways, this process has taken place in thousands of local unions, across local lines through the informal movements of women, Blacks, and Latinos, and through the national-level reform movements and campaigns of the last ten years. However, except for a handful of national campaigns on the scale of Miners for Democracy and Sadlowski's 1977 Steelworkers campaign, most of these movements, campaigns and events are invisible to the working-class public. Some of the strike movements described in Chapter 13 have had momentary visibility, but people often presume them to be the usual business union strike in which things return to normal when everyone returns to work. But many of these strikes have not been normal, either in their conduct or their outcome. Rather, they have had the character of a social movement and have changed the lives and consciousness of those who actively experienced them. Thus, if these various forms of working-class activity are taken together, the presumption of passivity within the class must be modified and the potential forces for change *within* the unions assessed as significant.

As has been argued, however, no real change in the balance of class forces is possible without the organization of the unorganized, both the millions in nonunion goods-producing firms and the tens of millions brought together by capital in various service enterprises. Measuring consciousness or activity is even harder among these workers. Polls, of course, indicate a willingness among a majority of nonunion workers to join a union given the chance. But the chance to join a union, these days, usually involves considerable risks. The question now, as always, is Who will take the first step? As noted earlier, the polls also indicate that Black, Latino, and women workers are the most favorably disposed to unionization – a fact borne out by the experience of recent organizing drives, from the fields to auto parts plants to textile mills. *Norma Rae*'s unprecedented alliance between white women and Black men (in the South, at that) offers a glimpse of what might happen if a reformed, realigned labor movement turned its attention as a mass movement to the many manufacturing and service employers who hire large numbers of women and minority workers.

The decline of the activist social movements of Blacks and women and the relative timidity of organizations like CLUW and CBTU seem to point to passivity in these quarters as well. But again, it must be remembered that people will follow the lines of least resistance before they will opt for confrontation. As I have argued, movements of the specially oppressed since the early 1970s have attempted to use the legal and conventional channels opened by earlier movements. These include the courts and electoral politics. While these arenas tend to be the natural terrain of middle-class activists, women and minority workers (union and nonunion) have also participated. The Jackson campaigns, for example, showed an increase in working-class support from 1983–84 to 1987–88, a sign that more working people were looking for a vehicle of social resistance. Indeed, the use of traditional channels to accomplish social goals is not a sign of working-class passivity, but of a conventional view of the normal means for redressing social ills that is shared even by most working-class and oppressed people in the US. These channels clearly offer fewer and fewer rewards. The potential of this search for social change to turn toward unionism, another traditional channel, is certainly there.

The potential for millions of workers to organize, however, depends on the attractiveness of unions. Unions that preside over the pauperization of the working class, that demonstrate no willingness to defend either the economic and special social interests of their members, that raise the banner of competitiveness, that are not organized along lines capable of influencing capital, and that offer no vision beyond nickels and dimes will not appear as a natural channel for workers to express social grievances. Thus, the fates of the movements to change the unions from the inside, the social movements among women and minority workers, and of the unorganized are inextricably linked. What is needed to unite these currents is a common vision of what unionism can be and how it could improve the lives of the millions who compose the US working class.

A New Vision for US Labor

Just as part of the human material for the transformation of unionism lies in the activists, leaders, and veterans of the union and social movements of the recent past, so the ideas that provide an outline of the direction of a new unionism have emerged from all of these attempts by sections of the working class to put their imprint on the social order. Additionally, a new unionism must draw on the positive traditions of past labor organizations in the US and elsewhere. In the US these traditions include the social inclusiveness, the rank-and-file democracy, the nascent egalitarianism, and the quest for universal justice that characterized, to one degree or another, the Knights of Labor, the Industrial Workers of the World, and the early CIO.

From Europe and the Third World, a new unionism in America can draw on a broader tradition of just what constitutes the labor movement. In the US the term *labor movement* is synonymous with the trade unions. But in most of the world, unions form only one part of the labor movement, which typically includes political parties, cooperatives and cultural, social and athletic organizations. In the US, working-class participation in politics, culture, social life, and athletics is typically commercialized and integrated across class lines to a greater extent than in Europe, the Third World or even Canada. A genuine labor movement would inevitably begin to evolve the means for recapturing the diverse cultures that coexist uneasily within the US working class from their commercialized, alienated, and distorted place in America's uniquely commercialized (and homogenized) popular culture. For the purposes of this book, however, the discussion of the conscious remaking of the working class will be limited to unionism and politics – using the concept of a labor movement in its broader historical meaning, rather than its narrow, business unionist sense.

As the composition and nature of the labor force and the work it performs changes, unionism must change as well. As noted in Chapter 9, such changes as have taken place are in precisely the wrong direction. Unions are chasing dues, not seeking new ways to match the changing organization of the employers. Unionism must return to the industrial structure, in both old and new industries, that gives unions their basic ability to take wages, benefits and conditions out of competition. In addition, it must seek new means (and revive old ones) that can follow the path of changing corporate organization and investment as its enters new lines of production. These would include cross- or multiunion formations such as stewards' councils, rank-and-file based coordinated bargaining, the use of corporate campaigns that mobilize workers across industrial lines to attack centers of capital, and, of course, the regularization of active solidarity through the recognition of picket lines and through various forms of mass action.

The enormous organizational changes required to re-create industrial unionism and active solidarity are not likely to come from today's business union bureaucracy, which benefits materially from the spread of general unionism. Nor is it simply a matter of electing a new set of more progressive bureaucrats. The restructuring of the unions must include the most thorough rank-and-file democracy possible. This is not simply because democracy is a nice thing or even because the rank and file are presumed to be more militant than bureaucrats, but because the working class cannot remake its own institutions unless it controls them.

In a number of ways, the struggles against concessions of the past several years and the solidarity efforts that have arisen with increasing regularity prefigure such developments. First, the fight against concessions took on a greater significance than the simple attempt by separate groups of workers to defend their incomes and working conditions: it became a fight against the introduction of competitive norms in collective bargaining. The significance of concessionary bargaining became clear to many during the P-9 strike, where this question became part of open debate as the older craft-style local bargaining mentality of most of the leadership of the UFCW clashed with the fight to stop the destruction of pattern bargaining. UFCW leaders saw pattern bargaining only in formalistic terms and failed to understand that the line had to be drawn somewhere in order to reestablish an upward pattern. The P-9ers' response was, 'If not here, where?' The fight against concessions was a fight in defense of industrial unionism.

In contrast, the business union bureaucracy seems to have completely missed the significance of concessionary bargaining as a way to fundamentally weaken unionism through the introduction of competition. They saw it only in terms of lost wages and benefits and, even at that, usually approved of it. In the same way, the top leadership of most international unions saw QWL and, more recently, the team concept, only in terms of the survival of unionized employers, ignoring the undermining effects of such schemes on the most basic level of unionism – in the workplace.

In the growing resistance to concessions, grass-roots activists have also frequently taken steps toward genuine solidarity. Recognizing that isolated strikes lose more often than not these days, they have formed local, cross-union solidarity committees in several cities. Activists around the country demonstrated a new level of consciousness in the impressive national solidarity campaigns around such struggles as the FLOC organizing drive and the Watsonville and P-9 struggles. The growing use of various corporate campaigns also represented an attempt by working-class people to match the illusive contours of capital with imaginative tactics.

To these developments must be added the even more embryonic efforts to establish grass-roots international links. The AFL-CIO's version of international solidarity is guided by the priorities of Corporate America and its foreign policy experts in Washington, isolating US workers and nurturing a narrow nationalism. But the internationalization of capital has undermined the conditions which once underwrote this alliance of labor and capital in foreign affairs. The AFL-CIO's justification for its policy has collapsed and opposition has arisen. As a result, a growing number of trade unionists have sought out direct contact with various overseas labor movements. These include not only the solidarity campaigns in support of unions in South Africa, Central America, Mexico, the Philippines, and most recently, South Korea, but US participation in the international networks based in specific industries or corporations.

The reshaping of the existing unions could also be catalyzed by unorganized workers seeking effective means of resistance to ever more aggressive employers. If unionization in the new mass service industries begins to take off, it will eventually run up against the inappropriate structures of today's unions, just as industrial workers in the first half of the 1930s found the old craft unions useless for their purposes. Industrial workers tried, first in the early 1920s and then in 1933–35, but met only defeat as the craft unions attempted to pull the workers within the same company and industry apart into separate organizations. Today, general unions not only fail to match the contours of the capital structure of their traditional jurisdictions, but have no relation to the potential jurisdictions among the unorganized. Thus, as more and more workers in firms such as Blue Cross or Beverly join unions, they will either abandon them as they fail to produce real change in their lives, or they will demand changes in the unions themselves.

As sections of the working class attempt to shape a new unionism in the ever changing economic climate of contemporary capitalism, they will inevitably confront the question of political action. Historically, the question of independent working-class political action has come up in every period when the working class attempts to create new unions. The notion that labor should take the lead in forming a party of the working class arose in the 1880s, culminating in scores of effective independent labor campaigns at the local level and a less effective national campaign. Attempts – some successful, most not – to form state-level labor or farmer-labor parties occurred in both the 1920s and 1930s as workers sought political protection for the unions they were forming. The rightward odyssey of the Democratic Party, the general debt crisis of the US economy (including the federal deficit), and the increased pressure of capital on the political process generally indicate that the Democrats are unlikely to make the sort of accommodation to a new unionism that they made in the 1930s. Thus, the concept of a labor party is likely to take on a new popularity as events unfold.

The British model of the creation of a labor party, or that often projected for the CIO in the 1940s, in which the labor bureaucracy itself leads a break from an existing capitalist party, seems unlikely for the United States. For one thing, the American labor bureaucracy tenacious-ly rejects such a course. In spite of its considerable loss of influence in the political arena, it remains linked to the establishment of the Demo-cratic Party, locally and nationally, by a multitude of relationships and deals. While the bureaucracy is well aware of its declining influence, it is still dependent on the Democrats at the local, state and national levels for whatever defensive legislation still seems within reach. A political break by one or more of the major internationals would have to be preceded by a rank-and-file rebellion capable of sweeping the bu-reaucracy away altogether.

A frequently cited reason for the failure of an independent working-class party to develop in the US is the winner-take-all, single-member constituency system of elections. Under this system, it is hard for a new political party to establish a presence in Congress, much less elect a presi-dent, because its candidates must defeat those of both old parties to gain any representation at all. Most third parties in American history have been small minority parties, and the winner-take-all system has in-hibited their ability to develop into mass alternatives to one or another of the two major parties. In reality, this argument simply says that so long as the two major parties maintain a relatively stable base in the elec-torate, it is difficult for a new party to become a genuine force in politics. In other words, a new working-class party cannot be born in the hum-drum of American politics as usual.

A new political party in the US will have to be the result of a con-fluence of the current breakdown of American party politics and the kind of mass movements from below that are also the basis for a new unionism. The more salient characteristics of the current dealignment of the two-party system are the decline of party loyalty and identification in the electorate, the difficulties both parties have in defining a program capable of holding their respective social bases together, and the mas-sive defection of voting-age citizens from the electorate since the early 1960s. Only slightly more than half the voting-age population votes in presidential elections, far fewer in all other types of elections, and least of all in primaries. While electoral participation for middle- and upper-class people runs about 70%, the figure for the working class is about

47%. Only about 25% of working-class people with incomes under $10,000 vote. As Walter Dean Burnham points out, two-thirds of the 'party of nonvoters' are working class. Not even Jesse Jackson's phenomenal showing in the 1988 primaries altered the low turnout rates among working-class people of all races. While participation rates in many primary states were greater than in 1984, they remained within the 25% to 35% range for Blacks and whites in all but two states. Jackson's crucial upset of Dukakis in Michigan was conducted among 3% of that state's electorate.[7]Such low voter participation even in an exciting race creates a potentially unstable political situation.

Mass movements and volatility in class relationships contain the potential to turn such political instability into a fundamental realignment along class lines. For one thing, the party of nonvoters overlaps with the unorganized section of the working class. Substantial self-organization into unions is certain to raise political awareness and create a new voting base that the Democrats are unable to reach with their developing centrist orientation. Also, any significant political break among unions at the local or state level that orients toward the nonvoters could establish footholds for a new party capable of winning single-member districts in relatively short order. It is in this manner, for example, that Canada's labor-based New Democratic Party has held on for thirty years without being able to win a national majority.

The catalyst for such a development need not come from the higher levels of the AFL-CIO in order to create the possibility of a successful new second party. The combination of a break by any major social constituency of the Democratic Party – for example, a large part of the Black vote, and the activation of significant numbers of working-class nonvoters could well serve as such a catalyst. It is for this reason that the vision of a break from the Democrats by the social forces backing Jesse Jackson in the 1988 Democratic primaries is so tantalizing. Just as the potential to organize the unorganized in the 1960s lay in the dynamic of Black workers, so both a new social unionism and a working-class political party could well be catalyzed by sections of the Black community.

A full-blown labor movement operating in the economic, political, and cultural arenas would alter much in American culture. The weight of Black, Latino and women workers in both existing and newly organized unions lays the basis for a confrontation with racism and sexism, for example. Such a movement could address the dismal meaning of old age in the US. It could lead the fight for the jobs and/or income necessary to take on the problems of the Black underclass. At the deepest level, it could challenge the domination of business/individualist values in American culture.

A true labor movement should project values that are counter to those of capital. Embodied in the slogan 'An Injury to One Is an Injury to All' is an ethic in which labor takes social responsibility for all working people. This responsibility spans race, sex, age and region. It is the opposite of the irresponsible business ethic in which the competitive struggle of each against all is imagined to advance the common welfare. Labor values are ultimately collective values counterposed to the selfishness that passes for individualism in contemporary America. The fundamental values embodied in the historic concept of a labor movement are also the antidote to the narrow 'interest group' perception that most people have of unions today. 'I got mine' unionism cannot inspire anyone outside its narrow confines. Labor's rebirth requires even more than new tactics or new forms of organization: it requires a vision that allows the millions facing downward mobility to see labor as the carrier of justice.

Prognosis

In the twilight of the Reagan years, the capitalist social order in the United States became more transparent. A change in the balance of social forces and a new economic polarization fed on one another to alter the old political and industrial arrangements that underwrote the stability of American social life. The growing gap of income and wealth that opened between the working class, on the one hand, and the middle and upper classes, on the other, revealed an articulated class society that was not supposed to exist in America. This visible class rigidity was not simply a matter of statistical abstractions, but of organized forces in motion. The working class, for its part, appeared in organizational disarray – its only organizations declining in size and power. The capitalist class seemed to grasp in its hands more and more of the strings that pulled on the institutions of power in the US.

The relative power shift was clearest in the field of labor relations. Here, class-level business organization, corporate reorganizations, overseas investment, outsourcing of all kinds, and new technology all provided tools to subdue labor. Government agencies that had once pretended to a measure of class neutrality stepped over the line to join the ranks of capital openly. Freed of old restraints, capital went even farther to reintroduce the use of scabs on a massive and regular scale. By the late 1980s, it had weakened the collective bargaining process more than at any time since the 1920s through the introduction of competitive norms in contract negotiations. What capital liked to call flexibility was, in fact, a rigid stand against all the traditional powers of trade unions to defend jobs and incomes.

In the political arena, the changed balance of class forces reflected itself in the general shift to the right of the entire political discourse of the 1980s. This shift to the right occurred not only between the two major parties, but within each of them. The catalyst for this shift was, of course, the economic crisis that emerged in the late 1960s as a crisis of profitability and that reached a new stage in the late 1980s as world financial markets entered a period of increased volatility. Thomas Byrne Edsall capsulized the nature of the shift: 'The economic crisis of the past decade has cut to the heart of a tradition in American politics, particularly in Democratic politics, playing havoc with that party's tradition of capitalizing on a growing and thriving economy in order to finance a continuing expansion of benefits for those toward the bottom of the income distribution.'[8]

To be sure, the Democrats have rebuffed organizational efforts to upset their relationship to the status quo in the past, but they have generally had something to give in return. They spurned the Mississippi Freedom Democrats in 1964, but they had also passed the Civil Rights Act of that year, and went on to pass the Voting Rights Act of 1965 and the Great Society programs. By contrast, Jesse Jackson and his supporters faced a stone wall in 1984 on the question of reforming the Democratic Party and received no legislative payoff in return. The most anyone discussed as compensation in the wake of Jackson's 1987–88 campaign were federal appointments for Black dignitaries.

The institutional changes wrought by capital in both the economic and political arenas have created a rigidity in the American social system that has been absent for several decades. Both collective bargaining and the traditional ability of the Democratic Party to alleviate the most extreme consequences of capitalism have been important elements in maintaining social peace throughout modern US history. Capital's tighter grip on these two major institutions of social give-and-take makes a flexible response to challenges from the working class more difficult. The price of capital's tighter grip is thus the disorganization of the American way of co-optation.

This new political and social rigidity places severe programmatic limits on the country's political and economic leaders. The now universal theme that social spending to alleviate poverty and unemployment should be sharply limited has disarmed both Republicans and Democrats in the certain event of a new recession. The sanctity of the market and of private property in business has left Democrats as well as Republicans with no means of addressing the devastation of America's have-not regions. The shared belief that US labor costs were out of line with global competitive realities has made both parties accomplices in the pauperization of the working class. The international stock market crash of October 1987 has oddly reinforced the belief that austerity is the only way to achieve financial stability and a competitive position in world markets.

No sign of the co-optive genius that in the past prevented social upheavals from taking radical directions appears on the horizon. As Thomas Ferguson and Joel Rogers point out, previous shifts back to liberal reformism have always been preceded by changes in opinion and priorities in capitalist circles, and in their associated intellectual centers, by the appearance of a new wave of politicians ready to translate upper-class opinion into economic and social policy. This was true of the New Deal, where businessmen from capital-intensive industries who saw the need for a shift from conservative dogma allied themselves with a wing of the Democratic Party that had already projected a new electoral strategy based on the urban working-class/ethnic vote (experimented with in the 1928 campaign of Catholic Al Smith). This shift preceeded the New Frontier as well.[9] While it is always possible to see the stray liberal (for example, Felix Rohatyn in the business world or Tom Harkin in politics) as the prophet of a new turn, it seems abundantly clear that the major trend in ruling circles is toward an austerity consensus in which only the programmatic specifics are matters for debate.

On the other side of the equation, working-class opinion already stood in opposition to capital's economic priorities. Ferguson and Rogers cite a legion of studies and polls over the years demonstrating that the majority of Americans hold liberal to populist economic views, regardless of their particular social or religious beliefs. The most recent of these indicate a shift away from the conservative business values of the Reagan era.[10] Tony Mazzocchi and Les Leopold described this shift in the *Multinational Monitor:* 'the majority of the public still believes that business must be strictly regulated, not unleashed; that social programs need to be expanded, not slashed; and that more public spending for jobs and environmental protection is needed, not less. Nevertheless, the Democratic Party is making a bid to recapture the support of the business elite and, of course, corporate PAC money.'[11]

Rigidity above and universal social and economic decline below portend social confrontation somewhere down the road. Predictions about the timing and form of such historic processes are usually wrong and none will be attempted here. It is only worth reemphasizing that the working class often turns to forms of organization it is familiar with, such as unions, and then transforms them to meet the challenges of the day. I have argued that such a transformation in today's terms would mean a social unionism that would seek to deal with capital at the level of industry and finance, in the political arena, and even internationally.

Another dimension of any prognosis concerning union organization or social confrontation lies in the cyclical nature of the economy. Recession tends to have a paralyzing effect on working-class struggle in its downward phase. The perception that capital can be fought usually awaits some sign of economic improvement – even a very weak one. Yet social desperation is ultimately unpredictable. The aggressive young labor movements in such countries as South Africa, Brazil, the Philippines, El Salvador, and South Korea have arisen in societies that have far greater levels of unemployment – indeed, several have nearly bottomless pools of reserve labor. They have arisen in the face of government repression that is more severe than anything seen in the US in decades. In some cases, they are based in growth industries (as in South Korea and Brazil), while in others they exist and fight in the midst of crisis-ridden economies (as in El Salvador, the Philippines, and, recently, South Africa). In all, these new unions play a leading role in a broader social and/or national struggle and are seen as allies of all the poor and oppressed. They survive and even grow largely because of this broader social role. The lesson for US labor should be clear. A recession may retard the development.of a new unionism, but if the consciousness is there it is not likely to prevent its emergence for long.

There is, of course, another, more dire scenario for the postcrash world economy – that of disastrous global depression. The world debt crisis creates the possibility of an economic chain reaction that could plunge virtually the entire world into a depression on the scale of the 1930s or even greater. So far, capital and its governments have proved able to contain the financial collapse that is always lurking around the corner as the first signs of recession emerge. But there is no existing international institutional arrangement sufficient to guarantee indefinite management of this debt structure. Should a financial collapse accompany a downturn in the business cycle, a deep depression would almost certainly be the result. The level of poverty and human misery would probably be unprecedented. In the Third World it would mean massive starvation and the collapse of more than a few governments. What it would mean in the US, Canada, Japan or Europe is harder to envision. But it would certainly spell the end of social stability as it has existed since 1945. Under such circumstances, a rethinking of the value of unregulated markets would surely occur, but the current rigidities in both the thinking and institutional controls of capital would retard capital's ability to respond rapidly or effectively. The continuing leadership crisis (reflected, for example, in US party politics) would deepen.

While the downward phase of a deep depression would also tend to paralyze the working class for a time, it is not likely to spell the end of its capacity to struggle. That is, capitalist economies continue to function even during depressions, and upturns, even weak ones like that of 1934–36, encourage worker resistance and class struggle. This is even more likely to be the case when significant numbers of working-class people perceive their plight as collective, rather than individual, and see their increased economic hardship as an injustice.

In the final analysis, under any of foreseeable circumstances, the ability of the working class or large sections of it to break out of organizational and political paralysis depends on the growth of a shared vision of plausible lines of action. Business unionism has no such vision. It has, in fact, exhausted its ability to defend working-class living standards – the ability it used to justify its hegemony as the only legitimate form of working-class organization in the United States for forty years. With its acceptance of the competitive norms of business itself, business unionism has become, like migration or the acceptance of low-wage employment, one of the lines of least resistance still open to workers. It will be used as such for years to come, and its limits will continue to be tested by workers taking the first steps toward rebellion. But ultimately it will be replaced: either by a more sinister form of capitalist domination or by a new unionism and new labor movement powerful enough to challenge capital.

The fight for a new labor movement is not tomorrow's fight. It has been under way for many years. Its pioneers have made mistakes and taken dead-end paths, but they have also pointed to new, more promising ones. Its current activists are drawn from every corner of the working class and embody its diverse experience. Increasingly, this band of fighters, still a tiny minority of their own class, recognize each other as allies and kindred spirits. The convergence of hundreds of struggles in the resistance to concessions and the embryonic solidarity movements have taught more and more workers that they no longer fight alone. They have experienced setbacks and defeats and the trauma that comes with the loss of a familiar way of life. But they have also experienced the uniquely human warmth of collective responsibility and mutual aid that comes with such a struggle. They have seen the old industrial order die and wondered what the future holds in store. But their speculation is not that of the detached observer or the hapless victim. Through their actions, the fighters of the American working class, in their growing numbers, have begun to shape that uncertain future.

Notes

Introduction

1. Alice Kessler-Harris, 'Trade Unions Mirror Society in Conflict Between Collectivism and Individualism', *Monthly Labor Review*, August 1987, p. 32.

2. Ibid.

3. Lane Kirkland, 'It Has All Been Said Before...' in Seymour Martin Lipset, ed., *Unions in Transition: Entering the Second Century*, San Francisco 1986, p. 394.

4. Harry Braverman, *Labor and Monopoly Capital: The Degradation of Work in the Twentieth Century*, New York 1974; David Montgomery, *The Fall of the House of Labor: The Workplace, the State, and American Labor Activism, 1865–1925*, New York 1987.

5. Council of Economic Advisers, *Economic Report of the President,1986*, Washington 1986, pp. 261, 298.

6. *FOSATU Workers News*, August 1985.

Chapter 1

1. *Labor Notes*, February 1987.

2. Jack Stieber, 'Steel', in Gerald G. Somers, ed., *Collective Bargaining: Contemporary American Experience*, Madison, Wis. 1980, p. 181.

3. John Lacombe and Joan Borum, 'Major Labor Contracts in 1986 Provide Record Low Wage Adjustments', *Monthly Labor Review*, May 1987, p. 11; US Bureau of Labor Statistics, *Handbook of Labor Statistics*, Washington 1985, pp. 332–33.

4. Daniel J. B. Mitchell, 'Shifting Norms in Wage Determination', *Brookings Papers on Economic Activity*, vol. 2 1985, pp. 584–85.

5. Leo Troy, 'The Rise and Fall of American Trade Unions: The Labor Movement from FDR to RR', in Seymour Martin Lipset, ed., *Unions in Transition: Entering the Second Century*, San Francisco 1986, p. 87; 'New Data on Workers Belonging to Unions, 1986', *Monthly Labor Review*, May 1987, p. 36.

6. Troy, 'Rise and Fall', p. 81; 'New Data', *Monthly Labor Review*, May 1987, p. 36.

7. Richard Freeman and James Medoff, *What Do Unions Do?*, New York 1984, p. 53.

8. Ibid., p. 49.

9. Manning Marable, *How Capitalism Underdeveloped Black America*, Boston 1983, p. 40.

10. Freeman and Medoff, *What Do Unions Do?*, p. 64.

11. US Bureau of the Census, *Statistical Abstract of the United States, 1986*, Washington

1985; 'New Data', *Monthly Labor Review*, May 1987, pp. 36, 77; BLS, *Survey of Current Wage Developments*, March 1986, p. 46.

12. Bureau of the Census, *Statistical Abstract, 1986*, p. 420; *Monthly Labor Review*, May 1987, p. 76.

13. AFL-CIO, *The Polarization of America: The Loss of Good Jobs, Falling Incomes and Rising Inequality*, Washington 1986, p. 15.

14. 'New Data', *Monthly Labor Review*, May 1987, p. 84; US Department of Labor, 'News', 27 March 1987, 24 April 1987, 22 May 1987.

15. *AFL-CIO News*, 27 June 1987.

16. AFL-CIO, *Polarization*, pp. 27, 39.

17. Barry Bluestone et al., 'The Great American Job Machine: The Proliferation of Low-Wage Employment in the US Economy', mimeo, prepared for the US Congressional Joint Economic Committee, December 1986, p. 17.

18. BLS, *Handbook, 1985*, pp. 72–73; *Monthly Labor Review*, May 1987, p.65.

19. AFL-CIO, *Polarization*, pp. 13–14; National Committee for Full Employment, 'The Jobs Outlook for June, 1987', press release, 5 June 1987.

20. Francis Horvath, 'The Pulse of Economic Change: Displaced Workers of 1981–85', *Monthly Labor Review*, June 1987, pp. 10–11.

21. AFL-CIO, *Polarization*, pp. 67–68, 70, 74.

22. *Dollars and Sense*, December 1985, p. 6.

23. *The Unifier*, December 1986.

24. AFL-CIO, *Polarization*, p. 46.

25. Ibid., pp. 48–50.

26. Bureau of the Census, *Statistical Abstract, 1986*, p. 395.

27. AFL-CIO, *Polarization*, pp. 51–53.

28. Ibid., p. 50.

29. William D. Nordhaus, *Brookings Papers on Economic Activity*, vol. 1 1974, pp. 180–81; Organization for Economic Co-operation and Development, *Profits and Rates of Return*, Paris 1979, pp. 122–25.

30. One of the best examples of a probusiness judgement of this sort was the June 1985 issue of *Business Week*, which featured a multipart article called 'The Reindustrialization of America'. A popular book on the subject from a perspective critical of business was *The Deindustrialization of America* (New York 1984) by Barry Bluestone and Bennett Harrison.

31. Jane Slaughter, *Concessions and How to Beat Them*, Detroit 1983, pp. 16–17, 22–23.

32. Charles Craypo, *The Economics of Collective Bargaining: Case Studies in the Private Sector*, Washington 1986, p. 6; US Bureau of the Census, *Survey of Current Wages*, April 1983, 1984, 1985, 1986; Daniel J. B. Mitchell, 'Shifting Norms', vol. 2 1985, p. 576.

33. Council of Economic Advisers, *Economic Report of the President, 1986*, Washington 1986, p. 354.

Chapter 2

1. David Brody, *Workers in Industrial America: Essays on the 20th Century Struggle*, New York 1980, pp. 173–75; Bureau of Labor Statistics, *Handbook of Labor Statistics, 1980*, Washington 1980, pp. 411–12.

2. BLS, *Handbook, 1980*, p. 411.

3. Nelson Lichtenstein, *Labor's War at Home: The CIO in World War II*, Cambridge, Mass. 1982, pp. 221–30; BLS, *Handbook, 1980*, p. 411.

4. Brody, *Workers in Industrial America*, pp. 175–176.

5. David Montgomery, *Workers' Control in America*, Cambridge, Mass. 1979, p. 165.

6. BLS, *Handbook, 1980*, p. 411.

7. Art Preis, *Labor's Giant Step*, New York 1964, p. 155.

8. Brody, *Workers in Industrial America*, p. 114.

9. Lichtenstein, *Labor's War at Home*, p. 51.

10. BLS, *Handbook, 1980*, p. 153.

11. Philip S. Foner, *Organized Labor and the Black Worker, 1619–1973*, New York 1974, p. 243.

12. Herbert Garfinkel, *When Negroes March*, New York 1969, p. 56; Mike Davis, *Prisoners of the American Dream: Politics and Economy in the History of the US Working Class*, London 1986, pp. 81–82; Foner, *Organized Labor and the Black Worker*, pp. 238–69; Preis, *Labor's Giant Step*, p. 271; August Meier and Elliott Rudwick, *Black Detroit and the Rise of the UAW*, New York 1979, passim.

13. Nancy Gabin, 'Women Workers and the UAW in the Post–World War II Period: 1945–1954', in Daniel J. Leab, ed., *The Labor History Reader*, Urbana, Ill. 1985, pp. 407–408.

14. Gabin, 'Women Workers', p. 410; Preis, *Labor's Giant Step*, p. 272; Patricia Cayo Sexton, 'A Feminist Union Perspective', in B. J. Widick, ed., *Auto Work and Its Discontents*, Baltimore 1976, pp. 18–22.

15. Sumner M. Rosen, 'The CIO Era, 1935–55', in Julius Jacobson, ed., *The Negro and the American Labor Movement*, New York 1968, pp. 200–201.

16. Paddy Quick, 'Rosie the Riveter: Myths and Realities', *Radical America*, July–August, 1975, pp. 124–25; Bureau of the Census, *Statistical Abstract of the United States, 1986*, Washington 1986, p. 398.

17. Meier and Rudwick, *Black Detroit*, pp. 214–15.

18. Rosen, 'The CIO Era', pp. 200–208; Meier and Rudwick, *Black Detroit*, pp. 175–221.

19. Meier and Rudwick, *Black Detroit*, pp. 175–222.

20. Preis, *Labor's Giant Step*, pp. 257–75; Lichtenstein, *Labor's War at Home*, pp. 221–30.

21. Lichtenstein, *Labor's War at Home*, p. 118; see also Brody, *Workers in Industrial America*, p. 180.

22. Lichtenstein, *Labor's War at Home*, p. 119.

23. Brody, *Workers in Industrial America*, pp. 184–85; William Serrin, *The Company and the Union: The "Civilized Relationship" of the General Motors Corporation and the United Automobile Workers*, New York 1974, pp. 169–71; Albert Rees, 'Productivity, Wages, and Prices', in Richard A. Lester, ed., *Labor: Readings on Major Issues*, New York 1965, pp. 328–31.

24. Robert Michels, *Political Parties: A Sociological Study of the Oligarchical Tendencies of Modern Democracy*, New York 1962, p. 280.

25. Richard A. Lester, *As Unions Mature*, Princeton, N.J. 1958, pp. 160–67.

26. Montgomery, *Workers' Control*, pp. 165–66.

27. Irving Bernstein, *Turbulent Years: A History of the American Worker, 1933–1941*, Boston 1969, p. 74; Irving Louis Horowitz, ed., *Power, Politics and People: The Collected Essays of C. Wright Mills*, New York 1962, p. 97; David Milton, *The Politics of US Labor: From the Great Depression to the New Deal*, New York 1982, pp. 130–31.

28. Lichtenstein, *Labor's War at Home*, pp. 180–82.

29. Ibid., pp. 179–80.

30. Lichtenstein, *Labor's War at Home*, p. 226; Serrin, *The Company and the Union*, pp. 135–38.

31. Milton, *Politics of US Labor*, pp. 156–60.

32. Ibid., p. 122.

33. Preis, *Labor's Giant Step*, pp. 323–413; Milton, *Politics of US Labor*, pp. 160–67.

34. Brody, *Workers in Industrial America*, p. 227.

35. Joshua Freeman, 'Delivering the Goods: Industrial Unionism during World War II', in Leab, *Labor History Reader*, pp. 392–98; Lichtenstein, *Labor's War at Home*, pp. 194–97.

36. Lichtenstein, *Labor's War at Home*, p. 173.

37. Preis, *Labor's Giant Step*, pp. 241–43.

38. Milton, *Politics of US Labor*, pp. 121–47; Brody, *Workers in Industrial America*, pp. 224–25; Lichtenstein, *Labor's War at Home*, pp. 174–76.

39. James C. Foster, *The Union Politic: The CIO Political Action Committee*, Columbia, Mo. 1975, p. 44; Lichtenstein, *Labor's War at Home*, pp. 175–76.

40. Brody, *Workers in Industrial America*, pp. 217–20.

41. Davis, *Prisoners of the American Dream*, p. 87.

42. Ibid., p. 92.

Chapter 3

1. BLS, *Handbook, 1980*, p. 61.
2. BLS, *Handbook, 1980*, p. 412.
3. Manuel Castells, *The Economic Crisis and American Society*, Princeton, N.J. 1980, pp. 104–109.
4. Michael Kidron, *Western Capitalism Since the War*, London 1968, p. 39.
5. Michael Kidron, *Capitalism and Theory*, London 1974, pp. 16–23; Kidron, *Western Capitalism*, pp. 38–56.
6. Kidron, *Western Capitalism*, p. ix.
7. Council of Economic Advisers, *Economic Report of the President, 1986*, Washington 1986, pp. 262, 305, 311, 351.
8. BLS, *Handbook, 1980*, pp. 206–26.
9. BLS, *Handbook, 1980*, pp. 402, 412; Troy, 'The Rise and Fall of American Trade Unions: The Labor Movement from FDR to RR', in Lipset, *Unions in Transition*, p. 87.
10. BLS, *Employment and Earnings, United States, 1909–78*, Washington 1979, p. 51.
11. Preis, *Labor's Giant Step*, pp. 424–27.
12. BLS, *Employment*, p. 51; BLS, *Handbook, 1980*, p. 412.
13. Harry M. Douty, 'Some Problems of Wage Policy', in Lester, *Labor: Readings on Major Issues*, p.314.
14. Robert Zieger, *American Workers, American Unions, 1920–1985*, Baltimore 1986, p. 137.
15. Jack Stieber, *Governing the UAW*, New York 1962, pp. 131–32.
16. Bert Cochran, *Labor and Communism: The Conflict that Shaped American Unions*, Princeton, N.J. 1977, p. 326.
17. Cochran, *Labor and Communism*, pp. 325–26; Stieber, *Governing the UAW*, pp. 67–91.
18. Stieber, *Governing the UAW*, p. 141.
19. Ibid., p. 131.
20. Philip W. Nyden, *Steelworkers Rank-and-File: The Political Economy of a Union Reform Movement*, New York 1984, pp. 27–37.
21. Lloyd Ulman, *The Government of the Steel Workers' Union*, New York 1962, pp. 40–53; Nyden, *Steelworkers Rank-and-File*, pp. 36–37.
22. Ulman, *Government*, pp.73–74; Preis, *Labor's Giant Step*, pp. 355–57.
23. Cochran, *Labor and Communism*, p. 107; Preis, *Labor's Giant Step*, pp. 225, 391.
24. Cochran, *Labor and Communism*, pp. 323–24.
25. Ibid., p. 339.
26. Ronald W. Schatz, *The Electrical Workers: A History of Labor at General Electric and Westinghouse, 1923–60*, Chicago 1983, pp. 181, 184.
27. Nyden, *Steelworkers Rank-and-File*, p. 41.
28. H. W. Benson, 'Apathy and Other Axioms', in Irving Howe, ed., *The World of the Blue-Collar Worker*, New York 1972, pp. 221–22.
29. Bert Cochran, ed., *American Labor in Midpassage*, New York 1959, p. 2.
30. David Herreshoff, 'Books about Labor', in Cochran, *American Labor in Midpassage*, pp. 174–75; Charles Craypo, *The Economics of Collective Bargaining: Case Studies in the Private Sector*, Washington 1986, p. 41.
31. Craypo, *Economics of Collective Bargaining*, p. 40.
32. David Riesman, *The Lonely Crowd: A Study of the Changing American Character*, New Haven 1961, p. 174.
33. Herman Benson, *Democratic Rights for Union Members: A Guide to Internal Union Democracy*, New York 1979, pp. 182–83.
34. Zieger, *American Workers, American Unions*, p. 138.
35. B. J. Widick, 'Black Workers: Double Discontents', in Widick, *Auto Work*, pp. 56–57.
36. John Kenneth Galbraith, *The Affluent Society*, Boston 1984, p. 116.
37. Ray Ginger, *Eugene V. Debs: The Making of an American Radical*, New York 1970, p. 113.

38. Marc Karson, *American Labor Unions and Politics, 1900–1918,* Boston 1965, p. 117.

39. Sidney Lens, *The Crisis of American Labor,* New York, 1959, p. 74.

40. Ibid., p. 81.

41. Ibid.

42. Cochran, *Labor and Communism,* p. 339.

43. Bernstein, *Turbulent Years,* p. 400.

44. Brody, *Workers in Industrial America,* p. 216.

45. Ibid., pp. 216–17.

46. Jack Ranger, *Next – A Labor Party!,* Long Island City, N.Y. 1948, p. 33.

47. Lens, *Crisis of American Labor,* p. 167.

48. Ranger, *Next – A Labor Party!,* p. 35.

49. Foner, *Organized Labor and the Black Worker,* pp. 255–58; Meier and Rudwick, *Black Detroit,* passim.

50. Lens, *Crisis of American Labor,* pp. 211–12.

51. Meier and Rudwick, *Black Detroit,* p. 219.

52. Preis, *Labor's Giant Step,* pp. 512–15.

53. Ibid., p. 514.

54. Eric Thomas Chester, *Socialists and the Ballot Box: A Historical Analysis,* New York 1985, pp. 44–45.

55. Cochran, *American Labor,* p. 14.

56. Lens, *Crisis of American Labor,* p. 215.

57. Ulman, *Government,* pp. 51–52.

58. William H. Miernyk, 'Coal', in Gerald G. Somers, ed. *Collective Bargaining: Contemporary American Experience,* Madison, Wis. 1980, pp. 25–26.

59. Jack Stieber, 'Steel', in Somers, *Collective Bargaining,* pp. 164–67.

60. Serrin, *The Company and the Union,* pp. 170–72.

61. Craypo, *Economics of Collective Bargaining,* pp. 51–52.

62. Bureau of National Affairs, *Basic Patterns in Union Contracts,* Washington 1986, p. 1.

63. Lens, *Crisis of American Labor,* p. 215

64. Bureau of Labor Statistics, *Directory of National Unions and Employee Associations, 1971,* Washington 1972, pp. 88–89.

65. Stieber, *UAW,* p. 92; John Herling, *The Right to Challenge: People and Power in the Steelworkers Union,* New York, 1972, pp. 121, 317; BLS, *Directory, 1971,* p. 89.

66. Lens, *Crisis of American Labor,* p. 223.

67. BLS, *Employment and Earnings, United States, 1909–78,* Washington 1979, pp. 20, 52, 136, 288, 352–53, 455, 672–73, 681–82, 709–10.

68. BLS, *Handbook, 1980,* p. 190.

69. Freeman and Medoff, *What Do Unions Do?,* p. 61.

70. BNA, *Patterns,* p. 27; Somers, *Collective Bargaining,* pp. 26–27; Steven Brill, *The Teamsters,* New York 1978, p. 208; Lens, *Crisis of American Labor,* pp. 215–16.

71. BNA, *Patterns,* p. 13; Bureau of the Census, *Statistical Abstract of the United States, 1986,* Washington 1985, p. 101.

72. Serrin, *The Company and the Union,* pp. 171–73; BNA, *Patterns,* p. 41.

73. Brody, *Workers in Industrial America,* pp. 194–95.

74. Somers, *Collective Bargaining,* p. 27.

75. Charles P. Larrowe, *Harry Bridges: The Rise and Fall of Radical Labor in the U.S.,* New York 1972, pp. 352–55.

76. Craypo, *Economics of Collective Bargaining,* pp. 68–70.

77. Harold Levinson, 'Pattern Bargaining: A Case Study of the Automobile Workers', in Lester, *Labor: Readings on Major Issues,* p. 247.

78. BLS, *Employment,* pp. 20, 136, 288, 352–53, 681–82; Craypo, *Economics of Collective Bargaining,* p. 32.

79. Herling, *Right to Challenge,* pp. 68–69.

80. BLS, *Handbook, 1980,* p. 415.

81. Serrin, *The Company and the Union,* p. 4

82. Zieger, *American Workers,* p. 138.

Chapter 4

1. Michael Harrington, *The Other America: Poverty in the United States*, Baltimore 1962, pp. 149, 192.

2. Foner, *Organized Labor and the Black Worker*, pp. 270–72; Sidney Peck, 'The Economic Situation of Negro Labor', in Jacobson, *The Negro and the American Labor Movement*, p. 219.

3. BLS, *Handbook, 1980*, p. 61; BLS, *Employment and Earnings, 1909–78*, Washington 1979, pp. 2, 51.

4. Foner, *Organized Labor and the Black Worker*, pp. 271–72.

5. Kerner Commission, *Report of the National Advisory Commission on Civil Disorders*, New York 1968, p. 240.

6. Martin Luther King, Jr., *Stride Towards Freedom: The Montgomery Story*, New York 1958, pp. 34–43; Preis, *Labor's Giant Step*, p. 517; Foner, *Organized Labor and the Black Worker*, p. 316.

7. Robert H. Zieger, *American Workers*, p. 174; BLS, *Handbook, 1980*, p. 151.

8. Foner, *Organized Labor and the Black Worker*, pp. 312–22.

9. Ibid., p. 325; see also Jacobson, *The Negro and the American Labor Movement*, passim.

10. Foner, *Organized Labor and the Black Worker*, pp. 323–24; Meier and Rudwick, *Black Detroit*, pp. 219–20.

11. Foner, *Organized Labor and the Black Worker*, pp. 328–29; Zieger, *American Workers*, p. 174.

12. Foner, *Organized Labor and the Black Worker*, pp. 334–36.

13. Ibid., pp. 335–54; James A. Geschwender, *Class, Race and Worker Insurgency: The League of Revolutionary Black Workers*, New York 1977, pp. 54–55.

14. Zieger, *American Workers*, p. 175; Geschwender, *Class, Race and Worker Insurgency*, pp. 54–55.

15. Julius Jacobson, 'Coalitionism: From Protest to Politicking', in Burton Hall, ed., *Autocracy and Insurgency in Organized Labor*, New Brunswick 1972, pp. 324–345.

16. BLS, *Handbook,1980*, pp. 412, 78, 190.

17. J. David Greenstone, *Labor in American Politics*, New York 1969, pp. 322–43.

18. Zieger, *American Workers*, p. 186.

19. Stan Weir, 'Forces Behind the Reuther-Meany Split', *New Politics*, Summer 1966, pp. 13–21; Foner, *Organized Labor and the Black Worker*, pp. 376–77.

20. Kerner Commission, *Report*, pp. 252–55.

21. Marable, *How Capitalism Underdeveloped Black America*, p. 30.

22. Kerner Commission, *Report*, pp. 143–50.

23. Preis, *Labor's Giant Step*, p. 42.

24. B. J. Widick, *Detroit: City of Race and Class Violence*, Chicago 1972, pp. 186–94.

25. Foner, *Organized Labor and the Black Worker*, p. 372.

26. Ray Marshall, 'Black Workers and Unions', in Irving Howe, *The World of the Blue-Collar Worker*, pp. 257–58.

27. Adam Fairclough, 'Was Martin Luther King a Marxist?', in C. Eric Lincoln, *Martin Luther King, Jr.: A Profile*, New York 1984, pp. 228–42.

28. Foner, *Organized Labor and the Black Worker*, pp. 378–83.

29. Zieger, *American Workers*, p. 190.

30. Leo Troy, 'Rise and Fall', in Lipset, *Unions in Transition*, pp. 81–82.

31. George Strauss, 'Union Maturity and Management Strength', in Lester, *Labor: Readings on Major Issues*, p. 129.

32. B. J. Widick, *Labor Today: The Triumphs and Failures of Unionism in the United States*, Boston 1964, p. 55.

33. Kimberly Moody, 'Government Intervention in the Steel Settlement', *New Politics*, Summer 1965, pp. 58–59.

34. Mike Urquhart, *The Grievance Procedure and the Challenge to Management's Control of Production*, unpublished paper, New School for Social Research, pp. 41–52.

35. Brody, *Workers in Industrial America*, p. 201; Widick, *Auto Work*, p. 9.

36. Harry Braverman, *Labor and Monopoly Capital: The Degradation of Work in the Twentieth Century*, New York 1974, pp. 195–97, 213–23; David Noble, *Forces of Production: A So-*

cial History of Industrial Automation, New York 1986, pp. 265–323.

37. Strauss, *Union Maturity,* pp. 126–27.

38. BLS, *Handbook, 1980,* pp. 206–207; Council of Economic Advisers, *Economic Report of the President, 1977,* Washington 1977, pp. 277, 282; T. P. Hill, *Profits and Rates of Return,* Paris 1979, p. 124.

39. Stan Weir, 'A New Era of Labor Revolt', mimeo, Berkeley 1966, p. 307; Brody, *Workers in Industrial America,* p. 209.

40. BLS, *Handbook, 1980,* p. 415.

41. William Serrin, *The Company and the Union,* pp. 191–95, 285.

42. Jack Trautman, 'Postal Workers Fight Back', pamphlet, Detroit 1975, pp. 4–6.

43. Samuel R. Friedman, *Teamster Rank and File: Power, Bureaucracy, and Rebellion at Work and in a Union,* New York 1982, pp. 136–68.

44. Kim Moody and Jim Woodward, *Battle Line: The Coal Strike of '78,* Detroit 1978, pp. 29–30.

45. Serrin, *The Company and the Union,* pp. 283–85; Geschwender, *Race, Class and Worker Insurgency,* pp. 199–203.

46. Harvey Swados, *A Radical's America,* Boston 1962, pp. 117–18.

47. Special Task Force of the Secretary of Health, Education and Welfare, *Work in America,* Cambridge, Mass. 1980, p. 19 and passim.

48. Heather Ann Thompson, 'Detroit: Wildcat 1973', mimeo, Senior Honors Thesis, University of Michigan 1985, passim.

49. Ernest Mandel, *The Second Slump: A Marxist Analysis of Recession in the Seventies,* London 1978, p. 26; Council of Economic Advisers, *Economic Report, 1986,* pp. 231–32; BLS, *Handbook, 1980,* pp. 61, 73.

Chapter 5

1. Council of Economic Advisers, *Economic Report of the President, 1978,* Washington 1978, p. 378.

2. Mandel, *The Second Slump,* pp. 28–29.

3. Council of Economic Advisers, *Economic Report of the President, 1979,* Washington 1979, p. 282; US Department of Commerce, *Economic Indicators,* September 1979, p. 29.

4. William D. Nordhaus, 'The Falling Share of Profits', *Brookings Papers on Economic Activity,* vol. 1 1974, pp. 169–208; *Morgan Guaranty Survey,* September 1979, p. 11; Hill, *Profits and Rates of Return,* p. 23.

5. Ernest Mandel, *Late Capitalism,* London 1975, p. 276.

6. Council of Economic Advisers, *Economic Report, 1986,* p. 376; BLS, *Handbook, 1980,* pp. 465–67.

7. Stephen S. Cohen and John Zysman, 'The Myth of a Post-Industrial Economy', *Technology Review,* February/March 1987, p.59.

8. *Economic Notes,* October 1985, p.2; Leo Troy, 'The Rise and Fall', in Lipset, *Unions in Transition,* p. 87.

9. Barry Bluestone and Bennett Harrison, *The Deindustrialization of America: Plant Closings, Community Abandonment, and the Dismantling of Basic Industry,* New York 1982, pp. 160–70.

10. Ronald W. Schatz, *The Electrical Workers: A History of Labor at General Electric and Westinghouse, 1923–60,* Chicago 1983, pp. 232–36.

11. Bluestone and Harrison, *Deindustrialization of America,* pp. 164–70; Michael Storper and Richard Walker, 'The Spatial Division of Labor: Labor and the Location of Industries', in Larry Sawers and William K. Tabb, eds., *Sunbelt, Snowbelt: Urban Development and Regional Restructuring,* New York 1984, pp. 19–43.

12. Bureau of the Census, *Statistical Abstract, 1986,* p. 744; BLS, *Employment and Earnings, United States, 1909–78,* Washington 1979, p. 51; Council of Economic Advisers, *Economic Reports, 1986,* p. 304.

13. Bluestone and Harrison, *Deindustrialization of America,* pp. 160–62.

14. Bureau of the Census, *Statistical Abstract, 1978*, pp. 578, 821; Federal Trade Commission, *Quarterly Financial Report for Manufacturing, Mining, and Trade*, issues for 1977–79, passim.

15. Craypo, *Economics of Collective Bargaining*, p. 199.

16. US Senate, Committee on Governmental Affairs, 'Interlocking Directorates Among Major U.S. Corporations', Washington 1978, pp. 123–25, 280; Martin Mayer, *The Bankers*, New York 1974, p. 528; US Senate, Committee on Governmental Affairs, 'Voting Rights in Major Corporations', Washington 1978, pp. 2, 3, 258.

17. *Business Week*, 10 September 1979, p. 72.

18. *Labor Notes*, December 1986; February 1987; Craypo, *The Economics of Collective Bargaining*, p. 173.

19. Craypo, *Economics of Collective Bargaining*, p. 173.

20. *The National Provisioner*, 23 May 1987, pp. 5, 24; *International Labour Reports*, July/August 1987, pp. 11–15.

21. Moody and Woodward, *Battle Line*, pp. 50, 64, 81–85.

22. Ibid., pp. 47–50, 66.

23. *Labor Notes*, 25 October 1984.

24. Barbara Doherty, *The Struggle to Save Morse Cutting Tool: A Successful Community Campaign*, North Dartmouth, Mass. 1985, p. 7.

25. Ibid., pp. 2–11.

26. Ibid., pp. 12–19; *New York Times*, 15 June 1986.

27. AFL-CIO, *Coordinated Bargaining: Labor's New Approach to Effective Contract Negotiations*, Washington n.d., p. 6.

28. Ibid., pp. 9–10.

29. Labor Institute, 'Shifting Balance of Power: An Education Program for UAW-Region 9A', mimeo, 1986, p. 5; Bureau of the Census, *Statistical Abstract, 1986*, p. 797.

30. Bureau of the Census, *Statistical Abstract, 1981*, p. 833.

31. *Newsweek*, 1 October 1979, p. 53.

32. Bluestone and Harrison, *Deindustrialization of America*, pp. 113–14.

33. Ibid., pp. 141–42.

34. Bureau of the Census, *Statistical Abstract, 1986*, pp. 305, 327, 532.

35. Bluestone and Harrison, *Deindustrialization of America*, pp. 173–75.

36. United Nations, *Yearbook of National Accounts Statistics*, 1971 and 1981, passim.

37. Barry Bluestone, Bennett Harrison, and Lucy Gorham, 'Storm Clouds on the Horizon: Labor Market Crisis and Industrial Policy', mimeo, Brookline, Mass. 1984, pp. 35–36.

38. Noble, *Forces of Production*, p. 348.

39. Braverman, *Labor and Monopoly Capital*, pp. 378–86.

40. Noble, *Forces of Production*, pp. 350–51.

41. Bluestone and Harrison, *Deindustrialization of America*, pp. 162–63.

42. *Business Week*, 6 April 1984.

43. *Fortune*, 23 January 1984.

44. Barry Bluestone and Bennett Harrison, 'Why Corporations Close Profitable Plants', *Working Papers*, May-June 1980, pp. 16–17.

45. Barry Bluestone, 'Deindustrialization and the Abandonment of Community', in John C. Raines, Lenora E. Berson, and David McI. Gracie, eds., *Community and Capital in Conflict: Plant Closings and Job Loss*, Philadelphia 1982, pp. 55–57.

46. Bureau of the Census, *Statistical Abstract, 1986*, p. 744.

47. Bureau of National Affairs, 'Report by the House Labor-Management Subcommittee on Failure of Labor Law', *Daily Labor Report*, 4 October 1984, p. D2; Freeman and Medoff, *What Do Unions Do?*, pp. 221–23.

48. Mary Gibson, *Workers' Rights*, Totowa, N.J. 1983, p. 88.

49. BNA, 'Report by the House', pp. D-2, D-3; Freeman and Medoff, *What Do Unions Do?*, p. 223; National Labor Relations Board, *Annual Reports*, Washington 1970–80.

50. Mimi Conway, *Rise Gonna Rise: A Portrait of Southern Textile Workers*, Garden City, N.J. 1979, pp. 24–25; Gibson, *Worker's Rights*, pp. 87–88.

51. BNA, 'Report by the House', p. D6.

52. Gibson, *Worker's Rights*, pp. 88–89; Conway, *Rise Gonna Rise*, pp. 206–13.

53. Interview with Charles McDonald, AFL–CIO Department of Organizing, 11 October 1984; BNA, 'Report by the House', p. D4; *Industrial Relations*, Winter 1980, p. 103.

54. Henry S. Farber, 'The Extent of Unionization in the United States', in Thomas A. Kochan, ed., *Challenges and Choices Facing American Labor*, Cambridge, Mass. 1985, p. 18.

55. Bluestone and Harrison, *Deindustrialization of America*, p. 165.

56. Anil Verma and Thomas A. Kochan, 'The Growth and Nature of the Nonunion Sector within a Firm', in Kochan, ed. *Challenges and Choices*, pp. 92–94.

57. Ibid., pp. 94–95.

58. Ibid., pp. 95–111.

59. Corporate Data Exchange (CDE), *CDE Handbook: Labor Relations*, New York 1982, passim; Freeman and Medoff, *What Do Unions Do?*, p. 226.

60. Freeman and Medoff, *What Do Unions Do?*, p. 223; *Wall Street Journal*, 2 October 1984, p. 1.

61. Richard Freeman, 'Why Are Unions Faring Poorly in NLRB Representation elections?', in Kochan, *Challenges and Choices*, pp. 50–51.

62. Thomas Byrne Edsall, *The New Politics of Inequality*, New York 1984, p. 151.

63. Kochan, *Challenges and Choices*, p. 66.

64. Stanley Aronowitz, *Working Class Hero: A New Strategy for Labor*, New York 1983, pp. 128–33.

Chapter 6

1. G. William Domhoff, *The Powers That Be*, New York 1979, pp. 67–79; Thomas Ferguson and Joel Rogers, *Right Turn: The Decline of the Democrats and the Future of American Politics*, New York 1986, pp. 51–52.

2. Edsall, *New Politics of Inequality*, p. 128.

3. Center to Protect Workers Rights, *The War on Wage Protection: The Business Offensive*, Washington 1979, pp. 9–17.

4. Laurence Shoup, *The Carter Presidency and Beyond*, Palo Alto, Calif. 1980, pp. 167–168; Edsall, *New Politics of Inequality*, pp. 120–21.

5. Bill Keller, 'The State of the Unions', *Congressional Quarterly Weekly*, 28 August 1982.

6. Edsall, *New Politics of Inequality*, pp. 129–32.

7. Ibid., p. 131.

8. *New York Times*, 6 November 1984.

9. *Wall Street Journal*, 11 September 1978.

10. *Wall Street Journal*, 26 July 1982; 17 October 1983.

11. Elizabeth Drew, *Politics and Money*, New York 1983, pp. 51–52.

12. Ferguson and Rogers, *Right Turn*, p. 144.

13. *In These Times*, 7–13 September 1983, p. 5; Ferguson and Rogers, *Right Turn*, p. 145.

14. Walter Dean Burnham, *The Current Crisis in American Politics*, New York 1982, pp. 173, 191, 262.

15. Burnham, *Current Crisis*, pp. 260–62, 294; Edsall, *New Politics of Inequality*, pp. 57–66.

16. Paul Craig Roberts, *The Supply-Side Revolution*, Cambridge, Mass. 1984, pp. 81–88; John Palmer and Isabel Sawhill, *The Reagan Record*, New York 1984, p. 304; Edsall, *New Politics of Inequality*, pp. 149–50.

17. US Congress, *Joint Economic Report, 1979*, Washington 1979, p. 3.

18. Roberts, *Supply-Side Revolution*, p. 63.

19. Shoup, *Carter Presidency*, pp. 21–62.

20. Jeff Frieden, 'The Trilateral Commission: Economics and Politics in the 1970s', in Holy Sklar, ed., *Trilateralism: The Trilateral Commission and Elite Planning for World Management*, Boston 1980, pp. 61–70.

21. Shoup, *Carter Presidency*, p. 169.

22. Ibid., pp. 47, 105.

23. Barry Bosworth, James Duesenbury and Andrew Carron, *Capital Needs in the Seventies,* Washington 1975, p. 4.

24. Council of Economic Advisers, *Economic Report,* 1979, p. 126.

25. Kim Moody, 'Wage Guidelines – The Road to Austerity', Detroit 1979, pp. 1–15.

26. Council of Economic Advisers, *Economic Report, 1979,* p. 55.

27. Standard & Poor, 'Labor Costs: Special Report', *Industry Surveys,* 10 December 1981, p. 2; Myron Gordon, 'Corporate Bureaucracy, Productivity Gain, and Distribution of Revenue in U.S. Manufacturing, 1947-77', *Journal of Post-Keynesian Economics,* Summer 1982, p. 489.

28. BLS, *Handbook, 1980,* pp. 190, 303; Bureau of the Census, *Statistical Abstract, 1986,* p. 469.

29. Shoup, *Carter Presidency,* pp. 179–81.

30. Jane Slaughter, *Concessions and How to Beat Them,* Detroit 1983, pp. 10–12, 16.

31. Arthur Shostak and David Skocik, *The Air Controllers' Controversy: Lessons from the PATCO Strike,* New York 1986, p. 77.

32. James McGregor Burns, *The Power to Lead,* New York 1984, pp. 58–63.

33. *Washington Post Weekly,* 4 March 1985.

34. Drew, *Politics and Money,* pp. 38–44.

35. *AFL-CIO News,* 17 May 1986.

36. Shostak and Skocik, *Air Controllers' Controversy,* pp. 103–22.

37. Council of Economic Advisers, *Economic Report, 1986,* p. 293; Michael Urquhart, 'The Employment Shift to Services', *Monthly Labor Review,* April 1984, pp. 15–21; *UAW Washington Report,* 30 May-6 June 1986.

38. Frank Ackerman, *Hazardous to Our Wealth,* Boston 1984, pp. 100–104; Bureau of the Census, *Statistical Abstract, 1986,* pp. 354, 376; *Monthly Labor Review,* April 1985, p. 79.

39. Bureau of the Census, *Statistical Abstract, 1985,* p. 325; Palmer and Sawhill, *The Reagan Record,* pp. 204–205.

40. Jules Bernstein and Laurence Gold, 'Mid-life Crisis: The NLRB at Fifty', *Dissent,* Spring 1985, pp. 214–15.

41. Thomas Ferguson and Joel Rogers, 'Mondale's Right Turn', *Texas Observer,* 13 June 1986, pp. 9–12; Kim Moody and Bill Denny, 'Eyes Right: The Democrats' Line of March', *Changes,* May-June 1985.

42. Ferguson and Rogers, *Mondale's Right Turn,* pp. 3–5.

43. Ibid., pp. 8–9; Moody and Denny, 'Eyes Right', p. 16.

44. Ferguson and Rogers, *Right Turn,* pp. 143–44.

45. *Wall Street Journal,* 20 November 1987.

46. *Business Week,* 27 November 1987, p. 210; 9 November 1987, p. 164; *Wall Street Journal,* 11 November 1987; 19 November 1987.

47. *Newsweek,* 23 November 1987, pp. 18–19.

48. Tony Mazzocchi and Les Leopold, 'The Politics of Labor: A Third Party in the Making', *Multinational Monitor,* February 1987, p. 15.

49. *Time,* 9 November 1987; David Moberg, 'Iowa Six-Pack: Great Taste or Less Filling?', *In These Times,* 18–24 November 1987.

Chapter 7

1. AFL–CIO, *Memo From COPE,* 26 September 1977.

2. UAW, *Ammo,* vol. 19, no. 6 1978.

3. Marick F. Masters and John Thomas Delaney, 'Contemporary Labor Political Investments and Performance', *Labor Studies Journal,* Winter 1987, pp. 220–37.

4. Douglas Fraser, Letter of resignation from the Labor-Management Group, 19 July 1978, reprinted in Kim Moody, ed., *Political Directions for Labor,* Detroit 1980, pp. 29–30.

5. Ibid., p. 31.

6. Ibid., p. 32.

7. UAW, *Ammo,* vol. 19, no. 6 1978.

8. Brody, *Workers in Industrial America*, pp. 247–54; Progressive Alliance, 'A Call to Action', in Moody, *Political Directions*, pp. 33–37.

9. George Poulin, 'Speech to the International Association of Machinists' Legislative Conference, January 23, 1979', in Moody, *Political Directions*, pp. 45–48.

10. *Labor Notes*, 28 April 1981; 20 May 1981; 26 August 1981; Mark Levitan, 'The UAW, the Progressive Alliance, and the Paralysis of Social Unionism', *Changes*, July-August 1979, p. 24.

11. *Labor Notes*, 22 September 1979.

12. Brody, *Workers in Industrial America*, p. 250; *Labor Notes*, 22 June 1979; 23 October 1979.

13. Harley Shaiken, *Work Transformed: Automation and Labor in the Computer Age*, New York 1984, pp. 236–37.

14. Reginald Stuart, *Bailout: America's Billion Dollar Gamble on the 'New' Chrysler Corporation*, South Bend, Ind. 1980, pp. 103–17; Serrin, *The Company and the Union*, p. 34; *Labor Notes*, 22 June 1979; 21 August 1979.

15. *Labor Notes*, 21 August 1979, 20 November 1979; Slaughter, *Concessions*, pp. 10, 16.

16. Stuart, *Bailout*, pp. 134, 170–75; Slaughter, *Concessions*, p. 16; *Labor Notes*, June 1986.

17. Stuart, *Bailout*, pp. 142–43.

18. Ibid., pp. 138–42.

19. *Labor Notes*, 27 January 1981.

20. Bill Parker, 'Plant Closings & the Alternatives: The Chrysler Experience', mimeo, April 1982, pp. 11–14.

21. *Washington Post*, 18 September 1981.

22. Samuel Bowles, David Gordon, and Thomas Weiskopf, 'Industrial Policy – Now the Bad News', *The Nation*, 4 June 1983, p. 705.

23. United Auto Workers, 'Blueprint for a Working America', special issue, *Solidarity*, May 1983; United Auto Workers, *Washington Report*, July 1983.

24. AFL-CIO, *American Federationist*, 22 October 1983, pp. 5–7.

25. International Association of Machinists, *Let's Rebuild America*, Washington 1983, passim.

26. Sidney Blumenthal, 'Drafting a Democratic Industrial Plan', *New York Times Magazine*, 28 August 1983.

27. Harold Meyerson, 'Labor's Risky Plunge into Politics', *Dissent*, Summer 1984, pp. 285–87.

28. *Labor Notes*, January 1985; Meyerson, 'Labor's Risky Plunge', pp. 286–90.

29. *Labor Notes*, 20 November 1984.

30. *Labor Notes*, December 1987.

31. *AFL-CIO News*, 4 January 1986; 15 February 1986; 19 April 1986; various issues from 1982 through 1986.

32. Moody and Denney, 'Eyes Right', pp. 19–20.

33. Burnham, *Current Crisis*, pp. 259–62.

Chapter 8

1. *Labor Notes*, 27 January 1981.

2. Parker, 'Plant Closings & the Alternatives', p. 17.

3. *Labor Notes*, 27 January 1981; Slaughter, *Concessions*, pp. 10–16.

4. Slaughter, *Concessions*, pp. 11–12.

5. *Labor Notes*, 24 February 1982.

6. *Labor Notes*, 22 April 1982.

7. *Labor Notes*, 24 March 1982; 22 April 1982.

8. *Labor Notes*, August 1982; Slaughter, *Concessions*, pp.16–25.

9. Freeman and Medoff, *What Do Unions Do?*, p. 56.

10. *Business Week*, 14 June 1982, p. 66; Craypo, pp. 71–72; 115–39; *Labor Notes*, 21 January 1982; 24 February 1982.

11. *Labor Notes*, 29 March 1983; 26 October 1983; 22 November 1983; 20 December 1983; 26 January 1984; 26 April 1984; 26 July 1984; May 1985.

12. Mitchell, 'Shifting Norms', pp. 584–85.

13. Slaughter, *Concessions*, p. 10.

14. Mitchell, *Shifting Norms*, pp. 584–86.

15. Freeman and Medoff, *What Do Unions Do?*, p. 54; BLS, *News*, 27 January 1984; 24 January 1985; 27 January 1986; 27 January 1987.

16. *Wall Street Journal*, 26 June 1987; BLS, *News*, 24 January 1985; 27 January 1987.

17. BLS, *News*, 24 January 1985; 27 January 1986; BNA, 'What's New in Collective Bargaining Negotiations & Contracts', 13 February 1986; George Reuben, 'Labor-Management Scene in 1986 Reflects Continuing Difficulties', *Monthly Labor Review*, January 1987, p. 37.

18. Slaughter, *Concessions*, pp. 37–38.

19. Braverman, *Labor and Monopoly Capital*; Noble, *Forces of Production*; Shaiken, *Work Transformed*.

20. Mike Parker, *Inside the Circle: A Union Guide to QWL*, Detroit 1985, pp. 29–30.

21. Peter Cappelli and Timothy H. Harris, 'Airline Union Concessions in the Wake of Deregulation', *Monthly Labor Review*, June 1985, p. 37.

22. Herbert Hill, 'Race, Ethnicity and Organized Labor: The Opposition to Affirmative Action', *New Politics*, Winter 1987, pp. 33–52; Craypo, *Economics of Collective Bargaining*, pp. 80–110.

23. Freeman and Medoff, *What Do Unions Do?*, passim; David Lewin, 'Public Employee Unionism in the 1980s: An Analysis of Transformation', in Lipset, *Unions in Transition*, pp. 241–64.

24. *Labor Notes*, December 1985.

25. *Wall Street Journal*, 18 Juné 1984.

26. Conference Board, 'The Labor Outlook 1984', The Conference Board Research Bulletin 150, 1983, p. 11.

27. UAW Local 160, *Tech Engineer*, January-February 1984; Pete Kelly, President, UAW Local 160, 'Minority Report: An Analysis of the Short-Comings of the 1984 General Motors Contract', Warren, Mich. 1984.

28. *Business Week*, March 1984.

29. *Labor Notes*, September 1986; February 1987.

30. Slaughter, *Concessions*, pp. 34–35; US Department of Commerce, *1986 U.S. Industrial Outlook*, Washington 1986, pp. 55: 4-8; *Labor Notes*, 20 March 1979.

31. *Labor Notes*, 25 March 1980; May 1985.

32. UFCW, *1986 Report on the U.S. Meat Packing Industry and the Challenges Workers Face*, Washington 1986, Section I, pp. 1–8; *Labor Notes*, 24 February 1982.

33. *Wall Street Journal*, 4 August 1983; *Labor Notes*, April 1986.

34. *Labor Notes*, April 1986.

35. UFCW, *1986 Report*, Section V, pp. 1–2; *Wall Street Journal*, 19 May 1986; *Labor Notes*, October 1986, June 1987.

36. *Labor Notes*, 22 May 1980; 19 June 1980.

37. *Labor Notes*, 23 November 1981.

38. *Labor Notes*, 24 February 1981; 27 October 1981; Slaughter, *Concessions*, p. 41.

39. Parker, *Inside the Circle*, p. 32.

40. Eric Mann, 'UAW Backs the Wrong Team', *The Nation*, 14 February 1987, pp. 172–74.

41. *Labor Notes*, February 1987; *Detroit Free Press*, 12 February 1987.

42. *Wall Street Journal*, 16 March 1987.

43. Ibid.

44. *Labor Notes*, December 1986.

45. Mann, 'UAW Backs the Wrong Team', p. 171.

46. Peter Capelli and Robert B. McKersie, 'Labor and the Crisis of Collective Bargaining', in Kochan, *Challenges and Choices*, p. 236.

47. Craypo, *Economics of Collective Bargaining*, p. 173.

48. Parker, 'Plant Closings', p. 13.

49. *Detroit Free Press*, 3–13 March 1987.

50. UFCW, *1986 Report*, Section IV, p. 2.

51. *Detroit Free Press,* 12 February 1987; Paul A. Eisenstein, 'What's Right with GM', *Metropolitan Detroit,* March 1987, p. 117.
52. Standard & Poor, 'Labor Costs', *Industry Surveys,* 10 December 1981, p. 3.
53. Slaughter, *Concessions,* p. 53.
54. Ibid., pp. 53–54.
55. *Labor Notes,* September 1985.
56. Parker, *Inside the Circle,* p. 34.
57. Ibid., p. 7.
58. Ibid., p. 114–15.
59. *Labor Notes,* January 1987.
60. Ibid.

Chapter 9

1. *Labor Notes,* February 1986.
2. Lewin, 'Public Employee Unionism', in Lipset, *Unions in Transition,* pp. 245, 252.
3. *Labor Notes,* April 1986.
4. AFL-CIO, Committee on the Evolution of Work, *The Changing Situation of Workers and their Unions,* Washington 1985, p.30.
5. *Wall Street Journal,* 18 January 1985.
6. AFL-CIO, *Changing Situation,* p. 30.
7. Chaison, *When Unions Merge,* pp. 33–35, 168–75; Larry T. Adams, 'Labor Organization Mergers, 1979–84: Adapting to Change', *Monthly Labor Review,* September 1984, pp. 23–24; *Labor Notes,* September 1986.
8. Gary N. Chaison, *When Unions Merge,* Lexington, Mass. 1986, pp. 95–96; Roger Horowitz, 'From UPWA to UFCW: Meatpacker Unionism Gutted', *Against the Current,* No. 6, November/December 1986, pp. 6–10; interviews conducted from 1984 through 1986 with various UFCW members and staff members, mostly on a confidential basis.
9. *Wall Street Journal,* 18 January 1985.
10. Horowitz, 'From UPWA to UFCW', pp. 8–9.
11. Ibid., pp. 12–14; interviews 1984–86; confidential interviews in July 1987.
12. Chaison, *When Unions Merge,* p. 120.
13. Association for Union Democracy, *Union Democracy Review,* July 1987.
14. Association for Union Democracy, *Union Democracy Review,* January 1987.
15. *Labor Notes,* November 1986.
16. *Labor Notes,* June 1986, February 1987, April 1987.
17. *Labor Notes,* March 1987; May 1987.
18. *Supermarket News,* 5 May 1986.
19. Michael Urquhart, 'The Employment Shift to Services', *Monthly Labor Review,* April 1984, pp. 15–21; Council of Economic Advisers, *Economic Report, 1986,* pp. 298–99; BLS, *Handbook, 1980,* p.156.
20. US Bureau of the Census, *Statistical Abstract, 1986,* pp. 400–404; BLS, *Employment,* p. 803; Wayne J. Howe, 'The Business Services Industry Sets Pace in Employment Growth', *Monthly Labor Review,* April 1986, pp. 29–35; Labor Institute, 'Shifting Balance of Power', p. 16.
21. Myron J. Gordon, 'Corporate Bureaucracy, Productivity Gain, and Distribution of Revenue in US Manufacturing 1947–77', *Journal of Post-Keynesian Economics,* Summer 1982, p. 486.
22. Harold Meyerson, 'Labor's Risky Plunge into Politics', *Dissent,* Summer 1984, p. 291.
23. 'America's Restructured Economy', *Business Week,* 1 June 1981, pp. 44–66.
24. Davis, *Prisoners of the American Dream,* pp. 216–19.
25. Bluestone and Harrison, 'The Great American Jobs Machine', mimeo, December 1986, pp. 5–17.
26. AFL-CIO, *The Changing Situation,* pp. 14–15.

27. Lane Kirkland, 'It Has All Been Said Before...', in Lipset, *Unions in Transition*, p. 397.

28. Troy, *Rise and Fall*, pp. 86–87; BLS, *Handbook, 1980*, p. 412; Courtney D. Gifford, *Directory of U.S. Labor Organizations, 1984–85 Edition*, Washington 1984, p. 2.

29. Troy, *Rise and Fall*, pp. 80–84; Lewin, 'Public Employee Unionism', in Lipset, *Unions in Transition*, p. 244.

30. Larry T. Adams, 'Changing Employment Patterns of Organized Workers', *Monthly Labor Review*, February 1985, p. 29; Bureau of the Census, *Statistical Abstract 1986*, p. 295.

31. Gifford, *Directory*, pp. 2, 64; Adams, *Changing Employment Patterns*, p. 29.

32. Bureau of the Census, *Statistical Abstract 1986*, p. 295.

33. Adams, *Changing Employment Patterns*, pp. 27–29; *Economic Notes*, October 1985, p. 2.

34. Lewin, 'Public Employee Unionism', in Lipset, *Unions in Transition*, p. 244.

35. National Urban League, *The State of Black America 1983*, New York 1983, p. 102; BLS, *Handbook 1985*, pp. 49–53.

36. Deborah E. Bell, 'Unionized Women in State and Local Government', in Ruth Milkman, ed., *Women, Work & Protest: A Century of U.S. Women's Labor History*, Boston 1985, p. 283.

37. Lewin, 'Public Employee Unionism', in Lipset, *Unions in Transition*, pp. 241–64.

38. Joseph C. Goulden, *Jerry Wurf: Labor's Last Angry Man*, New York 1982, pp. 61–99.

39. Adams, *Changing Employment Patterns*, pp. 23–24.

40. Chaison, *When Unions Merge*, p. 117.

41. Adams, 'Labor Organization Mergers', pp. 22–24; *Wall Street Journal*, 18 January 1985; Chaison, *When Unions Merge*, p. 117.

42. *Labor Notes*, February 1986.

43. Bureau of the Census, *Statistical Abstract, 1986*, pp. 150, 404, 414; Lewin, 'Public Employee Unionism', in Lipset, *Unions in Transition*, p 244.

44. Richard U. Miller, 'Hospitals', in Gerald G. Somers, ed., *Collective Bargaining: Contemporary American Experience*, Madison, Wis. 1980, pp. 373–78; Bureau of the Census, *Statistical Abstract, 1986*, pp. 103, 107.

45. US Department of Commerce, *U.S. Industrial Outlook, 1986*, Washington 1986, p. 54–62.

46. Bureau of the Census, *Statistical Abstract, 1986*, pp. 414, 526; *Economic Notes*, October 1985, p. 11; US Department of Commerce, *U.S. Industrial Outlook 1986*, Washington 1986. p. 57–63.

47. AFL-CIO, *The Changing Situation*, pp. 27–29.

48. Standard & Poor, 'Labor Costs', *Industry Surveys*, 10 December 1981, p. 3.

49. US Bureau of the Census, *Statistical Abstract, 1986*, p. 414

Chapter 10

1. Jack Stieber, 'Steel', in Somers, *Collective Bargaining*, pp. 186–89.

2. Ken Morgan, *The Steel Industry and the United Steelworkers of America: The Crisis Within*, Detroit 1978, pp. 11, 18; Bureau of the Census, *Statistical Abstract, 1977*, p. 820; Standard & Poor, 'Labor Costs', *Industry Surveys*, 10 December 1981; BLS, *Employment and Earnings*, p.138.

3. Nyden, *Steelworkers Rank and File*, pp. 71–77; Ken Morgan, 'Steelworkers Build a Movement', *Changes*, February 1979, pp. 21–23.

4. Nyden, *Steelworkers Rank and File*, pp. 77–86.

5. Ibid., pp.88–89, 135.

6. Ibid., p. 133; David Bensman and Roberta Lynch, *Rusted Dreams: Hard Times in a Steel Community*, New York 1987, pp. 132–35.

7. *Labor Notes*, 24 April 1979.

8. See Chapter 8, Table 6; BLS, *Employment and Earnings*, July 1984; Indiana University Northwest, *State of Steel: A Data Resource Book*, mimeo, 1982, p. 15.

9. *Labor Notes*, 20 November 1979.

10. *Labor Notes*, December 1979.

11. Mike Stout, 'Reindustrialization from Below: The Steel Valley Authority', *Labor Research Review*, Fall 1986, pp. 19–33.

12. *Labor Notes*, 25 March 1980; 21 August 1980.

13. Nyden, *Steelworkers Rank and File*, pp. 94–101.

14. Ibid., p. 96; *Labor Notes*, 26 August 1982; 23 November 1982; 29 March 1983.

15. *Labor Notes*, 23 February 1984; 22 March 1984.

16. Friedman, *Teamster Rank and File*, pp. 124–34; Brill, *The Teamsters*, pp. 22–69.

17. Ken Paff, TDU international organizer, interview, 3 April 1987.

18. *Labor Notes*, 20 March 1979; Friedman, *Teamster Rank and File*, pp. 116–23.

19. *Labor Notes*, 20 March 1979; Charles R. Perry, *Deregulation and the Decline of the Unionized Trucking Industry Philadelphia*, 1986, pp. 59, 87–105.

20. Teamsters for a Democratic Union, *TDU: 10 Years and Going Strong*, Detroit 1986, p. 13.

21. Friedman, *Teamsters Rank and File*, pp. 210–13.

22. TDU, *10 Years*, pp.14–15; Friedman, *Teamsters Rank and File*, pp. 214–15.

23. TDU, *Organizers Manual*, Detroit 1978; Teamster Rank & File Education and Legal Defense Foundation (TRFE & LDF), *Steward's Manual*, Detroit 1986; TRFE & LDF, *Teamster Rank & File Legal Rights Handbook*, Cleveland 1978; TRFE & LDF, *You and Your Teamster Pension Fund*, Cleveland 1977; TRFE & LDF, *Getting the Most from Your Grievance Procedure*, Detroit 1979; Ken Paff, interview.

24. *Convoy*, October 1978; *Convoy-Dispatch*, April 1980, May 1980.

25. TRFE & LDF, *Steward's Manual*, p. 2.

26. *Convoy*, May 1979, June 1979.

27. *Convoy Dispatch*, November/December 1979, January 1983.

28. *Convoy Dispatch*, April 1981, January 1986, April 1987; Ken Paff, interview.

29. *Convoy Dispatch*, October 1983; TDU, *10 Years*, p. 26.

30. *Convoy Dispatch*, June/July 1987.

31. *Labor Notes*, July 1986; December 1986; *Convoy Dispatch*, January 1987.

32. TDU, *10 Years*, p. 16.

33. Ibid.; *Convoy Dispatch*, January 1987.

34. *Labor Notes*, 27 October 1981; 21 January 1982; 24 March 1982.

35. *Labor Notes*, 23 November 1981; 22 April 1982; 23 November 1982.

36. *Labor Notes*, 26 August 1987; interviews and discussions throughout 1986–87.

37. *Labor Notes*, June 1986, July 1986, September 1986; *Union Democracy Review*, No. 35, July 1983, and No. 53, July 1986; Jack Metzgar, 'Running the Plant Backwards', *Labor Research Review*, Fall 1985; *The Voice of New Directions*, June/July 1987; *Convoy Dispatch*, May 1987.

38. *Labor Notes*, July 1987, August 1987.

39. Diane Feeley, 'Unemployment Grows, A New Movement Stirs', *Monthly Review*, December 1983, pp. 119–24; Laura McClure, labor writer for *The Guardian*, interview, July 1987.

40. Eric Mann, 'Keeping Van Nuys Open', *Labor Research Review*, Fall 1986, pp. 35–44.

41. Stout, 'Reindustrialization from Below, pp. 19–33; Tri-State Conference on Steel, 'A Summary of a Plan to Reconstruct Pittsburgh's Steel Industry', mimeo, 1984.

42. Benson, *Democratic Rights*, pp. 241–42.

43. Ibid., passim; *Union Democracy Review*, various issues from 1974 through 1987.

44. *American Labor*, various issues from 1982 through 1987.

45. Institute for Labor Education and Research, *What's Wrong with the U.S. Economy*, New York 1982; The Labor Institute, 'Hometowns against Shutdowns', 1986; interviews with Institute Director Les Leopold and OCAW Local 8-760 President Stanley Fischer.

46. *Labor Research Review*, issues from 1982 to 1987.

47. This account of the history and role of *Labor Notes* is based on the author's experience as a staff member since its founding in February 1979, as well as a rereading of most *Labor Notes* publications.

Chapter 11

1. *The Detroit News*, 19 July 1987.
2. Marable, *How Capitalism Underdeveloped Black America*, pp. 242–53; *The Minority Trendsletter*, April/May 1987.
3. Marable, *How Capitalism Underdeveloped Black America*, p. 242.
4. *Detroit Free Press*, 12 December 1983.
5. Hill, 'Race, Ethnicity and Organized Labor', pp. 68–71; Foner, *Organized Labor and the Black Worker*, pp. 430–31.
6. Foner, *Organized Labor and the Black Worker*, pp. 436–39.
7. Hill, 'Race, Ethnicity and Organized Labor', p. 71.
8. *Detroit Free Press*, 19 October 1983.
9. *In These Times*, 20–26 November 1985; *Detroit Free Press*, 3 July 1986.
10. *Detroit Free Press*, 13 June 1984; *AFL-CIO News*, 16 June 1984.
11. Douglas G. Glasgow, *The Black Underclass: Poverty, Unemployment and Entrapment of Ghetto Youth*, New York 1981. pp. 151–52.
12. Foner, *Organization of Labor and the Black Worker*, pp. 431–33.
13. *Labor Notes*, 24 June 1982.
14. Manning Marable, *Black American Politics: From the Washington Marches to Jesse Jackson*, London 1985, p.269.
15. Marable, *Black American Politics*, p. 187.
16. Bureau of the Census, *Statistical Abstract, 1986*, pp. 249, 251, 252.
17. Marable, *Black American Politics*, pp. 172–231.
18. Sheila D. Collins, *The Rainbow Challenge: The Jackson Campaign and the Future of U.S. Politics*, New York 1986, pp. 91–92; Marable, *Black American Politics*, passim.
19. Dan Georgakis and Marvin Surkin, *Detroit: I Do Mind Dying – A Study in Urban Revolution*, New York 1975, pp. 183–208, 223–25; Edward Greer, *Big Steel: Black Politics and Corporate Power in Gary, Indiana*, New York 1979, pp. 111–32; *The Minority Trendsletter*, April/May 1987.
20. Collins, *Rainbow Challenge*, p. 91.
21. Marable, *How Capitalism Underdeveloped Black America*, pp. 163–66, 242.
22. Greer, *Big Steel*, pp. 39, 100–104; Georgakis and Surkin, *Detroit*, pp. 223–24.
23. Marable, *Black American Politics*, pp. 227–38; *The Minority Trendsletter*, April/May 1987.
24. Marable, *Black American Politics*, p. 250.
25. Ibid., pp. 107–24.
26. Ibid., pp. 247–80.
27. Adolph L. Reed, Jr., *The Jesse Jackson Phenomenon: The Crisis of Purpose in Afro-American Politics*, New Haven 1986, pp. 13–16.
28. Marable, *Black American Politics*, p. 173; Reed, *Jackson Phenomenon*, pp.13–16.
29. Marable, *Black American Politics*, p. 172.
30. Greer, *Big Steel*, p. 31.
31. Ibid.
32. Thomas Landess and Richard Quinn, *Jesse Jackson and the Politics of Race*, Ottawa, Ill. 1985, pp. 34–82.
33. Collins, *Rainbow Challenge*, pp. 254–67.
34. *Newsweek*, 21 March 1988; *Detroit Free Press*, 27 and 28 March 1988.
35. *Labor Notes*, August 1985, September 1985.
36. Manning Marable, 'The Contradictory Contours of Black Political Culture', in Mike Davis et al., *The Year Left 2*, London 1987, p. 13.

Chapter 12

1. BLS, *Handbook, 1985*, pp. 14, 15, 18, 19; *Monthly Labor Review*, February 1987, pp.

58, 59.

2. BLS, *Handbook, 1985*, p. 183.

3. Bureau of the Census, *Statistical Abstract, 1986*, p. 424; Bureau of the Census, *Statistical Abstract, 1977*, pp. 406, 418.

4. Ruth Milkman, 'Women Workers, Feminism, and the Labor Movement since the 1960s', in Ruth Milkman, ed., *Women, Work, and Protest: A Century of Women's Labor History*, Boston 1985, pp. 301–304.

5. Barbara Ann Solz, *Still Struggling: America's Low-Income Working Women Confronting the 1980s*, Lexington, Mass. 1985, pp. 177–83; Milkman, 'Women Workers', in Milkman, *Women, Work, and Protest*, pp. 307–10.

6. Milkman, 'Women Workers', in Milkman, *Women, Work, and Protest*, p. 306; *Wall Street Journal*, 22 August 1980.

7. Bureau of the Census, *Statistical Abstract, 1986*, pp. 39, 398.

8. *Labor Notes*, 20 November 1979.

9. Diane Balser, *Sisterhood and Solidarity: Feminism and Labor in Modern Times*, Boston 1987, pp. 87–149.

10. Coalition of Labor Union Women, Press Release, 2 September 1980; *Wall Street Journal*, 22 August 1980.

11. Milkman, 'Women Workers', in Milkman, *Women, Work, and Protest*, p. 312.

12. *Labor Notes*, 21 August 1979.

13. *Labor Notes*, 22 June 1979; 21 August 1979; 21 December 1981.

14. *Labor Notes*, 20 February 1979.

15. Mon Valley Media, 'Women of Steel', video, Pittsburgh 1985.

16. Mary Frank Fox and Sharlene Hesse-Biber, *Women at Work*, Palo Alto, Calif. 1984, pp. 98, 114.

17. Cindy Cameron, 'Noon at Nine to Five: Reflections on a Decade of Organizing', *Labor Research Review*, Spring 1986, pp. 105–106; Milkman, 'Women Workers', pp. 316–17.

18. *Labor Notes*, 21 July 1979.

19. Ibid.

20. Milkman, 'Women Workers', in Milkman, *Women, Work, and Protest*, p. 315; Cameron, 'Noon at Nine to Five', pp. 106–109.

21. Cameron, 'Noon at Nine to Five', p. 109.

22. Hill, 'Race, Ethnicity and Organized Labor', pp. 37–43.

23. James D. Cockcroft, *Outlaws in the Promised Land: Mexican Immigrant Workers and America's Future*, New York 1986, p. 142.

24. BLS, *Handbook, 1980*, p. 28; BLS, *Handbook, 1985*, p. 26.

25. Hector Ramos, 'Latino Caucuses in U.S. Labor Unions', *Race and Class*, Spring 1986, p. 71.

26. Cockcroft, *Outlaws*, pp. 194, 206; Ramos, *Latino Caucuses*, p. 69.

27. Bureau of the Census, *Statistical Abstract, 1986*, p. 424.

28. Hill, 'Race, Ethnicity, and Organized Labor', pp. 53–60, 80.

29. Ramos, *Latino Caucuses*, pp. 71–74.

30. Ibid., pp. 74–76; *Labor Notes*, February 1986.

31. Cockcroft, *Outlaws*, pp. 195–97.

32. *Labor Notes*, 22 June 1979.

33. *Labor Notes*, 22 June 1979; 21 August 1979; 25 September 1980.

34. *Labor Notes*, August 1985; September 1985; April 1986.

35. Eric Mann, 'Keeping Van Nuys Open', *Labor Research Review*, Fall 1986, pp. 35–44; Ramos, *Latino Caucuses*, pp. 76–77; *Labor Notes*, January 1986.

36. Tom Berry and Deb Preusch, *AIFLD in Central America: Agents as Organizers*, The Inter-Hispanic Education Resource Center, 1986, p. 3.

37. Ibid., pp. 4–6.

38. Penny Lernoux, *Cry of the People: The Struggle for Human Rights in Latin America*, New York 1980, p. 211.

39. Berry and Preusch, *AIFLD*, pp. 7–8.

40. Lernoux, *Cry of the People*, pp. 211–12; Maria Helena Moreira Alves, *State and Opposition in Military Brazil*, Austin, Tex. 1985, p. 6.

41. *Labor Notes*, August 1986.

42. *Wall Street Journal*, 31 December 1985.
43. Barry and Preusch, *AIFLD*, p. 9; *Labor Notes*, May 1986, June 1987.
44. J. Michael Luhan, 'AIFLD's Salvadoran Labor Wars', *Dissent*, Summer 1986, pp. 340–49; Labor Report on Central America, March/April 1987, May/June 1987.
45. National Labor Committee in Support of Democracy and Human Rights in El Salvador, 'The Search for Peace In Central America', New York 1984, pp. 3–5.
46. *Labor Notes*, 26 October 1983.
47. *Racine Labor*, 29 November 1985; *The Labor Link*, Fall 1985.
48. *International Labour Reports*, January/February 1986.
49. *Labor Notes*, January 1985.
50. *Labor Notes*, April 1987, June 1987.
51. Michael Moore, 'Made in Mexico', *Multinational Monitor*, February 1987, pp. 4–6.
52. Bluestone, Harrison, and Gorham, 'Storm Clouds on the Horizon', pp. 18, 35–36.
53. Charles H. Smith, Jr., 'The Multinational Corporation: Shadow and Substance', in Robert F. Banks and Jack Stieber, eds., *Multinationals, Unions and Labor Relations in Industrialized Countries*, Ithaca, N.Y. 1977, p. 37.
54. North American Congress on Latin America, 'Electronics: The Global Industry', *Latin America and Empire Report*, April 1977, p. 4.
55. Shaiken, *Work Transformed*, p. 235.
56. Burton Bendiner, 'World Automotive Councils: A Union Response to Transnational Bargaining', in Banks and Stieber, *Multinationals*, pp. 186–91; Peter Waterman, *For a New Labour Internationalism: A Set of Reprints and Working Papers*, Birmingham 1984, pp. 89–96; IUF, 'We Will Neither Go Nor Be Driven Out', A Special Report by the IUF Delegation on the Occupation of the Coca-Cola Bottling Plant in Guatemala', Washington 1984, pp. 1–4; *Labor Notes*, 23 May 1984.
57. *Labor Notes*, July 1987.
58. Jeroen Peijnenburg, 'Workers in Transnational Corporations: Meeting the Corporate Challenge', in Waterman, *For a New Labor Internationalism*, pp. 109–17; *Labor Notes*, 25 October 1984, June 1986.
59. *International Labour Reports*, May/June 1985.
60. *Labor Notes*, May 1987.
61. Ibid.
62. *International Labour Reports*, March/April 1987; *Labor Notes*, June 1987.

Chapter 13

1. BLS, *News*, 6 March 1987.
2. *New York Times*, 4 May 1986.
3. *Labor Notes*, 21 August 1981.
4. Charles Perry, *Union Corporate Campaigns*, Philadelphia 1987, pp. 15, 95, 99–100; *Labor Notes*, 26 July 1984; September 1985.
5. Perry, *Corporate Campaigns*, p. 20.
6. Corporate Campaign, Inc., 'Curing Labor's Ills: Outline of a Strategy to Reverse the Decline of the U.S. Labor Movement', mimeo, New York 1987, pp. 1–4.
7. Perry, *Corporate Campaigns*, pp. 15, 92, 185–92.
8. AFL-CIO, *Developing New Tactics: Winning with Coordinated Corporate Campaigns*, Washington 1985.
9. Corporate Campaign, *Curing Labor's Ills*, pp. 4–5.
10. *Labor Notes*, May 1987.
11. *Labor Notes*, 22 November 1983.
12. *Labor Notes*, 22 November 1983; 20 December 1983.
13. *Labor Notes*, 28 June 1984; March 1985.
14. *Labor Notes*, 25 October 1984; April 1985; February 1986.
15. *Labor Notes*, September 1985.
16. Quoted in Kim Moody, 'U.S. Labor – Is Concessions Tide Turning?', *Against the*

Current, January-February 1986, p. 13.

17. *Labor Notes,* September 1985.

18. Peter Rachleff, 'The Hormel Strike: Turning Point for the Rank and File Labor Movement', *Socialist Review,* No. 89, September-October 1986, p. 74; *Labor Notes,* April 1985.

19. Kim Moody and Roger Horowitz, 'Debate in Labor Growing as P-9 Strikers Continue the Battle', *Against the Current,* May-June 1986, p. 9.

20. Affidavit of James V. Guyette, U.S. District Court for the District of Minnesota, 16 May 1986, pp. 1–5, 8–10; Fred Halstead, *The 1985–86 Hormel Meat-packers Strike in Austin, Minnesota,* New York 1986, pp. 14–16.

21. UFCW, *Leadership Update,* February 1986, p. 2; Halstead, *Hormel Strike,* pp.16–17.

22. , Affidavit of James V. Guyette, p. 6.

23. James V. Guyette, 'Affidavit in Support of Plaintiff's Motion for Preliminary Injunction', *Local P-9* v. *UFCW,* U.S. District Court, District of Columbia.

24. *Labor Notes,* April 1985.

25. Barb Collette, Speech at the November 1986 *Labor Notes* Conference; Madeline Krueger, 'United Support Group Continues P-9ers' Fight', *Against the Current,* May-June 1987, pp. 12–14.

26. *Labor Notes,* April 1985; Ray Rogers, Speech at the November 1986 *Labor Notes* Conference.

27. Hormel Rank and File Fight Back, 'The Hormel Struggle Continues', Austin, Minn. 1986, p 3.

28. Interviews and discussions with Ray Rogers and Ed Allen, September 1986; P-9 activists Kathy Buck, Dick Shatuck, Pete Kennedy, Pete Winkels, Cecil Cain, and United Support Group member Barb Collette in Austin in October 1986 and Detroit in November 1986; and numerous telephone discussions with Dick Blin, editor of the *Duluth Labor World,* and Pete Rachleff, chairman of the Twin Cities P-9 Support Committee, over the course of two years.

29. Rachleff, 'The Hormel Strike', pp. 86–87.

30. Interviews, as cited above.

31. Affidavit of James V. Guyette, pp.4–5.

32. UFCW, 'Position Paper on Local P-9/Hormel, Austin Situation', mimeo, October 1985; Rachleff, 'The Hormel Strike', p. 79.

33. UFCW, *Leadership Update,* February 1986, passim; Rachleff, 'The Hormel Strike', pp. 79–80.

34. Statement by the AFL-CIO Executive Council on the Hormel Strike, February 1986, Bal Harbor, Florida.

35. *Labor Notes,* April 1986; *Guardian,* 19 February 1986; *In These Times,* 26 February-11 March 1986; Lance Compa, 'A Second Look at the Hormel Strike', mimeo, June 1986, passim.

36. Rachleff, 'The Hormel Strike', p. 80; *Labor Notes,* March 1986.

37. *Labor Notes,* May 1986, June 1986, July 1986; U.S. Court of Appeals for the Eighth District, No. 86-5262 MN, 'Statement of the Case', 20 August 1986, p. 1.

38. *Labor Notes,* May 1986, June 1986; Interviews, as cited above.

39. *Labor Notes,* October 1986, July 1987.

40. *Labor Notes,* January 1987, April 1987.

41. *Labor Notes,* July 1986, September 1986.

42. *Labor Notes,* June 1987.

43. 'Watsonville Roundtable', *Forward,* January 1987, p. 13.

44. Frank Bardacke, 'Watsonville: How the Strikers Won', *Against the Current,* May-June 1987, pp. 15–17.

45. *Labor Notes,* April 1987.

46. 'Watsonville Roundtable', *Forward,* p. 6.

47. *Labor Notes,* December 1985; Ken Paff, TDU international organizer, interview, 3 April 1987.

48. *Labor Notes,* December 1985; 'Watsonville Roundtable', *Forward,* p. 4.

49. *Labor Notes,* December 1986.

50. *Labor Notes,* April 1987.

51. Bardacke, 'Watsonville', p. 15; *Labor Notes,* April 1987.

Chapter 14

1. International Metal Workers Federation, *Changing Patterns of Collective Bargaining* Geneva 1986, pp. 3–4.

2. Pradeep Kumar, 'Organized Labor in Canada and the United States: Similarities and Differences', *Queen's Papers in Industrial Relations*, Kingston, Ontario 1987, Tables 1 and 2.

3. Burnham, *Current Crisis*, pp. 183–87.

4. E. P. Thompson, *The Making of the English Working Class*, New York 1963, pp. 9–12.

5. David Montgomery, *The Fall of the House of Labor: The Workplace, the State, and American Labor Activism, 1865–1925*, New York 1987, pp. 5–9, passim.

6. Baldemar Velasquez, Speech at 1986 *Labor Notes* Conference; Ken Paff, TDU international organizer, interview, 3 April 1987.

7. Burnham, *Current Crisis*, p. 262; Joshua Cohen and Thomas Ferguson, *Rules of the Game*, Boston 1986, pp. 24–28.

8. Edsall, *New Politics of Inequality*, p. 14.

9. Ferguson and Rogers, *Right Turn*, pp. 46–57.

10. Ibid., pp. 12–24.

11. Mazzocchi and Leopold, 'The Politics of Labor', p. 15.

Index

372